365 Daily Readings from Biblical History

FASCINATING
PEOPLE
OF BIBLE
THE

365 Daily Readings from Biblical History

FASCINATING
PEOPLE
OF BIBLE
THE

CHRISTOPHER D. HUDSON

WITH DAVID BARRETT AND BENJAMIN D. IRWIN

BARBOUR
PUBLISHING

Cover image: © National Galley, London Art Resource, NY

Published by Barbour Publishing, Inc., P.O. Box 719, Uhrichsville, Ohio 44683, www.barbourbooks.com

Our mission is to publish and distribute inspirational products offering exceptional value and biblical encouragement to the masses.

 Member of the Evangelical Christian Publishers Association

Printed in the United States of America.

Introduction

Therefore, since we are surrounded by so great a cloud of witnesses,
let us also lay aside every weight and the sin that clings so closely,
and let us run with perseverance the race that is set before us.
HEBREWS 12:1 NRSV

Bible studies and Sunday school classes can fill our minds with many important facts. Through them we learn names of cities, recount historical events, and memorize favorite verses. And though every bit of Bible knowledge we learn can be worthwhile, sometimes we forget one of the most basic characteristics of the Bible: that it's a book about people.

Though these men and women lived thousands of years before us, we share a similar human journey. Together we enjoy the pleasures of life and learn to look to God when faced with devastating pain. Along with them, we experience the excitement of young love, the challenges of raising a family, and the complexities of trying to live for God in a fallen world.

Though we're separated by the years, we're joined by a common human spirit, and we serve a God who spans the ages. As we live in our modern communities, we have the opportunity to learn from those who have gone before us—both from the good and the bad.

Because it is our conviction that we have something to learn from every person in the Bible, we've placed the following profiles in random order rather than organizing them using a prescribed theme or program. (If you're looking for someone in particular, an alphabetical index can be found in the back of this book.) We pray that as you read the stories of these lives, you will find your own life changed as well.

Day
1

*"Then bring near to you Aaron your brother, and his sons with him,
from among the people of Israel, to serve me as priests—
Aaron and Aaron's sons, Nadab and Abihu, Eleazar and Ithamar."*

EXODUS 28:1 ESV

I t's not what you know, but who you know" can only get you so far. In the end,
you will still be held responsible for your own actions.

As Aaron's firstborn son, Nadab witnessed the plagues in Egypt, saw God's
people delivered through the Red Sea, and enjoyed the daily manna delivered to
the Hebrew camp (Exodus 16). He tasted the waters of Marah and Elim (Exodus
15), saw water flow from a rock (Exodus
17), and probably saw for himself the tab-
lets containing the Ten Commandments
(Exodus 20). Being the son of Aaron and
the nephew of Moses, Nadab certainly had
a front-row seat from which to witness
God's miraculous show of power.

NADAB

First Son of Aaron

Nadab also became one of Israel's
first priests—a position that he qualified
for because he descended from Aaron. He represented the people's sacrifices and
concerns to God and helped care for the holy objects of worship. Because of his
position, he was allowed to approach God on Mt. Sinai along with seventy elders of
Israel (Exodus 24:1, 9).

But pedigree and position did not spare Nadab and his brother from God's
judgment when they made an offering to God that did not meet His holy standards.
Nadab and his brother were instantly killed, providing the people with a powerful
reminder that God's holiness is not to be taken lightly by anyone.

SPIRITUAL INSIGHT

A commitment to Christian service can sometimes fizzle into
complacency. While you might begin a ministry with the greatest of
intentions, the constant repetitive tasks of the work may cause you
to lose sight of its impact or holiness before God. Pray for a fresh and
reverent perspective as you continue to serve in the ways God has
appointed for you.

But Moses' hands grew weary, so they took a stone and put it under him, and he sat on it, while Aaron and Hur held up his hands, one on one side, and the other on the other side. So his hands were steady until the going down of the sun.
EXODUS 17:12 ESV

Acts of heroism may come disguised as fairly simple gestures.

While Joshua and his army wielded their swords and shields against the Amalekites, the true heroes that day observed the fight from the top of a nearby hill. The Bible records that Moses, Aaron, and Hur climbed a hill in the vicinity of the conflict in order to watch Israel fight at Rephidim. With the battle raging below, Moses raised his hands in prayer to God. As long as Moses kept his hands raised, Israel secured the upper hand in the battle. But when Moses grew tired and lowered his hands, the Amalekites began to win the battle.

HUR

The Hero from Behind the Scenes

Hur became a military hero that day by faithfully doing the simplest of tasks: helping Moses raise his tired arms. After finding a rock for Moses to sit on, Aaron stood on one side of Moses and Hur on the other. Together they held his arms up until the sun set. Because of Hur's unpretentious contribution, the Israelites crushed the enemy army.

In addition to his place in this story, Hur is also noted as serving as a leader to the people. When Moses went to Mount Sinai, he left Aaron and Hur behind as his representatives to handle disputes and conflicts that might arise while he was gone (Exodus 24:14).

RELATED INFORMATION

Descendants of Esau, the Amalekites lived near the desert region of Paran—which lies along the southern border of the Promised Land. In addition to the battle involving Hur, the Amalekites skirmished with Israel during the time of the judges (Judges 8). They remained Israel's enemies until King David finally soundly defeated them (1 Samuel 15, 27, 30; 2 Samuel 8).

When the woman saw that the fruit of the tree was good for food and pleasing to the eye, and also desirable for gaining wisdom, she took some and ate it. She also gave some to her husband, who was with her, and he ate it.
GENESIS 3:6

It's sobering to realize that a lifetime of good can be forever marred by a single sin or poor decision, and the consequences can be seemingly immeasurable. In the case of Eve, the consequences of her sin affected the entire world for the rest of time.

As most people know, Eve was the first woman, created by God from a rib from Adam's side. She and Adam lived in a beautiful garden in perfect harmony with God and with the rest of creation—until she and Adam chose to disobey and eat from the one tree that they were forbidden to eat from in all the garden.

EVE

The First Woman and
Mother of All People

Certainly when Eve ate the fruit, she never imagined all the harm that her sin would cause. Yet that is the nature of sin. It looks pleasing and harmless, but the final result is always death. No amount of blaming each other or the serpent, who tempted her to eat the fruit, could change the sad consequences that would forever plague Adam and Eve and all their descendants. Forced to leave the garden, their lives—and the lives of all who have come after them—would now be marked by hard work, pain, and sorrow.

RELATED INFORMATION

After Adam and Eve were forced to leave the garden, Eve gave birth to Cain and Abel. Years later, Cain killed Abel out of jealousy, but God gave Eve another son named Seth. Eve likely had other sons and daughters as well (Genesis 5:4).

*But Esau ran to meet him and embraced him
and fell on his neck and kissed him, and they wept.*
GENESIS 33:4 ESV

Often just when you think you know someone, that person does something completely unexpected, and you're left scratching your head trying to make sense of it all. Esau must have been someone like that.

Esau was the older twin brother of Jacob; they were the sons of Isaac and grandsons of Abraham. As the oldest sibling, Esau was entitled to the family birthright, which granted him leadership of the extended family and a double portion of his father's inheritance. But Esau revealed his disregard for his birthright when he sold it to Jacob for a bowl of stew. Later Jacob made sure to seal the deal by tricking his father into blessing him as the one receiving the birthright (Genesis 25–27).

ESAU

Brother of Jacob

When Esau realized that his birthright was lost forever, he became furious with Jacob and wanted to kill him. So Jacob fled far away to Paddan Aram (Genesis 27:42–28:5).

After many years, Jacob returned to Canaan, and along the way he heard that Esau was coming to meet him. Jacob feared for his life, thinking that Esau was still looking to exact revenge on him for stealing the birthright. When Esau caught up with him, however, he ran to Jacob and kissed him! The two brothers were finally reconciled (Genesis 32–33).

RELATED INFORMATION

Esau became the ancestor of the Edomites, who lived in the mountainous area to the southeast of Israel (Genesis 36:9). The rivalry between Jacob and Esau appears to have continued through their descendants, the Israelites and the Edomites. The Israelites fought several battles with the Edomites throughout their history (2 Samuel 8:13; 2 Kings 8:21; 14:1–7).

Now I, King Artaxerxes, order all the treasurers of
Trans-Euphrates to provide with diligence whatever Ezra
the priest, a teacher of the Law of the God of heaven, may ask of you.
EZRA 7:21

Have you ever had someone who displays little interest in godly things ask you to pray about something he or she is facing? It always jolts us a bit to realize that even the most ardent unbelievers, deep down, may have some regard for God, even if their interest in Him is mostly self-serving. This was clearly the case for King Artaxerxes of Persia.

Artaxerxes ruled over the vast kingdom of Persia during the days of Ezra and Nehemiah. Decades earlier, many Jews had been sent into exile under the Babylonians, and then the Persians defeated the Babylonians and absorbed their territory into their empire. King Cyrus was the first to decree that Jews were free to return to Jerusalem and rebuild the temple. Years later, Artaxerxes would make a similar decree and grant Ezra funds to maintain the rebuilt temple and offer sacrifices. His reasoning is made clear in his letter to Ezra: "Why should there be wrath against the realm of the king and of his sons?" (Ezra 7:23).

ARTAXERXES

King of Persia

Artaxerxes may have merely been concerned about stacking the deck of divine providence in his favor, but it was regard for the Lord nonetheless. And it also provided generous funds for building up God's temple in Jerusalem.

When unbelievers ask us to pray for them, it is tempting to harbor thoughts like, *Why should I ask God to do anything for them when they don't seem to care about following Him at all?* But this is not an attitude of grace and mercy. At the same time, God may already be working in their hearts to bring about repentance, and their request reveals the true regard they have for Him in their hearts. Instead of harboring resentment, respond with a grace-filled, "Yes, I will certainly pray for you"—and do it!

Now the man Moses was very humble,
more than any man who was on the face of the earth.
NUMBERS 12:3 NASB

Arguably Israel's greatest prophet, Moses left behind one of the strongest legacies in the Bible. As God's anointed leader, he led the people from Egypt to the Promised Land, appointed priests and judges, created a place of worship, delivered God's law, wrote the first five books of the Bible, and frequently interceded on behalf of the people. With this exceptional résumé, it's easy to envy a character like Moses. Who wouldn't want to accomplish so much?

For Moses, though, the road to each accomplishment included a great many difficult and rocky places as it twisted and turned. After becoming a fugitive from Pharaoh's court, Moses scratched out a living in the desert of Midian as a shepherd for forty years (Exodus 3). Once commissioned by God, Moses then risked his life by bringing bad news and judgment to Pharaoh (Exodus 4–12). And though God gave him the task of confronting Pharaoh, Moses lacked natural speaking ability and needed to rely on his brother, Aaron, to be his mouthpiece (see Exodus 4:10).

MOSES

Greatest Hebrew Prophet

Securing the freedom of the Hebrew people led to more difficulty for Moses. Instead of being heralded as a hero, he became the object of the Israelites' complaints and rebellion (see examples in Exodus 15–17; Numbers 14, 16).

In spite of all his illustrious achievements as God's appointed leader, Moses was not perfect. As a consequence for Moses' disobedience (Numbers 20), God did not allow him to cross into the land. Instead, God graciously allowed Moses to view the Promised Land that God had reserved for His people (Deuteronomy 34).

RELATED INFORMATION

Moses' life illustrated that the price of leadership is often loneliness. During the difficult times of leading the people through the wilderness, Moses faced opposition from those who should have been his closest allies. Leadership is difficult and lonely work. What leaders need to experience your support?

Luke alone is with me. Get Mark and bring him with you,
for he is very useful to me for ministry.
2 TIMOTHY 4:11 ESV

Mark (also called John Mark) is a shining example of the power of God to redeem failed disciples. If you read only the book of Acts, you might come away thinking that Mark was simply another sad example of an unfaithful believer gone astray, and that was the end of the story. Not true.

Mark was a relative of Barnabas (Colossians 4:10) and was among the first believers in the early church. He accompanied Paul and Barnabas on their first missionary journey (Acts 13:5), but it seems that when things got rough, Mark decided to pack up and head home to Jerusalem (Acts 13:13; 15:37–38). Later, when Paul and Barnabas were considering making a second missionary journey, Paul

MARK

Coworker of Paul and Gospel Writer

was firmly decided that Mark should not be allowed to come (Acts 15:39).

Fortunately, the story doesn't end there. Barnabas, the great encourager, took Mark along to Cyprus, perhaps on a second missionary trip through Barnabas's home region (Acts 15:39). Apparently this second opportunity for Mark to show himself faithful paid off, because by the time Paul wrote Colossians and Philemon, he was referring to Mark as his fellow worker (Colossians 4:10; Philemon 1:24). Paul's great regard for Mark comes through most clearly late in his life in his second letter to Timothy, where Paul describes Mark as helpful in the ministry (2 Timothy 4:11). Even Peter later referred to Mark as a son (1 Peter 5:13).

DID YOU KNOW?

Church tradition says that Mark composed the second Gospel from Peter's sermons. In the first half of the second century, an early church leader named Papias wrote, "Mark, having become the interpreter of Peter, wrote down accurately whatsoever he remembered. It was not, however, in exact order that he related the sayings or deeds of Christ. For he neither heard the Lord nor accompanied Him. But afterwards, as I said, he accompanied Peter, who accommodated his instructions to the necessities [of his hearers]."

*David then asked Ahimelech the Hittite and Abishai son of Zeruiah,
Joab's brother, "Who will go down into the camp with me to Saul?"
"I'll go with you," said Abishai.*

1 Samuel 26:6

Abishai had all the makings of a great warrior—loyalty, courage, prowess—but at times he also seemed to be easily led astray by his bloodthirsty brother Joab.

Without a doubt, Abishai was a loyal soldier, fully devoted to his uncle David. When David was fleeing from Saul, Abishai was the one who volunteered to risk his life by going with David at night into Saul's camp (1 Samuel 26:6). He was also protective of David's honor as well, asking David to allow him to kill Shimei for insulting the king (2 Samuel 16). He even came to David's rescue in a battle against the Philistines (2 Samuel 21:16–17).

ABISHAI

One of David's Mighty Men

Abishai was also an able warrior and commander, demonstrating his military prowess in several battles against the Edomites and the Arameans and Ammonites. His military exploits earned him a place of honor among David's mighty men (2 Samuel 23:18–19).

Unfortunately, however, Abishai was also very loyal to his brother Joab, who led him to be an accomplice to vengeful, bloodthirsty deeds. Abishai conspired with Joab to avenge his brother Asahel's death by killing Abner, another commander (2 Samuel 3:30). Abishai also seems to have turned a blind eye to Joab's jealous murder of yet another commander named Amasa (2 Samuel 20).

SPIRITUAL INSIGHT

Many Christians today resemble Abishai: They have all the makings of great warriors for God, but they allow family ties to keep them from fully obeying Him. Perhaps it is the godly wife and mother who turns a blind eye to her husband's disregard for godliness in front of their children. Perhaps it is the young man who desires to follow God but accompanies his brother in sinful things. Whatever your situation, don't allow family relationships to undermine your devotion to follow God.

*Because Ahaziah had no son, Joram succeeded him as king
in the second year of Jehoram son of Jehoshaphat king of Judah.*
2 KINGS 1:17

Day
9

King Jehoram (or Joram) of Israel was a man marked by trouble. He experienced political unrest from the time he first ascended the throne, and his life was cut short by the hand of a usurper.

JEHORAM

King of Israel

Jehoram was a son of wicked King Ahab. When Ahab's older son, Ahaziah, died without an heir, Jehoram ascended to the throne. The Moabites had already declared their independence from Israel during his brother's short reign, and Jehoram joined up with the king of Judah and the king of Edom to try to regain control over the Moabites. Though the Israelite coalition fiercely attacked Moab and virtually overran their land, they were unable to capture the capital city of Kir-hareseth, and it appears that Moab remained independent for the rest of Israel's history.

Later Jehoram invited the king of Judah to accompany him in an attempt to recover the town of Ramoth-gilead from the Arameans. During the battle, Jehoram was wounded, and he returned to Jezreel to recover. The king of Judah also came to visit him. Then Jehu, one of Jehoram's commanders, left the battle and killed Jehoram and the king of Judah. Jehu then assumed the throne and established his own dynasty instead of Jehoram's.

RELATED INFORMATION

Jehoram's assassin, Jehu, had been anointed by the prophet Elisha to become king of Israel and to bring judgment on the family of Ahab (2 Kings 9). More than seventy members of Ahab's family and forty-two family members of the king of Judah would be killed by Jehu.

*He blessed them that day and said,
"In your name will Israel pronounce this blessing:
'May God make you like Ephraim and Manasseh.' "
So he put Ephraim ahead of Manasseh.*
GENESIS 48:20

From Joseph to David to many of the first Christians, one of the key themes that is repeated throughout the Bible is God's favor being shown to those who are regarded by the world as less important. Ephraim is yet another example of this wonderful habit of God.

EPHRAIM

Son of Joseph and Father of a Half-Tribe of Israel

Ephraim was born the younger son of Joseph, who had been sold into slavery in Egypt by his older brothers. By the providence of God, Joseph rose to a very high position in the Egyptian kingdom, and Pharaoh gave him a wife from among the Egyptian priestly classes. This wife bore him two sons, Manasseh and Ephraim.

When the time came for Joseph's father, Jacob, to bless his grandsons, Joseph brought the boys to him and placed Manasseh, who was the firstborn, at Jacob's right hand, expecting him to receive the greater blessing. But Jacob chose instead to give the greater blessing to Ephraim, the younger. No reason is given for why he chose to do this; he simply did it.

Eventually Ephraim's descendants would become one of the most prominent tribes of Israel, and the northern kingdom would even be referred to at times as Ephraim.

SPIRITUAL INSIGHT

In the thinking of the world, it is those who demonstrate themselves as especially deserving who should receive special honor or blessing from God or others. But that is not God's way. In God's kingdom, the first are last, and the last are first (Matthew 20:16). God chooses to bless us simply because of His good pleasure and grace, not because of anything we have done (Romans 9:15–16; Ephesians 2:8–9).

Now Elihu had waited before speaking to Job because
they were older than he. But when he saw that the
three men had nothing more to say, his anger was aroused.
JOB 32:4–5

E lihu in the book of Job is a bit of an enigma. He seems to come out of nowhere, ready to set things straight with both Job and Job's friends, yet in the end, he, too, seems to fall short of truly addressing Job's concerns.

We don't hear about Elihu until the last several chapters of Job (Job 32–37). By this point in the story, Job has experienced great suffering, the reasons for which are not at all clear to him, for he was a righteous man. Three of Job's friends have come to visit him and then begin to offer various reasons why Job must be experiencing

ELIHU

Friend of Job

suffering. For the most part, their reasons boil down to a basic belief that all suffering is the result of sin on the part of the sufferer, so Job must have sinned in some way.

Finally, with no previous mention of his existence in the story, Elihu speaks. He begins by saying that he was waiting to speak because he is younger than the other friends, but he has become frustrated by their failure to adequately explain the reason for Job's troubles. Then he begins his monologue, mostly saying that there is a disciplinary role in suffering and that this should be accepted. But even if Elihu's words are true, why would Job, a righteous man, be disciplined by God?

Eventually Elihu's words are cut off by the Lord (Job 38:1), who speaks from the storm to address Job, and this brings all disputing to a close.

RELATED INFORMATION

Elihu is described as a Buzite, which may mean that he was descended from Nahor, Abraham's brother (Genesis 22:20–21). The descendants of Buz appear to have lived somewhere in the desert of Arabia near the desert oases of Tema and Dedan (Jeremiah 25:23–24).

But the angel said to her, "Do not be afraid, Mary, you have found favor with God. You will be with child and give birth to a son, and you are to give him the name Jesus."

LUKE 1:30–31

Mary is, of course, best known as the virgin who gave birth to the Messiah—one of the most celebrated miracles in the Bible. But the New Testament also portrays Mary as a refreshingly human figure. In the Gospels, she is often characterized by her motherly concern for her son.

MARY

Mother of Jesus

Twelve years after Jesus' miraculous birth, He accompanied His parents and their relatives and friends to Jerusalem for the Passover. When the time came to return home, Jesus lagged behind, wanting to spend more time among the rabbis in the temple. After three days of panicked searching, Mary and Joseph finally caught up with their son. The relief was obvious in Mary's words: "Son, why have you treated us like this? Your father and I have been anxiously searching for you" (Luke 2:48).

Years later, as Jesus began drawing large crowds—and as opposition started to form in some corners—Mary and her sons made a thirty-mile journey, intending to "take charge of him" (Mark 3:21). In all likelihood, Mary was concerned for Jesus' well-being; she simply wanted to protect her son from the ever-growing (and, no doubt, ever more demanding) crowds, not to mention the murmuring religious authorities who accused Jesus of being demon-possessed.

The Gospel of John provides yet another fleeting glimpse of Mary—this time at the foot of her son's cross. In the midst of His agony, Jesus spoke to His mother one last time. The sheer courage it must have taken to witness her son's execution is astounding. One of Jesus' final acts before giving up His spirit was entrusting His mother to the care of His most beloved disciple, John (John 19:26–27). Even at the climax of redemptive history, Jesus paused to make sure the mother who had loved Him so well was cared for.

SPIRITUAL INSIGHT

The crucifixion was not the first time Mary demonstrated extraordinary courage. Submitting herself to God's plan meant risking years of scorn—and perhaps worse. In all likelihood, most would have scoffed at her account of the angelic visitation and miraculous conception. What's more, the Mosaic law stated that a betrothed virgin who slept with another man was to be stoned. Mary, however, demonstrated great trust in God's ability to protect her.

Wail, O gate! Howl, O city! Melt away, all you Philistines!
A cloud of smoke comes from the north,
and there is not a straggler in its ranks.
ISAIAH 14:31

From the time of the judges and lasting for the duration of the monarchy, the Philistines were a thorn in Israel's side. They had settled in the Promised Land long before God's chosen people arrived; but like the Israelites, they started out as immigrants from a distant land.

PHILISTINES

Enemies of Israel

The Philistines—from which we get the word *Palestine*—were also known as the Sea Peoples. It is believed they originated from the Aegean Sea region, which comprises mainland Greece, Turkey, and the islands in between. Being accustomed to the sea, the Philistines settled the coastal region of the Promised Land, from the border with Egypt in the south to Gaza in the north.

On their way into the Promised Land, the Israelites took the longer route in order to avoid "Philistine country" (Exodus 13:17). In an allusion to what was to come, the writer of Exodus noted that the Israelites were not yet prepared for war.

Eventually war was what they got. Having failed to subdue the Philistines during the conquest, the Israelites often found themselves oppressed by the Philistines during the time of the judges. The Philistine threat was undoubtedly a factor in Israel's desire for a king. After three centuries of conflict, the Israelites wanted a strong leader to fight for them (see 1 Samuel 8:20). Their first choice, Saul, proved largely ineffective—he was, in fact, eventually killed in battle with the Philistines. However, Saul's successor, King David, managed to subdue the Philistines during his reign.

DID YOU KNOW?

Before he was king, David lived under the protection of Achish, the Philistine ruler of Gath. David was very nearly pressed into service to fight against his fellow Israelites, but at the last minute, Achish changed his mind on the advice of his military commanders, who did not trust David (see 1 Samuel 28:1–2, 29).

[Noah] also said, "Blessed be the LORD, *the God of Shem!*
May Canaan be the slave of Shem."
GENESIS 9:26

Going into the ark prior to the great Flood, Shem had no children. After the waters receded, though, Shem became the ancestor of many great nations— including the chosen people of Israel.

Shem was the oldest son of Noah, the most righteous man on earth at the time. (Not that there was much competition.) Shem and his brother, Japheth—the youngest of Noah's three sons—seemed to follow in their father's footsteps, un-like the middle child, Ham.

SHEM

Noah's Son

The writer of Genesis recorded just one incident from Shem's life, but it was enough to reveal his character. After the Flood, Noah returned to his original livelihood: farming. Specifically, Noah decided to plant a vineyard. It is possible that Noah was the first person to do so—which would make Noah the world's original winemaker. Noah, however, enjoyed a little too much of his own harvest and became drunk on the wine he had made. Intoxicated, Noah retired to his tent, where he lay naked and unconscious. Ham walked in on his exposed father and seemed to find the situation amusing.

Ever since Adam and Eve's fall from grace in the Garden of Eden, nakedness had become synonymous with shame. Instead of doing the honorable thing and covering his father's nakedness—and thereby his shame—Ham told Shem and Japheth about it, apparently thinking they would find the situation as entertaining as he did. Shem, however, showed his father the respect he deserved; he and Japheth discreetly covered Noah, taking care to walk backwards into the tent so as not to see their father's nakedness.

It may seem like a silly episode, but the real issue was one of honor. Ham failed to demonstrate even the most basic respect for his father. Shem, on the other hand, did the right thing—and his descendants were rewarded for his honorable behavior.

DID YOU KNOW?

Shem is regarded as the ancestor of Semitic people groups, including the Jews. According to Luke, Jesus descended from Shem's third son, Arphaxad (see Luke 3:36).

I commend to you our sister Phoebe,
a servant of the church in Cenchrea.
ROMANS 16:1

Scholars debate whether Phoebe was a deacon in the formal sense of the word or some kind of lay servant or minister. Either way, she was a woman of prominence who made a significant contribution to the church—not just for those in Paul's day but for all the ages.

Paul provided little detail concerning the woman mentioned in the closing chapter of Romans—only that Phoebe was from Cenchrea, a seaport near Corinth (located in present-day Greece). It is likely that Paul wrote his letter to the Roman church while staying either at Corinth or nearby Cenchrea.

PHOEBE

Prominent Woman in the
Early Church

When Paul described Phoebe as a servant, he used the Greek word *diakonos.* Elsewhere in the New Testament, the same word is used for the formal office of deacon. Many scholars believe that it is impossible to tell whether this is the sense of the word that Paul intended in Romans 16:1, but it is clear that Phoebe was an important member of the church and played a vital role in supporting Paul's ministry. Perhaps she provided encouragement or financial assistance or hospitality—or all of the above. Very likely, Paul and Phoebe worshipped side by side in the church at Cenchrea.

Over time, Paul developed great trust in Phoebe. The reference to her near the end of Romans was meant to serve as a letter of introduction. Evidently it was Phoebe who delivered Paul's letter to the church at Rome—a six-hundred-mile journey over land and sea. Without Phoebe, the great servant of the church, we would not have in our possession what is perhaps Paul's greatest theological contribution: the letter to the Romans.

DID YOU KNOW?

The name Phoebe, which means "radiant," was another name for the Greek goddess Artemis. It is likely that Paul's friend Phoebe was a pagan convert to the Christian faith—perhaps even a former worshipper of Artemis.

*Now if perfection was through the Levitical priesthood
(for on the basis of it the people received the Law),
what further need was there for another priest to arise
according to the order of Melchizedek, and not be designated
according to the order of Aaron?*

HEBREWS 7:11 NASB

O rdinary leaders often become remarkable leaders because of extraordinary support. While Moses was arguably the greatest Hebrew leader during Bible times, much of his success came with the help of his brother, Aaron. Aaron stood alongside Moses as they confronted Pharaoh, and he compensated for Moses' weakness by often serving as Moses' spokesperson (see Exodus 4:10). And though Moses served as the principal leader of the Hebrew people, Aaron also held an important position of influence.

It was Aaron's staff that became a snake before Pharaoh (Exodus 7:10). That same staff also turned Egypt's water into blood (Exodus 7:19), brought frogs on the Egyptians (Exodus 8:5), and caused gnats to swarm the Egyptians (Exodus 8:16). Aaron and his sons became the first Hebrew priests appointed by God (Exodus 28:3). The significance of their role as intermediaries between God and the Hebrews became clearly evidenced when they interceded for the people after the rebellion of Korah, Dathan, and Abiram (Numbers 16).

AARON

Brother of Moses

While Aaron usually provided loyal assistance to Moses, he also experienced some notable failures as a supporter. For example, Aaron and his sister, Miriam, received a sound reprimand from God when they spoke against Moses for marrying a Cushite (Numbers 12:1–15). On another occasion, Aaron buckled under the pressure of the people and created a golden calf while Moses communed with God away from the camp (Exodus 32). As the people approached the Promised Land, Aaron died at the age of 123 on Mount Hor (Numbers 33:39).

SPIRITUAL INSIGHT

Though generally a good priest, Aaron's imperfection became an important theological symbol. In spite of faithful service to the people of God, Hebrew priests could not provide the perfect intercession required to obtain God's complete forgiveness. Their service illustrated the need for something more, something better. God met that need through the perfect priesthood initiated by Jesus Christ (see Hebrews 5:4; 7:11).

*When two years had elapsed, Felix was succeeded by Porcius Festus.
And desiring to do the Jews a favor, Felix left Paul in prison.*
ACTS 24:27 ESV

F estus just wanted to do his job. He had been appointed by the Romans to replace Felix as governor of Judea, and in the transfer of leadership, he had inherited a unique prisoner named Paul.

Paul did not fit the reputation most people ascribe to prisoners. He was well educated and respectful, and he desired to live rightly before God and others. Why was he here?

The Jewish leaders had been hounding Festus to transfer Paul to Jerusalem to stand trial there (because they secretly wanted to assassinate him along the way), but Paul refused and appealed his case to Caesar. As Paul waited to leave for Rome, Festus discussed Paul's case with some visiting dignitaries and called for Paul to speak to them to help him make sense of the case.

FESTUS

Governor of Judea

As Paul spoke, Festus became so puzzled by what Paul was saying about Jesus that he called Paul insane. Paul continued, however, and even tried to persuade the dignitaries themselves to become Christians.

After Paul was finished, the dignitaries informed Festus that Paul could have been set free if he had not appealed to Caesar, but Festus was now bound by Paul's appeal, so he sent him to Rome.

RELATED INFORMATION

The dignitaries who were visiting Festus were Agrippa II and his wife, Bernice. Agrippa II was the last of the descendants of Herod to rule over Judea, because it was during his reign that the First Jewish-Roman War (against the Romans) occurred, and after that the Romans took more direct control over the region.

*When it was time for Elizabeth to have her baby,
she gave birth to a son. Her neighbors and relatives heard
that the Lord had shown her great mercy, and they shared her joy.*

LUKE 1:57–58

F ew joys in life are felt as deeply as that of a mother who is blessed with a child after many years of struggling to become pregnant. This was the wonderful experience of Elizabeth, and we are privileged to share in her joy year after year as we read the scriptures surrounding the Christmas story.

ELIZABETH

Mother of John the Baptist

Elizabeth was the wife of a priest named Zechariah, and both of them served God blamelessly. Elizabeth was also a relative of Mary, who would later give birth to Jesus. When we first read about Elizabeth and her husband, they are already very old, and they have been unable to bear any children (Luke 1:5–7).

But once, while Zechariah was on duty in the temple, an angel appeared to him and announced that Elizabeth would have a son, and they were to name him John (whom we know as "John the Baptist").

About the same time, an angel appeared to Mary and announced that she would give birth to Jesus and that Elizabeth would also bear a child. When Mary went to visit Elizabeth, Elizabeth was filled with the Holy Spirit, and her child leaped in her womb. In a wonderful testament of faith and humility, Elizabeth asked, "Why am I so favored, that the mother of my Lord should come to me?" (Luke 1:43).

Elizabeth did indeed give birth to a son, and they named him John, as the angel had instructed. All her neighbors and relatives shared in her great joy.

RELATED INFORMATION

Mary's visit to Elizabeth was no small event. She was already expecting a child, and it would have taken her about three days to travel from Nazareth to the hills of Judea. She then stayed with Elizabeth for about three months before making the same journey back to Nazareth—three months further along in her pregnancy (Luke 1:39, 56).

*Then Zerubbabel the son of Shealtiel, and Joshua the
son of Jehozadak, the high priest, with all the remnant
of the people, obeyed the voice of the LORD their God,
and the words of Haggai the prophet, as the LORD
their God had sent him. And the people feared the LORD.*
HAGGAI 1:12 ESV

In a big game with only an inning or two left, every baseball coach worth his salt knows to bring in his ace "closer," a pitcher whose sole job is to stop the other team from scoring runs and ensure victory.

The prophet Haggai must have been an amazing closer.

Many prophets had spent nearly their whole lives relaying God's messages to His people but with little positive response. Haggai's prophetic ministry, on the other hand, appears to have spanned only four months, but by God's providence it resulted in the completion of the second temple.

HAGGAI

Prophet of Judea
after the Exile

The first temple had been destroyed by the Babylonians several decades earlier, and now many Jews had returned from exile and had begun to rebuild the temple. The project had been at a standstill for many years due to opposition from hostile neighbors, but the Lord began to stir the hearts of the Jewish leaders once again through the words of Haggai and Zechariah. These two prophets called for the people to finish what they had started, and the people responded.

RELATED INFORMATION

Haggai may have been very old when he delivered his prophecies to God's people, because Haggai 2:3 seems to imply that he saw the first temple with his own eyes before it was destroyed. The first temple was destroyed over sixty-five years before Haggai delivered his messages.

Obadiah was a devout believer in the LORD.
While Jezebel was killing off the LORD's prophets,
Obadiah had taken a hundred prophets and hidden them in two caves,
fifty in each, and had supplied them with food and water.

1 KINGS 18:3–4

In most people's catalogs of spiritual heroes, it is unlikely that Obadiah ranks very high. Yet even though Obadiah may not have demonstrated great bravery in the face of danger, he served the Lord nonetheless, and his efforts no doubt preserved the lives of many godly people.

OBADIAH

Servant of Ahab

Obadiah was in charge of wicked King Ahab's palace, yet he himself was a devout believer. When evil Queen Jezebel began to destroy the prophets of the Lord, Obadiah hid one hundred of them in a cave and provided them with food and water.

During this time there was a severe famine, and Ahab and Obadiah went looking for water for his animals. While Obadiah was searching in one area, the prophet Elijah approached him and told him to tell Ahab that he was there. Obadiah was very concerned, however, because Ahab had already been looking everywhere for Elijah to arrest him, and Obadiah feared that Elijah would disappear again and make Obadiah out to be a liar to Ahab. Elijah understood Obadiah's concern and promised to appear before Ahab that day.

RELATED INFORMATION

When Elijah appeared before Ahab, he challenged him to bring hundreds of the prophets of Baal and Asherah to Mount Carmel for a contest to see who was the true God. When the Lord showed Himself to be the true God, Elijah and the people of Israel killed the prophets of Baal and Asherah.

The name of Amram's wife was Jochebed daughter of Levi,
who was born to Levi in Egypt; and she bore to Amram:
Aaron, Moses, and their sister Miriam.
NUMBERS 26:59 NRSV

Jochebed was a risk-taker. Although the Bible doesn't give us a detailed biography of Moses' mother, it does disclose the results of the courageous choices she made.

When the Egyptian Pharaoh ordered the death of all newborn Hebrew boys in order to slow the slaves' population growth, Jochebed took decisive action to protect the life of her tiny son. The risks she took on Moses' behalf often go unnoticed:

JOCHEBED

Mother of Moses, Aaron, and Miriam

- Jochebed risked punishment by defying the king's orders and letting her son live.
- She secretly hid her newborn baby for three months (Exodus 2:2).
- She risked her child's life by placing the infant in a floating basket in the Nile. She could not have known if this daring action would result in the baby being lost downstream, being discovered and killed, being drowned, being eaten by Nile crocodiles, or being discovered and spared.
- She risked exposure by having Miriam, her daughter, watch the basket and then approach the Egyptian princess with an offer of aid.

Though bold, Jochebed's choices were not reckless. A descendant of Levi, she had faith that God could intervene and save the boy she viewed as "a fine baby" (Exodus 2:2 NRSV).

SPIRITUAL INSIGHT

Faith can be risky. We don't know what other risks Jochebed may have taken and how those turned out, but we do know that in this case God fulfilled His plan for the Hebrew people because of the risks she took. Doing what is right isn't always easy, and it can often be accompanied by a fair amount of risk. But when faith-based risks and God's plan coincide, the results can change the world.

*All these latter kings joined forces in the Valley of Siddim
(the Salt Sea). For twelve years they had been subject to
Kedorlaomer, but in the thirteenth year they rebelled.*
GENESIS 14:3–4

Like so many other rulers in the Bible, Kedorlaomer is yet another example of a king who may have been more powerful than the other kings around him, but he was no match for someone empowered by God.

Kedorlaomer was the king of Elam, an old and powerful kingdom in the

KEDORLAOMER

King of Elam

time of Abraham. Though Elam was several hundred miles away from Canaan, Kedorlaomer's reach in Abraham's time was so great that he was able to rule over even some of the Canaanite kings, including five cities near the Dead Sea. Eventually, however, those kings banded together and rebelled against Kedorlaomer, so he formed a coalition of four kings and attacked them. He defeated them, but as he was returning to Elam, he carried off Abraham's nephew Lot. When Abraham learned of this, he gathered together 318 men from his household—a significant number for a household, but probably no match for a coalition of four kings—and headed off to rescue Lot. Abraham no doubt shocked Kedorlaomer's forces when he defeated them and rescued Lot, showing that God was surely watching over Abraham and Lot (Genesis 14).

RELATED INFORMATION

The five cities that were allied against Kedorlaomer—Sodom, Gomorrah, Admah, Zeboiim, and Zoar—are referred to elsewhere as the cities of the plain (Genesis 13:12, 19:24–25). Lot lived near the city of Sodom, which was later destroyed by the Lord for its wickedness. Of these cities, archaeologists have only been able to find Zoar, but it is possible that the other cities lay along the eastern shore of the Dead Sea.

They bound [Jesus] and brought him first to Annas,
who was the father-in-law of Caiaphas, the high priest that year.
JOHN 18:12–13

Annas appears to have been astute, wealthy, powerful, and politically influential, yet in the end, he will always be known among Christians as the man who, together with his son-in-law Caiaphas, presided over Jesus' trial before the Sanhedrin and handed Him over to be crucified by the Romans.

ANNAS

High Priest of Israel during Jesus' Time

Annas, a prominent Sadducee, had been appointed as high priest by the Romans in AD 6, and he held that post for ten years until they deposed him. For the next few decades, his sons and one son-in-law occupied the office of high priest, but Annas wielded so much influence over them that he continued to be referred to as high priest as well (see Luke 3:2; Acts 4:6).

Annas accrued much of his vast wealth from sales of sacrificial animals, oil, and other required items in the temple area. It was almost certainly his business dealings in the temple that prompted Jesus to denounce those who made the temple a "den of robbers" (Mark 11:15–19).

When Jesus was first arrested, He was brought to the house of Annas, and then He was sent to Caiaphas, Annas's son-in-law. Later Jesus would be handed over to the Romans, who would crucify Him just as the Jewish leaders had requested (John 18).

RELATED INFORMATION

Annas and his son-in-law Caiaphas were also present during the trial of Peter and John, who had been arrested for preaching about Jesus in the temple area (Acts 4).

24

When Herod saw Jesus, he was greatly pleased, because for a long time he had been wanting to see him. From what he had heard about him, he hoped to see him perform some miracle.

LUKE 23:8

In his heart, Herod Antipas was probably not much different than many unbelievers today—they are intrigued by Jesus' life and teachings, but in the end they will never truly believe in Him, because they aren't willing to surrender their lives to Him.

Herod Antipas was one of the sons of Herod the Great, the king who ruled over all Judea and Galilee when Jesus was born. After Herod died, his kingdom was divided among his sons Archelaus, Antipas, and Philip. Antipas was given the regions of Perea and Galilee, where Jesus grew up and conducted most of His ministry.

HEROD ANTIPAS

Tetrarch over Galilee

Herod Antipas appears to have been intrigued with both John the Baptist and Jesus (Mark 6:20; Luke 23:8). When John criticized Antipas for taking his brother Philip's wife, he had John arrested and put in prison, but he still liked to listen to him. Later, however, he bowed to his wife's schemes to have John beheaded. When Pilate was looking for a way to pass the buck regarding the accusations against Jesus, he sent Him to Antipas, who thought he would have a front-row seat to one of Jesus' miracles. When Jesus failed to meet his expectations, he let his soldiers mock Jesus and sent Him back to Pilate. That is the last we hear of any interaction Herod Antipas had with Jesus.

SPIRITUAL INSIGHT

There is certainly some good in being attracted to Jesus' life and message, but ultimately Jesus must be seen as more than a mere wonder-worker or moral teacher. He must be seen as our Lord and our only way to God (John 14:6; Romans 10:8–10).

When Simon saw that the Spirit was given at the laying
on of the apostles' hands, he offered them money and said,
"Give me also this ability so that everyone on whom I lay
my hands may receive the Holy Spirit."
ACTS 8:18–19

Before the gospel came to Samaria, Simon was a minor phenomenon with a major ego. Pretending to be someone important—perhaps even claiming to be the incarnation of God Himself (depending on the meaning of the phrase "Great Power" in Acts 8:10)—Simon wowed the people with his sorcery, convincing them that he exercised control over the spiritual realm. In a time when most people assumed the existence of a spiritual world—and believed that it was not likely a benevolent force—sorcerers like Simon were in great demand.

SIMON

The Sorcerer

But all that was before the arrival of Philip, the man famous for taking the gospel to unexpected places. As a follower of the resurrected Jesus, Philip possessed a power that made Simon look like the conjurer of cheap tricks by comparison. Even Simon was impressed—so much so that he "believed and was baptized" (Acts 8:13).

However, Simon seems to have been drawn to the power rather than to its source. When Peter and John came to impart the Holy Spirit to the Samaritan believers, Simon was beside himself. Desperate for his former glory, he offered the apostles money in exchange for the ability to dispense God's Spirit. After all, he had spent years pretending to do just that; now, he thought, the real thing was within his grasp!

How wrong he was. Enraged, Peter reduced Simon to a whimpering wreck, denying him any part in their ministry and warning him to beg God's forgiveness before it was too late. Nothing more is said about Simon, except that he begged Peter to pray on his behalf—now afraid to even speak to the God whose power he just tried to purchase.

SPIRITUAL INSIGHT

Simon had a fundamentally flawed understanding of the Holy Spirit. While Peter and John freely shared the Spirit, empowering all who believed, Simon saw the Holy Spirit as a means of gaining power for himself—some deep magic that he could dispense for a price. Peter and John did not use their status to control others but to release them from sin so they could experience Christ's promise of true liberation.

"For I tell you that unless your righteousness surpasses that of the Pharisees and the teachers of the law, you will certainly not enter the kingdom of heaven."

MATTHEW 5:20

Pharisees are a notorious and sometimes misunderstood group in the New Testament. While they provided one of the chief sources of opposition to Jesus, they actually had more in common with Him than some other Jewish religious groups of the day.

Some may be surprised to learn that Jesus shared two of the Pharisees' most important theological commitments. Unlike their rival Sadducees, Pharisees firmly believed in the bodily resurrection—a fact the apostle Paul later used to his advantage when he appeared before the Sanhedrin, a ruling body comprised of both Pharisees and Sadducees. On the basis of their shared belief in the resurrection, the Pharisees sided with Paul.

PHARISEES

Jewish Religious Leaders

Jesus and the Pharisees also shared a deep devotion to the Torah, the Jewish law contained in the first five books of the Old Testament. The Pharisees were mainly preoccupied with how to interpret and apply the law, while Jesus insisted that He came not to abolish but to fulfill (that is, to give the ultimate interpretation or meaning to) the law (see Matthew 5:17).

Nevertheless, the New Testament records a profound rift between Jesus and the Pharisees. Out of their zeal for correct interpretation of the law, they had turned it into a burden. Often, their efforts to keep the letter of the law caused them to miss the *spirit* of the law, such as when they carefully tithed the smallest spices while neglecting matters of justice, mercy, and faithfulness (see Matthew 23:23–24). As lay leaders, the Pharisees were held in high esteem among the people—something they relished (see Luke 11:43). Because of this, it is no surprise that they vigorously opposed anyone who represented a threat to their power and influence. As the ultimate fulfillment of the law, Jesus represented precisely such a threat.

DID YOU KNOW?

The Pharisees were not necessarily united in their opposition to Jesus. The Gospel of John mentions one Pharisee, Nicodemus, who sought a personal meeting with Jesus and even defended Him (briefly) to his fellow Pharisees.

On that day Gad went to David and said to him,
"Go up and build an altar to the LORD
on the threshing floor of Araunah the Jebusite."
2 SAMUEL 24:18

As great as King David was, much of his greatness was no doubt due in part to the guidance of other spiritual leaders—leaders like Gad, the prophet.

Gad is referred to in the Bible as a "seer," which is basically a prophet, someone who receives special messages from God. Gad appears to have been with David from his earliest days while he was on the run from Saul. He informed David not to stay in the stronghold (perhaps the fortress of Masada) and to return to the land of Judah (1 Samuel 22:5).

We don't hear about Gad again until many years later, after David had been firmly established as king and had ordered a census to be taken throughout Israel. Gad informed David of the consequences of his actions and offered him three options for punishment. Gad also told David to build the altar (of the temple) on the place where the plague was stopped (2 Samuel 24).

GAD

Prophet during David's Time

It seems that Gad also helped David station where the various clans of Levites would be in the temple that David's son Solomon would eventually build (2 Chronicles 29:25). Gad recorded many of the events of David's reign so that others could read about them afterward for generations to come (1 Chronicles 29:29).

RELATED INFORMATION

Another prophet who was closely linked with David's reign was Nathan. He relayed the message that God planned to build David a lasting dynasty and that David's son would build the temple (2 Samuel 7). Nathan was also the one who confronted David about his sin of adultery with Bathsheba (2 Samuel 12).

Meanwhile, the Midianites sold Joseph in Egypt to Potiphar,
one of Pharaoh's officials, the captain of the guard.
GENESIS 37:36

Potiphar was very fortunate to be master of a slave whose every move was blessed by God. Unfortunately, Potiphar's good fortune was not destined to last.

Potiphar was an important individual—a high-ranking official in Pharaoh's court. His obvious wealth is confirmed by the fact that he was able to afford a slave in the first place. After a few weeks with Joseph, however, Potiphar must have been thinking that he had gotten quite a bargain.

Potiphar quickly recognized the divine blessing on Joseph, and soon the latter was more than a common slave; he was Potiphar's personal attendant. Thanks to Joseph, Potiphar did not have a care in the world—at least as far as his household was concerned—for he had Joseph to look after everything for him. Joseph managed everything at home and in Potiphar's fields. All Potiphar had left to worry about was what to eat for dinner.

POTIPHAR

Owner of Joseph

Unfortunately for Potiphar, he should have been a bit more worried about his wife, who eventually became attracted to his talented, young attendant. Joseph, however, clung to his integrity and resisted each of her advances. Frustrated and rejected, Potiphar's wife sought revenge, falsely accusing Joseph of attempted rape. Potiphar fell for the ruse, believing himself a fool to have trusted Joseph so completely. He had Joseph put into the royal prison; it was the second time Joseph found himself bound against his will.

However, God's blessing did not end when Joseph was taken from Potiphar's household. Joseph continued his rise to prominence, while Potiphar and his devious wife faded into obscurity.

DID YOU KNOW?

Potiphar is part of an interesting pattern in Joseph's story. Three times Joseph found favor in the eyes of a superior—first as the favorite of his own father, then with Potiphar, and finally with Pharaoh himself. Each time, Joseph encountered some kind of trial—first being sold into slavery, then being imprisoned, and finally coming face-to-face with the brothers who betrayed him—only to triumph in the end.

*When David came to Mahanaim, Shobi the son of Nahash
from Rabbah of the Ammonites, and Machir the son of
Ammiel from Lo-debar, and Barzillai the Gileadite from
Rogelim, brought beds, basins, and earthen vessels, wheat, barley,
flour, parched grain, beans and lentils, honey and curds and sheep
and cheese from the herd, for David and the people with him to eat.*
2 SAMUEL 17:27–29 ESV

T here are always plenty of "friends" around when times are good, but true friends stick by us even when times are hard. Barzillai was indeed a friend of David. And David made sure he was good to Barzillai in return.

Late in David's reign as king of Israel, his son Absalom rebelled against him and attempted to usurp the throne. Absalom's rebellion had gained such momentum that David and those still loyal to him were forced to flee Jerusalem to a town named Mahanaim on the other side of the Jordan River (2 Samuel 15–17). When he arrived, several friends of David showed their loyalty to him by providing for the basic

BARZILLAI

Friend of David

needs of David and his men. Barzillai was one of those who provided food and supplies.

When the rebellion was put down and David was returning to Jerusalem, Barzillai accompanied David to the Jordan River to send him on his way (2 Samuel 19). In return for the kindness that Barzillai had shown, David invited Barzillai to come live with him in Jerusalem. Barzillai politely declined, saying that he was too old even to enjoy the comforts the king enjoyed at his palace. So Barzillai sent another friend in his place, and David blessed Barzillai. Later David instructed Solomon to continue to grant a place at his table for the sons of Barzillai (1 Kings 2:7).

RELATED INFORMATION

The story of Barzillai and David is a perfect example of ancient Near Eastern hospitality. A guest (which David was to Barzillai) was to be hosted and protected at great cost, even to the detriment of one's family. A good host also accompanied his parting guest for the first portion of his continuing journey. Likewise, such hospitality was expected to be repaid, even if the offer of repayment was merely an empty gesture and not really expected to be accepted.

*King Joash did not remember the kindness
Zechariah's father Jehoiada had shown him but killed his son.*
2 CHRONICLES 24:22

King Joash of Judah should have paid more attention to the Lord's words to Cain: "If you do not do what is right, sin is crouching at your door; it desires to have you, but you must master it" (Genesis 4:7). Perhaps then he would not have turned so remarkably from good to bad during his reign.

JOASH

King of Judah

The very fact that Joash was even alive to reign was a result of the gracious hand of God and the heroic acts of others. When he was just a baby, Joash's father was murdered, and his grandmother saw this as her opportunity to rule Judah. She murdered the entire royal family—her own grandchildren—except for one: Joash. Jehosheba, a member of the royal family and the wife of a priest named Jehoiada, stole him away and hid Joash in the temple precincts for six years. Then Jehoiada arranged for the people to crown Joash king at seven years of age (2 Kings 11).

For the first part of Joash's reign, Jehoiada remained an adviser to him, and he did what was pleasing to the Lord. He even arranged for the temple to be repaired. But once Jehoiada died, Joash began to listen to the officials of the land, who led him to worship idols. Later, Jehoiada's son Zechariah prophesied against this wickedness, but Joash ordered that he be stoned to death. Because of his treacherous act toward Jehoiada's son, Joash's own officials killed him while he slept (2 Chronicles 24).

RELATED INFORMATION

Athaliah, the daughter of wicked King Ahab of Israel, was the woman who tried to kill Joash along with all the royal family (see 2 Kings 8:26). Presumably her mother was Jezebel, Ahab's idolatrous wife.

"You say to God, 'My beliefs are flawless and I am
pure in your sight.' Oh, how I wish that God would speak,
that he would open his lips against you."
Job 11:4–5

In reality, Zophar just wanted the same thing that his tortured friend Job longed for. They both wanted God to speak. However, they had very different ideas of what God would say if and when He did speak.

Zophar was one of three friends to visit Job after every imaginable disaster had struck. In response to Job's complaints, Zophar spoke twice; he was always the third of Job's friends to speak. Unfortunately, the extra time did not make his words any wiser than those of his two friends, Eliphaz and Bildad. In many ways, Zophar was the

ZOPHAR

Job's Friend

most insistent of the three. He was convinced that Job had done something wrong to merit God's punishment—for surely all of Job's misery could only be the result of divine punishment.

Job, however, would have none of it. In the third and final round of debate, Zophar—apparently exasperated by his friend's dogged proclamations of innocence—did not even bother to speak. It was just as well, too. When God finally spoke, He didn't exactly bring words of comfort to Job, but His response was nonetheless a vindication of Job's integrity. Job's friends, on the other hand, found themselves on the receiving end of God's anger. However, Zophar and the others did as they were instructed, offering expensive sacrifices as burnt offerings to God, who heard Job's prayers on their behalf. Zophar who once insisted that his friend repent of some unknown (and nonexistent) sin—discovered that he was the one who needed to repent.

SPIRITUAL INSIGHT

Zophar and his friends did one thing right in their interaction with Job. Upon arriving—only to discover their friend in such a miserable state—they tore their robes and sprinkled dust on their heads as a sign of mourning and solidarity. Then they sat and said nothing for a full week, giving Job the chance to speak first—and only when he was ready. In a world obsessed with easy answers and quick solutions, sometimes the best thing we can do for hurting friends is simply to sit with them.

[Elijah] replied, "I have been very zealous for the LORD God Almighty. The Israelites have rejected your covenant, broken down your altars, and put your prophets to death with the sword. I am the only one left, and now they are trying to kill me too."

1 KINGS 19:14

Even the greatest of God's servants can become overwhelmed by circumstances. Just ask Elijah, God's prophet to Israel during the evil reign of King Ahab.

Elijah was called by God to prophesy against the wickedness of Ahab and the Israelites during one of the darkest times in its history. King Ahab and his wife, Jezebel, had been promoting idolatry throughout the land and were trying to rid the land of the prophets of the Lord. Elijah faithfully and courageously confronted Ahab repeatedly about his sins and witnessed various miracles from God.

ELIJAH

Prophet of Israel

Perhaps the greatest confrontation between Elijah and Ahab took place on Mount Carmel. There Elijah called for hundreds of the prophets of Baal and Asherah to meet him and see which God or gods answered their prayers to consume a sacrifice. When Elijah's God proved victorious over the other gods, Elijah instructed the people to kill all the prophets of Baal and Asherah.

Having just witnessed this amazing miracle, however, Elijah fled for his life to Horeb (Mount Sinai) to escape the wrath of Jezebel. Along the way, and even while he was there speaking with God, Elijah expressed despair that he was the only one left who worshipped God.

God answered him by giving him some very direct commands of what to do next, and He assured him that he was not alone, for there were still seven thousand others in Israel who refused to bow down to idols. Elijah obeyed and anointed Elisha to succeed him in his ministry.

SPIRITUAL INSIGHT

When you feel overwhelmed in your walk with God, take heart in knowing that God is always in control—and He can raise up others to help even when it seems that no one else cares about God.

One of the criminals who hung there hurled insults at him:
"Aren't you the Christ? Save yourself and us!"
LUKE 23:39

The precise identity of the men crucified alongside Jesus remains a mystery—as do their specific crimes. Though both died on their crosses, the two men experienced very different fates.

THE THIEVES WHO WERE CRUCIFIED

Died alongside Jesus

The three Gospels that mention the "thieves" (as tradition has come to identify them) refer to them in three different ways. According to Matthew, the two men were "robbers" or "rebels," depending on how the text is translated. Luke referred to them as "criminals," while Mark ambiguously described them as "those crucified with" Jesus.

Though it is not possible to state conclusively, it may be that the two men crucified next to Jesus were actual rebels, guilty of the crime (treason) for which Jesus was wrongfully condemned.

At first, both criminals were defiant and joined in the insults being hurled at Jesus. Who knows what motivated their vitriol—perhaps they did not think Jesus was "worthy" of being crucified alongside them. Or perhaps their agony simply revealed the worst of their characters. For whatever reason, though, one of the criminals had a change of heart, recorded only in Luke. Rebuking the other condemned man, he turned to Jesus and asked to be remembered in His kingdom—a powerful demonstration of his last-minute belief that not even death could keep God's kingdom from breaking into our world through the man who was dying next to him.

DID YOU KNOW?

Jesus' promise to the believing criminal (Luke 23:43) contains an interesting ambiguity. The meaning of the word "today" is reasonably straightforward, but what it refers to is less clear. It could be an indication that Jesus and the criminal would be together in paradise later that same day. Or Jesus simply may have been saying, in effect, "Today I'm telling you. . ." The lack of punctuation in the oldest Greek manuscripts makes interpreting this nuance of the verse challenging.

And he carried away Jehoiachin to Babylon. The king's mother,
the king's wives, his officials, and the chief men of the land
he took into captivity from Jerusalem to Babylon.
2 KINGS 24:15 ESV

The life of Jehoiachin, one of the last kings of Judah, is a portrait of sadness, both for him and for his people. It seems that the only bright rays of hope that shone during his life came briefly at the beginning and then again at the end. The first bright ray shone at his birth, in that his grandfather Josiah was still king of Judah. Josiah brought about revival throughout the country, repaired the temple, and even expanded his territory to reclaim much of the land of Israel that had been lost to Assyria many years earlier.

JEHOIACHIN

Exiled King of Judah

Later, however, Josiah was killed in a battle with Pharaoh Neco of Egypt, and Neco installed Josiah's son Eliakim as king, changing his name to Jehoiakim. Jehoiakim was the father of Jehoiachin. Soon after this, King Nebuchadnezzar of Babylon gained control of Judah and exiled Jehoiakim, and many other Judeans, to Babylon when the puppet king rebelled against him. Jehoiachin then became king in place of his father but reigned only three months before he, too, was exiled to Babylon by Nebuchadnezzar. Jehoiachin remained in Babylon for over thirty-seven years.

Jehoiachin's second ray of hope shone during his final days, when the new king of Babylon released Jehoiachin from prison and gave him a seat of honor above all the other captive kings. Jehoiachin was allowed to eat with the king of Babylon for the rest of his days (Jeremiah 52:31–34).

> **DID YOU KNOW?**
>
> Zedekiah, another son of Josiah and the uncle of Jehoiachin, was the only other king to rule over Judah after Jehoiachin. Zedekiah was originally called Mattaniah until the Babylonians changed his name.

But the magicians of Egypt did the same by their secret arts;
so Pharaoh's heart remained hardened, and he would not
listen to them; as the Lord had said.
EXODUS 7:22 NRSV

When Moses and Aaron confronted Pharaoh in Egypt, members of Pharaoh's court opposed them and tried to duplicate Moses and Aaron's miraculous signs. While the book of Exodus doesn't reveal the names of these rivals, Hebrew tradition preserves their memory as Jannes and Jambres—which the apostle Paul also affirms (2 Timothy 3:8).

God had given Moses and Aaron specific miracles to help persuade Pharaoh to release God's people from their slavery. By trying to duplicate these miracles, Pharaoh's magicians hoped to keep the people of God enslaved in Egypt.

JANNES AND JAMBRES

Pharaoh's Magicians Who Opposed Moses

Although Jannes and Jambres managed to copy many of God's miraculous signs, they could not do so universally. Exodus 8 records that these magicians failed to replicate the plague of gnats, and Exodus 9:11 records that the plague of boils had affected them so badly that they could not stand before Pharaoh.

Throughout Israel's history, these men served as an archetype of those who fight against the progress of God's plan and His gospel message. Paul wrote: "As Jannes and Jambres opposed Moses, so these people, of corrupt mind and counterfeit faith, also oppose the truth" (2 Timothy 3:8 NRSV). Their actions made these men appropriate symbols of opposition to God's deliverance of His people.

DID YOU KNOW?

These magicians became popular villains throughout Israel's history. Not only were their names preserved as the magicians of Pharaoh's court, but Hebrew tradition also refers to these men as sons of Balaam, as those who incited Aaron to build the golden calf, and as having died at the crossing of the Red Sea. Though physically impossible for Jannes and Jambres to be linked in actuality to each of these episodes, their mention in each reveals the place these men occupied in the Hebrews' hearts and minds.

*[The LORD] brought up against them the king of the Babylonians,
who killed their young men with the sword in the sanctuary,
and spared neither young man nor young woman, old man or aged.
God handed all of them over to Nebuchadnezzar.*

2 CHRONICLES 36:17

As powerful as they were, ultimately the Babylonians functioned as a tool in the hand of God. Unfortunately, God eventually needed to use that tool to bring judgment on His people.

The Babylonians lived in the southern part of what is now known as Iraq, between the Tigris and Euphrates rivers. They gained prominence under the reign of Hammurabi, who united several smaller states and codified the laws of the nation. Around 729 BC the Assyrians began to rule over them, but by 612 BC the Babylonians had joined with the Persians to break free from their grip and take over much of their kingdom, including the regions of Israel and Judah.

BABYLONIANS

Nation That Exiled
the People of Judah

Soon after this, the Babylonians became directly involved in Judean affairs as different kings rebelled against them. The Babylonians under Nebuchadnezzar eventually attacked the capital city of Jerusalem in 586 BC, destroyed the city and the temple, and exiled virtually all the leading citizens to Babylon.

By 539 BC, King Cyrus of Persia captured the city of Babylon and decreed that all the Jews who had been exiled there could return to Judea.

RELATED INFORMATION

The capital of Babylonia was Babylon, which was located about fifty-five miles south of modern-day Baghdad. The walls of this city were immense, but Cyrus of Persia conquered the city by diverting the flow of the Euphrates River, which ran under the walls, thereby enabling his soldiers to enter the city.

I have become all things to all men so that by all possible means I might save some. I do all this for the sake of the gospel, that I may share in its blessings.

1 CORINTHIANS 9:22–23

Day
37

The apostle Paul, the New Testament figure second only to Jesus in prominence, was a man of single-minded devotion. His mission to bring the gospel to the Gentile world filled him with an unrelenting fervor that carried him across the Roman Empire. In retrospect, Paul's background made him the perfect choice for this God-ordained mission.

PAUL

Apostle to the Gentiles

Paul was born in the city of Tarsus (located in present-day Turkey), which was cosmopolitan and diverse; it was one of the leading university cities of its day. There Paul would have encountered all kinds of religious, cultural, and philosophical expressions.

But Paul was also devoted to the faith of his ancestors. He studied under Gamaliel, grandson of Hillel, the most famous rabbi of his day. As an adult, Paul bore all the markings of a rabbi. He even counted himself among the Pharisees.

Given his background, perhaps it is no surprise that God chose Paul to "carry my name before the Gentiles and their kings" (Acts 9:15) With one foot in the Jewish world and the other in the culture of the Gentiles, Paul was ideally suited to take the gospel from one to the other. His status as a Roman citizen—which suggests he belonged to the aristocracy—gave him enormous freedom as he traveled the empire. Paul used his citizenship not for his own gain, but to gain an audience with Caesar—knowing full well that to appeal to the Roman emperor (as only a Roman citizen could) was to put his very life at risk (see Acts 25:11). Paul's fate is not known. However, it is believed he gained his audience before Caesar—the dangerous Emperor Nero, to be precise—where he may well have become a martyr for the faith.

SPIRITUAL INSIGHT

Despite his justifiably revered status in church history, Paul comes across as a refreshingly human figure. He was passionate—capable of great fits of emotion. The book of Acts even records Paul's falling out with his colleague Barnabas (Acts 15:36–41). Paul knew that he was just a sinner—in his mind, "the worst of sinners" (1 Timothy 1:16)—who had been saved by God's immeasurable grace.

*And since the LORD had not said he would
blot out the name of Israel from under heaven,
he saved them by the hand of Jeroboam son of Jehoash.*
2 KINGS 14:27

W hen we see people who seem to have everything in life—lots of money, a great career, good health—it's tempting to think that God must somehow like them better than us. But the story of King Jeroboam II should show us that material blessings do not automatically equal approval from God.

JEROBOAM II

King of Israel

Like the king of Israel before him with the same name, King Jeroboam II of Israel did evil in the eyes of the Lord. Yet his reign appears to have been extremely successful in every other way. He reigned for a lengthy forty-one years, and his domain expanded considerably under his rule, virtually doubling in size (2 Kings 14). The Bible doesn't say anything about Jeroboam suffering any great difficulties during his reign (although the prophet Amos apparently prophesied that he would die by the sword—see Amos 7).

So does this mean that God actually *approved* of Jeroboam? Or that He didn't really care whether he was evil or not? Not at all. Rather, the Lord allowed these good things to come because of love for His people, not Jeroboam's behavior (2 Kings 14:26–27). As with ancient Israel, often what appears to be God's tolerance of evil is actually a demonstration of His mercy (2 Peter 3:9).

Then Miriam the prophetess, the sister of Aaron,
took a tambourine in her hand,
and all the women went out after her
with tambourines and dancing.
EXODUS 15:20 ESV

Siblings often bring out both the best and worst in each other. This certainly held true in Miriam's life.

As a young girl, she lived as a slave in Egypt. When Pharaoh's edict commanded that all newborn baby boys be killed, Miriam and her family worked to keep her newborn brother hidden. When they could no longer conceal Moses, Miriam's mother made a papyrus basket, waterproofed it with tar, and left the basket floating in the Nile River. She gave Miriam the job of watching the basket and the fate of her little brother. When Pharaoh's daughter discovered and adopted Moses, Miriam courageously approached the royal daughter and offered to find a suitable nurse for the baby, thereby bringing the family back together under safe conditions.

MIRIAM

Sister of Moses

Although Moses grew up and lived his early adult life near his sister, the two were separated for nearly forty years when Moses ran from Pharaoh (see Exodus 2). God reunited the siblings in the task of leading the people out of slavery and into the Promised Land (see Micah 6:4). Along the way, Miriam became jealous of Moses (see Numbers 12:1–2). When she and her brother, Aaron, began to display their jealousy, God struck her with leprosy for seven days to discipline her for her insolence (see Numbers 12:14).

In her adult life, Miriam is often best remembered for leading the people in song and worship after they crossed the Red Sea (Exodus 15:20–21).

DID YOU KNOW? Miriam was the first woman in the Bible with the title of prophetess (Exodus 15:20).

*Then Amaziah sent messengers to Jehoash son of Jehoahaz,
the son of Jehu, king of Israel, with the challenge:
"Come, meet me face to face."*

2 KINGS 14:8

When King Amaziah of Judah challenged King Jehoash of Israel to battle, he definitely bit off more than he could chew. But it seems as if this followed the general character of Amaziah, who had a habit of acting without fully thinking through the situation.

AMAZIAH

King of Judah

Amaziah had taken over the throne of Judah when his father was assassinated by his own officials (2 Kings 12:19–21). Amaziah appears to have started out strong, because the Bible describes him as doing "right in the eyes of the LORD" (2 Kings 14:1–3). But his commitment was not wholehearted, because he allowed the pagan shrines to remain in the land.

Perhaps in a rush to amass enough troops to fight Edom, Amaziah rashly hired mercenaries from Israel to add to the troops that came from Judah. When a prophet warned him not to use mercenaries from Israel to fight the battle, Amaziah simply dismissed them and headed off to war with Edom. In the meantime, the mercenaries, no doubt angry that they would not share in any spoils of victory, attacked several Judean towns.

Amaziah defeated the Edomites, but he also brought back their gods and worshipped them. The battle victory must have gone to his head, too, because he soon challenged King Jehoash of Israel to battle. Despite Jehoash's warnings, Amaziah would not back down, and Jehoash thoroughly defeated him, even destroying part of Jerusalem's wall and looting the temple (2 Kings 14:8–14).

In the end, Amaziah was assassinated by his own people from Jerusalem, just as his father had been (2 Kings 14:18–20).

RELATED INFORMATION

Amaziah's defeat at the hands of Jehoash should have come as no surprise. Jehoash proved himself to be an able military leader by defeating the Arameans in three separate battles to recover Israelite towns that they had taken (2 Kings 13:25).

*Then Judas (not Judas Iscariot) said,
"But, Lord, why do you intend to show
yourself to us and not to the world?"*
JOHN 14:22

T haddaeus was one of the original twelve apostles. Little is known about him, however. In fact, there is just one biblical passage that records anything Thaddaeus ever said or did—and that passage used a different name for him.

The Gospel writers Matthew and Mark referred to this disciple as Thaddaeus, perhaps the name by which he is most commonly known. Luke and John, however, identified him as "Judas son of James" (see, for example, Luke 6:16 and Acts 1:13).

His only speaking role captured in scripture was recorded by John and came during the final week of Jesus' life. As the disciples shared one last meal with their rabbi before His crucifixion, Jesus spoke words of comfort, promising to send the Holy Spirit to His followers. Only they would be able to see Jesus and experience

THADDAEUS

Disciple of Jesus, Also Known as Judas

His love. The world—that is, those who did not embrace Jesus—would not be able to see Him.

Thaddaeus (or Judas, as he was called in John's story) was confused. He and the other disciples expected a Messiah who would gather all Israel to Himself, throw off the yoke of Roman oppression by force, and reveal Himself to the world. To Thaddaeus's way of thinking, Jesus had it backwards. Why, he wondered, would the Messiah only want to reveal Himself to the disciples? How, then, could He force the entire world to bow down to His authority?

Jesus' answer to Thaddaeus's question contained a powerful lesson that the disciples struggled to understand until after Jesus ascended back to heaven. Jesus did not intend to coerce the world into submission. Rather, He planned to reveal Himself to those who loved Him—that is, those who obeyed His teaching. Perhaps this was a bit less dramatic, but ultimately it proved a far more effective way to build a kingdom.

DID YOU KNOW?

Thaddaeus seems to be an idiomatic name meaning either "large hearted" or "courageous." Christian tradition says that most of the disciples (including Thaddaeus) met martyrs' deaths. It seems this large-hearted and courageous disciple preached the gospel message to the end.

*The commander himself was alarmed when he realized that
he had put Paul, a Roman citizen, in chains.*

ACTS 22:29

In all likelihood, Lysias just wanted the trouble to go away. Roman commanders were employed to maintain order—with brutal force, if needed—not mediate disputes. Lysias commanded the garrison at Jerusalem, one of the most volatile outposts in the Roman Empire. When the entire city seemed to explode in uproar over the apostle Paul, Lysias tried repeatedly to diffuse the situation, to no avail.

LYSIAS

Protected Paul during a Riot

A group of Jews from Asia had accused Paul of bringing Gentiles into the court of Israel in the temple. When a crowd began beating Paul, Lysias and his troops intervened. First, Lysias granted Paul's request to address the crowd, perhaps hoping Paul could explain the situation to their satisfaction. Paul's speech had the opposite effect: The moment he announced his call to preach to the Gentiles, the crowd erupted anew.

Lysias decided to try another course of action, ordering Paul to be flogged by one of his centurions. This plan nearly backfired when Paul revealed that he was a Roman citizen—beating him would have been illegal. Paul, who was born a citizen, gained the upper hand over Lysias, who admitted he had had to purchase *his* citizenship.

Lysias's third attempt at restoring order—by calling a meeting of the Sanhedrin (the Jewish ruling council)—fared no better. This time it seemed even Paul worked to undermine him, deliberately throwing the Sanhedrin into a furious debate over the resurrection.

With the help of Paul's nephew, Lysias intercepted a plot to assassinate Paul and decided the time had come to move Paul up the chain of command, referring the matter to Felix, governor of Judea—and doubtless experiencing no small amount of relief.

SPIRITUAL INSIGHT

Lysias did not realize it, but he played an important part in God's plan for Paul's life. The night after Paul appeared before the Sanhedrin, God revealed that he was to testify in Rome, capital of the world's most powerful empire. By referring Paul's case to Felix, Lysias unwittingly took the first step in fulfilling the divine plan.

John replied in the words of Isaiah the prophet,
"I am the voice of one calling in the desert,
'Make straight the way for the Lord.'"
JOHN 1:23

J ohn the Baptist was a man who clearly understood his calling: He was to prepare the way for the Messiah. So when the time came for Jesus to begin His ministry, John willingly directed others to Him and allowed his own powerful ministry to take a backseat to Jesus.

John was Jesus' relative, and his own birth, like Jesus', was foretold by the angel Gabriel (Luke 1). John grew up to be a prophet, living in the desert and dressing in clothing similar to Elijah's (2 Kings 1:8; Matthew 3:4). He preached the message, "Repent, for the kingdom of heaven is near"—the same message Jesus would later preach (Matthew 4:17) after John baptized

JOHN THE BAPTIST

Forerunner of Jesus

Him. Jesus held John in very high esteem, declaring that no man has ever been greater than he (Matthew 11:11). John's ministry and his call for repentance were so widespread that years after his death he had followers as far away as Ephesus (Acts 19:1–5).

As great as John's ministry was, however, he always understood that his role was to point to One who was greater: Jesus. John knew that Jesus was so great in comparison to him that he was not even worthy to untie Jesus' sandals (Mark 1:7).

John met his death when he was thrown in prison for speaking out against Herod Antipas's marriage to his brother's wife. Herod's wife eventually asked for John's head on a platter, and Herod ordered that it be done.

SPIRITUAL INSIGHT

John modeled the attitude that all believers should follow as we point others to Jesus. We may be serving Christ in a way that is very powerful and beneficial to many people, but ultimately Jesus is greater than anything we are doing. The time may come for us to allow our ministry to be overshadowed or even replaced by other things Jesus is doing, and we should imitate John's example and willingly allow that to happen.

Moses was willing to dwell with the man,
and he gave his daughter Zipporah to Moses.
EXODUS 2:21 NASB

Zipporah's appearance in the Bible's story line begins with murder. She neither witnessed nor participated in the slaying, but she enters the biblical narrative when she marries a fugitive wanted for murder: Moses.

Moses' name usually invokes the image of a bold leader and spiritual giant, but that wasn't always the case. At one time, Moses lived the life of an adopted prince in Pharaoh's palace. Then one day, Moses murdered an Egyptian for abusing a Hebrew slave. Though Moses tried to hide his crime by burying the body, Pharaoh heard what Moses had done, and the future Bible hero became an outlaw (Exodus 2).

ZIPPORAH

Wife of Moses

After running over a hundred miles, Moses made it to the land of Midian, located east of the Sinai Peninsula. While resting there, he saw seven sisters, caring for their flock, fighting the harmful treatment of other shepherds. Seeing their trouble, Moses chased off their abusers and proceeded to water the sisters' flock. Their father, Jethro, rewarded Moses' kindness by inviting him to live with them and by ultimately giving his daughter Zipporah to him in marriage. Together, Moses and Zipporah had two sons, named Gershom and Eliezer.

To survive as a shepherdess in the desert region of Midian, Zipporah must have been an industrious and resourceful woman. Those survival skills would have served her and Moses well as they lived together in the desert of Midian for forty years. These decades provided essential training for the overwhelming task that lay ahead: successfully leading the people of Israel through the desert to the Promised Land.

> **DID YOU KNOW?**
>
> Moses was about forty years old when he fled from Pharaoh's palace. He lived in Midian for approximately forty years and returned to lead God's people to the Promised Land at age eighty. After leading the people through the desert for forty years, Moses died at the age of 120.

Then Jeremiah took another scroll and gave it to Baruch the scribe,
the son of Neriah, who wrote on it at the dictation of Jeremiah all
the words of the scroll that Jehoiakim king of Judah had burned
in the fire. And many similar words were added to them.
JEREMIAH 36:32 ESV

The story line is familiar enough: Someone has written a scathing article against ongoing evil, and now he is being attacked. Sound like the lead news story from a couple of weeks ago? Actually, it's the story of Baruch, the personal scribe of the prophet Jeremiah, who demonstrated his faithfulness by willingly risking his life to record and recite Jeremiah's messages from God.

Baruch may have come from a noble family, since he appears to have been related to a staff officer who was exiled to Babylon along with all the other leading families of Judah (Jeremiah 51:59). Nevertheless, his high position did not deter him from linking his fate to that of Jeremiah, who was often harassed and even imprisoned by Judean leaders for his messages of judgment.

BARUCH

King of Persia

We first hear of Baruch when he helps Jeremiah with the process of purchasing land in his hometown. After that Jeremiah dictated a message of divine judgment for the nation of Judah and instructed Baruch to read it before the people at the temple. Baruch did so, and the message led the king to put out an order for the arrest of Baruch and Jeremiah (Jeremiah 36). The Lord kept them hidden, however, and eventually Baruch accompanied Jeremiah to Egypt along with the other exiles who were fleeing from the wrath of the Babylonians (Jeremiah 43:1–7).

RELATED INFORMATION

The Bible does not record anything further about Baruch after he accompanied Jeremiah to Egypt, but the early church leader Jerome wrote that some people in his day believed that Baruch died soon after arriving in Egypt. In 1975 a seal of Baruch was believed to have been discovered.

Day
46

*But the king of Assyria discovered that Hoshea was a traitor,
for he had sent envoys to So king of Egypt, and he no longer paid
tribute to the king of Assyria, as he had done year by year.
Therefore Shalmaneser seized him and put him in prison.*

2 KINGS 17:4

Based on what we read about him in the Bible, Hoshea must have been a gambler, but it seems his luck—or rather, the mercy of God—ran out when he chose to bet against the king of Assyria.

HOSHEA

King of Israel

Hoshea enters the biblical scene as the assassin and usurper of King Pekah of Israel (2 Kings 15:30). This treacherous act alone demonstrates that Hoshea chose to live dangerously and take great risks. The high stakes of his choices become even more apparent, however, when we realize that he did this immediately after the Assyrians had captured much of Israel's territory and deported many of the people to Assyria (2 Kings 15:29). Hoshea must have known that he was taking over a kingdom that was very much on the ropes with Assyria, and his fate was now tied to Israel's.

Nevertheless, Hoshea continued taking risks—both for himself and for Israel as a nation—when he sent secret envoys to Egypt to try to gain their support against Assyria. The risk did not pay off, however, because when he refused to continue paying tribute to Assyria, the Egyptians failed to show up. The Assyrians came and besieged Hoshea's capital city of Samaria until it finally fell three years later. The kingdom of Israel came to an end, and the Assyrians deported many Israelites to Assyria and other cities far away.

RELATED INFORMATION

King Hezekiah of Judah attempted a similar act of refusing to pay tribute to Assyria, but the city of Jerusalem survived due to the Lord's intervention (2 Kings 18–19). Perhaps this was due to Hezekiah's dependence upon the Lord, rather than on foreign powers, for help against Assyria.

After him, Abdon son of Hillel, from Pirathon, led Israel.
He had forty sons and thirty grandsons,
who rode on seventy donkeys. He led Israel eight years.
JUDGES 12:13–14

It's often what *isn't* mentioned that really tells the story. For example, if someone filling out a job application fails to answer why he or she left a previous job, it's very likely that this information would make the applicant look bad. It's hard to say for sure, but the Bible's short record of Abdon may be saying as much by what it doesn't say as by what it says.

The Bible does make it clear, though, that Abdon must have been a very wealthy man. It is impressive enough that he could have fathered and raised forty sons, but it is a truly incredible achievement to provide each of them—as well as each of his thirty grandsons—with his own donkey to ride. To connect that to today, it would be like saying he bought each of them his own car!

ABDON

Judge of Israel

But curiously absent from his record is any mention of his deeds or of Israel's deliverance from any oppressing nation. That may be because he never really performed any amazing deeds or helped to rescue Israel from anyone. He may have simply been the most influential person around when the nation needed to fill the role of judge. We don't know for sure, but that seems to be the implication from the Bible's account (Judges 12:13–15).

RELATED INFORMATION

Abdon came from the town of Pirathon in the hill country of Ephraim. This otherwise unknown town was also the home of Benaiah, the head of David's bodyguard (2 Samuel 23:30).

*Gehazi, the servant of Elisha the man of God, said,
"See, my master has spared this Naaman the Syrian,
in not accepting from his hand what he brought.
As the LORD lives, I will run after him and
get something from him."*

2 KINGS 5:20 ESV

W hen Paul warned his protégé Timothy that "the love of money is a root of all kinds of evil" (1 Timothy 6:10), he may well have been thinking of Gehazi. This relatively minor character from the Old Testament demonstrates that greed can get the best of anyone—even a servant of one of God's greatest prophets.

Gehazi was the servant of Elisha and had assisted him in some of the most amazing miracles of the Old Testament, including raising a young boy from the dead. Yet even after witnessing all these great acts of God, Gehazi allowed himself to be seduced by greed and even tried to deceive Elisha to hide his guilt.

GEHAZI

Servant of Elisha

It all started when an Aramean commander named Naaman came to Elisha for healing from his leprosy. After Naaman was healed, he offered a gift to Elisha to show his gratefulness, but Elisha declined. Gehazi, however, must have seen the incredible treasure that Naaman was offering Elisha, because he immediately schemed to collect some for himself. He ran back to Naaman and told him that Elisha changed his mind and requested 150 pounds of silver (about $24,000 today) and two sets of clothing for some other prophets! Gehazi then hid the items, returned to Elisha, and lied to cover up his sin. Elisha knew better, however, and told Gehazi that Naaman's leprosy would now cling to him and his descendants forever.

> **SPIRITUAL INSIGHT**
>
> From Achan (Joshua 7) to Gehazi (2 Kings 5) to Judas (Matthew 26:14–16), greed has always been a temptation for God's people— even for those who work closely with godly leaders. Be careful not to fall into the sin of greed, which is really idolatry at its core (Colossians 3:5).

*And as he reasoned about righteousness and self-control and
the coming judgment, Felix was alarmed and said,
"Go away for the present. When I get an opportunity
I will summon you."*
ACTS 24:25 ESV

S adly, if Felix lived among us today, he almost certainly would fit right in with
many churchgoers. His general attitude seems to have been that he was interested
and acquainted with Christianity ("the Way"), but when push came to shove, he
would dismiss it if it wasn't convenient.
And the gospel is not convenient.

Felix was governor of Judea during the
time of Paul, and he was renowned for his
corruption and self-interest. When Paul
was arrested in the temple at the end of
his third missionary journey, he was taken
to the Roman headquarters at Caesarea
on the coast of Palestine, and Felix heard

FELIX

Governor of Judea

Paul's case there. Felix delayed passing judgment on the case, but in the meantime
invited Paul to speak to him and his wife (who was a Jew) about Christianity.
When Paul touched on the unpleasant issues of righteousness, self-control, and
judgment, Felix grew afraid and quickly dismissed Paul, telling him that he would
send for him when he found it convenient.

Felix continued to speak with Paul from time to time, all the while hoping
that Paul would offer him a bribe to be released. Eventually the Romans replaced
Felix with another governor named Porcius Festus.

SPIRITUAL INSIGHT

Felix's actions make it clear that he was not really interested in
giving his life to Jesus Christ. He was only curious about Christianity
and the benefits it might offer him. In what ways might you be like
Felix? Are there aspects about the Christian life or the gospel that
you prefer to ignore or modify? In the end, a gospel that lacks hard
things is really no gospel at all.

So they searched for a beautiful girl throughout all the territory of Israel, and found Abishag the Shunammite, and brought her to the king.

1 KINGS 1:3 NASB

The Bible is a foreign book to most people. Even for those who grew up reading the Bible and attending church regularly, the Bible captures stories and messages from a different culture. The Middle Eastern traditions are very different than the twenty-first-century Western culture that many Christians live in. Because of this profound cultural difference, Abishag's story strikes us as unusual.

Abigshag was a beautiful young woman who was pressed into service of an elderly King David. As he aged, he had trouble staying warm at night no matter how many blankets they put on his bed. Rather than risk smothering their king, his servants enlisted Abishag—a Shunammite virgin. Her primary job was to sleep next to the king and keep him warm. Though she slept in the king's bed, Abishag remained a virgin.

ABISHAG

Nurse of King David

Abishag's closeness to the king put her in the center of controversy after David died. Though Solomon had become king, his brother Abiathar had his own eyes on the crown and made a play for power by requesting Abishag's hand in marriage. Solomon would not allow the union, and because Solomon interpreted the request as a political threat, he had Abiathar put to death the same day.

DID YOU KNOW?

As king, David had the right to conscript any man or woman into his service. The prophet Samuel had warned the people of a king's power. He said, "These will be the ways of the king who will reign over you: he will take your sons and appoint them to his chariots and to be his horsemen. . . . He will take your daughters to be perfumers and cooks and bakers. He will take the best of your fields and vineyards and olive orchards and give them to his courtiers. . . . He will take your male and female slaves, and the best of your cattle and donkeys, and put them to his work. He will take one-tenth of your flocks, and you shall be his slaves" (1 Samuel 8:11–17 NRSV).

"When you come to the Ammonites, do not harass them or provoke them to war, for I will not give you possession of any land belonging to the Ammonites. I have given it as a possession to the descendants of Lot."

DEUTERONOMY 2:19

O ften it is the people closest to us who are the hardest to get along with. The Ammonites and the Israelites were no exception.

AMMONITES

Neighboring Nation of Israel

The Ammonites were a people group descended from a man named Ben-Ammi, who was the son of Abraham's nephew Lot (Genesis 19:38). They lived on the eastern border of Israel, just south of the Jabbok River. They had occupied their territory before the Israelites came up from Egypt to live in the Promised Land of Canaan. The Lord specifically instructed the Israelites not to take any Ammonite territory as they claimed other land in the region (Deuteronomy 2:19).

The Ammonites' relationship with the Israelites was one of almost constant tension and sometimes even outright aggression. The Law of Moses forbade any Ammonite from entering the tabernacle area (Deuteronomy 23:3). The Ammonites took part in several alliances against Israel during the time of the judges (Judges 3:13; 10:7; 11:4), and they continued to attack Israel during the reign of Saul (1 Samuel 11:1).

David eventually brought them under the rule of Israel (2 Samuel 12:26–29), but they regained their independence after Israel split into two kingdoms. Various Israelite kings continued to struggle against them (2 Chronicles 20:1; 26:8; 27:5). The Ammonites remained a source of tension even when the Babylonians and Persians ruled over both the Israelites and the Ammonites (Nehemiah 4:7–8; Jeremiah 40:14).

The Ammonites worshipped the god Molech, who was often associated with child sacrifice (Leviticus 18:21; 2 Kings 23:10; Jeremiah 32:35). The Israelites were often guilty of worshipping this god as well.

RELATED INFORMATION

The capital of Ammon was Rabbah, located at modern-day Amman. After the city was conquered by the Greeks, it was renamed Philadelphia and listed among the cities of the Decapolis.

*By faith Abraham, even though he was past age—
and Sarah herself was barren—was enabled to become
a father because he considered him faithful
who had made the promise.*

HEBREWS 11:11

Sarah's story is one of belief mixed with doubt. As such, she is a character to which many readers can easily relate.

Most students of the Bible are well acquainted with Sarah's lack of faith. Her skepticism when God promised Abraham a son is understandable—after all, she had more than enough reason to believe this could never happen. Sarah had aged well beyond childbearing years when God spoke to her husband for the first time. Also, Sarah and Abraham were nearly parted from each other on at least two occasions—both times thanks to Abraham's own apparent lack of faith. In strikingly similar episodes, two rulers—first the king of Egypt, then the king of Gerar—took Sarah to be their wife. To save his own skin, Abraham had passed off Sarah as his sister (which was half true, since, in addition to being husband and wife, Sarah and Abraham were half siblings).

SARAH

Abraham's Wife

However, God's plan for Sarah would not be thwarted—not by outside events and not even by Sarah's own actions. Having long since given up on the hope of bearing a son, Sarah gave her servant Hagar to Abraham, in accordance with an ancient Mesopotamian custom. This union had the desired effect: Hagar gave birth to Ishmael. But things soured when Sarah turned on Hagar.

Despite her many doubts, however, Sarah was not entirely without faith. After all, she stood by Abraham during the entire twenty-five years that transpired between the first promise and its eventual fulfillment in the birth of Isaac. She may have laughed at the thought of a son, but she did not entirely abandon hope. In fact, the prophet Isaiah held up Sarah as a model of trust in God's faithfulness, counseling the people to "look to Abraham, your father, and to Sarah, who gave you birth" (Isaiah 51:2).

DID YOU KNOW?

As further evidence of Sarah's faith, it is possible to translate Hebrews 11:11 as a statement about her: "By faith even Sarah, who was past age, was enabled to bear children because she considered him faithful who had made the promise" (see NIV footnote to Hebrews 11:11).

As Jesus went on from there, he saw a man named Matthew sitting at the tax collector's booth. "Follow me," he told him, and Matthew got up and followed him.
MATTHEW 9:9

Matthew sat at the crossroads of commerce. His tax collector's booth in Capernaum probably looked out on the Via Maris, one of the most important trading routes in the Roman Empire.

MATTHEW

Tax Collector Turned Disciple

Local tax collectors were employed by the empire to keep Rome's coffers filled. They had a reputation for charging more than even Rome demanded and pocketing the extra—a habit that did not win many friends in occupied territories such as Galilee. In the ancient Jewish world, a tax collector's word was of no value in court, his presence was unwelcome at the synagogue, and even his own family might disown him.

Few would have approached Matthew's collection booth willingly—yet Jesus did. To some, it may seem strange that Matthew left behind a lucrative trade in order to wander the countryside with an itinerant preacher. Jesus, however, may have been one of the only people to offer Matthew an invitation of any kind. He may have been the first to look into Matthew's eyes—the eyes of one who, according to popular wisdom, should have been His enemy—and see a human being created in the image of God.

In that moment, Matthew left the crossroads of commerce to walk the crossroads of history. Not only did he accept Jesus' invitation—and extend one of his own, inviting Jesus to dinner—Matthew authored the Gospel that bears his name. Matthew wrote his account primarily for a Jewish audience—for the very people who had once despised him.

SPIRITUAL INSIGHT

Matthew's dinner party caused great controversy among the religious leaders, mainly because the guest list contained so many tax collectors and "sinners"—in other words, people who deliberately violated God's law. The religious authorities were offended because fellowship with sinners was believed to contaminate—and in the ancient world, one of the most intimate forms of fellowship was sharing a meal. Jesus' response revealed that where others saw potential for contamination, Jesus saw an opportunity to bring healing and wholeness.

But Omri did evil in the eyes of the LORD and sinned more than all those before him. He walked in all the ways of Jeroboam son of Nebat and in his sin, which he had caused Israel to commit, so that they provoked the LORD, the God of Israel, to anger by their worthless idols.

1 KINGS 16:25–26

Perhaps more is known about Omri from outside scripture than from the Bible itself. In fact, Omri is regarded as the most politically and militarily important monarch to sit on the throne of the northern kingdom of Israel. That, however, was not enough to salvage his reputation in the eyes of God.

OMRI

King of Israel

With Omri's rise to power, Israel enjoyed a time of relative stability after a brief but intense period of volatility. Omri's dynasty endured for almost five decades—no small accomplishment by Israelite standards.

Omri's predecessor, Zimri, reigned for a mere seven days. Having murdered the previous king, Zimri declared himself ruler of Israel. At the time, Omri was leading the Israelite army in a siege against a Philistine stronghold. The military rejected Zimri's appointment as king, preferring their commander instead. So Omri marched on Israel's capital, which he took easily. Before he could be killed by Omri, Zimri committed suicide, setting his palace on fire. After besting yet another contender for power, Omri secured his place on the throne, which he occupied for twelve years.

As king, Omri made a number of strategic moves. Most importantly, he built the city of Samaria on a hill and made it his base of operations. The new Israelite capital was a much more defensible site than the one Omri had subdued. From the Bible we know that Omri lost territory to neighboring Syria (see 1 Kings 20:34), but extrabiblical sources reveal that he pressed his advantage against Moab, taking some of their lands. It is likely that Omri orchestrated a political arrangement with the Phoenicians, which led to his son Ahab's marriage to Jezebel.

For all his diplomatic and military success, the Bible judged Omri a failure. Not only did he persist in the idolatry of Israel's kings, but the writer of 1 Kings concluded that Omri was even more sinful than any of his predecessors.

SPIRITUAL INSIGHT

It may seem surprising that the Bible did not include more details of Omri's reign, particularly since his tenure was reasonably well documented in extrabiblical sources. Omri's story is a useful reminder that God does not value success as the world defines it—what truly shapes a person's legacy is his or her faithfulness to the Lord.

The name of the one [son of Moses] was Gershom
(for he said, "I have been an alien in a foreign land").
EXODUS 18:3 NRSV

Day
55

Gershom's story doesn't follow the expected plotline. It would be logical to assume that as the firstborn son of Moses, Gershom would rise to a significant position of leadership or power in the developing Hebrew nation. However, God did not choose Moses' children as his successors. Instead, in a surprising plot twist, God chose Joshua to lead His people into the Promised Land.

While still living in Midian, Moses and Zipporah welcomed Gershom into their family. Moses chose the name Gershom, which means "stranger" or "cast out," as a reference to his recent escape from Egypt. When God commissioned him to return to Egypt and lead the Israelites out of slavery, Moses took his wife and their son, Gershom, and began the journey to Egypt. On the way, Gershom became the object of an important lesson in obedience.

GERSHOM

First Son of Moses

As a Hebrew, Moses should have circumcised his son, yet he had neglected to obey this command of God (Genesis 17). Before Moses could act as God's messenger, he needed to learn the importance of following God's commands himself. Fortunately, Zipporah recognized the error, moved quickly to circumcise their son, and averted God's judgment on their family.

SPIRITUAL INSIGHT

God doesn't value bloodlines like we often do. Instead, God looks at the heart of a person and builds His kingdom and plan around willing servants. That's an important reminder for children of Christian parents or for Christian parents as they raise their own children: Faith is not transferred like DNA. Each person must interact with God on his or her own initiative. Every individual is responsible for personally pursuing spiritual growth. No one inherits a relationship with God.

*Then, leaving her water jar, the woman went back to the town
and said to the people, "Come, see a man who told me
everything I ever did. Could this be the Christ?"*
JOHN 4:28–29

The Samaritan woman must have hated coming to fetch water day after day from the well—all that work, all that gossip about her and her shameful marital situation—but it was at that very well that she found the source of *living* water, which truly satisfies and brings eternal life.

The Samaritans lived in the north-central part of Israel, and they were descended from both Jews and foreign peoples who had been relocated to Israel by the Assyrians hundreds of years earlier. Jews and Samaritans typically despised each other.

SAMARITAN WOMAN

Woman Who Met Jesus at a Well

When Jesus was traveling from Jerusalem to Galilee, He took the most direct route and passed through Samaria where He met a woman at a well at midday. Jesus spoke to her and offered her living water that brings eternal life, rather than merely water from the well that needed to be fetched day after day. Jesus revealed to the woman that He was aware of her many marital relationships and her current situation of living with a man who was not her husband, and taught her about true worship. She was amazed and went back to her town to tell everyone about Jesus. Many Samaritans turned to Jesus because of the woman's testimony (John 4).

DID YOU KNOW?

In the language of Jesus' day, the word for "living" water is the same for "running" water—like a river. The Samaritan was initially interested in Jesus' offer of "living/running" water to avoid having to come to the well each day. Jesus, however, gave her something that truly satisfies the soul.

*But Jehosheba, the daughter of King Jehoram, took Joash son
of Ahaziah and stole him away from among the royal princes
who were about to be murdered and put him and his nurse
in a bedroom. Because Jehosheba, the daughter of King
Jehoram and wife of the priest Jehoiada, was Ahaziah's sister,
she hid the child from Athaliah so she could not kill him.*

2 CHRONICLES 22:11

E ver heard of Jehosheba? Probably not. Yet if it weren't for her quick thinking
and brave actions, the entire royal dynasty of Judah—the descendants of David
and the ancestors of Jesus—would have
been wiped out.

JEHOSHEBA

Woman Who Saved the Infant Joash from Death

The Bible contains only two verses
about Jehosheba (2 Kings 11:2; 2 Chronicles
22:11), but those two verses speak volumes
about the character of this brave woman.
She was the daughter of King Jehoram
and the sister of King Ahaziah of Judah,
so she was of royal blood. She was also
married to an influential priest named Jehoiada, suggesting that she possessed
an understanding and concern for spiritual things and God's laws.

After a man named Jehu killed King Ahaziah, his mother, Athaliah, seized
the opportunity to rule and began killing off the entire royal family. Jehosheba
acted quickly, however, and saved her one-year-old nephew Joash by hiding him
in the temple with herself and her husband. After six years, her husband staged a
coup to overthrow Athaliah and place Joash on his rightful throne (2 Chronicles
23–24).

RELATED INFORMATION

After Joash became king, he did what was right in God's eyes while
Jehoiada was alive; but after Jehoiada died, Joash listened to the people
of the land and worshipped idols. He even killed Jehoiada's son when
he prophesied against their wickedness (2 Chronicles 24).

Day
58

*Now the sons of Israel set out from Beeroth Bene-jaakan
to Moserah. There Aaron died and there he was buried
and Eleazar his son ministered as priest in his place.*

DEUTERONOMY 10:6 NASB

Wise people learn from the mistakes of others. Eleazar appears to have possessed this ability. When Eleazar became Israel's second high priest (succeeding his father, Aaron), he took the office with the sound judgment he learned from watching the failures of his father and his brothers. Although his father had served God devotedly, he also failed by betraying his office on two different occasions. Once he jealously opposed Moses (Numbers 12), and another time he led the people into idolatry by building a golden calf (Exodus 32). Then, in Leviticus 10, we read how Eleazar's older brothers died for their disrespect of God.

ELEAZAR

Third Son of Aaron

While not perfect, Eleazar avoided repeating the mistakes of his father and brothers as he served God as priest and then as high priest (Numbers 20:25–29). During his twenty years of ministry, he assisted Moses by taking a census (Numbers 26:3) and helping to appoint Joshua to serve as the leader of the people (Numbers 27:18–21). And when Joshua became the Hebrew leader, he helped settle the people in the Promised Land (Joshua 14:1). Eleazar served so faithfully that the high priestly line remained in his family off and on throughout Israel's monarchy.

RELATED INFORMATION

The duties of high priest included making an annual atonement for the sins of the entire Hebrew nation. Once a year, on the Day of Atonement, the high priest entered the tabernacle's Holy of Holies with the people's offering (Leviticus 16). In addition, the high priest sought God's will for the people through the use of the Urim and Thummim, which were similar to dice used to cast lots (Numbers 27:21). You can study further about the role of the high priest and the vestments in Exodus 28:2–43, 39:1–31; Numbers 4, 8, and 18.

But Naboth replied, "The LORD forbid
that I should give you the inheritance of my fathers."
1 KINGS 21:3

Naboth fell victim to a desperate king's bid for absolute power, the likes of which other kings enjoyed. There was only one problem: Israel's kings were not supposed to be like other kings.

Naboth owned a vineyard adjacent to King Ahab's palace in Jezreel. When Ahab wanted to expand his property so he could plant a vegetable garden, he offered to buy Naboth's vineyard or replace it with a better one—whichever Naboth preferred.

Naboth, however, refused. His rejection of such a lucrative business opportunity may seem strange to modern readers, but at the time it was the only natural response of a God-fearing Israelite. Inheritance was everything to ancient Jewish families. They had been taught that the land they occupied belonged to God—it was entrusted to

NABOTH

Vineyard Owner
Murdered by Ahab

them as an ongoing inheritance. Naboth's ancestors had parceled out the land to each family and tribe in Israel. Each allotment was supposed to stay in the family, passed down from generation to generation (see Numbers 36:7). Even those who forfeited their inheritance by falling into debt were supposed to have it returned in the Year of Jubilee (see Leviticus 25:23–28).

By turning down Ahab's offer, Naboth demonstrated his respect for the Jewish concept of inheritance. He also reminded Ahab of another distinctly Jewish principle: the limited power of kings. The Israelite king—unlike other rulers—could not do whatever he pleased. He was subject to God's law, just like everyone else. And that meant respecting Naboth's inheritance.

Unfortunately for Naboth, Ahab's scheming wife Jezebel had the vineyard owner falsely accused of blasphemy and stoned to death. Naboth was vindicated in the end, as both Ahab and Jezebel met a grisly fate in punishment for their crime.

DID YOU KNOW?

Naboth's murder echoed a warning given by the prophet Samuel years earlier. When Israel first demanded a king, Samuel warned them that such a monarch would eventually overstep his bounds and "take the best of your fields and vineyards and olive groves" (see 1 Samuel 8:14).

*Micaiah declared, "If you ever return safely,
the Lord has not spoken through me." Then he added,
"Mark my words, all you people!"*
1 Kings 22:28

MICAIAH

Imprisoned Prophet

Micaiah's greatest crime was refusing to tell the Israelite king what he wanted to hear. It is ironic, then, that the one time Micaiah actually tried saying what Ahab wanted him to say, the king wouldn't have it.

Ahab sought an alliance with Judah's King Jehoshaphat to attack neighboring Aram in hopes of reclaiming the Israelite city of Ramoth Gilead. Jehoshaphat was willing to cooperate, but on one condition: "First seek the counsel of the Lord," he insisted (1 Kings 22:5). Ahab obliged, summoning four hundred pagan prophets, who unblinkingly promised success. Jehoshaphat was not convinced, however; he asked whether there were any true prophets of the Lord left in Israel. Apparently, there was just one who was still on speaking terms with the court of Ahab: Micaiah. The mere mention of his name must have put Ahab in a foul mood. "I hate him because he never prophesies anything good about me," he complained (1 Kings 22:8).

Jehoshaphat insisted, however, and Micaiah was summoned. It is possible that Micaiah had given Ahab counsel before, only to have it ignored or thrown back in his face. This time, Micaiah opted for sarcasm, repeating exactly what the false prophets had declared: "The Lord will give [Ramoth Gilead] into the king's hand" (1 Kings 22:15). Suspicious, Ahab demanded the truth, so Micaiah obliged. Not only did he predict Ahab's death in battle, but he claimed that God had sent an evil spirit into the four hundred prophets in order to entice Ahab into battle.

That news did not go over well. The leader of the false prophets, Zedekiah, slapped Micaiah, and the king ordered God's true prophet thrown into prison. Micaiah's fate is unknown, but his prophecy was vindicated when Ahab fell in battle with Aram.

DID YOU KNOW?

One of the most puzzling things about this story is the fact that Jehoshaphat joined Ahab in battle, despite Micaiah's prediction. After narrowly escaping death, Jehoshaphat returned to Jerusalem, where a seer named Jehu rebuked him for allying himself to Ahab. Apparently Jehoshaphat failed to get the message; later he forged a trading alliance with Ahab's successor—and paid dearly for it (see 2 Chronicles 19:1–3; 20:35–37).

So Hilkiah the priest, and Ahikam, and Achbor, and Shaphan,
and Asaiah went to Huldah the prophetess, the wife of Shallum
the son of Tikvah, son of Harhas, keeper of the wardrobe
(now she lived in Jerusalem in the Second Quarter),
and they talked with her.

2 KINGS 22:14 ESV

Everyone wants a straight shooter when in a tight spot, because the only words that have a chance of bringing real help are those that give an honest assessment of the situation. The prophetess Huldah was just the person Josiah needed when all Israel was in a tight spot.

In the years leading up to Josiah's time, the people of Israel had been sinning rampantly and repeatedly, and their actions were leading God to bring the judgments warned about in Deuteronomy 27–28. Things had gotten so bad that apparently even a book of the Law (what we would call the Bible) had been completely lost (2 Kings 22:8–13).

HULDAH

Prophetess during
King Josiah's Reign

When this book was found during extensive temple renovations, it was read to King Josiah, and it told of the terrible judgments that awaited God's people because of their disobedience. Josiah knew right away that this was serious, and he needed someone who could tell him the truth about just what the nation was facing—he needed to hear the words of the prophetess Huldah.

Huldah told Josiah's officials that the nation would indeed experience judgment, but Josiah himself would be spared this judgment, as it would occur after his death. After this, Josiah went throughout the country, tearing down pagan shrines and abolishing idolatry wherever he found it. Eventually the Lord still brought judgment on the nation because of the sin of the people and their leaders, but Josiah was able to delay this punishment and promote godliness in his lifetime.

RELATED INFORMATION

The Bible says that Huldah lived in the second district of Jerusalem. This was a relatively new section of the city that had developed as the city expanded westward. Hezekiah had enclosed this portion of the city with a new wall many decades earlier.

*An angel of the Lord appeared to him in a dream and said,
"Joseph son of David, do not be afraid to take Mary home as your
wife, because what is conceived in her is from the Holy Spirit."*

MATTHEW 1:20

Along with great pride, most new fathers feel some amount of anxiety over the new responsibilities they face. But no one has ever really understood the burden placed on Joseph's shoulders: raising the Son of God. Where's the manual for that one? Who would you ask for advice?

JOSEPH

Earthly Father of Jesus

Even before Jesus was born, however, Joseph had faced a great deal, and his good character was already beginning to show. When he learned that his fiancée, Mary, was pregnant with a child that wasn't his, he mercifully planned to divorce her quietly and spare her public disgrace. Then an angel appeared to him in a dream and told him that he should marry her—because the baby was conceived by the Holy Spirit and would be the Savior of the world (Matthew 1:18–21).

When Mary gave birth to Jesus, Joseph watched, no doubt amazed, as people came from far and near to worship the baby as the divine King. Then an angel appeared to him again and warned him to take his family to Egypt to avoid being killed by King Herod. Later Joseph returned to his hometown of Nazareth, where he continued to raise Jesus, the Savior of the world (Matthew 2).

When Jesus was twelve, Joseph and Mary were reminded again of Jesus' true identity when they found Him in the temple astounding the teachers with His questions. Jesus reminded them that the temple was His true Father's house, so it should be no surprise that He would be there (Luke 2:40–52).

RELATED INFORMATION

Joseph was apparently a carpenter by trade (Matthew 13:55), and he must have passed these skills on to Jesus as well, because Jesus is also referred to as a carpenter in one of the Gospels (Mark 6:3).

*"This is the service of the. . .clans as they work at the Tent
of Meeting under the direction of Ithamar son of Aaron, the priest."*
NUMBERS 4:33

People of God aren't always known for their rousing sermons or devout prayer life. Even though Ithamar may have had those traits, he was best known for being a strong administrator. As the fourth son of Aaron, he served the Lord as a priest. While his father and brother served God as the people's high priest, Ithamar faithfully served God with his administrative skills—which may have seemed less inspirational to some.

ITHAMAR

Fourth Son of Aaron

As the treasurer of the tabernacle (Exodus 38:21), Ithamar's responsibilities included counting the offerings from the people and allocating funds for building the tabernacle. Today's church treasurers work with cash and computer programs, but the gifts Ithamar received and cataloged included various precious metals, assorted costly stones, and expensive fabrics. These would have required storehouses that needed to be organized and guarded.

In addition to his role as treasurer, Ithamar also held the role of foreman. He oversaw the Gershonites and Merarites (Numbers 4:24–33) when the tabernacle, curtains, posts, and bases were taken down, moved, and reassembled at a new location. Their job needed to be done quickly so that the tabernacle was transported and in place before the ark of the covenant arrived (Numbers 10:21). Even though the tabernacle was designed to be moved, the extensive amount and weight of material involved made this a difficult job requiring good organization in order for it to be completed on time.

SPIRITUAL INSIGHT

A large, movable tent, the tabernacle became the holy place of worship for the Hebrew people during their time in the wilderness. You can study it further by exploring the design (Exodus 25–27) and reading about the furniture found inside (Exodus 25, 27). The tabernacle was not the ultimate place of worship for God's people. God designed it to represent heaven—where His people will one day worship Him (Hebrews 8–9).

*And he said, "Hagar, servant of Sarai,
where have you come from, and where are you going?"
"I'm running away from my mistress Sarai," she answered.*

GENESIS 16:8

Have you ever felt so alone that it seemed like no one cared if you lived or died? Hagar knew these feelings—twice.

Hagar was the maidservant of Sarah (named Sarai at the time), the wife of Abraham. God had promised Abraham and Sarah that they would have many descendants, but because of her advanced age, Sarah had not been able to conceive. Sarah came up with her own plan B that involved the socially accepted practice of allowing her maidservant, Hagar, to conceive for her. After Hagar became pregnant with Abraham's child, however, she began to look down on Sarah, and Sarah began to mistreat her in return. Eventually Hagar fled into the desert to escape. Along the way, the Lord spoke to her and told her to return to Sarah, and He would raise up her child to be the father of a great nation—though that would not be the people of Israel.

HAGAR

Sarah's Maidservant
and Mother of Ishmael

A while after Hagar gave birth to Ishmael, Sarah became angry with her again, and this time Sarah sent her away into the desert with Ishmael. When Hagar ran out of water and prepared for Ishmael to die of thirst, the Lord appeared to her again and reiterated His promise to make Ishmael into a great nation. He also showed her a nearby well, and she and Ishmael were saved from certain death.

SPIRITUAL INSIGHT

There are times when we will be mistreated by others, and we may feel like no one cares what happens to us—but God always sees us, and He always cares (Psalm 139). We can trust ourselves to Him and know that He is working for our good even in the midst of wrongs that we may be experiencing (Genesis 50:18–20; Romans 8).

Day
65

"But now your [Saul's] kingdom will not endure;
the LORD has sought out a man after his own heart
and appointed him leader of his people, because you
have not kept the LORD's command."
1 SAMUEL 13:14

W hether it's a eulogy at a funeral or a bit of reminiscing at the dinner table, it always seems like the best things are said about people when they are not around to hear it. In David's case, God's highest praise of him was spoken not to David but to Saul when the Lord was rebuking him for his unfaithfulness.

Understandably, David is famous for many things throughout his life—mostly good, but some bad. As a boy, he killed the giant Goliath and played the harp to soothe Saul's troubled spirit. Later he was forced to flee from Saul when Saul tried to kill him. After David assumed the throne of Israel, he fought a number of battles and established Israel as the dominant power in the region.

DAVID

King of Israel

Still later, David committed adultery with Bathsheba and arranged for her husband's death. After he repented, David made preparations to build a new temple to replace the tent that housed the ark of the covenant, although it was actually his son Solomon who built the temple. All the while, David composed psalms expressing his love for God and calling on God to rescue him from his enemies.

So was God's highest praise of David about one of David's many accomplishments? Or about his skillful composition of praise songs? No. It was simply that David was "a man after [God's] own heart" (1 Samuel 13:14). That is what made David truly great in the eyes of God.

SPIRITUAL INSIGHT

As we strive to honor God in life, what should be our highest aspiration? That we accomplish great things for God? That we live a godly life? Certainly these are noble goals. But ultimately our chief concern should be that we seek to have a heart that reflects the heart of God. No other praise could be greater.

The LORD has sworn and will not change his mind:
"You are a priest forever, in the order of Melchizedek."
PSALM 110:4

In Genesis, Melchizedek was an obscure priest—a minor figure in Abraham's narrative. But to the writer of Hebrews, Melchizedek was a forerunner of the Messiah Himself.

The Old Testament identifies Melchizedek as "king of Salem" and "priest of God Most High" (Genesis 14:18). *Salem* was a contraction of *Jerusalem*, the city that became capital of the Promised Land and home to God's temple. In other words, Melchizedek was a priest before there was even a priesthood—he was king of God's holy city long before it had a temple.

When Abraham defeated Kedorlaomer's forces and rescued his nephew Lot, Melchizedek met him with bread and wine and blessed him in the name of God Most High. Abraham, in turn, gave Melchizedek a tenth of the spoils from his victory—the first tithe recorded in scripture.

MELCHIZEDEK

Priest-King of Jerusalem

Centuries later, when the writer of Hebrews pressed his case that Jesus was the ultimate priest, he appealed to the example of Melchizedek. Skeptics might have claimed that Jesus could not be regarded as a priest, since He did not descend from the tribe of Levi. But Hebrews notes that long before there was a Levite priesthood, there was Melchizedek. Jesus, then, was a priest "in the order of Melchizedek" (Hebrews 7:11). Furthermore, by the time of the Levite priesthood, the roles of priest and king had been carefully separated, whereas Melchizedek was *both* priest and king. Once more the writer of Hebrews compared Jesus to Melchizedek, concluding that Jesus is the high priest "who sat down at the right hand of the throne of the Majesty in heaven" (Hebrews 8:1). Melchizedek's brief story served as a preview of what was to come in the person and work of Jesus Christ.

*Now Aaron's sons, Nadab and Abihu, each took his censer,
put fire in it, and laid incense on it; and they offered unholy
fire before the LORD, such as he had not commanded them.*
LEVITICUS 10:1 NRSV

God holds spiritual leaders to a strict standard. This principal was illustrated by Abihu, the second son of Aaron, who served as a priest for the Hebrew people (Exodus 6:23). Abihu's position meant that he had great responsibilities as he represented the people and the sacrifices they offered God. His priestly clothes set him apart from the masses and emphasized his special role in the community. The people likely gave him their rapt attention when he offered them priestly instruction. They respected his work in the tabernacle as he took great care with the holy articles located there.

However, being a popular religious leader or respected member of the ministry did not give Abihu a free pass when it came to revering God. Early in the wilderness experience of the people of Israel, Abihu and his older brother, Nadab, became reckless in the offerings they brought to God. Rather than take the best care in

ABIHU

Second Son of Aaron

preparing their sacrifice, they carelessly created an incense offering from common fire rather than from the holy fire source that God had ordained (see Leviticus 10:1–2). God's judgment on their irreverence came with speed and severity; fire consumed both brothers even as they were in the midst of their insolent act.

God's immediate reprimand came through Moses when He reminded Aaron and the people. "By those who come near Me I will be treated as holy, and before all the people I will be honored" (Leviticus 10:3 NASB).

SPIRITUAL INSIGHT

God expects every person to treat Him and His instructions with utmost reverence and respect. No pulpit is too big, no ministry is too important, and no position is too prestigious to be exempted from this requirement.

*Abel also brought of the firstborn of his flock and of their fat portions.
And the LORD had regard for Abel and his offering.*
GENESIS 4:4 ESV

Abel became the world's first victim to violent crime. The son of Adam and Eve, Abel died at the hands of his older brother Cain. Before this fateful day, Abel lived in a small human village made up only of his own family. As a family might do in this scenario, they divided the jobs among different members: Cain farmed the earth and Abel cared for the herds of animals.

ABEL

Son of Adam and Eve

During the course of time, the two brothers offered a sacrifice to God. Abel offered his gift from his herds and Cain from his fields. While we can't know for certain the reason God accepted one sacrifice and not the other, the biblical narrative reveals that Abel's offering obtained God's approval. Cain, on the other hand, received a reprimand. While we don't have further details of the story, we see into Cain's heart through his next action: the murder of his brother. The anger and jealousy in Cain's heart may have been the exact reason God had rejected his sacrifice. In contrast, Hebrews 11:4 records, "By faith Abel offered to God a more acceptable sacrifice than Cain, through which he was commended as righteous, God commending him by accepting his gifts. And through his faith, though he died, he still speaks" (ESV).

While there has been much speculation about the nature of the two sacrifices, it may simply be that Abel's act of worship was offered by faith and Cain's was offered with an angry spirit of jealousy and obligation.

SPIRITUAL INSIGHT

There are many reasons to attend and get involved in church. Even steps taken to grow in your spiritual life can be cloaked with spiritual reasons that mask a concern for appearances or the need to match other people's expectations. The jealous need for acceptance and approval can result in your doing good activities like Cain—but doing them without the heart motivation of which God approves.

In the course of time, Amnon son of David fell in love with Tamar, the beautiful sister of Absalom son of David.

2 SAMUEL 13:1

The tragic rape of Tamar ruined an innocent girl's life and upset the balance of power in Israel.

Tamar and Amnon were half siblings; they shared a common father (David) but different mothers. Over time, Amnon grew obsessed with Tamar, to the point where it began to affect his physical well-being. With the aid of one of his advisers, Amnon concocted a plan to lure Tamar to his bedroom—pretending to be ill, he duped the king into sending Tamar to him—and he raped her.

Tamar protested, trying to persuade Amnon that his behavior would bring disaster on them both.

But Amnon was not to be deterred. Sadly, as so often happens when something (or someone) is unjustly taken by force, Amnon grew to despise Tamar almost immediately. The object of his obsession was now an object of revulsion. Tamar was humiliated, and her father, David, and full brother Absalom were enraged. However, David's fury does not seem to have materialized into action. While David fumed, Tamar took refuge in Absalom's house, her future prospects ruined by Amnon's lust.

When his father failed to defend Tamar's honor, Absalom took matters into his own hands and conspired to kill his half brother Amnon. In doing so, he struck down David's firstborn and presumed heir to the throne. Absalom, the third son of David, would eventually lose his own life, causing the throne to pass to Solomon.

TAMAR

Daughter of King David

DID YOU KNOW?

The story of Tamar and Amnon bears a number of unfortunate parallels to the account of David's own infidelity. In each case, the guilty party used an unwitting accomplice to fetch the victim. Just as David had used Joab to summon Bathsheba's ill-fated husband, so now David found himself the pawn in Amnon's plan to rape Tamar. Also, just as David's sin had resulted in the loss of a son, now Amnon's sin would lead to the death of not just one but two sons of David. Sometimes history has a tragic way of repeating itself.

Then I [Isaiah] said, "For how long, O Lord?" And he answered: "Until the cities lie ruined and without inhabitant, until the houses are left deserted and the fields ruined and ravaged, until the LORD has sent everyone far away and the land is utterly forsaken."

ISAIAH 6:11–12

W anted: dedicated employee who will faithfully proclaim messages of judgment to people who will reject and despise you. All efforts will produce little noticeable results and will end in complete destruction." It's unlikely that a job posting like that would garner many applicants. Yet that is essentially the job to which the prophet Isaiah was called by God.

ISAIAH

Prophet of Israel and Judah

Isaiah was probably closely affiliated with the royal court, given his relatively easy access to the king (Isaiah 7:3). But at some point in his life, the Lord, in His royal splendor, appeared to him in a vision (Isaiah 6), and Isaiah's life was forever changed. He was called to prophesy God's messages of judgment and restoration to His people, but God also warned him that the people would not listen and would eventually experience destruction. Even Isaiah's own children bore prophetic names: Shear-Jashub ("A Remnant Shall Return") and Maher-Shalal-Hash-Baz ("Swift Is Spoil, Speedy Is Prey").

Isaiah faithfully carried out his solemn and weighty task to the very end. He began prophesying a few decades before the fall of the northern kingdom of Israel and ended a few decades after this event.

Isaiah's efforts were not really futile, though, for his words were recorded for later generations in the book of Isaiah. Many of these prophecies foretold the Messiah, who would redeem His people from their bondage.

RELATED INFORMATION

Isaiah is the Old Testament book most quoted in the New Testament. Jesus quoted Isaiah 6:9–10, which speaks of the people's callous hearts, when His disciples asked why He spoke in parables rather than in direct statements (Matthew 13:13–15).

*In the land of Uz there lived a man whose name was Job.
This man was blameless and upright;
he feared God and shunned evil.*
JOB 1:1

Suffering the consequences of our wrong actions can be painful, but it pales in comparison to the pain that we feel when we suffer for no apparent reason of our own. That is why Job's painful experiences move us so deeply.

Job was a very successful man, with seven sons, three daughters, and a wealth of livestock. In fact, "he was the greatest man among all the people of the East." The Bible also makes it clear that Job was a righteous man. In a single day, however, nearly all his earthly blessings were snatched away: All his animals were either stolen or destroyed, and every single one of his children died in a terrible tragedy. Yet "in all this, Job did not sin by charging God with wrongdoing" (Job 1).

JOB

King of Persia

But Job's sufferings were not over yet. He himself was stricken with terrible sores from head to toe, and even his own wife prodded him to give up on God (Job 2). Finally, some of Job's friends came to mourn with him; but in the end, each of them spent great energy trying to convince Job that he had caused his own suffering by some hidden sin.

In all of this, God was holding Job up as an example of a truly righteous man, someone who would remain faithful even when undergoing terrible suffering. That does not mean that Job did not question what God was doing and express anger over his condition. When God finally did answer Job, however, He made it clear that His ways are far above human ways and cannot truly be understood by human beings.

Job humbly recognized his place before God, and God blessed him once again with even more children and livestock.

RELATED INFORMATION

The book of Job is written in both poetry and prose. The prose sections include the introductory section (which sets the scene and informs the reader of the dialogue between God and Satan) and the conclusion (which describes Job's restoration and blessing). The rest of the book is written in Hebrew poetry.

*So Moses listened to his father-in-law
and did all that he had said.*
EXODUS 18:24 NASB

Once Jethro gave his daughter to Moses in marriage, he didn't expect her to move back home. Moses had shown kindness to Jethro's family, and Jethro welcomed him into his home and rewarded him with marriage to Zipporah, one of his seven daughters. The marriage gave Jethro confidence that his daughter would be cared for after he died. He must have been surprised when she arrived at his home while Moses was still alive and well.

JETHRO

Moses' Father-in-Law

Earlier in their story, they all lived together in Midian. At one point, God called Moses to return and lead the Hebrew people out of captivity. Jethro blessed Moses, said good-bye to his daughter and grandchildren, and sent them all on their journey back to Egypt. Moses, his wife, and their children endured the journey, witnessed the plagues brought on the Egyptians, and walked through the Red Sea together.

Though we don't know Moses' reasons, we read that he sent his wife and children back to Midian to live with Jethro after God miraculously delivered the Hebrews from Egypt. Perhaps Moses felt the upcoming journey would be too difficult or too dangerous for his family. Or perhaps he felt his own responsibilities would keep him from caring for his family properly. While we don't know his reasons, we do know that Jethro did not accept his daughter and grandchildren back as permanent guests but rather escorted them back to their proper place with Moses (Exodus 18).

Moses greatly respected Jethro and received his family back from him. And while Jethro visited with Moses, he helped God's leader prioritize and delegate (Exodus 18:13–23). Jethro's wise counsel proved to be a valuable lesson early in Moses' forty-year ministry of leading God's people.

DID YOU KNOW?

Jethro was also known as Reuel, which was probably his given name. The name Jethro was actually a title, which means "His Excellence." Jethro is referred to by both names in Exodus and Numbers.

Achish trusted David and said to himself,
"He has become so odious to his people, the Israelites,
that he will be my servant forever."
1 SAMUEL 27:12

Achish must not have been a very good judge of character, because David seems to have had him wrapped around his little finger.

Achish was the king of the Philistine city of Gath. We first read of Achish when David fled to him from Saul, who was trying to kill him out of jealousy. David sought asylum with Achish, but he quickly feared for his life in Gath as well, because his great reputation as a mighty warrior of Israel had preceded him there. So David pretended to be insane, and Achish left him alone (1 Samuel 21:10–15).

ACHISH

King of Gath
during David's Time

David soon left Gath and gathered six hundred men with him while he lived in the cave of Adullam and elsewhere throughout Judah. He later returned to Gath to escape Saul, and Achish granted David the town of Ziklag as his home. David continued to deceive Achish by attacking various Philistine villages and telling Achish that he had attacked Israelite villages (1 Samuel 27). Achish became so trusting of David that he included his men among the Philistine forces that were gathering for battle against Israel in the Jezreel Valley. But the other Philistine commanders smelled a rat, and they wisely forbade David and his men to join them (1 Samuel 28–29).

RELATED INFORMATION

David had dealings with the city of Gath even before he met Achish. The giant Goliath, whom the young David defeated with his sling, was from Gath, and David had retrieved Goliath's sword just before going to Achish at Gath.

*Philip went down to a city in Samaria and proclaimed the
Christ there. When the crowds heard Philip and saw the miraculous
signs he did, they all paid close attention to what he said.*

ACTS 8:5–6

In His great commission to the disciples, Jesus revealed that His gospel was to smash all ethnic, national, and cultural barriers. Philip the evangelist embraced the inclusive nature of the gospel with inspiring zeal.

Philip was first mentioned as one of seven men chosen by the apostles to care for the widows who belonged to the Jerusalem church. Even this seemingly small service was a barrier-breaking act—Philip and his colleagues were responsible for making sure that the widows were treated equally, regardless of whether they were Hellenistic (Greek) or Hebraic Jews.

Later, when Saul's persecution scattered the church of Jerusalem, Philip seized the opportunity to go to Samaria. By extending the good news of Jesus, the Jewish Messiah, to the Samaritans, Philip shattered another centuries-old barrier.

PHILIP

Evangelist

The great evangelist was not finished with his barrier-breaking career, either. Having been directed by an angel, Philip journeyed from Jerusalem to Gaza, meeting an Ethiopian eunuch along the way. This man had two strikes against him. First, he was not Jewish (not even part Jewish, as the Samaritans were). Second, as a eunuch, Jewish law regarded him as ritually unclean—he was, in effect, "damaged goods." Yet Philip did not hesitate to sit with the eunuch and explain the gospel to him. The real test, however, came when the eunuch asked to be baptized. By agreeing to perform the ancient purification ritual, Philip acknowledged that in God's eyes, the eunuch was clean, pure, and whole.

Philip's life became the first of many signs that the good news of Jesus is for all people.

DID YOU KNOW?

The name Philip means "one who loves horses" in Greek. In the case of Philip the evangelist, this turned out to be an appropriate name, since he had to run up to a horse-drawn chariot in order to engage the Ethiopian eunuch in conversation! (See Acts 8.)

When Delilah saw that [Samson] had told her everything, she sent word to the rulers of the Philistines, "Come back once more; he has told me everything." So the rulers of the Philistines returned with the silver in their hands.
JUDGES 16:18

Day
75

From stealing petty cash at work to selling illegal drugs, some people will do anything for money. Delilah was even willing to hand over her lover Samson to his worst enemies.

Delilah lived in the Valley of Sorek during the time of the judges of Israel, when powerful Samson was wreaking havoc on the Philistines. This key valley linked the Israelites with their enemies the Philistines, so it was a constant area of conflict. The Bible doesn't say if Delilah was a Philistine or an Israelite, but she proved to be disloyal to Samson and harmful to Israel as a result (Judges 16).

DELILAH

Woman Who Learned the
Secret of Samson's Strength

Samson was an Israelite and a Nazirite from birth, meaning he had been specially dedicated to God and was not allowed to cut his hair or drink alcohol (Judges 13:3–5). Samson fell in love with Delilah, and the Philistine rulers immediately saw an opportunity to get to Samson. They offered to pay her a huge sum of money if she would tell them the secret of Samson's strength. She agreed and tried three times to get Samson to tell his secret, but he lied to her each time. Finally, he agreed to tell her where his strength came from: his Nazirite vow, which was confirmed by his long hair.

Delilah sent word to the Philistines, who came and cut Samson's hair while he slept. When Samson awoke, his amazing strength was gone, and the Philistines took him away captive. Eventually he would regain his strength for one last act, which would destroy many Philistines as well as himself.

RELATED INFORMATION

Several other people in the Bible appear to have taken Nazirite vows for some or even all of their life, including Samuel (1 Samuel 1–2), John the Baptist (Luke 1:13–17), and possibly even Paul (Acts 18:18; 21:23).

*By faith Rahab the prostitute did not perish with those
who were disobedient, because she had given
a friendly welcome to the spies.*
HEBREWS 11:31 ESV

Y ou rarely hear the word *righteous* used to describe a prostitute, but that's how the Bible depicts Rahab (James 2:25). Though God did not condone her occupation, Rahab's faith in God and her protective actions of the Hebrew spies made her righteous in God's eyes.

RAHAB

Righteous Prostitute

When the Hebrew people were finally ready to take possession of the Promised Land, Joshua sent two spies into Jericho to size up the enemy (Joshua 2). The spies found safe refuge in the home of a prostitute, where it would not have been unusual for people to be seen coming and going. With such potential activity, the men found her residence a practical place to hide and spend the night. While at her home, the spies were buoyed by the city residents' fear of the Hebrews and by the help extended to them by Rahab.

In exchange for her protection, the spies gave Rahab instructions that would keep her and her family safe during the upcoming battle. By following these directives, her life was spared when the city was ravaged. As her final reward, she received an honored place in Israel's history; for in addition to New Testament references that laud her faith, some Jewish traditions indicate that Rahab became the wife of Joshua, the Hebrew leader.

RELATED INFORMATION

The story of Rahab goes beyond the pages of Joshua and continues into the New Testament Gospels. Tucked in the genealogy of Jesus, we find an unlikely ancestor of the long-awaited Messiah: Rahab. By including unlikely women like Rahab (the prostitute) and Tamar (the woman who had a child with her own father-in-law), God revealed that the Messiah would be the Savior of all people—the likable *and* the undesirables (Matthew 1:5).

When Jehoshaphat king of Judah returned safely to his
palace in Jerusalem, Jehu the seer, the son of Hanani,
went out to meet him and said to the king,
"Should you help the wicked and love those who hate the LORD?
Because of this, the wrath of the LORD is upon you."
2 CHRONICLES 19:1–2

J ehu was no respecter of persons. He faithfully called sin "sin" no matter if it was being committed by the very wicked or the very righteous.

Jehu was a prophet whose ministry spanned the reigns of King Baasha of Israel and King Jehoshaphat of Judah. The Bible only ascribes two prophecies to him, but these prophecies reveal that Jehu was unswerving in his faithfulness to carry out his prophetic duties.

Jehu's first prophecy was given during the reign of Baasha, a wicked king who promoted idolatry throughout Israel. Because of Baasha's wickedness, Jehu announced that Baasha's family would die humiliating deaths. This prophecy came true several years later after a man named Zimri assassinated Baasha's son Elah, took over the kingdom, and killed off Baasha's entire family.

JEHU

Prophet of Israel and Judah

Years later, Jehu prophesied again, this time against Jehoshaphat, who was generally regarded as a righteous king in the Bible, because he agreed to join forces with wicked King Ahab of Israel and fight the Arameans. Jehu prophesied that the "wrath of the LORD" was upon him, although it is not clear what exactly this meant. Even so, Jehu recognized that Jehoshaphat had done many things well.

SPIRITUAL INSIGHT

When a person who generally lives a godly life falls into sin, it is tempting to turn a blind eye to his or her wrongdoing. But sin is sin no matter who commits it, and we do a person no favors by pretending it is not important or harmful.

Joseph took the body, wrapped it in a clean linen cloth, and placed it in his own new tomb that he had cut out of the rock. He rolled a big stone in front of the entrance to the tomb and went away.

MATTHEW 27:59–60

Perhaps it was something about Jesus' crucifixion that finally got through to Joseph of Arimathea. Perhaps it was seeing all that his Savior was willing to do for him that made him shake off his fears and boldly ask for the body of Jesus. Whatever it was, Joseph clearly showed his true colors that day as one of Jesus' followers.

Everything the Bible has to say about Joseph's background appears in four verses—one in each of the four Gospels (Matthew 27:57; Mark 15:43; Luke 23:51; John 19:38). Joseph was from the Judean town of Arimathea, twenty-one miles northwest of Jerusalem, and he was rich. Though he was a member of the Council—the Sanhedrin, the ruling assembly of the Jews—he did not consent to the crucifixion of Jesus. He was also a good and upright man, a follower of Jesus who was waiting for the kingdom of God.

JOSEPH OF ARIMATHEA

Owner of the Tomb in Which Jesus Was Laid

The only negative thing that we read about Joseph is that he kept his belief in Jesus a secret because he feared the Jews—that is, until Jesus died. For whatever reason, that day Joseph was emboldened to ask Governor Pilate for the body of Jesus, and he wrapped it in a clean linen cloth and laid it in his own new tomb—an undeniable public declaration of his regard for Jesus.

SPIRITUAL INSIGHT

Are you living like Joseph of Arimathea regarding your faith in Christ? Are you afraid of what others might think of you or do to you if you openly admit that you are one of His followers? Perhaps taking a long look at all that Jesus has done for us on the cross might give you new boldness to declare to others that you believe in Him.

Now the king was attracted to Esther more than to any of the other women, and she won his favor and approval more than any of the other virgins. So he set a royal crown on her head and made her queen instead of Vashti.

ESTHER 2:17

V ashti may have been a woman ahead of her time. In today's world, she would certainly be praised for her resolute claim to her rights. Feminists today would applaud her refusal to parade before King Xerxes' party guests as mere eye candy.

Whether she refused to come because she was busy, angry, not feeling well, or sticking to principles, we don't know. But what we do know is that refusing to come when the king summoned you was certainly not an offense that could be easily overlooked. Not only was her act seen as defiant, but Xerxes and his counselors feared that if Vashti went unpunished, women throughout the nation would be inspired to rebel against their husbands.

VASHTI

Deposed Queen

Though this reasoning smacks of chauvinism to our modern sensibilities, it was no small offense to the king and people of ancient Persia.

Queen Vashti was stripped of her title, which paved the way for Esther's rise to royalty. During the ancient Near Eastern equivalent of a royal beauty contest, Esther caught the king's attention and worked her way into his heart.

Vashti probably never understood why these events transpired in her life, and she may have felt that she had been denied fair treatment. And though these feelings would be natural, the events in her life led to the saving of the Hebrew people. Because Persia's new queen had Xerxes' ear, Esther was able to save her people from certain destruction.

Many of us don't get the chance to see how troubling events in our lives work toward God's plan or the greater good. However the story of Vashti and Esther serves as a reminder that God uses all kinds of events to ensure His greater plan is advanced.

DID YOU KNOW?

Xerxes is known in history for his unsuccessful assault on Greece early in his reign. It is possible that this event took place just before or after the great banquet described in Esther 1.

Day
80

"Observe what I command you this day. Behold,
I will drive out before you the Amorites, the Canaanites,
the Hittites, the Perizzites, the Hivites, and the Jebusites."

EXODUS 34:11 ESV

The Canaanites were a constant aggravation to the Hebrew people. Although the Bible does reference the names of some specific people groups (for example, the Ammonites and the Edomites), the term *Canaanites* seemed to be a broad name used for any of the people living in the land of Canaan. Generally, these people worshipped regional idols referred to as Baal and Asherah.

THE CANAANITES

Enemies within the
Promised Land

The Hebrews' first military conflict with the Canaanites came after God's people initially spied the land but refused to take it based on the advice of ten unfaithful spies. After seeing God's judgment and experiencing His displeasure, the Hebrews tried to take the land with their own strength rather than follow God's ordained plan. Though urged by Moses not to attempt the battle, the people persisted and were soundly defeated by the Amalekites and the Canaanites (Numbers 14:40–45).

Later when Joshua led the people into the Promised Land, the Israelites failed to completely remove the Canaanites from the land. As a result, these enemies remained a constant threat during the time of the judges (see Joshua 3, 7, 9, and 17). In addition to their military threat, their spiritual culture exerted a negative influence on the Hebrew people.

RELATED INFORMATION

Baal was the name given to a sun god or chief male god for a specific region, and Ashtoreth was the supreme female divinity associated with the moon. The worship of both these false gods began to influence God's people as they took possession of the Promised Land. Because the Hebrew people never completely expelled the practice, the worship of these false gods extended through the exile of the Hebrew people (Jeremiah 7:9). While the worship of Baal included incense, sacrifice, and occasional slashing of oneself, the worship of Ashtoreth may have gone as far as to include human sacrifice and perverse sexual sins.

"My father," she replied, "you have given your word to the LORD. Do to me just as you promised, now that the LORD has avenged you of your enemies, the Ammonites."

JUDGES 11:36

T he story of Jephthah and his daughter raises some difficult questions, such as whether Jephthah should have gone ahead with his sacrifice. Even so, one thing is clear: Jephthah's daughter must have been a very devoted daughter and very concerned that her father remain true to his word.

JEPHTHAH'S DAUGHTER

Became Her Father's Regret

Jephthah was a man who had become judge of Israel by leading the Israelites to victory against the Ammonites who were oppressing them. Jephthah had been driven from his brothers, but the leaders of Israel brought him back in order that he might help them win the battle. As Jephthah was preparing to battle the enemy, he made a rash vow to the Lord by promising to sacrifice the first thing that came out of his house to greet him when he returned home after victory. Though that is a promise we have trouble understanding today, it was a vow he intended to keep.

Jephthah was indeed victorious. To his surprise, his daughter was the first to greet him as he arrived home. Despite Jephthah's regret, his daughter urged her father to remain true to his vow before the Lord and offer her as a sacrifice. The only thing she requested was some time to go away into the hills with her friends for two months to mourn that she would die before ever marrying (Judges 11).

RELATED INFORMATION

Apparently the fate of Jephthah's daughter left such an impression on the people of Israel that they initiated a custom in which the young women would go out for four days to commemorate her death (Judges 11:39–40).

Day 81

Baasha killed Nadab in the third year of
Asa king of Judah and succeeded him as king.
1 KINGS 15:28

The dynasty of Jeroboam, king of Israel, came to an abrupt end with his son Nadab in the late tenth century BC.

More than twenty years before Nadab's reign, his father Jeroboam had revolted against Solomon. According to the prophet Abijah, God intended to punish Solomon's idolatry by cutting his kingdom in two. The northern portion, Israel, would go to Jeroboam, who was offered the chance to build a lasting dynasty to match David's—if only he would devote himself fully to God.

NADAB

King of Israel

Nadab's father, however, had other plans. He reasoned that if his people continued to worship the Lord—which meant recurring trips to the temple in Jerusalem, the capital of the southern kingdom—their loyalties would eventually revert back to the line of David. So Jeroboam made two golden calves for Israel to worship, setting a precedent that would haunt the country for the remainder of its days.

As a result, Jeroboam forfeited the prospect of a lasting dynasty—his family's hold on power ended with the brief tenure of Nadab. Jeroboam's son reigned for just two years. While attacking a Philistine stronghold in the southwest part of his kingdom, Nadab was assassinated by a man named Baasha—very likely one of Nadab's own military commanders. Unlike the kingdom to the south, there would be no lasting dynasty for the northern kingdom of Israel.

DID YOU KNOW?

Nadab means "noble" in Hebrew, an ironic name for someone who "did evil in the eyes of the LORD" (1 Kings 15:26). He shared his name with one of Aaron's sons, a priest who was struck down for offering "unauthorized fire" to God (see Leviticus 10:1).

*When Jesus saw his mother there, and the disciple
whom he loved standing nearby, he said to his mother,
"Dear woman, here is your son."*
JOHN 19:26

T he disciple whom Jesus loved." What title could anyone possibly want more
than this? This title was the distinct privilege of the apostle John, the writer of the
Gospel and letters that bear his name (John
13:23; 19:26; 21:7, 20).

We first read about John when he is
chosen along with his brother James to leave
his profession as a fisherman and become
one of Jesus' disciples. John and his brother
must have been somewhat of a rowdy pair,
because Jesus nicknamed them "Sons of
Thunder" (Mark 3:17). Nevertheless, John

JOHN

Apostle

held some special place in Jesus' heart, because he was included in Jesus' "inner
circle" of followers (Mark 5:37; 9:2; 13:3; 14:33) and was specifically given the
responsibility to take care of Jesus' mother as Jesus neared death (John 19:26–27).

Soon after Jesus' resurrection, John and Peter healed a crippled man and were
thrown into prison for preaching in the name of Jesus (Acts 3–4). Later John
and Peter were sent to Samaria to confirm the genuineness of some Samaritans'
conversion to Christianity (Acts 8). Years later John apparently moved to Ephesus,
where he established his ministry among the churches of western Asia Minor.
Near the end of his life, John was exiled to the island of Patmos off the coast of
Asia Minor, and there he wrote the book of Revelation, a vision of the final days
of the world.

SPIRITUAL INSIGHT

While John's title as "the disciple whom Jesus loved" certainly sets
him apart as one who enjoyed a special relationship with Jesus, all
believers in a sense can also claim this privileged title, for we are all
followers (disciples) whom Jesus loves.

"Phinehas the son of Eleazar, son of Aaron the priest, has turned back my wrath from the people of Israel, in that he was jealous with my jealousy among them, so that I did not consume the people of Israel in my jealousy."

NUMBERS 25:11 ESV

P hinehas did not shy away from confrontation. When the people of Israel faced the temptation to stray from the strict, orthodox teachings of God's law, Phinehas took the crucial steps to correct the error. Having seen (or heard about) the steps God took to quell the unholy acts of Korah, Abihu, and Nadab, Phinehas knew the necessity of taking drastic action to bring the people back in line.

PHINEHAS

Protector of Orthodox Faith

On one occasion, Hebrew men began to stray from God by indulging in idolatry and sexual sins with women from Midian. One particularly brazen man paraded a Midianite woman through the people of Israel and into his tent. The Bible records that "When Phinehas. . .saw this, he left the assembly, took a spear in his hand and followed the Israelite into the tent. He drove the spear through both of them—through the Israelite and into the woman's body" (Numbers 25:7–8). As a result, the plague that God had brought against the people was stopped.

On another occasion, certain tribes were suspected of building their own altars in competition to the one that the tabernacle housed. Since God had ordained only one altar, Phinehas explored and resolved the situation (Joshua 22). On yet another occasion, the tribe of Benjamin committed a horrific rape and murder (Judges 20). When the Benjamites remained unrepentant for their actions, Phinehas led the ensuing fight against his own countrymen. Phinehas's courage and moral strength made him one of the best-known defenders of God's law.

There is a lesson to be learned from Phinehas. While Christians may disagree about finer points of doctrine or worship practices, they cannot make exceptions when it comes to the core message of the gospel. When Phinehas saw the people leave the faith and stray into idolatry, he boldly confronted them. While some lines of doctrinal differences may not be worth splitting hairs over, others are worth defending to the end.

Whenever the day came for Elkanah to sacrifice, he would give portions of the meat to his wife Peninnah and to all her sons and daughters. But to Hannah he gave a double portion because he loved her, and the LORD had closed her womb.

1 SAMUEL 1:4–5

Elkanah plays a relatively minor role in the story of Hannah and Samuel, but even so, he serves as a positive example of godly love that goes against the grain of culture.

Elkanah was the husband of two wives, Hannah and Peninnah. Peninnah had children, but Hannah did not, and this was a source of great tension between the two wives. In the culture of Bible times, one of the most important roles a woman could fulfill was to bear children for her husband. If she was unable to do that, she was often

ELKANAH

Husband of Hannah

despised or ignored by her husband and treated disdainfully by other women. In fact, Peninnah would often provoke Hannah because of this and cause her to become very sad and upset whenever they went up to worship at the tabernacle at Shiloh.

Elkanah, however, demonstrated godliness by going against the grain of his culture and showing true love for his wife Hannah. When they would offer sacrifices and then prepare to eat the meal as part of the sacrifice, Elkanah would give Hannah a double portion of food as a demonstration of his care for her even while she was unable to bear children.

Later the Lord blessed Hannah and Elkanah and allowed Hannah to become pregnant. She eventually gave birth to the great prophet Samuel.

> **RELATED INFORMATION**
>
> The priest who presided over the tabernacle during Elkanah's time was Eli, who gave a blessing to Hannah that she might be able to conceive. Years later, Samuel would be raised by Eli in the tabernacle, and he would even replace him as priest.

The ark of the LORD remained in the house of Obed-Edom the Gittite for three months, and the LORD blessed him and his entire household.

2 SAMUEL 6:11

There is some debate over the precise identity of the man named Obed-Edom. What implications can be drawn from his involvement with the ark of the covenant depend in large part on the true nature of his background.

After David's first attempt to bring the ark to Jerusalem had ended in disaster—one of its escorts, Uzzah, died when he touched the ark—the king abandoned his plans, fearing a further outbreak of God's wrath. Instead, David left the ark in the care of Obed-Edom, a Gittite. But why did David choose Obed-Edom? And why did God bless Obed-Edom's entire household for the three months that the ark remained in his care?

OBED-EDOM

Temporary Keeper
of the Ark

In the first possible scenario, Obed-Edom seems a perfectly logical choice for a temporary caretaker. Some scholars believe that he was a Levite, a member of the Jewish priestly class. This interpretation rests on the assumption that "Gittite" is a reference to the Levitical town of Gath Rimmon. The parallel account in 1 Chronicles may support this interpretation, mentioning Obed-Edom in connection with a number of Levite priests and identifying him as one of the "doorkeepers for the ark" (see 1 Chronicles 15:23–24). As a priest, Obed-Edom would have known exactly how to care for the ark, treating it with appropriate respect, in contrast to Uzzah.

A more bizarre possibility is that Obed-Edom was a Philistine—which is likely the case if "Gittite" refers not to a Levitical town but to the Philistine city of Gath, as it does in 2 Samuel 15:18. A Philistine seems like a strange choice for a caretaker, especially since the Philistines had once managed to seize the ark in battle with the Israelites. If Obed-Edom was a Philistine, then being entrusted with the ark—then invited to be one of its doorkeepers—was an extraordinary honor indeed. Some scholars see Obed-Edom as an example of the value God placed on foreigners, long before the gospel was taken to the Gentiles.

Either way, Obed-Edom enjoyed a tremendous honor, and he received God's blessing for his faithful service.

DID YOU KNOW?

Further adding to the mystery surrounding Obed-Edom is the significance of his name. It means "servant of Edom." In this instance, however, the servant of Edom became the servant of the one true God instead.

And the donkey said to Balaam, "Am I not your donkey,
on which you have ridden all your life long to this day?
Is it my habit to treat you this way?"
NUMBERS 22:30 ESV

The tale of Balaam and his talking donkey fascinates children, but his story carries a greater significance than what may be seen on the surface. When examined more deeply, the biblical narrative regarding Balaam ultimately points to the power and supremacy of God.

Biblical and archaeological history both confirm that Balaam was a renowned seer in the ancient world. When Balaak, king of Moab, felt threatened by the Hebrews, he summoned Balaam. He hoped to hire Balaam to curse the Hebrews.

BALAAM

Prophet with
a Talking Donkey

Even though Balaam was a spiritual person, there is no indication that he was a true prophet of God. He did, however, appear to know of God's power and feared Him enough to turn down Balaak's initial request. When Balaak persisted with offers of financial gain, Balaam agreed to meet him. (Read the entire story in Numbers 22–24.) On Balaam's trek to Moab, God confronted the seer with profound reminders of His power: an angel with a flaming sword and a talking donkey (Numbers 22:27–28). With a stern rebuke and severe warning, God permitted Balaam to proceed on his journey. Arriving at his destination with God's admonition fresh in his mind, Balaam refused to curse the people of God but blessed them three times instead.

Balaam's story illustrates how the power of God trumps the evil intents of others. By using a talking donkey and a sinful seer, God showed that He can use anyone or anything to accomplish His plan—even unwilling or unusual participants.

SPIRITUAL INSIGHT

Balaam's story includes more than the episode involving a talking donkey. Revelation 2:14 and Numbers 31:16 reveal that Balaam instructed Balaak to lead the Israelites into idolatry and sexual sin. Balaam's story ended when he died in battle against the Israelites as recorded in Numbers 31:16.

[Moses' other son] was named Eliezer, for he said, "My father's God was my helper; he saved me from the sword of Pharaoh."

EXODUS 18:4

When parents choose names today, they often select names that sound distinctive or pretty. However, in ancient times baby names often became biographical landmarks that corresponded to a time in the family's life. For example, after Moses became a fugitive from Pharaoh, he married Zipporah, and together they had their first son whom they named Gershom (which means "stranger" or "cast out"). Moses likely selected that name as he contemplated his transition from the life of an adopted prince to that of a fugitive shepherd.

ELIEZER

Moses' Second Son

While Moses apparently reflected on his change in status during these early years in Midian's desert, he did not dwell indefinitely on what he had lost. This is evident in the name he gave his second son: Eliezer (which means "God is my help"). Even though Moses had to flee for his life, he could see ways that God had helped him. He recognized how his life had been spared as an infant. He acknowledged the miracle of having been adopted and raised by Pharaoh's daughter. He could see how he had successfully escaped certain judgment from Pharaoh. He perceived how he had been protected by God as he fled across the desert of Sinai. He identified how God had led him to a new home in Midian, and how He had given him a successful vocation and a family. While Moses could have continued to look at all he had lost, instead he reflected on what God had done for him.

SPIRITUAL INSIGHT

Moses' life illustrates that when life is difficult, we still have the opportunity to choose our perspective. Moses could have wasted his final years complaining about all that he lost. He could have looked at the desert of Midian and bitterly compared his rural home to the palaces of Egypt. Instead, Moses chose to see God's hand of protection and help at work in his life. By giving his son the name Eliezer, he reminded himself that "God is our help" every time he called to his child. You have the same opportunity to choose your perspective. How has God helped you?

*Then Zedekiah son of Kenaanah went up and slapped Micaiah
in the face. "Which way did the spirit from the LORD go
when he went from me to speak to you?" he asked.*
1 KINGS 22:24

Zedekiah and his four hundred companions had an easy job. Claiming to speak
on behalf of God, they merely told the king of Israel exactly what he wanted to
hear. They did not care whether the advice they dispensed corresponded to the
actual will of God.

Ahab, the infamously evil king of Israel,
had invited his counterpart from Judah to
join him in going to war against Aram.
There was just one catch: Jehoshaphat, the
southern king, wanted confirmation from
the Lord. So Ahab obligingly supplied four
hundred prophets who chimed, as if on
cue, "Go, for the Lord will give [Ramoth

ZEDEKIAH

False Prophet

Gilead] into the king's hand" (1 Kings 22:6). Jehoshaphat was not falling for
it—he saw through the prophetic ruse and demanded that Ahab produce a true
prophet of the true God.

This alone must have been enough to set Zedekiah, the ringleader of the
four hundred prophets, on edge. Unfortunately for him, though, Jehoshaphat
got exactly what he wanted—and perhaps more than he bargained for—when
Micaiah arrived. Somewhat reluctantly, Micaiah gave Ahab the real story, revealing
that God, in fact, did want Ahab to attack Aram, but that it would not end well
for the Israelite king. Micaiah accused Zedekiah of being nothing more than a
mouthpiece for the "lying spirit" (1 Kings 22:23) that God had sent in order to
entice Ahab into foolish combat.

Zedekiah had heard enough. He got up and slapped Micaiah—a move
designed to humiliate—and sarcastically demanded to know when God's spirit had
suddenly stopped speaking through him in order to go and whisper into Micaiah's
ear. Not one to take things lying down, Micaiah told Zedekiah that he would find
out on the day he went into hiding. Neither prophet was heard from again.

> **DID YOU KNOW?**
>
> It is not known how and when Micaiah's prediction against Zedekiah
> came to pass. However, Micaiah accurately prophesied Ahab's death
> in battle, so it's reasonable to assume he was right about Zedekiah,
> too. Zedekiah may have feared retribution, having been the one who
> encouraged Ahab to go to war in the first place. In that case, perhaps
> he went into hiding upon receiving word that Ahab was dead.

And Elisha prayed, "O LORD, open his eyes so he may see."
Then the LORD opened the servant's eyes, and he looked and saw
the hills full of horses and chariots of fire all around Elisha.

2 KINGS 6:17

Throughout his entire ministry, Elisha was a man acutely aware of God's presence and power. He never lacked confidence in God's watchful care of him, and he seemed to call upon God's power as naturally as he carried out all his other tasks.

ELISHA

Prophet of Israel and Successor of Elijah

Perhaps this confidence was a result of witnessing firsthand all the ways that God watched over his mentor, Elijah, through even the most threatening of situations. Elijah had promised that if Elisha saw him taken up to heaven in a fiery chariot, he would receive a double portion of the spirit that rested on Elijah. Elisha did indeed see this, and the truth of this promise is evidenced by the fact that he performed twice as many miracles as Elijah.

Some of the miracles that Elisha took part in included curing the salty water of Jericho, witnessing Israel's miraculous victory over Moab, providing oil (and later a son) for a Shunammite woman, raising the Shunammite woman's son from the dead, curing some poisonous stew, healing Naaman's leprosy, causing an axhead to float in water, predicting that the Arameans would give up their siege of Samaria, and foretelling King Jehoash's victories over the king of Aram.

*So they brought to the people of Israel a bad report
of the land that they had spied out, saying, "The land,
through which we have gone to spy it out, is a land that
devours its inhabitants, and all the people that we
saw in it are of great height."*
NUMBERS 13:32 ESV

Though belonging to some of the most influential people in Hebrew history, the names of Shammua, Shaphat, Igal, Palti, Gaddiel, Gaddi, Ammiel, Sethur, Nahbi, and Geuel remain largely unrecognized. Though their names have been lost to obscurity, their reputations have not. These names belong to the ten spies who turned public opinion against Moses, and who led the people to give in to fear rather than obey God's instructions. When Caleb and Joshua tried to remind the people of God's promises to be with them, this vocal

THE TEN SPIES

Majority Who Were Very Wrong

majority convinced the people to believe in the dangers they had seen in the land instead of the power of the unseen God who led them there. Rather than listen to Joshua and Caleb, the people rallied behind the majority and threatened to stone the two men who acted with faith. (See the story in Numbers 13–14.)

Though the people had seen God defeat the Egyptian army, had followed the cloud by day and fire by night, had drunk water from a rock, and had eaten the miraculous manna, the threat of the Canaanite armies overwhelmed them with fear—and they wept and complained against Moses. As a result of these actions, God sentenced His obstinate people to live as nomads in the wilderness for forty years. During that time, every adult over the age of twenty years would die because God forbade anyone to enter the land who had treated Him with contempt (Numbers 14:23). Only Joshua and Caleb survived this judgment.

What fate awaited the ten spies who led the people into disobedience? Numbers 14:36–37 records, "And the men whom Moses sent to spy out the land, who returned and made all the congregation complain against him by bringing a bad report about the land—the men who brought an unfavorable report about the land died by a plague before the LORD" (Numbers 14:36–37 NRSV).

SPIRITUAL INSIGHT

The majority can often be right, but greater numbers do not assure accuracy. Following God's standards and directions is always the right choice, no matter how unpopular they may be.

The name of the Israelite who was killed with the Midianite woman was Zimri son of Salu, the leader of a Simeonite family.
NUMBERS 25:14

Zimri's brazen act of sexual immorality cost him and his partner their lives, his family its honor, and 24,000 lives of his countrymen in a resultant plague.

To be fair, Zimri was not the only one engaging in sexual immorality. According to the book of Numbers, the men of Israel at the time were being enticed by Moabite women. The problem was not that these women were foreigners per se. After all, many foreigners played valuable roles in Israel's story—Ruth (another Moabite woman and ancestor of both David and Jesus) being just one example. The problem was that these women worshipped false gods. The sexual immorality described in Numbers 25 was intimately connected to their pagan worship. Temple prostitution played a significant part in many religions of the day—but it was not to be so with Israel.

ZIMRI

Son of Salu

Zimri, then, was just one of many in Israel to pursue this destructive path. But he chose the worst possible time to do so. Just as Moses was ordering Israel's judges to kill any man who was guilty of sexual immorality—and just as the people were gathered outside the tent of meeting, weeping in a public display of their repentance—Zimri marched into the camp with a Midianite woman. In front of everyone, including Moses, he entered the tent. Apparently he thought that ritual prostitution was the order of the day.

One of the priests, however, had other ideas. Phinehas, a grandson of Aaron, followed the pair into the tent—spear in hand. With one sweeping motion, he impaled Zimri and his Midianite partner, Kozbi.

Thousands more died in the subsequent plague that was sent to punish the Israelites. Phinehas was rewarded for his zeal. Zimri, on the other hand, brought shame upon his family—particularly his father, Salu, who was named in the account of his son's shocking behavior.

DID YOU KNOW?

From this moment on, God ordered the Israelites to regard the Midianites as enemies. God did not take lightly the efforts of those who tried to lead His people astray.

But Joseph said to [his brothers], "Don't be afraid.
Am I in the place of God? You intended to harm me,
but God intended it for good to accomplish what is now being done,
the saving of many lives."
GENESIS 50:19–20

J oseph was no victim. Though the Bible recounts episode after episode of wrongs being done to him, Joseph knew—or perhaps learned—that ultimately God was in charge of everything, and He was working all things together for the good of His people.

JOSEPH

Favorite Son of Jacob

Joseph was the eleventh and favorite son of Jacob, and his favored status earned him resentment from his brothers, who eventually sold him as a slave to some merchants traveling to Egypt (Genesis 37). Once there, Joseph was sold to a royal official named Potiphar, who quickly recognized and benefited from Joseph's administrative gifts. Later Potiphar's wife falsely accused Joseph of assaulting her, and he was thrown into prison (Genesis 39).

While in prison, Joseph demonstrated the ability to interpret dreams, and he was brought before Pharaoh to explain some troubling dreams. Joseph correctly foretold a great famine that was going to come upon the whole world, so Pharaoh elevated him to second in command of the kingdom. The famine drove Joseph's brothers to Egypt for food as well, and after a series of interactions with them, Joseph revealed his identity to them (Genesis 40–45).

Joseph's brothers feared that he would seek revenge on them for selling him into slavery, but Joseph recognized that God was orchestrating the events of his life for the good of His people—and that he should not assume the role of God and repay his brothers for their wrongs against him (Genesis 50).

King Asa also deposed his grandmother Maacah
from her position as queen mother.
2 CHRONICLES 15:16

As the king's wife, Maacah enjoyed great power at a crucial juncture in Israel's history. Unfortunately, she was anything but a positive influence.

Maacah's husband, Rehoboam, was the first king of Judah after God's people split into northern and southern kingdoms. She seems to have impacted her husband's judgment—though it's not as though he needed help making bad decisions. After all, it was Rehoboam's arrogance that led to the separation of Israel and Judah in the first place.

MAACAH

Rehoboam's Wife

Rehoboam followed his father's example by taking several wives and concubines (though not as many as Solomon). But Maacah was the clear favorite. Even though Maacah wasn't his first wife, Rehoboam decreed that her son Abijah would be the future king of Judah.

However, the writer of 2 Chronicles denounced Rehoboam as a failure because "he had not set his heart on seeking the LORD" (12:14). From details gathered later in the story, it becomes evident that Maacah was part of the problem. Instead of worshipping the God of Israel, Maacah aligned herself with Asherah, a Canaanite mother goddess. She even set up an Asherah pole, perhaps in Jerusalem itself. The chronicler's disgust went beyond words—her behavior was simply "repulsive."

Ultimately, Rehoboam's favoritism toward Maacah proved to be her undoing. Maacah's son Abijah, handpicked for the throne by Rehoboam, was little better than his parents in God's eyes—but his son Asa was another story. Asa devoted himself fully to God. As such, he deposed his grandmother—who was, by this time, queen mother—and burned the Asherah pole she had erected.

Strange as it might seem in light of her shameful legacy, Jesus was a direct descendant of Maacah. According to Matthew's genealogy, Jesus' ancestors include (among others) Maacah's grandson Asa, her son Abijah, and her husband, Rehoboam. This largely dysfunctional family is a testimony to God's ability to bring good from even the most broken situations.

*But Doeg the Edomite, who was standing with Saul's officials,
said, "I saw the son of Jesse come to Ahimelech son of Ahitub at Nob.
Ahimelech inquired of the LORD for him; he also gave him provisions
and the sword of Goliath the Philistine."*

1 SAMUEL 22:9–10

It's difficult to read the story of Ahimelech without feeling some sense of deep anger at his fate. He was simply doing his God-given job as priest, but it wound up getting him and most of his family brutally killed.

Ahimelech and his family were priests who lived at Nob, only a couple of miles from Gibeah, the capital of Israel during Saul's reign. Soon after David fled from Saul, who had grown jealous of David's popularity and success, David visited Ahimelech and asked him for some bread and some weapons. David was careful not to mention to Ahimelech that he was fleeing from Saul. One of Saul's servants named Doeg happened to be there at the time.

AHIMELECH

Priest Who Helped
David Escape Saul

Later, Doeg informed Saul that David had visited Ahimelech before he fled to Gath, and Saul summoned Ahimelech's family to come to him. Ahimelech admitted that he helped David, but he truthfully indicated that he often helped David and did not know why that day was any different. Saul ordered Doeg to strike down Ahimelech and his family, and he did, killing eighty-five priests (1 Samuel 21–22).

RELATED INFORMATION

Ahimelech's son Abiathar escaped Saul's massacre at Nob and fled to David. Later it seems that David made Abiathar his personal priest who would consult the Lord to find out what David should do when facing certain circumstances (1 Samuel 23:6–12; 30:7–8).

*When Johanan son of Kareah and all the army officers who were
with him heard about all the crimes Ishmael son of Nethaniah
had committed, they took all their men and went to fight
Ishmael son of Nethaniah.*

JEREMIAH 41:11–12

W e are all gray. As difficult as it is to accept, the truth is that every human being is always capable of both the most noble and the most heinous of deeds. Johanan was no different.

When the Babylonians invaded Judah and carried away most of the nobles and other leaders, Johanan was among the "army officers and their men. . .still in the open country" (Jeremiah 40:7) who escaped capture. The Babylonians appointed a man named Gedaliah as governor over those who remained in the land, and Johanan and the other captains agreed to submit to Gedaliah's authority.

JOHANAN

Pursued the Assassin of Gedaliah

When Ishmael, who was one of the captains, assassinated Gedaliah and took other Judeans captive, Johanan courageously chased after him and rescued the captives (Jeremiah 41–42).

Immediately after this heroic deed, however, Johanan and the other leaders made plans to flee to Egypt to escape the wrath of the Babylonians over the assassination of Gedaliah. They consulted the prophet Jeremiah, who warned them not to go, but they chose to disobey the Lord and go anyway—and they took Jeremiah with them. It is likely that they died there, just as Jeremiah had prophesied (Jeremiah 42:15–16).

If we truly understand that we are all capable of the best and the worst of deeds at any time, then there is no room for judging others—nor is there any room for pride. We are no better than anyone else, and no one else is any better than us. We are all sinners in need of God's grace (Ephesians 2:8–9).

For a man named Demetrius, a silversmith, who made silver shrines of Artemis, brought no little business to the craftsmen.
ACTS 19:24 ESV

O ne thing is clear about Demetrius: He loved silver. From the silver shrines he made of the goddess Artemis to the silver coins he received from selling them, silver was definitely first and foremost in his mind.

Demetrius lived in the great city of Ephesus in Asia Minor, the location of the temple of Artemis. People traveled from all over the Roman world to visit this temple, which was listed by the ancient historian Herodotus as one of the Seven Wonders of the World. Demetrius was a leader among the silversmiths and other craftsmen who made shrines and other trinkets for people paying homage to Artemis, so he had a vested interest in making sure the temple remained a top attraction throughout the world.

Enter Paul and his coworkers. After two years in Ephesus, Paul's evangelistic work was so successful that it apparently began to threaten the popularity of the temple of Artemis itself (Acts 19:24–27). So Demetrius and his fellow craftsmen incited a riot against Paul and his coworkers, and Paul decided to leave for Macedonia. The

DEMETRIUS

Silversmith of Ephesus

Bible records nothing further of Demetrius, but the temple of Artemis remained popular for generations to come—so he very possibly was able to continue on with his silver business.

DID YOU KNOW?	The Ephesian temple of Artemis that existed in Paul's day was first built around 550 BC at the expense of Croesus, the wealthy king of Lydia. The temple met its demise at the hand of an arsonist in AD 356.

*Samuel continued as judge over Israel all the days of his life.
From year to year he went on a circuit from Bethel to
Gilgal to Mizpah, judging Israel in all those places.*

1 SAMUEL 7:15–16

Delivering good news does not seem to have been a part of Samuel's job description very often. Yet he was so important to Israel's history that he came to be known as a second Moses (see Jeremiah 15:1).

Like so many others in scripture—Isaac, Samson, and John the Baptist, for example—Samuel was a miracle baby. After pleading with God in the sanctuary at Shiloh, Samuel's mother finally conceived. Hannah had promised that her firstborn son would be devoted to God's service. True to her word, Hannah brought the young boy to Shiloh, where he served under the care of Eli the priest.

SAMUEL

Prophet and Judge

Samuel's first encounter with God required him to deliver unsettling news to Eli. God had spoken to Samuel, telling him that his mentor was about to be judged for his failure to restrain his wicked sons, who also served in the sanctuary.

Years later, the Israelites demanded that Samuel appoint a king. God told Samuel to grant the people's request, and then He gave Samuel more bad news to deliver: Israel would come to regret the day they asked for a king. Kings had a way of oppressing their people—seizing their lands and taxing the fruits of their labors. Samuel's prophetic words were fulfilled when Solomon's greed wound up splitting the kingdom in two.

The first choice of king, a man named Saul, proved a disaster, giving Samuel the opportunity to deliver yet another dose of unwelcome news: Saul would not sit long on the throne, and none of his descendants would follow him. Even in death, Samuel delivered bad news for those who disobeyed the Lord. When a desperate King Saul consulted a medium (or witch) at Endor, the figure of Samuel appeared from beyond the grave, telling Saul that he would not live to see another sunset.

DID YOU KNOW?

Such was Samuel's reputation that the elders of Bethlehem trembled when the elderly prophet arrived in their town. However, this time Samuel brought good tidings—guided by God, he anointed David to be Saul's replacement.

Cain said to his brother Abel, "Let us go out to the field."
And when they were in the field, Cain rose up
against his brother Abel, and killed him.
Genesis 4:8 nrsv

J ealousy kills. And while Cain had intended only to kill his brother, the effects of his jealousy reached further than he could have imagined.

As the firstborn son of Adam and Eve, Cain became the third person to inhabit the earth. Together with his parents (and later his other brothers and sisters), Cain began to care for the earth and became a farmer (Genesis 4:2). But soon Cain—once the greatest achievement of Adam and Eve (Genesis 4:1)—became the scourge of his family when anger and jealousy drove him to murder his own brother. Not only did

CAIN

Son of Adam and Eve

Cain's anger result in Abel's death, but it also brought painful consequences in his own life. God drove Cain away from his family to live as an outcast in the land of Nod. Cain's jealousy first destroyed his brother's life and the family's unity, and then it shattered his own life as well. First John 3:12 records, "We must not be like Cain who was from the evil one and murdered his brother. And why did he murder him? Because his own deeds were evil and his brother's righteous" (1 John 3:12 nrsv)

Although Cain showed no remorse for his crime, he still received God's gracious protection and was allowed to begin his own family and community in the land of Nod. Cain's sons and grandsons became the fathers of music, cattle keepers, and craftsmen who worked with bronze and iron (Genesis 4:22).

Did You Know?

The phrase, "Am I my brother's keeper?" originated with Cain. He said this to God after murdering his brother (Genesis 4:9).

*Zimri, one of his officials, who had command of half his chariots,
plotted against him. Elah was in Tirzah at the time, getting
drunk in the home of Arza, the man in charge of the palace at Tirzah.
Zimri came in, struck him down and killed him in the twenty-seventh
year of Asa king of Judah. Then he succeeded him as king.*

1 KINGS 16:9–10

Sometimes it seems as if certain kings of Israel were so devoid of good that the
Bible hardly goes to the trouble of mentioning anything about them. This must
have been the case with Elah.

ELAH

King of Israel

Elah was born to Baasha, who had
assassinated Nadab, the son of wicked Jeroboam. By assassinating Nadab, Baasha was
carrying out judgment on the family of Jeroboam for its wickedness, yet Baasha's own
family, including Elah, was also wicked. Just
as Jeroboam had done, Baasha and Elah
practiced idolatry and promoted it throughout
Israel. As a result, a prophet named Jehu
foretold the demise of Baasha's family as well.

So while Elah was getting drunk at the home of the man in charge of his
palace, one of his officials, Zimri, assassinated him and reigned for seven days
in his place. Zimri also killed all the other members of Baasha's family, fulfilling
Jehu's prophecy.

RELATED INFORMATION

It is interesting that the small town of Gibbethon figures twice in
the story of Elah. At Gibbethon, Baasha assassinated Nadab and
usurped the throne. Years later, after Zimri assassinated Elah and
usurped the throne, the people of Israel declared Omri king instead
of Zimri while they were besieging the town of Gibbethon.

This sin of the young men was very great in the LORD's sight,
for they were treating the LORD's offering with contempt.
1 SAMUEL 2:17

It's nothing new for unbelievers to accuse religious leaders of being people who are simply out to benefit themselves. But what is really infuriating is when those charges are exactly right. Hophni and his brother Phinehas would have fit right in with the worst of these hypocrites.

Though their father Eli was a good priest (and strong role model for Samuel—his young protégé), he failed to raise sons that followed his God-honoring ways. Rather than treat their priestly office with reverent humility, Hophni and his brother mistreated the people, abused their sacrifices, and went as far as enjoying inappropriate

HOPHNI

Wicked Son of Eli

sexual liaisons at the very tabernacle itself. Rather than treat God and their office with deserving awe, they made a mockery of God and His commands.

When the Philistines mobilized their army against the Israelite people, Hophni and Phinehas rallied the people by taking the ark of the covenant into battle. For two brothers who didn't fear God or His commands, it is easy to see how they would irreverently place the ark at the front lines either as a lucky charm or a tactic to manipulate and motivate the people.

Rather than guarantee their victory, the ark was captured—the people of God were routed, and these two evil priests met their deaths on the battlefield.

SPIRITUAL INSIGHT

Hophni and his brother Phinehas serve as reminders for every faith-filled parent. Though Eli was a priest and leader of Israel, he failed to address the wicked practices of his two sons. It is not enough to focus on your own faith or to be perceived as a leader in the eyes of others if your own family doesn't receive the attention it needs.

Then the prophet poured the oil on Jehu's head and declared, "This is what the LORD, the God of Israel, says: 'I anoint you king over the LORD's people Israel. You are to destroy the house of Ahab your master, and I will avenge the blood of my servants the prophets and the blood of all the LORD's servants shed by Jezebel.'"

2 KINGS 9:6–7

From bombing abortion clinics to spreading lies about political candidates, there are many ways God's people have gone wrong in their attempts to do right. Perhaps we should all take a lesson from the life of Jehu, king of Israel.

The Bible makes it clear that the Lord had appointed Jehu, the commander of Israel's troops, to bring an end to the reign of evil King Joram of Israel and to wipe out Ahab's family for its wickedness. The Lord even instructed the prophet Elisha to anoint Jehu for this very task (2 Kings 9).

JEHU

King of Israel

The problem was that Jehu appears to have allowed his zeal to turn into an unbridled lust for violence, and he eventually showed more interest in destroying others than in carrying out the Lord's will.

Jehu began his rampage by returning to Jezreel from battle and killing King Joram of Israel, King Ahaziah of Judah, and Jezebel, the widow of Ahab. Immediately after this, he went to Samaria and arranged for the death of seventy sons of Ahab (2 Kings 10). Then he killed forty-two relatives of King Ahaziah. Finally, he arranged for many of the prophets and priests of Baal to be assembled in the temple of Baal, and he slaughtered them all and destroyed the temple.

The Lord's disapproval of Jehu's excessiveness was made clear by the prophet Hosea, who said that the Lord would punish the house of Jehu for his massacre at Jezreel (Hosea 1:3).

SPIRITUAL INSIGHT

Have you ever allowed zeal for righteousness to disintegrate into simple hatred toward others? Don't misuse the name of the Lord by allowing your sinful desires to replace the Lord's call for promoting righteousness.

*Jehoiada and his sons brought out the king's son and put the
crown on him; they presented him with a copy of the covenant
and proclaimed him king. They anointed him and shouted,
"Long live the king!"*
2 CHRONICLES 23:11

Whether true or not, popular culture has associated priests and other religious leaders with various things: morality, studiousness, peacefulness, and even clumsiness. When was the last time you heard of a priest arranging a coup against the king and installing another ruler instead? But that's what Jehoiada did during the reign of Queen Athaliah of Judah.

Jehu murdered Judah's King Ahaziah. When Ahaziah's mother (Athaliah) saw that her son had been killed, she became consumed with power and killed the remaining members of the royal family—thinking she had established herself as a queen without a rival. But without her knowledge, Jehoiada's wife saved one-year-old Joash, one of Ahaziah's sons, by stealing him away and hiding him in the temple. Six years later, Jehoiada overthrew Athaliah and restored Joash to his rightful throne. Jehoiada accomplished this by arming the other temple workers with spears and shields that David had placed in the temple (2 Chronicles 23).

JEHOIADA

Priest Who Helped
King Joash

Jehoiada continued to advise young King Joash for the rest of his life, even arranging his marriages to two women. He and Joash also made arrangements to repair the temple, which had fallen into disrepair under the rule of Athaliah (2 Chronicles 23).

Unfortunately, after Jehoiada died, Joash turned to idolatry and even killed Jehoiada's own son, Zechariah, who had prophesied against Joash's wickedness.

RELATED INFORMATION

Joash eventually paid for his treachery against Jehoiada's son. After Joash had been wounded in a battle against the Arameans, Joash's own officials killed him while he slept, and his son Amaziah became king (2 Chronicles 24).

*And the L*ORD *raised up an adversary against Solomon,*
Hadad the Edomite. He was of the royal house in Edom.

1 KINGS 11:14 ESV

From workplace grudges to family feuds to bitter divorces, hatred dies hard. In the case of Hadad the Edomite, hatred lasted a lifetime.

Hadad was only a boy when David sent his commander Joab to subdue Edom, a country to the southeast of Israel. Joab spent six months trying to kill off all the men of Edom, but Hadad, who belonged to a ruling family of Edom, escaped to Egypt with some other officials. There Pharaoh gave him asylum and treated him very well for many years, even giving Hadad one of his daughters in marriage.

HADAD

Enemy of Solomon

Apparently time does not heal all wounds. Once Hadad learned that David and Joab had died, he urged Pharaoh to allow him to return to Edom, even though he had spent virtually his whole life in Egypt and even had a son by his Egyptian wife. Pharaoh agreed to let him return, and after that Hadad apparently became a constant source of trouble for Solomon, David's son (1 Kings 11).

RELATED INFORMATION

The Edomites were distant relatives of the Israelites. Jacob (the father of the Israelites) and Esau (the father of the Edomites) were twin brothers (Genesis 25). Despite the family connection, however, the Edomites remained in constant tension with the Israelites throughout their history, and several of the Old Testament prophets (including Isaiah, Jeremiah, Ezekiel, Amos, Obadiah, and Malachi) foretold Edom's doom. Ironically, in the time of the New Testament, Israel was ruled by several Idumeans (Edomites)—King Herod and his descendants.

*Now the daughter of Pharaoh came down to bathe at the river,
while her young women walked beside the river. She saw the basket
among the reeds and sent her servant woman, and she took it.*
EXODUS 2:5 ESV

God can use anyone—even pagans—to accomplish His plan. Just look at Pharaoh's daughter; she became a key instrument in God's plan to deliver His people out of Egypt and into the Promised Land. As she approached the Nile River one day to bathe, she found baby Moses floating in a basket of reeds. Rather than let the baby wash away or die, she rescued Moses and made the amazing choice to adopt him as her own son.

PHARAOH'S DAUGHTER

Moses' Adopted Mother

While Pharaoh's daughter could not have assumed the Egyptian throne (based on her gender), her sons would be in line to inherit the kingship. And while we don't know where Moses, her newly adopted son, would have fallen in regard to potential brothers, we do know that Moses would have received the royal upbringing, education, and training fit for an Egyptian prince. John Wesley said of Moses: "Those whom God designs for great services he finds out ways to qualify them. Moses, by having his education in a court, is the fitter to be a prince, and king in Jeshurun; by having his education in a learned court (for such the Egyptian then was), is the fitter to be an historian; and by having his education in the court of Egypt, is the fitter to be employed as an ambassador to that court in God's name."

Though Pharaoh's daughter did not follow God, He used her compassion and devotion to save Moses' life and equip him for the important work that lay forty years down the road. Likewise, God can use unsaved people as tools in our lives to accomplish His purposes now and in the future.

RELATED INFORMATION

The world's longest river, the Nile, was the central reason for Egypt's early economic and social success. Without the river, Egypt would have been absorbed into the Sahara to its west. The river provided water and the fertile ground needed for development and predictable farming cycles. This allowed Egypt to become a breadbasket for that region of the world even when other nearby regions experienced famine.

"To obey is better than sacrifice, and to heed is better than the fat of rams. . . . Because you have rejected the word of the LORD, he has rejected you as king."

1 SAMUEL 15:22–23

As far as disasters go, Saul's time on the throne was an unmitigated one. At first, the man with the impressive physique tried to resist his appointment as king of Israel. He did not consider himself suited to the job. He was, as he reminded Samuel, a member of "the smallest tribe of Israel"; his clan was "the least of all the clans of the tribe of Benjamin" (1 Samuel 9:21). Apparently, many of Saul's own subjects were inclined to agree. After his first coronation, some openly questioned whether Saul was up to the job of delivering Israel.

SAUL

Israel's First King

Soon, however, Saul won over the doubters when he rallied a massive army to come to the aid of Jabesh Gilead, just east of the Jordan River. The victory prompted a second coronation ceremony—this one marked by the people's enthusiastic celebration of their new king.

Unfortunately, Saul's triumph was short-lived. For the rest of his reign, he proved erratic and unstable. More than once he failed to listen to the prophet Samuel—as a result, Samuel announced that the throne would be taken from Saul. When God chose David as Saul's successor, the king of Israel became even more dangerously paranoid. Though David would not lift a finger against him, Saul made repeated attempts on the young warrior's life. So obsessed was Saul that he slaughtered eighty-five priests suspected of aiding David and even began neglecting his royal duties. While Saul schemed, it was left to David to deliver the town of Keilah from the Philistines—the very enemy whom Saul had been raised up to fight.

Saul's life ended in humiliating defeat to the Philistines. His failure was complete, and the nation of Israel was in disarray.

SPIRITUAL INSIGHT

Despite being enemies, David never completely lost his regard for Saul. Such was David's honor that on the first occasion when he spared Saul's life, he was "conscience-stricken" over merely cutting a corner of his robe (see 1 Samuel 24:5). When Saul was finally killed, David responded with a touching lament for Israel's fallen king (2 Samuel 1:19–27). Long before Jesus came, David demonstrated what it looks like to "love your enemies" (see Matthew 5:44).

[Apollos] began to speak boldly in the synagogue;
but when Priscilla and Aquila heard him, they took him aside
and explained the Way of God to him more accurately.
ACTS 18:26 NRSV

Everyone can use help understanding the gospel better. When Paul's coworkers Priscilla and Aquila first met Apollos at Ephesus, it was obvious that he was a very gifted teacher of the scriptures (Acts 18:24–25). But even he was lacking in certain aspects of his understanding about the gospel, and he needed Priscilla and Aquila's helpful correction to set him straight.

Apollos had all the credentials to be a key leader in the early church:
- He was well educated.
- He came from Alexandria, one of the most important centers of learning in the ancient world.
- He understood the Old Testament—and even Jesus—very well.
- He spoke about Jesus with great fervor.

APOLLOS

Christian Preacher and Coworker of Paul

With all these credentials, Apollos—and everyone around him—could have easily assumed that he didn't need help understanding God better. But when Priscilla and Aquila listened to his passionate preaching in the synagogue, they must have sensed that Apollos didn't have some things quite right. So they hospitably invited Apollos to their home and explained to him what was still missing in his understanding of the gospel.

Through Priscilla and Aquila's loving and insightful help, Apollos became an even greater preacher about Jesus. The Bible says that he traveled to Corinth and was a great help to the church (Acts 18:27). He even helped Paul in his ministry there (see 1 Corinthians 4:6).

SPIRITUAL INSIGHT

Never think that you or anyone else has ever fully "got it" with the good news about Jesus. From the newest believer to the most gifted preacher or Bible teacher, anyone can use help understanding Jesus better. Don't let pride keep you from learning more about God from others—and don't mistakenly think that someone else can be completely trusted to have it all figured out.

*Isaac reopened the wells that had been dug in the time of his father
Abraham, which the Philistines had stopped up after Abraham
died, and he gave them the same names his father had given them.*

GENESIS 26:18

In a world that celebrates pioneers and trailblazers, it is easy to underestimate the importance of those who faithfully carry on what others have established. But a brief look at the life of Isaac, the son of Abraham and father of Jacob, will show that such people are just as critical to God's plan as those who are marking a new trail for others.

Isaac's greatest claim to fame was simply that he was the son of Abraham and Sarah, the child that was promised by the Lord to carry on Abraham's name and make him into a great nation.

As a young man, Isaac was nearly sacrificed by his father in a test of obedience, but at the last second the Lord stopped Abraham and showed him a ram to sacrifice instead. Later Abraham acquired a wife for Isaac from Haran, the land of his ancestors, and Isaac and Rebekah gave birth to the twins Esau and Jacob.

ISAAC

Son of Abraham and
Father of Jacob

Much of Isaac's adult life consisted simply of maintaining and bolstering the abundance handed down to him by his father.

He continued to look after his extensive herds of livestock, and he repeatedly reopened wells that his father had dug that had been stopped up by jealous neighbors.

In his later years, Isaac bestowed his blessing on his sons and unwittingly granted the greater blessing of birthright to the younger son, Jacob, who had deceived him into thinking he was the older son.

SPIRITUAL INSIGHT

It is often tempting to think that we are nothing if we are not making waves. But the simple faithfulness of Isaac makes it clear that some of us are simply called to be devoted followers and faithful managers of the things handed down by others. Make a point to appreciate the role such people play, whether that be your role or the role of others around you.

*Behold, I will utterly sweep away Baasha and his house,
and I will make your house like the house of Jeroboam
the son of Nebat.*
1 KINGS 16:3 ESV

Someone should have warned Baasha, king of Israel, that what goes around comes around.

Baasha ascended to the throne of Israel by plotting against his own king, Nadab, who was the son of the wicked king Jeroboam. A prophet named Ahijah had foretold that because of Jeroboam's wickedness, all his male descendants would be killed and shamefully left unburied (1 Kings 14:1–18). When Baasha usurped the throne from Nadab, he carried out this terrible curse on Jeroboam's family (1 Kings 15:27–30).

BAASHA

King of Israel

But apparently Baasha himself didn't get the point of Ahijah's message. Rather than see God and His discipline behind the events that transpired, Baasha lived in total disregard of God and His commands. The Bible reports that Baasha lived just as wickedly as Jeroboam had. Because of this, another prophet prophesied that the very same fate would befall Baasha's family (1 Kings 15:33–16:4)—a curse that was carried out by yet another usurper named Zimri (1 Kings 16:10–13).

RELATED INFORMATION

Jeroboam and Baasha were not the only kings of Israel to experience the curse of having their families wiped out. This same curse was placed on Ahab for his wickedness, and the curse of being left unburied was placed on his wicked wife, Jezebel (1 Kings 21:20–24).

*Jacob was in love with Rachel and said,
"I'll work for you seven years in return for
your younger daughter Rachel."*
GENESIS 29:18

Rachel was the more beautiful of Laban's daughters and the better loved of Jacob's wives. However, for the first several years of marriage, she was unable to become pregnant. This combination of circumstances led to the great rivalry between Rachel and her sister, Leah.

Rachel and Jacob's story was a case of love at first sight. So strong was Jacob's affection that he offered to work seven years for Rachel's father, Laban—according to the writer of Genesis, these seven years "seemed like only a few days" (Genesis 29:20). However, Laban famously tricked Jacob (who was no stranger to treachery himself), and when Jacob awoke the morning after his wedding, he discovered that his new bride was not Rachel, but her older and less attractive sister, Leah.

RACHEL

Jacob's Second Wife

In response to Jacob's fury, Laban gave Rachel to him as well—in exchange for another seven years of labor. Jacob did not attempt to hide his favoritism. God, however, intervened by providing children for Leah while Rachel failed to become pregnant. This gave rise to a protracted competition in which Leah tried but failed to win her husband's affection by giving him sons. Not until many years had passed did God finally open Rachel's womb, enabling her to conceive and give birth to Joseph and later Benjamin—both of whom would become their father's favorites, perhaps because it was Rachel who bore them.

In addition to her competitive streak, Rachel had a talent for deception that matched her husband's. When the family fled from Laban (having grown their own flocks at Laban's expense), Rachel stole her father's household gods and managed to hide them from Laban when he came after them. Despite her deception and apparent idolatry, Rachel was remembered as one of the pillars of the Israelite nation.

The prophet Jeremiah made Rachel the personification of the entire nation of Israel, describing hers as the voice that refused to be comforted just before the restoration of God's people (see Jeremiah 31:15). Later Matthew quoted this prophecy when he described the slaughter of all of Bethlehem's sons under the age of two (see Matthew 2:13–18).

One of them, named Cleopas, asked him,
"Are you only a visitor to Jerusalem and do not know
the things that have happened there in these days?"
LUKE 24:18

Day
111

Have you ever imagined what it would be like to have Jesus Himself lead you through the scriptures, giving you a guided tour of all that the Bible says about Him? For a man in scripture simply known as Cleopas, that dream really came true.

CLEOPAS

Traveler to Emmaus with Jesus

On the very day that Jesus rose from the dead and the disciples found His tomb empty, Cleopas and another unnamed person were walking from Jerusalem to the small town of Emmaus about seven miles away. Along the way, Jesus came to them and began to talk with them as they walked—but they didn't recognize who He was. Jesus asked what they had been discussing, and they told Him about all that had happened to Jesus in Jerusalem—how some of the disciples had found the empty tomb, but that they had not seen Him yet.

Jesus recognized the doubt and uncertainty in their words, so He rebuked them for their slowness to believe God's words about Him through His prophets. Then He led them through the scriptures (the Old Testament at that time), showing them what was spoken about Him. When they reached Emmaus, Cleopas and his companion urged Jesus to share a meal with them. During the meal, they recognized Jesus, but He immediately disappeared! Right away they went and told the other disciples all that they had seen.

SPIRITUAL INSIGHT

Like Cleopas, when we are facing troubles and difficulties that we don't understand, we would do well to review and believe God's promises to us in the Bible. As we come to fully understand and accept those promises, we will find they provide us with abundant assurance that God loves us, that He is in control, and that He is continually working out His plans for us—plans for our good (Romans 8).

*In the twenty-third year of Joash son of Ahaziah
king of Judah, Jehoahaz son of Jehu became king of Israel
in Samaria, and he reigned seventeen years.*

2 KINGS 13:1

It is often said that there are no atheists in foxholes—meaning that even the most ardent atheist will appeal to a higher power for help when faced with imminent danger, though later he may continue to deny that God exists. Perhaps this was the case with Jehoahaz, who "sought the LORD's favor" when suffering the oppression of the Arameans, but continued to allow idolatry to flourish in Israel (2 Kings 13).

JEHOAHAZ

King of Israel

Jehoahaz was the son of Jehu, the Israelite commander who assassinated his king and became king in his place. The Bible makes it clear that Jehoahaz's reign was characterized by evil because he sinned in the same way that Jeroboam I did—by allowing idolatry to be practiced throughout Israel. Because of this, the Lord allowed the Arameans under Hazael and Ben-hadad to gain supremacy in the region and oppress Israel.

Though the Bible doesn't make clear exactly how, God provided a deliverer for Israel against the Arameans when Jehoahaz "sought the LORD's favor. . .for he saw how severely the king of Aram was oppressing Israel" (2 Kings 13:4). This deliverer may have been an Israelite leader, or it may have been another leader, such as the king of Assyria, who attacked Aram and caused them to withdraw from Israel. Nevertheless, the people of Israel continued to practice idolatry.

RELATED INFORMATION

The extent of Aram's power over Israel during Jehoahaz's reign can be seen by the fact that when he came to power, all of Gilead (the entire eastern half of the country) had already been lost to them during the reign of Jehu, his father (2 Kings 10:32–33).

Mordecai the Jew was second in rank to King Xerxes, preeminent among the Jews, and held in high esteem by his many fellow Jews, because he worked for the good of his people and spoke up for the welfare of all the Jews.
ESTHER 10:3

In one of the Bible's most ironic plot twists, God used Mordecai, a man who tried to conceal his Jewish identity, to save the Jews from annihilation.

Mordecai settled in Susa (present-day Iran), where he enjoyed a successful livelihood at the city gates, a hub of commerce in the ancient world. The Bible portrays Mordecai as a conflicted figure. On the one hand, he demonstrated compassion and courage. Mordecai adopted his orphaned cousin Esther as his own daughter, and he uncovered a plot to assassinate the Persian king. On the other hand, Mordecai advanced his and Esther's fortunes primarily by concealing their Jewish ethnicity.

Mordecai found his nemesis in Haman, a royal official who probably descended from the Amalekites. The Jews and Amalekites had been enemies since the days of Sinai, when the Amalekites attacked the Jewish people following their escape from Egypt. When Mordecai refused to pay homage to Haman, the latter sought to finish the work his ancestors had begun in the wilderness years before.

MORDECAI

Queen Esther's Uncle

Haman concocted a plan to exterminate the Jews—and personally arranged for Mordecai's execution. Just in time, however, the Persian king remembered Mordecai's life-saving service to him. Just as Haman was preparing to ask the king's permission to execute Mordecai, the king ordered him to pay homage to Mordecai instead. Mordecai and Esther, their Jewish identity no longer a secret, were able to undermine Haman's plot to exterminate the Jews. Haman, meanwhile, ended up being impaled on the very pole he had set up for Mordecai's execution.

SPIRITUAL INSIGHT

Mordecai's story, told in the book of Esther, contains no mention of God. Indeed, Mordecai and Esther do not seem to have been particularly religious—Esther, for example, seemed to ignore Jewish dietary laws by freely eating from the king's table (see Esther 2:9). However, Mordecai's story is filled with a number of improbable "coincidences," which serve as a reminder that God is always at work, even when He cannot be seen.

The LORD is good, a refuge in times of trouble. He cares for those who trust in him, but with an overwhelming flood he will make an end of Nineveh.

NAHUM 1:7–8

To some, Nahum's single-minded, relentless fury seems like a strange addition to the Bible. However, considering the subject of his fiery little book, Nahum's rage is perfectly understandable.

In contrast to other biblical prophets, Nahum restricted himself to one subject: Nineveh, the infamous capital of the Assyrian Empire. Assyria had toppled the northern kingdom of Israel roughly a century before Nahum prophesied. During the reign of Sennacherib, the Assyrians managed to subjugate Judah as well, forcing its king, Hezekiah, to pay tribute in the form of gold stripped from the temple (see 2 Kings 18:16).

NAHUM

Old Testament Prophet

Still, Nineveh's supremacy was not the primary reason for God's fierce judgment, as foretold by Nahum. Even Nahum acknowledged that God had used the Assyrian Empire to punish the wayward Israelites (see Nahum 1:12). But Nineveh and its kings were renowned for their cruelty. It was, to quote Nahum, a "city of blood. . .never without victims" (Nahum 3:1). In the wake of conquest, the Assyrians always left a gruesome scene: "many casualties, piles of dead, bodies without number, people stumbling over the corpses" (Nahum 3:3). Indeed, Nahum's depiction of Nineveh's bloodlust is confirmed by extrabiblical sources. During the siege of one city, the king of Nineveh intimidated his enemies by forming a pyramid out of the severed heads of those he had already slain. Assyrian troops did not hesitate to skin their victims alive or brutalize them in other ways.

It came as no surprise when Nahum predicted that all who learned of Nineveh's downfall would greet the news with applause. Just as God had once used Nineveh as an instrument of judgment, now He would turn the tables and bring cruel Nineveh to its knees.

SPIRITUAL INSIGHT

Despite the harshness of his message, Nahum believed firmly in God's compassion and mercy (see Nahum 1:7). In fact, he saw the downfall of Nineveh as a form of deliverance for Judah—an opportunity for them to resume their religious festivities and fulfill their vows (Nahum 1:15). Nevertheless, Nahum's words are a sobering reminder that a compassionate God cannot tolerate "endless cruelty" toward others (see Nahum 3:19).

Neither did Naphtali drive out those living in Beth Shemesh or Beth Anath; but the Naphtalites too lived among the Canaanite inhabitants of the land.

Day 115

JUDGES 1:33

NAPHTALI

Sixth Son of Jacob

The tribe of Naphtali, born out of struggle, wound up living in relative comfort—albeit a bit too close to the pagan influence of the Canaanites.

Naphtali's birth was part of a great contest between Leah and Rachel, two sisters who shared the same husband: Jacob. After Leah bore four sons, Rachel, who had not managed to become pregnant herself, took matters into her own hands, convincing Jacob to sleep with her servant, Bilhah. In their culture, any children that Bilhah bore would be regarded as Rachel's own. In time, Bilhah gave birth to two sons: Dan and Naphtali. While Rachel interpreted Dan's birth as divine vindication, she credited herself with the triumph when Naphtali was born. "I have had a great struggle with my sister, and I have won," she said (Genesis 30:8). Naphtali's name means "struggle" or "wrestler."

The struggle in which Naphtali was conceived wore on. Leah copied Rachel, giving Jacob her servant, Zilpah, who bore two sons. Then Leah gave birth to two more sons and a daughter, after which Rachel gave birth to two sons at last.

Years later, when an ailing Jacob blessed his sons, he declared Naphtali "a doe set free" (Genesis 49:21)—a description that seemed to suit Naphtali's inheritance in the Promised Land. The tribe of Naphtali settled in the hilly, northern reaches of Israel's territory, where they could easily enjoy relative autonomy as well as the bounty of some of the most fertile land Canaan had to offer.

The men of Naphtali, however, failed to drive out the Canaanites, preferring instead to subjugate them as forced laborers (see Judges 1:33)—ultimately making themselves vulnerable to pagan influence.

DID YOU KNOW?	The territory occupied by Naphtali later came to be known as Galilee. It was in this part of the Promised Land that Jesus spent the majority of His adult life, delivered most of His teachings, and performed most of His miracles.

And Jonathan made a covenant with David because he loved him as himself. Jonathan took off the robe he was wearing and gave it to David, along with his tunic, and even his sword, his bow and his belt.

1 SAMUEL 18:3–4

In a world that typically looks out for number one, we are amazed and even puzzled by people like Jonathan, King Saul's oldest son. In contrast with his father's flawed character, Jonathan repeatedly demonstrated himself to be brave, capable, and loyal.

We first read about Jonathan when he was leading a thousand Israelite warriors to attack the Philistines (1 Samuel 13). He and his armor-bearer risked their lives climbing a cliff to attack the Philistines and sent them into a panic. Jonathan's leadership qualities earned him the respect of his men, because they refused to allow Saul to kill Jonathan for unwittingly going against Saul's orders (1 Samuel 14).

JONATHAN

Son of Saul and Friend of David

Perhaps even more impressive than Jonathan's bravery is his selfless loyalty to David. Jonathan was poised to become the next king after his father, but David's own acts of bravery were establishing him as a leader among the people (1 Samuel 17). Jonathan could easily have seen David as a threat, but instead he became friends with David and pledged enduring loyalty to him and his descendants—even sealing his commitment by giving him his own robe and weapons (1 Samuel 18:1–4). Later he tipped David off to Saul's intent to harm him, and David had to flee (1 Samuel 20).

Jonathan died with his father in battle against the Philistines, and David composed a lament on his behalf (1 Samuel 31:1–2; 2 Samuel 1).

RELATED INFORMATION

David was true to the pledge that he and Jonathan made to each other and their descendants. Years after Saul and Jonathan died, David sought out one of Jonathan's sons, Mephibosheth, and granted him all the property of his grandfather Saul. David also allowed him to eat at his table like one of his own sons (2 Samuel 9).

But my servant Caleb, because he has a different spirit and has followed me fully, I will bring into the land into which he went, and his descendants shall possess it.

NUMBERS 14:24 ESV

Day
117

T he meaning of his name fit him well: *to rage with canine madness.* Just as a wild dog gives his undivided attention to ravenously attacking and devouring, so Caleb remained completely focused on God's command to take the Promised Land.

Sent to explore the land as one of the original twelve spies, Caleb (along with Joshua) tried to convince the people to carry out God's orders to take the land. When the people began to stray by following the counsel of the other ten spies, Caleb snapped, "We should by all means go up and take possession of it, for we shall surely overcome it" (Numbers 13:30 NASB). His unyielding devotion and determination to the task was obvious throughout his life.

God rewarded Caleb's tenacity when He promised him a place in the Promised Land. Though millions of Hebrew people left slavery in Egypt, only two endured the forty years in the wilderness and entered the Promised Land: Joshua and Caleb (Numbers 14:30).

CALEB

The Spy with a "Different" Spirit

Even as an old man, Caleb's doggedness did not wane. Once the major battles wound down, an eighty-five-year-old Caleb approached Joshua and said "I am still as strong today as I was in the day Moses sent me; as my strength was then, so my strength is now, for war and for going out and coming in. Now then, give me this hill country about which the LORD spoke on that day, for you heard on that day that Anakim were there, with great fortified cities; perhaps the LORD will be with me, and I will drive them out as the LORD has spoken" (Joshua 14:11–12 NASB). Joshua granted his request, and Caleb successfully settled the land of Hebron.

DID YOU KNOW?

By giving him the land of Hebron, Joshua rewarded Caleb's lifelong loyalty and devotion. Hebron, the city of the patriarchs, contained the tombs of Abraham, Sarah, Isaac, Jacob, Rebekah, and Leah.

*During this time some prophets came down from Jerusalem
to Antioch. One of them, named Agabus, stood up and through the
Spirit predicted that a severe famine would spread over the entire
Roman world. (This happened during the reign of Claudius.)*
ACTS 11:27–28

F rom the earliest days, God has used prophets to deliver special messages to His people, and this role continued into the early church through people like Agabus.

After Jesus was crucified and resurrected, the apostles began telling people about Him, and the church of the New Testament was founded in Jerusalem. Later people carried the gospel to places like Antioch in Syria, and local churches were formed there as well. A church leader named Barnabas teamed up with Saul (later called Paul), and they taught for one year in the church in Antioch.

AGABUS

Prophet of the
New Testament

During that time, some prophets came to Antioch from Jerusalem, including a man named Agabus, who prophesied that a severe famine would spread throughout the Roman world. In anticipation of this, the church in Antioch chose to send a gift of money with Saul and Barnabas to help those living in Jerusalem (Acts 11:25–30).

Later we hear from Agabus again at the end of Paul's third missionary journey. Paul was at Caesarea preparing to go up to Jerusalem, and Agabus bound him with his belt to signify how the Jewish leaders would bind Paul and hand him over to the Gentiles (Acts 21:10–11).

Both prophecies of Agabus eventually came true, showing that he was a legitimate prophet.

RELATED INFORMATION

Throughout his ministry, Paul delivered several gifts of money to the believers in Jerusalem. Mention of such a collection is made in Romans 15:25–28; 1 Corinthians 16:1; and 2 Corinthians 8–9.

The women said to Naomi: "Praise be to the LORD,
who this day has not left you without a kinsman-redeemer.
May he become famous throughout Israel!"
RUTH 4:14

Naomi needed a redeemer. Bereft of her husband and her sons, she had no one to care for her. At least that's how it seemed to her. Little did she know that God was already working to provide a redeemer.

Naomi was from Bethlehem in Judah, but a famine forced her and her family to move to the country of Moab on the other side of the Dead Sea. While there, Naomi's husband and two sons died. Eventually Naomi decided to return to Judah along with her Moabite daughter-in-law Ruth, who chose to leave her own family and people and follow Naomi and her God, the Lord.

When Naomi returned, she told her neighbors to stop calling her Naomi, which means "pleasant," and to call her Mara, which means "bitter," for she was suffering much. But God was already working to provide a redeemer for Naomi—a relative who would buy her property and marry Ruth to raise up a family with her in the name of her deceased husband.

NAOMI

Mother-in-Law of Ruth

Ruth began gleaning leftover grain from the fields of Naomi's distant relative Boaz, and Boaz took great interest in the younger woman. He lovingly provided for Ruth and Naomi and made sure Ruth was safe while she gleaned in his fields.

Eventually Boaz married Ruth and purchased the land of Naomi's, thereby ensuring that Ruth and Naomi would always be provided for. When Ruth bore a son to Boaz, the women of the town recognized the child as a redeemer who would help provide for Naomi (Ruth 1–4).

> **SPIRITUAL INSIGHT**
>
> According to the story, Naomi was blessed with not one but two redeemers—and the New Testament makes it clear that there is yet another Redeemer who always stands ready to help all who turn to Him: Jesus (Galatians 4:4–5; Titus 2:11–14).

*There was never a man like Ahab, who sold himself to do evil
in the eyes of the LORD, urged on by Jezebel his wife.*
1 KINGS 21:25

If the Bible gave a list of the most wicked women in history, Jezebel would almost certainly be at the top. Her life was marked by evil through and through, both by her own acts and the deeds she encouraged her husband to commit.

Jezebel was the daughter of King Ethbaal of Sidon (1 Kings 16:31), and she married King Ahab of Israel, probably to seal a political alliance between the two powers. Ahab had already demonstrated a love of idolatry and evil, and his marriage to Jezebel only compounded his sin.

Jezebel began to kill off the Lord's prophets, but Ahab's servant Obadiah secretly hid one hundred of them in a cave to save them. She personally supported hundreds of priests of Baal and Asherah (1 Kings 18:19), so when Elijah had them killed at the foot of Mount Carmel, Jezebel tried to kill him, too (1 Kings 19:1–2). She also arranged for a man named Naboth to be killed so that Ahab could seize his vineyard for himself (1 Kings 21).

JEZEBEL

Wicked Wife of
King Ahab of Israel

Jezebel's wickedness did not go unnoticed by the Lord, however. Elijah prophesied that one day her body would become like refuse and be eaten by dogs by the wall of the city of Jezreel. This prophecy eventually came true at the hand of a usurper named Jehu (2 Kings 9).

RELATED INFORMATION

Jezebel's hometown of Sidon was located in Phoenicia, whose people were famous throughout the ancient world for their extensive maritime activity. They had established trading colonies as far away as Spain and North Africa and were widely regarded as skilled sailors.

Thus Joseph, who was also called by the apostles Barnabas (which means son of encouragement), a Levite, a native of Cyprus . . .
ACTS 4:36 ESV

I f people from your church gave you a nickname, what would it be? The Great Helper? Miss Generous? Captain Gossip? We don't usually give people such overtly suggestive nicknames, but people in Jesus' day did. One such nickname for a leader in the early church was Barnabas, meaning "Son of Encouragement," and the nickname couldn't have been more fitting.

BARNABAS

Apostle and Coworker of Paul

We first hear of Barnabas, whose given name was Joseph, during the early days of the church. The Bible notes how at that time the believers were of one mind, and no one was needy—because from time to time believers would sell some possessions and bring the money to the leaders for distribution (Acts 4:32–35). Barnabas is mentioned as being one of those generous people.

Later, Barnabas is mentioned again as the one who stood up for Paul (also called Saul) before the other apostles in Jerusalem when Paul first became a believer (Acts 9:27). Barnabas also traveled to Tarsus, Paul's hometown, to ask him to join in ministry at Antioch (Acts 11:25). Barnabas went with Paul on their first missionary journey (Acts 13:1–3). At the outset of their second journey, Barnabas was such a believer in people that he could not bear to exclude his relative Mark, who had abandoned them on the first journey, even though Paul was insistent that Mark not be allowed to come (Acts 15:36–41).

SPIRITUAL INSIGHT

Barnabas's encouraging nature was so apparent to everyone that they nicknamed him Son of Encouragement. Take a moment to consider what your most recognizable traits are. Are you seen as a person who encourages? Who helps? Who gives? Or would others see you as someone who criticizes? Who avoids church work days? Who is tight-fisted? Ask God to help you become a person who is characterized by the fruit of the Spirit (Galatians 5:22–23).

Jehoram was thirty-two years old when he became king, and he reigned in Jerusalem eight years. He passed away, to no one's regret, and was buried in the City of David, but not in the tombs of the kings.

2 CHRONICLES 21:20

T hough few people would ever admit it, we have all known people whom we were more glad to see go than come. Perhaps we have even been that person to someone else. This was the attitude of the people of Judah toward their wicked king Jehoram (2 Chronicles 21:20), and as we learn more about his life, perhaps the reasons for this attitude will become clearer.

JEHORAM

King of Judah

Jehoram was the son of King Jehoshaphat, who is regarded as a good king. But it seems that Jehoram was given in marriage to Athaliah, the daughter of wicked King Ahab of Israel, and apparently she led him to become evil himself. Upon his ascension to the throne, Jehoram killed all his brothers, no doubt to secure his grip over Judah, and he promoted idolatry throughout the kingdom (2 Chronicles 21).

During his reign, the nation of Edom rebelled against Judah, and so did the Judean town of Libnah. Jehoram attacked Edom to try to regain control over it, but failed. Even his royal palace was attacked by Philistines and Arabs, who killed all of his sons except his youngest, Ahaziah. Because of his wickedness, Jehoram died of an incurable bowel disease, just as he had been warned in a letter from the prophet Elijah.

SPIRITUAL INSIGHT

As the Bible makes clear, marriage plays a very significant role in determining the direction of our life (2 Corinthians 6:14–18). For Jehoram, his marriage to Athaliah led him to practice all kinds of idolatry and wickedness, even though he had been raised by a father who wholeheartedly worshipped the Lord. We should make sure that we regard a person's spiritual walk as a critical factor in our choice of a mate or in our children's choice of a mate.

While Josiah was king, Pharaoh Neco king of Egypt went up
to the Euphrates River to help the king of Assyria.
King Josiah marched out to meet him in battle,
but Neco faced him and killed him at Megiddo.
2 KINGS 23:29

D uring the brief power vacuum that existed between the waning Assyrian Empire and the Babylonians' rise to power, Pharaoh Neco of Egypt played kingmaker in Judah.

Neco belonged to the twenty-sixth dynasty of pharaohs; his reign lasted just fifteen years. Shortly after his ascent to the throne, Neco sought to help the Assyrians, who were being pushed farther west by the emerging Babylonian superpower. The Assyrian capital of Nineveh had already fallen; now Assyria's army prepared to make its final stand near the Euphrates River, in present-day Iraq.

Josiah, the last good king of Judah, blocked Neco's path. The armies of Judah and Egypt met at Megiddo, where Neco tried to dissuade Josiah from interfering. Amazingly, the chronicler revealed that it was Neco and not Josiah who acted in accord with God's command. In the end, Josiah may have prevented Neco from

NECO

Pharaoh of Egypt

saving the Assyrians, but he did so at the cost of his own life. Neco's archers fatally wounded him on the battlefield.

With no Assyrian army left to save, Neco settled for a time in Riblah (present-day Syria). Having slain one Jewish king already, he imprisoned Josiah's successor, imposed a heavy tribute on Judah, and appointed Judah's next king, Jehoiakim.

However, Neco's influence over Judah was short-lived. Under Nebuchadnezzar's command, the Babylonian army drove Neco all the way back to his homeland. The Egyptian Empire would never again extend its reach into the Middle East. Its diminishment had been foretold by the prophet Jeremiah (see Jeremiah 46).

DID YOU KNOW?

Neco proved a more effective leader at home than on the battlefield. He began work on a canal connecting the Nile River to the Red Sea (though it was not completed until the Persians arrived under Darius). According to the Greek historian Herodotus, Neco's naval fleet circumnavigated Africa—two thousand years before the Portuguese explorer Vasco de Gama managed the same feat.

Naaman was an unlikely candidate for healing by a prophet from Israel. After all, he commanded the army of Aram (present-day Syria), one of Israel's adversaries.

Unfortunately, Naaman's reputation for valor was not enough to protect him from one of the most shameful diseases the ancient world knew: leprosy. Ironically, though, it was one of Naaman's prisoners of war who pointed the way to his eventual cure—a young Jewish servant girl suggested that Naaman visit the prophet Elisha.

NAAMAN

Syrian Army Commander

Naaman sought the blessing of his master, the king of Aram, who sent a hefty payment to Israel's king in order to procure Elisha's services. Naaman and his master seemed unaware that Israel's prophets answered not to human authorities, but to God alone. At first, the bribe had the opposite of the intended effect, alarming the Israelite king, who suspected the Arameans of trying to pick another fight. But Elisha intervened, sensing an opportunity to demonstrate the superiority of the one true God—both to Naaman and to Israel's own unbelieving king.

Elisha staged his encounter with Naaman to leave no doubt as to who was responsible for the miraculous healing that took place. By refusing to meet Naaman face-to-face, Elisha made him realize that healing came from God, not from the superstitious incantations of a human prophet (see 2 Kings 5:11). By demanding that Naaman wash in the Jordan River—instead of allowing him to wash in waters belonging to Aram and to Aram's gods—Elisha asserted the supremacy of Israel's God over Aramean idols.

The carefully orchestrated episode left its mark on Naaman, who declared afterward, "Now I know that there is no God in all the world except in Israel" (2 Kings 5:15). The irony of the story is that a pagan warrior's eyes were opened to what so few in Israel were able to see.

> **SPIRITUAL INSIGHT**
>
> Jesus mentioned Naaman as proof that ethnic or religious heritage does not entitle someone to God's favor. He noted that none of Israel's own lepers were healed in Elisha's time, but only Naaman (see Luke 4:24–27). Later Jesus commanded His followers to take the gospel to all nations, proving once more that God's love knows no geopolitical boundaries.

The LORD was with Jehoshaphat because in his early years he walked in the ways his father David had followed. He did not consult the Baals but sought the God of his father and followed his commands rather than the practices of Israel.

2 CHRONICLES 17:3–4

Even the godliest leaders are vulnerable to sin, yet God is still able to use these people to accomplish good things. Jehoshaphat is a perfect example of this truth.

On the whole, Jehoshaphat was a very godly king who worshipped the Lord and sought to promote godliness throughout the land. He appointed teachers of the law and judges throughout the land to teach the people right from wrong, settle disputes, and promote godliness (2 Chronicles 17:6–9; 19:4–11). As a result, the Lord gave him success as a military leader, and the neighboring peoples brought him gifts as a sign of their submission to him (2 Chronicles 17:10–13). The Lord also gave him victory over a great army of Moabites, Ammonites, and Meunites who were approaching Jerusalem to attack him (2 Chronicles 20).

JEHOSHAPHAT

King of Judah

Nevertheless, even Jehoshaphat evidenced susceptibility to sin. The root of his sin probably lay in his willingness to marry into wicked King Ahab's family, likely to seal a political alliance with him (2 Chronicles 18:1). Later Ahab persuaded Jehoshaphat to join him in an ill-fated battle to recover the town of Ramoth Gilead from the Arameans. He also partnered with Ahab's wicked son Ahaziah to launch a fleet of trading ships to sail to Ophir for gold, but the ships were wrecked by a storm before they ever launched (1 Kings 22:48–49; 2 Chronicles 20:35–37).

RELATED INFORMATION

Jehoshaphat's plan to launch trading ships for Ophir was likely inspired by his great-great-grandfather Solomon, who had done the same thing about a hundred years earlier (1 Kings 9:26–28). As with Solomon's venture, the ships were set to launch from Ezion Geber, a port on the Red Sea at the extreme southern border of Judah.

Day
126

"Thus says Cyrus king of Persia: The LORD, the God of heaven, has given me all the kingdoms of the earth, and he has charged me to build him a house at Jerusalem, which is in Judah."

EZRA 1:2 ESV

Have you ever witnessed the amazing hoopla that occurs every time the president of the United States travels anywhere? His mere presence in a city can shut down an airport or a major highway for hours! Security teams often travel to the site weeks in advance to ensure that the most powerful person on earth will be safe while he is there.

This was the sort of awe that accompanied King Cyrus the Great of Persia (modern day Iran). After establishing the Persian Empire, Cyrus quickly expanded his territory both westward and eastward, eventually conquering even the great Babylonian Empire. Though there were certainly other kingdoms that he did not conquer, such as Greece, Cyrus had clearly established himself as the most powerful ruler in the known world—and it is understandable why he would say that he had been given "all the kingdoms of the earth" (Ezra 1:2 NRSV).

CYRUS

King of Persia

Yet even the great Cyrus was ultimately merely a tool in the hands of the Lord. The book of Isaiah tells how the Lord said to Cyrus, "He is my shepherd, and he shall carry out all my purpose" (Isaiah 44:28 NRSV), and it foretold that Cyrus would rebuild the temple of the Lord in Jerusalem. Just as God said, Cyrus conquered Babylon and decreed that all the Jews who had been exiled to that city could return to their homeland and rebuild their temple.

DID YOU KNOW?

The ancient historian Herodotus records how Cyrus captured the city of Babylon by diverting water from the mighty Euphrates River, which protected several gates of the city, until the river was low enough to be crossed on foot by Cyrus's soldiers.

And the Levites, of the Kohathites and the Korahites, stood up to praise the L*ORD, the God of Israel, with a very loud voice.*
2 CHRONICLES 20:19 NRSV

Day 127

KOHATH

Son of Levi

Kohath never knew the legacy he left behind.

It fell to the descendants of Levi to transport the ark of the covenant, along with the lampstands and other tabernacle accessories. When the Hebrew camp was ready to move and the tabernacle needed to be transported, God entrusted Kohath's family with "the care of the most holy things" (Numbers 4:4).

Though their job required them to transport these holy items, they were prohibited from physically touching them. Numbers 4:15 reads, "And when Aaron and his sons have finished covering the sanctuary and all the furnishings of the sanctuary, as the camp sets out, after that the sons of Kohath shall come to carry these, but they must not touch the holy things, lest they die" (Numbers 4:15 ESV).

Carrying these special items wasn't easy. Considered too holy to be shuttled by a wagon or cart, these heavy golden objects were supported by beams and then carried between the shoulders of the men of this family (see Numbers 7:9). God instructed the Kohathites to demonstrate the utmost reverence and respect as they completed their task, indicating that even leering at the items inappropriately could result in His judgment (Numbers 4:20).

When the Hebrew people settled the Promised Land, Joshua rewarded Kohath's family for their faithful service through the years. As their reward, they were the first Levites to receive towns in which to settle (Joshua 21:4). Though Kohath never knew it, his service yielded an immense privilege for the descendants that came behind him.

DID YOU KNOW?

The legacy of the Kohathites continued through their service to Judah's monarchy. David organized them (as found in 1 Chronicles 23:12; 24:20–25), they worshipped along with Jehoshaphat (2 Chronicles 20:19), and Hezekiah commissioned them during the cleansing of the temple (2 Chronicles 29:12, 14).

"Sovereign Lord, as you have promised, you now dismiss your servant in peace. For my eyes have seen your salvation, which you have prepared in the sight of all people, a light for revelation to the Gentiles and for glory to your people Israel."

LUKE 2:29–32

Simeon spent his days waiting for the "consolation of Israel" (Luke 2:25). He was not alone. Many in Israel had longed for the Messiah who would deliver them, ever since Jerusalem had been conquered nearly six hundred years before.

In his Gospel, Luke revealed that Simeon was a righteous man filled with the Holy Spirit. Others may well have thought he was mad for being so certain that he would not die until he had laid eyes on the Messiah. But Simeon had been told as much by the Holy Spirit. As a result, Simeon remained watchful.

SIMEON

Blessed the Infant Jesus

Forty days after Jesus was born, Simeon got his wish. Joseph and Mary came to the temple to present Jesus to God, as was custom with every firstborn male. Overcome with emotion, Simeon took the child and rejoiced that the little bundle in his arms would bring salvation—not just for his people but for the Gentiles as well. Clearly, Simeon knew the Old Testament prophecies well and understood that the scope of God's redemptive plan knew no national or ethnic boundaries.

However, there was a darker side to Simeon's prophecy. So well did Simeon understand the prophecies concerning the Messiah that he anticipated the suffering that Jesus would bring upon Himself and those who followed Him. Simeon saw in the eyes of the baby Jesus One who would turn empires upside down. Mary in particular would share in Jesus' suffering.

Unsettling as his words may have been, Simeon was not troubled. He knew that all this was part of God's plan. And having been blessed to see the great deliverer face-to-face, the elderly prophet was prepared to die in peace.

The name Simeon comes from the Hebrew word for "to hear." It was an appropriate name for someone who spent his days listening carefully to the Holy Spirit. Simeon is proof of God's blessing for those who have open ears and, more important, open hearts for what God is doing.

He [Benaiah] was held in greater honor than any of the Thirty,
but he was not included among the Three.
And David put him in charge of his bodyguard.
2 SAMUEL 23:23

Day
129

P erhaps the most inspiring stories ever told revolve around others so completely devoted to something greater than themselves that they are willing to risk their very lives for it. Benaiah is a quintessential picture of such devotion.

Benaiah was from Kabzeel, a town in southern Judah, and he was the son of a man named Jehoiada. The only other information we know about Benaiah is about what he himself did. As one of David's bravest warriors, he killed two of Moab's best men. The story continues as he went down into a pit and killed a lion. Once he even disarmed a large Egyptian and killed him with his own weapon (2 Samuel 23:20–23)!

Probably as a reward for his bravery and wholehearted devotion, David put Benaiah in charge of his bodyguard, where Benaiah continued to demonstrate his loyalty to David. When Adonijah set himself up as king, Benaiah and his bodyguard unit were not invited to the coronation—probably because Adonijah knew that David had not authorized the event, and Benaiah would always side with David.

BENAIAH

Captain of David's Bodyguard

Benaiah's loyalty to David continued even under Solomon, whom David had appointed to be the next king. Benaiah faithfully and bravely carried out Solomon's orders to strike down Adonijah, Joab, and Shimei for their disloyalty to David, and he replaced Joab as the commander over the whole army.

DID YOU KNOW?

David's bodyguard was comprised of men from the Kerethites and Pelethites, who lived near the Philistines and may have been related to them. David may have gained their loyalty during the time that he sought refuge from Saul among the Philistines and lived at Ziklag.

*Now David was the son of an Ephrathite of Bethlehem in Judah,
named Jesse, who had eight sons. In the days of Saul
the man was already old and advanced in years.*

1 SAMUEL 17:12 ESV

As with many parents of famous children, what we know of Jesse comes largely by way of information about his son David. If it's true, however, that "the apple doesn't fall far from the tree," then Jesse must have been someone with a heart that was deeply devoted to God.

JESSE

Father of King David

Jesse had eight sons, the eighth of which was David. After the Lord rejected Saul as king, the Lord sent Samuel to Bethlehem to anoint one of Jesse's sons as king. All seven of Jesse's oldest sons were brought before Samuel, but it was Jesse's eighth son, David, whom Samuel anointed as the next king (1 Samuel 16). Soon after this, Saul sent messengers to Jesse asking him to send David to the palace to be his royal musician.

Jesse's three oldest sons joined Saul's army to fight against the Philistines (1 Samuel 17). Jesse sent David to carry food to his brothers and their commander. While David was there, he fought and killed the giant Goliath, establishing himself as a great warrior in the eyes of the Israelite people. Later David became king of Israel, and Jesse would forever become known as the father of David.

DID YOU KNOW? For a time, David left his father, Jesse, and his mother in the care of the king of Moab (1 Samuel 22:3–4), the country just across the Dead Sea from David's tribe of Judah. The Moabites were often enemies of the Israelites, but David needed a place for them to stay beyond the reach of Saul, who was seeking to kill David.

Now Korah the son of Izhar, son of Kohath, son of Levi,
and Dathan and Abiram the sons of Eliab, and On the son of Peleth,
sons of Reuben, took men. And they rose up before Moses, with a
number of the people of Israel, 250 chiefs of the congregation,
chosen from the assembly, well-known men.
NUMBERS 16:1–2 ESV

It's not every day the earth swallows up rebellious people. God clearly wanted to make a statement when He chose this as the punishment for Korah, Abiram, and Dathan. These three men, their families, and their followers reaped an unusual, but deserved, judgment for their insolence against God and Moses.

While Korah had a faithful following of 250 men, all three of these men held leadership roles in the Hebrew community. Yet Korah, a Levite, and the two brothers, Abiram and Dathan (from the tribe of Reuben), were jealous of Moses' unique leadership and the special relationship he

ABIRAM, KORAH, AND DATHAN

Led a Revolt against Moses

shared with God. They envied Aaron's position as priest to the people. This led them to incite the people to rebel against Moses and grumble against Aaron. Their charge: "For all in the congregation are holy, every one of them, and the LORD is among them. Why then do you exalt yourselves above the assembly of the LORD?" (Numbers 16:3 ESV). They failed to find contentment in what God had already given them, complaining instead that they wanted more.

Though Moses and Aaron interceded for these rebellious people (Numbers 16:22), God caused the earth to open underneath the three men, their families, and some of their followers. The remaining followers of Korah were destroyed by fire from heaven (Numbers 16:35).

Even after witnessing this supernatural execution, the people were slow to refocus their devotion to God and His appointed leaders—Moses and Aaron. Less than twenty-four hours later, the people of Israel rallied against Moses and Aaron and blamed them for the dramatic death of their popular community leaders. God acted again, sending a plague to strike down the entire assembly of people. When Moses and Aaron intervened on behalf of the people, God stopped the plague—but by that time it had already killed nearly fifteen thousand.

DID YOU KNOW?

These rebels, particularly Dathan and Korah, became symbols and archetypes of rebellious behavior throughout Israel's history. (See Numbers 26:9–10; Deuteronomy 11:6; Psalm 106:17.)

Day
132

"Put your sword back in its place," Jesus said to him,
"for all who draw the sword will die by the sword."
MATTHEW 26:52

Malchus was a personal servant to Caiaphas, the high priest who led the conspiracy to have Jesus arrested and killed. Probably on Caiaphas's orders, Malchus accompanied Judas and the party seeking to arrest Jesus while He prayed in the Garden of Gethsemane. As the situation threatened to explode into chaos, Malchus found himself very much in the wrong place at the wrong time.

MALCHUS

Caiaphas's Servant

Cornered, Jesus' disciples watched the horrifying scene unfold—one, however, decided to act. Peter unsheathed a sword and swung, severing Malchus's ear. It may have been the combination of instinct and adrenaline that drove Peter's hand. Or it may have been his failure to understand the true nature and purpose of Jesus' ministry. As Malchus writhed in pain, Jesus rebuked his attacker, warning Peter that "all who draw the sword will die by the sword" (Matthew 26:52).

Determined that no blood but His own be shed on His account, Jesus somehow managed to reach Malchus and heal his injury before being dragged away by the temple guard. Malchus, then, provided the object lesson in one last teaching to the disciples before Jesus' crucifixion—one final reminder that His kingdom would not come by force or be spread by the sword. What happened to Malchus after this incident—and whether he returned to his master, the man who plotted Jesus' murder—is unknown.

DID YOU KNOW?

While uncertain, the attack on Malchus may have had hidden significance. Assuming Malchus was a Levite, like his master and all who belonged to the priestly class, a defect like the loss of an ear would have rendered him unclean according to the Law of Moses. Malchus would have been forbidden from going anywhere near the temple (see Leviticus 21). If this was the case, then Jesus not only restored Malchus's ear—He restored his livelihood.

And if he rescued Lot, a righteous man,
who was distressed by the filthy lives of lawless men. . .
then the Lord knows how to rescue godly men from trials.
2 PETER 2:7, 9

Day
133

*R*ighteous is not the first word that usually comes to mind when the subject is a man named Lot.

Lot accompanied Abraham to the Promised Land. Once there, tensions grew as he and Abraham tried to tend their flocks on limited resources in a land that did not fully belong to them. Abraham proposed they go their separate ways and magnanimously gave Lot the choice of which direction to take—especially remarkable in a culture where the family patriarch's word was final. Lot chose what appeared to be the best land and eventually set aside the nomadic life in order to settle in one of the nearby cities, Sodom.

LOT

Abraham's Nephew

Lot seemed to resist the worst of Sodom's vice, which may explain why he was considered "righteous." He alone offered hospitality to the angelic visitors. Honorbound to protect his guests, he attempted to spare them from the angry mob—even though the offer of his own daughters understandably strikes modern readers as detestable. Lot even tried to warn his extended family of God's impending judgment.

His family, however, did not fare as well. Lot's wife ignored the angels' command, looked back on the city, and died as they fled. His daughters, convinced they had no hope of finding husbands, slept with Lot in order to become pregnant.

Nevertheless, Peter held Lot as an example of righteousness—proof that God can deliver His people from difficulty. Lot also benefited from Abraham's superior righteousness. The writer of Genesis sums up the story of Sodom by noting that God "remembered Abraham, and he brought Lot out of the catastrophe" (Genesis 19:29).

SPIRITUAL INSIGHT

Lot is famous for choosing what he considered the best land, while leaving his uncle to tend his flocks in a less hospitable environment. Lot's choice, however, proved disastrous for him and his family, while Abraham was rewarded with "offspring like the dust of the earth" (Genesis 13:16). The difference between the two came down to faith. Lot based his choice on what he could see, while Abraham trusted in what he could not see.

And Deborah said to Barak, "Up! For this is the day in which the Lord has given Sisera into your hand. Does not the Lord go out before you?" So Barak went down from Mount Tabor with 10,000 men following him.

Judges 4:14 esv

Deborah was a woman who knew what needed to be done and wasn't afraid to tell people. And apparently it was obvious to everyone else that she knew what she was talking about, because they listened.

DEBORAH

Prophetess and Judge of Israel

We first read about Deborah, who was married to a man named Lappidoth, when she was leading the Israelites as a prophetess. She had set up her court in the hill country of Ephraim, roughly in the middle of the nation, and people came to her to have their disputes settled (Judges 4:4–5).

At some point, the Lord made it clear to Deborah that a man named Barak in the northern part of Israel was supposed to lead the Israelites to fight against the Canaanites who lived near him. When she told Barak, he must have gotten cold feet—but he trusted Deborah, because he refused to go into battle unless she went with him (Judges 4:7–8). Deborah agreed to go, but she warned Barak that, as a result, he would forfeit the glory for the victory. In the end, Deborah and Barak won a great victory over the Canaanites, and they celebrated by singing a victory song together.

Did You Know?

The hill country of Ephraim, where Deborah set up her court, was home to several other early leaders of Israel. The judge Ehud lived there (Judges 3), as did the judge/prophet Samuel (I Samuel 7:15–17) and the first king, Saul (I Samuel 9:1–4).

For it was Adam who was first created, and then Eve.
1 TIMOTHY 2:13 NASB

Day
135

Adam knew both the privilege and the pain of being first. As the first person who ever lived, Adam had the honor of naming all the animals. He joyfully entered into the first marriage in a way that would be completely unique from every marriage that followed. He experienced an unparalleled relationship with God as he ate from the tree of life and walked with God in the Garden of Eden.

But Adam also experienced painful firsts. Together with his wife Eve, he was the first to disobey God, and his actions ushered sin into a perfect world. Sickness, death, pain, and a wealth of other difficulties came into not only the world but also his life as a result. While Adam knew the joy of welcoming the first baby into the world, he also knew the pain that came when that same son murdered his younger brother.

ADAM

First Man

The Bible gives Adam a significant theological role by contrasting him directly with Christ. While sin and death entered the world through Adam, forgiveness and eternal life came through Jesus Christ. First Corinthians 15:22 says, "For as in Adam all die, so also in Christ shall all be made alive" (1 Corinthians 15:22 ESV). While humanity's allegiances were once aligned with Adam, Christians align themselves instead with Christ who becomes the "author and perfecter of faith" (Hebrews 12:2 NASB).

> **SPIRITUAL INSIGHT**
> The theological importance of Adam (and his contrast in Christ) underscores the heart of the gospel message and Christian faith. Study more of the contrasts in Romans 5:12–21; 1 Corinthians 15:22, 45.

And the three sons of Zeruiah were there, Joab, Abishai,
and Asahel. Now Asahel was as swift of foot as a wild gazelle.

2 SAMUEL 2:18 ESV

Asahel was a valiant warrior who would not be distracted from pursuing the enemy. Unfortunately for Ahasel, however, this admirable character trait also led to his death.

ASAHEL

One of David's Mighty Men

Asahel (as well as his brothers Joab and Abishai) was a nephew of David by his sister Zeruiah, and had apparently demonstrated great valor as a warrior, for he was listed among David's mighty men (2 Samuel 23:24; 1 Chronicles 11:26). Beyond this, however, the only other information we have about Asahel comes from his death at the hands of Abner, the commander of Ish-Bosheth's army.

Ish-Bosheth was a son of Saul who fought against David to be the next king. During one of their battles, Asahel doggedly pursued Abner and would not heed Abner's call for him to give up the chase. Eventually Abner took his spear and killed Asahel. Joab, the commander of David's army, and his brother Abishai nursed their hatred of Abner for many months for killing their brother Asahel. Finally, they avenged their brother's death by arranging for Abner to come to Hebron and then killing him in the city gate.

RELATED INFORMATION

It is interesting to note that several of David's thirty-seven mighty men (including Asahel) came either from David's family or from the general area of Bethlehem, the town of David's family (2 Samuel 23). These include Abishai (David's nephew), Asahel (David's nephew), Elhanan (from Bethlehem), Ira (from Tekoa), Mebunnai (from Hushah), Maharai (from Netophah), and Heled (from Netophah).

Abraham left everything he owned to Isaac. But while he was still living, he gave gifts to the sons of his concubines and sent them away from his son Isaac.
GENESIS 25:5–6

Keturah's descendants were proof that blood is not necessarily thicker than water.

Genesis provides no background on Keturah—she is simply (and quickly) introduced as Abraham's second wife. They married some time after Sarah died and Abraham's son Isaac had begun his new life with his bride, Rebekah. In one of the Bible's most extensive genealogies, the chronicler does not even acknowledge Keturah as a full-fledged wife—merely as "Abraham's concubine" (1 Chronicles 1:32).

Nevertheless, Keturah bore Abraham six sons: Zimran, Jokshan, Medan, Midian, Ishbak, and Shuah. Keturah's sons, however, did not share in Abraham's inheritance—everything went to Isaac. Shortly before he died, Abraham sent Keturah's sons away, though he did not dismiss them empty-handed. Abraham may well have felt fatherly affection for the children he had with Keturah, prompting him to give each child an unspecified gift. Still, he wanted to put some distance between them and his beloved son Isaac.

KETURAH

Abraham's Second Wife

That distance would not prevent their stories from interweaving—sometimes with explosive results. Keturah's sons settled in Arabia, where one of them became the ancestor of the Midianites. It was Midianite merchants who sold Abraham's great-grandson Joseph into slavery in Egypt. Later Moses fled to Midian, where he married the daughter of a Midianite priest named Jethro. The Midianites conspired with Moab to curse the Hebrews as they entered the Promised Land—and during the time of Gideon, the Midianites were responsible for repeated incursions into Hebrew territory.

SPIRITUAL INSIGHT

Minor character though she was, Keturah played an important role in fulfilling God's covenant with Abraham. God did not just promise to make Abraham into a "great nation" (Genesis 12:2); He also swore that Abraham would become the father of "many nations" (Genesis 17:4). This promise was fulfilled, in part, through Keturah's offspring.

Day
138

God has numbered the days of your reign and brought it to an end. . . .
You have been weighed on the scales and found wanting.

DANIEL 5:26–27

Some people seem to live above the rules. The rich hire skilled lawyers to get them off the hook for their crimes. The powerful put pressure on judges and leaders to turn a blind eye to their wrongs. The crafty find ways to get around the law to keep their schemes from being found out. Sometimes it can even seem like such people go unnoticed even by God Himself. But God does see, and one day He will call all persons to account for what they have done. No one illustrates this better than Belshazzar, the king of Babylon.

BELSHAZZAR

King of Babylon

Many years earlier, Belshazzar's father, Nebuchadnezzar, had invaded the land of Judah and exiled many of God's people to Babylon. He also destroyed the temple and carried away many of the gold utensils to his palace. Later Belshazzar became king, and he held a great banquet for all his officials. During the festivities, he called for the gold utensils of the Lord's temple to be brought out, and they drank from them, praising the gods of gold, silver, bronze, iron, wood, and stone (Daniel 5:3–4). Just then the Lord caused a hand to appear, announcing that God had numbered Belshazzar's days, for he failed to measure up to God's standards. His kingdom would be handed over to the Medes and the Persians. That very night the prophecy came true, and Belshazzar was killed.

DID YOU KNOW?

Belshazzar was made coruler after his father left Babylon and lived in the desert town of Tema for over ten years. A few years before the Persians attacked Babylon, his father returned to defend his empire, and Belshazzar was put in charge of the city of Babylon itself. As the Bible records, however, Belshazzar was unable to stop the Persians from overtaking the city.

"This is what the LORD, the God of Israel, says: 'Long ago your forefathers, including Terah the father of Abraham and Nahor, lived beyond the River and worshiped other gods.'"

JOSHUA 24:2

In some families, little changes from one generation to the next. Terah witnessed a cataclysmic change in his own family as his son Abraham grew to become the family patriarch.

Terah lived in the Chaldean city of Ur, believed to have been located in what is today the southeastern corner of Iraq. There he raised three sons—one of whom died. Terah's surviving sons, Abram (later named Abraham) and Nahor, married, but only Nahor was able to produce offspring.

For reasons the text does not specify, Terah decided to uproot his entire family—including his children, daughters-in-law, and grandchildren—and migrate approximately eight hundred miles northwest to Haran, located in present-day Turkey. While the distance covered was great, the religious culture of Haran would have been familiar to Terah—the people of Ur and Haran worshipped variations of the same deity, the moon god.

TERAH

Father of Abraham

While Terah adjusted to life in his new hometown, God spoke to Abram, directing him to move on to a new land where he would worship an altogether new God—the one true God. The implication was that in leaving his father behind, Abraham would forever leave behind his father's gods as well. In all likelihood, Abraham never saw his father again.

SPIRITUAL INSIGHT

In his farewell speech to the Israelites, Joshua left no doubt that their ancestor Terah worshipped false gods: "And Joshua said to all the people, 'Thus says the LORD, the God of Israel: Long ago your ancestors—Terah and his sons Abraham and Nahor—lived beyond the Euphrates and served other gods' " (Joshua 24:2 NRSV). Though no parent is perfect, God is able to work in the lives of the people He chooses—no matter their upbringing.

"Do not be afraid of them, for I am with you and will rescue you," declares the LORD. Then the LORD reached out his hand and touched my [Jeremiah's] mouth and said to me, "Now, I have put my words in your mouth."

JEREMIAH 1:8–9

No one wants to be the one to pass on bad news, especially if the people you are speaking to don't really want to hear the truth. But this was the painful ministry that the prophet Jeremiah was called to even before he was born (Jeremiah 1:5).

JEREMIAH

Prophet of Judah

Jeremiah was probably only about twenty years old when the Lord informed him of his special calling to prophesy against His people. At first Jeremiah was reluctant, but the Lord told him not to fear the people, for He would be with him (Jeremiah 1:17–19). Jeremiah began his ministry in the days of the godly king Josiah, but he would eventually witness the destruction of Jerusalem and the temple at the hands of the Babylonians. All the while, he faithfully warned the people of the impending consequences of their wickedness and idolatry.

Jeremiah was often perceived as a traitor for preaching his messages of doom. Once some royal officials of Judah even put Jeremiah in an empty cistern until he was rescued by a Cushite named Ebed-Melech (Jeremiah 38).

After the Babylonians attacked Jerusalem and destroyed the temple, some fleeing Judeans took Jeremiah with them to Egypt, where he prophesied more messages of doom and probably spent the rest of his life.

SPIRITUAL INSIGHT

Have you ever faced a situation where you had to warn others about the consequences of their actions? Even if the people you are speaking to become angry or threaten you with harm, you do not need to fear—the Lord is with you, just as He was with Jeremiah.

Then the people of Israel cried out to the LORD, and the LORD raised up for them a deliverer, Ehud, the son of Gera, the Benjaminite, a left-handed man. The people of Israel sent tribute by him to Eglon the king of Moab.
JUDGES 3:15 ESV

Throughout history, people have associated left-handedness with all sorts of things, both good and bad: natural artistic talent, clumsiness, even misfortune. For Ehud, however, left-handedness put him at a great advantage for striking a crippling blow to the Moabites who were oppressing Israel during his time.

EHUD

Left-Handed
Judge of Israel

Ehud came from the tribe of Benjamin, who apparently were renowned in Israel for their many left-handed warriors (Judges 20:16; 1 Chronicles 12:2). The Moabites, however, were no doubt unaware of this tribe's distinctive warriors, and this ultimately led to their defeat.

King Eglon of Moab had attacked Israel and taken over the city of Jericho, called the City of Palms. Ehud was chosen to take the Israelites' tribute money to Eglon at Jericho. But Ehud brought another surprise for Eglon. Being left-handed, Ehud strapped a small sword to his right thigh. Since most people would have been right-handed and reached for their swords on their left thigh, Ehud's sword must have gone unnoticed by the Moabite guards, who would likely have been checking his left thigh for any weapons. After being granted access to the king to hand over the tribute money, Ehud drew his sword, killed Eglon, and escaped back to Israel to call his fellow Israelites to arms. The Israelites seized control of Jericho and even made Moab subject to them. Ehud continued to serve Israel as judge for the rest of his life.

RELATED INFORMATION	Jericho is one of the oldest known cities in the world, dating back several thousand years. Even though Ehud lived probably no more than a few hundred years after Israel entered the Promised Land of Canaan, Jericho would have already been a very old, established city.

Day

142

In Joppa there was a disciple named Tabitha
(which, when translated, is Dorcas),
who was always doing good and helping the poor.
ACTS 9:36

Dorcas was a continual witness to the power of God at work in her life, from her generosity with her possessions, to her own labors of love, to her amazing experience of being raised to life again by Peter.

DORCAS

Disciple Whom Peter Raised from the Dead

Dorcas, also known as Tabitha, lived in the town of Joppa, one of the few port cities of Israel. The Bible describes her as a disciple who was known and loved as a very generous woman toward the poor. She made clothing for others and was always doing good.

While Peter was ministering in the city of Lydda nearby, Dorcas became sick and died—and some believers brought Peter to see what had happened. When he arrived, some widows were mourning her death and showed Peter some clothes that Dorcas had made for them.

Peter sent everyone from the room and prayed to God. Then he turned to Dorcas, telling her to get up—and she did! News of this amazing miracle spread throughout Joppa, and many people believed in the Lord.

RELATED INFORMATION

Dorcas's generous gifts of clothing for others are made even more admirable when we realize that clothing was typically much more expensive in ancient times than it is today. The making of cloth and clothing was essentially an entirely manual process, so it took a long time to make a single item. As a result, clothing was expensive, and people could not usually afford many sets of clothing.

When he had said this, Jesus called in a loud voice,
"Lazarus, come out!"
JOHN 11:43

Lazarus and Jesus were so close that names did not need to be mentioned when word reached Jesus that His friend was ill. He was simply told, "The one you love is sick" (John 11:3).

Lazarus and his sisters, Mary and Martha, probably belonged to a wealthy family, as evidenced by the expensive perfume Mary poured on Jesus' feet after He raised Lazarus from the dead. It is possible the three siblings supported Jesus' ministry financially.

In any case, a deep bond existed between Lazarus and Jesus—so much so that Jesus willingly risked His life returning to Judea in order to "wake him up" (John 11:11). By the time Jesus arrived, however, Lazarus was unquestionably dead. John notes that Lazarus had been in the grave four days, which was significant because of the widely

LAZARUS

Raised from the Dead

held Jewish belief that the soul departed the body three days after death. In other words, people might have accepted the possibility that Lazarus could be raised within the first three days—that is, before he was truly, irreversibly dead, but any hope of resurrection evaporated after the fourth day.

Jesus, however, was undeterred.

Led to the tomb where Lazarus was buried, He became deeply troubled at the sight of Lazarus's sisters grieving—and almost certainly by His own grief as well. Jesus ordered Lazarus to come out of his tomb, and to the crowd's amazement, he obeyed.

No one knows how long Lazarus lived after being brought back to life, but this miracle set in motion the events that led to Jesus' own death and resurrection. Incensed at Jesus' growing popularity, the Pharisees decided the time had come to put Jesus to death.

SPIRITUAL INSIGHT

One thing is known about Lazarus's postresurrection life: Like Jesus, he became the target of an assassination plot. As far as the religious leaders were concerned, a living and breathing Lazarus was almost as great a threat to their authority as the One who had raised him. Lazarus's story, then, is a picture of the cost of following Jesus. With new life comes new risk—and new opportunity to sacrifice all for Christ.

*Jesus looked at him and loved him. "One thing you lack," he said.
"Go, sell everything you have and give to the poor, and you will have
treasure in heaven. Then come, follow me."*

MARK 10:21

Jesus once asked His followers "What good is it for a man to gain the whole world, yet forfeit his soul?" (Mark 8:36). One rich young ruler in Jesus' day apparently must have considered that a trade worth making.

THE RICH YOUNG RULER

Rich Young Ruler Who Refused to Follow Jesus

The young man certainly seemed genuine enough in his initial question to Jesus. He fell on his knees and said, "Good teacher. . .what must I do to inherit eternal life?" (Mark 10:17–22). But Jesus must have quickly seen through the question into the man's heart, because the Lord wasted no time showing the man he was wrong to think he could gain eternal life by doing the "right stuff." After establishing that the man was blameless in the more "traditional" commandments, Jesus put His finger on what was really the key issue for the rich young ruler: "Go, sell everything you have and give to the poor, and you will have treasure in heaven. Then come, follow me."

With the heart of the matter laid wide open before him, the man went away sad because he couldn't let go of his wealth—even to inherit eternal life!

SPIRITUAL INSIGHT

At its root, the gospel is not about doing good deeds or obeying commandments or even giving away our money. The gospel is about surrendering our lives to Jesus and gaining the only life we can truly have, anyway. What might you still be clinging to that is keeping you from surrendering your entire life to Jesus?

And over the people who remained in the land of Judah,
whom Nebuchadnezzar king of Babylon had left,
he appointed Gedaliah the son of Ahikam,
son of Shaphan, governor.
2 KINGS 25:22 ESV

N o, don't go in that door!" How often have we wanted to warn a character in a movie or a book not to do something, because he or she was oblivious to the danger that lay ahead? None of us is able to fully anticipate all that lies in store for each decision he or she makes. Unfortunately for Gedaliah, that meant death at the hands of an assassin.

Because of the rampant and enduring sin among God's people, God allowed the Babylonians to invade the land and take many of God's people captive to Babylon. Only the poorest were left in the land (2 Kings 24:14). The Babylonians then appointed Gedaliah, likely a man from Judah who was loyal to the Babylonians, as governor over the land (2 Kings 25; Jeremiah 40).

GEDALIAH

Governor of Judea

Many Judeans returned to Judah, and Gedaliah urged them to submit to the Babylonians so they could live in peace. King Baalis of Ammon (an enemy country of Judah), however, conspired with a Judean named Ishmael to kill Gedaliah. Another Judean named Johanan learned of the plot and even warned Gedaliah, but Gedaliah didn't believe him. The mistake proved to be fatal, for Ishmael and his men did indeed assassinate Gedaliah and all those with him at the time, including some Babylonian soldiers. Johanan chased after Ishmael and his men, but they managed to escape to Ammon.

DID YOU KNOW? The prophet Jeremiah was a contemporary of Gedaliah and even went to live with him after he was nearly sent into exile in Babylon (Jeremiah 39:14; 40:6).

*And the Lord did an amazing thing while Manoah and his
wife watched: As the flame blazed up from the altar toward heaven,
the angel of the Lord ascended in the flame.*

JUDGES 13:19–20

Any parent who watches a child turn out differently from what was hoped can appreciate the story of Manoah.

Manoah and his wife suffered two kinds of hardship: They lived under the yoke of the Philistines and they were childless. Still, when the angel of the Lord told Manoah's wife that she was going to bear a son who would deliver His people from the hated Philistines, Manoah found the courage to believe the impossible. He prayed for God to send the mysterious visitor once more—not because he didn't trust his wife, but because he wanted to know how they should raise their promised son.

MANOAH

Samson's Father

Manoah's faith was rewarded when the visitor returned to the awestruck couple. While the angel refused Manoah's hospitality—he had offered to prepare a young goat, no small delicacy in those days—he invited Manoah to make a burnt offering to God. Manoah did so, and while he and his wife watched, the angel rode the flame back to heaven. Only then did they realize that God Himself had visited them. Convinced they were about to die, Manoah needed his wife's reassurance that God would not accept their offering and promise them a son only to kill them.

Nevertheless, Manoah was destined to experience great anguish on account of the son that God provided. That son, Samson, was to be one of Israel's great deliverers—unfortunately, he fell far short of the godly example set by his parents. Much to their distress, Samson took a pagan wife from their enemies, the Philistines. It is not known whether Manoah lived to see his son's demise, but he certainly watched Samson take those first fateful steps toward personal destruction.

SPIRITUAL INSIGHT

For someone who lived in a patriarchal culture (and one where barren women were especially despised), Manoah demonstrated a surprising degree of respect for his wife. He took her word when she told him of the angelic visitation. Also, it was Manoah's wife who had the better understanding of things when the angel of the Lord disappeared in the flames of the couple's burnt offering.

Moreover, Manasseh also shed so much innocent blood
that he filled Jerusalem from end to end.
2 KINGS 21:16

Long life and a long reign were often taken as signs of God's favor. But Judah's longest reigning monarch proved the exception. During his fifty-five year reign, Manasseh led his people into shocking new depths of idolatry and immorality.

Ironically, Manasseh's father, Hezekiah, was one of Judah's great reformers—but Manasseh was determined to restore Judah's idolatry. He embraced an "all of the above" approach to religion—adopting the Baal cult of the Canaanites who once occupied the Promised Land, borrowing astrology from the Babylonians who would crush Jerusalem not one hundred years later, and reviving nature worship from the depths of early humanity. But for the writers of Kings and Chronicles, two acts in particular confirmed Manasseh's place as an object of revulsion: human sacrifice and the desecration of God's temple.

MANASSEH

King of Judah

Despite his long rule, Manasseh appears to have been no more than a client king, subject to the Assyrian Empire, the reigning superpower of the day. An ancient artifact called the Prism of Ashurbanipal identifies Manasseh as one of nearly two dozen regional kings who paid tribute to Assyria. At one point, Manasseh was dragged to Babylon on orders from the Assyrian king, something the chronicler took as proof of God's displeasure (see 2 Chronicles 33:10–13).

This humiliation proved to be a pivotal moment for Manasseh. Upon returning to Jerusalem, Manasseh removed pagan objects from the temple grounds and restored the altar by making fellowship and thank offerings to God. Manasseh stopped short of purging the whole country of its idolatry, however. Nonetheless, God was moved by Manasseh's willingness to humble himself.

DID YOU KNOW?

The author of 2 Chronicles reveals that Manasseh sacrificed humans "in the fire in the Valley of Ben Hinnom" (2 Chronicles 33:6). This valley, just outside Jerusalem, was so detestable that it became the primary image for hell in Jewish thought. The word *gehenna,* which Jesus used frequently for hell (see, for example, Matthew 5:22), came from the Hebrew name for this valley where Manasseh sacrificed his own son.

"Bezalel and Oholiab and every craftsman in whom the LORD
has put skill and intelligence to know how to do any work in the
construction of the sanctuary shall work in accordance with
all that the LORD has commanded."

EXODUS 36:1 ESV

Given the Bible's strong emphasis on godly living and faithfulness to the Lord, it might be tempting to think that such things as art and architecture are essentially secular, second-class concerns of God. The Lord's commission to Bezalel, however, proves this idea very wrong.

BEZALEL

Builder of the Tabernacle

While Moses was on Mount Sinai, the Lord gave him very specific plans regarding how His people were to live and worship. Part of those plans included the construction of the tabernacle, essentially a mobile worship tent that housed the ark of the covenant and the altar. The Lord gave very specific instructions regarding how the tabernacle was to be built and how the priests were to dress and perform their duties. The Lord designated a man named Bezalel to head a team of artists to produce all the objects involved in worship. These people were skilled in working with gold, silver, bronze, stone, wood, and even fabric, and they were to use their skills to glorify God and lead others to glorify Him in worship. Their work would become a lasting part of the worship of God's people as they offered their sacrifices and prayers at the tabernacle generation after generation.

SPIRITUAL INSIGHT

Bezalel and those he trained were commissioned to a very noble calling, and they used their artistic skills to bring glory to God for generations to come. God continues to endow His people with gifts for the purpose of glorifying Himself and leading others to glorify Him as well (1 Corinthians 12; Romans 12). How might you use the gifts God has given you to glorify Him and lead others to do the same?

*It seemed good also to me to write an orderly account for you,
most excellent Theophilus, so that you may know the certainty
of the things you have been taught.*
LUKE 1:3–4

Surprisingly little is known about the man who wrote a quarter of the New Testament. What is known, however, is that Luke brought his unique set of skills to bear—including his expertise as a physician and his keen eye for detail—in writing an account of the life of Jesus and the early church.

Luke was not an eyewitness to Jesus' ministry. At the beginning of his Gospel, he described himself as a researcher who "carefully investigated everything" (Luke 1:3). Of the four Gospels, Luke's has the most in common with classical Greek literature—its sophisticated style of writing reflects favorably on the author's education.

LUKE

Paul's Traveling Companion

However, Luke was no ivory tower academic, writing about things from afar. Luke was friends with the apostle Paul. Beginning with Paul's second missionary journey, the two men became traveling companions. (Notice Luke's use of the pronoun "we" starting in Acts 16:10.) As such, Luke witnessed firsthand many of the incidents recorded in the book of Acts. He may well have suffered imprisonment and persecution alongside Paul. He was there with Paul when a ship bound for Crete broke apart, nearly drowning everyone on board. Some believe he put his medical training to use at key moments, such as when Paul was bitten by a snake on the island of Malta.

Luke was part doctor, part historian, and part adventurer—but most of all, he was a dedicated, articulate, compelling advocate for the good news of Jesus Christ.

DID YOU KNOW?

Luke is probably the only Gentile author represented in the New Testament. Near the end of his letter to the Colossians, Paul included Luke in a list of Gentile companions who sent their greetings to the believers in Colosse (see Colossians 4:14).

Now when Athaliah the mother of Ahaziah saw that her
son was dead, she arose and destroyed all the royal family.
2 KINGS 11:1 ESV

At times it is simply astounding how pervasive the effects of one person's sin can be. From the alcoholic to the busybody to the self-indulgent, one person's sin can affect not only those around that person but also those who come after him or her. Athaliah is a sad demonstration of the pervasiveness of her father, Ahab's, sin.

ATHALIAH

Queen of Judah

Most Bible readers are already familiar with the wicked deeds of King Ahab of Israel (including his clashes with the prophet Elijah), but few realize that his sin continued even in the life of his daughter Athaliah. Athaliah married Jehoram, the oldest son of the godly king Jehoshaphat of Judah, and soon her wicked influence became visible. Jehoram "did evil in the eyes of the LORD," and the same was said of Ahaziah, the son born to him and Athaliah (2 Kings 8:18, 27). After Ahaziah was killed by Jehu (2 Kings 9:27), Athaliah saw her chance to seize the throne—and she attempted to kill off all the royal family of Judah. Only young Joash escaped as his aunt stole him away and hid him with a nurse in the temple for six years.

After six years of Athaliah's rule over Judah, a priest named Jehoiada staged a rebellion and brought out Joash to anoint him as king. Athaliah was killed, and the wicked influence of Ahab finally came to an end. The pervasive sin of Athaliah stands as a strong reminder to watch our own lives carefully for unchecked sinful attitudes or behaviors.

Athaliah's wickedness (and that of her father, Ahab) extended even into the temple of the Lord, for at some point her sons "had broken into the temple of God and had used even its sacred objects for the Baals" (2 Chronicles 24:7).

But when Pharaoh saw that there was a respite,
he hardened his heart and would not listen to them,
as the LORD had said.
EXODUS 8:15 ESV

Day
151

P haraoh's determination to maintain power caused him to discount the obvious hand of God. Although the Bible doesn't record the name of this Pharaoh (many scholars think it may have been Menephtah, son of Ramses II), it does tell of his ill-fated resolve.

PHARAOH

King with a Hard Heart

As king of Egypt, Pharaoh struggled to maintain the power and order of the land. The vast Hebrew population provided a significant labor source and played an important role in Egypt's economy. As slaves, they helped build the infrastructure of the land—creating construction supplies and buildings (Exodus 5). If Pharaoh had yielded to Moses' demands, it would have dealt a blow to the kingdom, the economy, and his personal prestige.

Through Moses and Aaron, God inflicted Egypt with ten plagues designed to induce Pharaoh to release the Hebrew people and send them on their way to the Promised Land (Exodus 7–12). While many of the plagues initially motivated Pharaoh to release God's people, he changed his mind and held on to the people as soon as God removed the pain of the plague from the land. These plagues included turning the water into blood, infestations of frogs, lice, flies, and the death of cattle. They also included the infliction of boils, hail, locusts, and darkness.

Despite his grasping for power and his efforts to hold his kingdom's economy together, Pharaoh finally relented when the plagues became personal. The tenth plague (the killing of the firstborn son) directly affected Pharaoh's life and succession plan. Seeing his own dead son finally persuaded the king to release the people.

SPIRITUAL INSIGHT

Pharaoh's stubbornness is no different than that of many in the world today. When they read of supernatural events in the Bible or hear of answered prayer, they explain away God's hand and continue to ignore the reality of God. Be careful that you don't dismiss your own blessings as good fortune or the mere fruits of your own hard work. Thank God for the times He answers your prayers.

*Then a man named Jairus, a ruler of the synagogue,
came and fell at Jesus' feet, pleading with him to come to his house
because his only daughter, a girl of about twelve, was dying.*
LUKE 8:41–42

It's the reason ambulances are allowed to run red lights and emergency rooms stand ready to deal with virtually any life-threatening situation: Life is fragile, and time is critical when emergencies arise. Surely this was what Jairus must have been thinking when he came to Jesus, fell at His feet, and pleaded for Him to come and heal his dying daughter (Luke 8:40–56). And if we find ourselves perplexed by Jesus as He took time to find out who touched His garment amid a great crowd, we are probably thinking the same thing about life.

JAIRUS

Synagogue Official Whose Daughter Died

But Jesus didn't see things that way. There is no mention of urgency in His pace, no mention of concern about whether they would reach the girl in time to help her. And even when someone informed Jesus along the way that Jairus's daughter had already died, no mention is made that Jesus expressed any despair. The Bible doesn't record Jairus's reaction, but he may have wondered whether Jesus really cared what happened to his daughter. But Jesus responded this way not because He was uncaring, but because He knew He had no reason to worry—His Father was in complete control of the situation (Luke 8:50).

When Jesus finally arrived at the house, He simply made His way to where the girl was, took her by the hand, and raised her to life again. Such is the power of God—and the reason that we, too, can always find great assurance and peace in Him.

*Andrew, Simon Peter's brother, was one of the two
who heard what John had said and who had followed Jesus.
The first thing Andrew did was to find his brother Simon and tell him,
"We have found the Messiah" (that is, the Christ).*
JOHN 1:40–41

P eter is usually considered the foremost among Jesus' apostles. But he may not have even come to know Jesus had it not been for his brother Andrew's zeal in finding the Messiah then telling his brother about Him.

The Gospels of Matthew and Mark give the appearance that Jesus just happened upon His first disciples, fishermen on the Sea of Galilee, when He called them (Matthew 4:18–20; Mark 1:16–18). But John's Gospel gives the impression that Andrew had been looking for the Messiah

ANDREW

One of Jesus'
Twelve Apostles

at the time that Jesus called him. Andrew appears to have already been a follower of John the Baptist, who then pointed out the Messiah to him (John 1:35–40). Andrew's unmistakable zeal to share the Messiah with his brother as well further supports the idea that Andrew had already been looking for Jesus.

In any event, Andrew's simple belief in Jesus, and his immediate witness to the people close to him, gives all believers an inspiring example to follow.

RELATED INFORMATION

Andrew, his brother Peter, and Philip all came from the town of Bethsaida. While there is some dispute as to the location of this city, it is usually placed at the northeast corner of the Sea of Galilee. Herod Philip rebuilt this city in honor of Julia, the daughter of Caesar Augustus.

*David and the chiefs of the service also set apart for the service
the sons of Asaph, and of Heman, and of Jeduthun,
who prophesied with lyres, with harps, and with cymbals.*

1 CHRONICLES 25:1 ESV

A nd now the choir and choir director have a special message from the Lord. . . ."
When is the last time you heard an announcement like that in church? But that
is exactly the role that David assigned Asaph and his descendants for the worship
of the Lord at the temple. They were to lead the people in singing and music, but
their ministry was also considered prophecy—that is, their words were considered
special messages from the Lord.

ASAPH

Temple Worship Leader

Asaph was first assigned his new
role as worship leader when David was
organizing the worship at the new temple
to be built by his son Solomon. Asaph and
his descendants performed their new roles
well, and the temple was filled with the
glory of the Lord (2 Chronicles 5:12–14).
Over the years that followed, many of the
songs that Asaph and his descendants
wrote were included in the book of Psalms.

Their words continued to be regarded as special messages from the Lord, as
evidenced during the reign of Jehoshaphat. At that time, a coalition of Moabites,
Ammonites, and Edomites were threatening to attack Jerusalem, and a descendant
of Asaph named Jahaziel received a special message from the Lord that encouraged
Jehoshaphat to trust in the Lord. Jahaziel even prophesied that the enemy coalition
would be at a certain place the next day and that Jehoshaphat and his men should
stand firm against them. As a result, Jehoshaphat was moved to worship the Lord,
and they experienced a great victory (2 Chronicles 20:15–18).

DID YOU KNOW?

Asaph is even referred to in 2 Chronicles 29:30 as a "seer," a term
usually used of prophets such as Samuel or Amos (I Samuel 9:19;
I Chronicles 9:22; 26:2; 29:29; Amos 7:12).

"Simeon and Levi are brothers—
their swords are weapons of violence."
GENESIS 49:5

Day
155

Levi, Jacob and Leah's third son, brutally demonstrated his skill with a sword when he and his brother Simeon avenged their sister Dinah.

Dinah had been raped by a local Canaanite named Shechem. When Shechem and his father, Hamor, arrived to propose a marriage uniting the two families (Shechem was enamored with Dinah), Jacob's sons devised a cunning plan for vengeance. As the defining mark of God's covenant with Abraham, they insisted Shechem and all those affiliated with him be circumcised if they wanted to form a union with Jacob's family. Hamor and Shechem believed this was an opportunity to enrich themselves by absorbing Jacob's family and its wealth into their own—so they hastily agreed.

While Hamor and his men were recovering from their painful surgeries, Jacob's sons swooped down on their settlement. Levi, with his brother Simeon, led the charge, killing all the men of the town, while their brothers plundered the place and took the women and children for themselves.

LEVI

Jacob's Son

On his deathbed years later, Jacob recalled Levi's propensity for violence, criticizing his anger, fury, and cruelty (see Genesis 49:5–7). As punishment for Levi's aggression, Jacob warned that his descendants would have no territory to call their own—rather, they would be scattered throughout the Promised Land.

Jacob's promise came true—though God turned it into more of a blessing than a curse. In the wilderness, the descendants of Levi rallied to Moses after the Israelites worshipped the golden calf. As a reward, Moses promised the Levites they would be "set apart" for God (Exodus 32:29). Both promises came true: The Levites did not receive a tribal inheritance, but as priests to the nation, they served as mediators between God and His people.

DID YOU KNOW?

The book of Leviticus, which contains the priestly law, is named for Levi's descendants.

Ish–bosheth, Saul's son, was forty years old when he began to reign over Israel, and he reigned two years. But the house of Judah followed David.

2 SAMUEL 2:10 ESV

Ish-bosheth appears to have been a man who was easily manipulated by others. As David was rising to power throughout Israel, Saul and several of his sons died in battle on Mount Gilboa. Abner, Saul's commander, apparently believed that he had a better chance of retaining his favored position under one of Saul's sons than under David—so he took Ish-bosheth (also called Ish-baal) and made him king over the northern tribes of Israel, while David became king only over the southern tribe of Judah.

ISH-BOSHETH

King of Israel and Rival to David

Later, when Ish-bosheth accused Abner of being disloyal, Abner threatened to hand Ish-bosheth's kingdom over to David, and Ish-bosheth was too afraid even to rebuke him. Soon after this, David demanded that Ish-bosheth return Michal, David's former wife, to him. (Earlier, Saul had given her to another man when she helped David escape from Saul.) Ish-bosheth appears to have followed David's every word, despite her new husband's desperate tears (2 Samuel 3).

Finally, when David's commander, Joab, killed Abner, Ish-bosheth's courage failed (2 Samuel 4:1), and eventually Ish-bosheth himself was assassinated by two of his own men.

RELATED INFORMATION

Ish-bosheth reigned over the northern tribes for two years from the city of Mahanaim, which was located across the Jordan River and along the Jabbok River. This is the same city to which David later fled when his son Absalom rebelled against him, and it became the capital of one of Solomon's administrative districts (1 Kings 4:14). That suggests it must have been a key city of the northern kingdom during the time of David and Solomon.

"The scepter will not depart from Judah, nor the ruler's staff from between his feet, until he comes to whom it belongs and the obedience of the nations is his."
GENESIS 49:10

JUDAH

Fourth Son of Jacob

Judah is best known as the forefather of Israel's leading tribe. His family produced the royal bloodline that included both David and the Messiah. Judah enjoyed this position of honor because he was given his father's blessing—a blessing that, by custom, should have gone to the firstborn son.

Judah's path to preeminence was unlikely, to say the least. When his brothers decided to get rid of Joseph (the youngest member of their family), it was Judah who stepped in and persuaded them not to kill the boy. However, Judah's plan was little better than theirs—he suggested they sell Joseph into slavery instead.

Years later, Judah was given a once-in-a-lifetime opportunity for redemption. In Egypt to beg for food—and unaware that the official listening to their plea was in fact their long-lost brother, Joseph—the sons of Jacob found themselves in a crisis rapidly going from bad to worse. Joseph threatened to enslave the youngest son, Benjamin—at which point Judah intervened, offering to take Benjamin's place. The one who had sold Jacob's favorite son into slavery now volunteered to become a slave himself in order to spare another of Jacob's favorite sons.

This selfless act opened the door for Joseph's reconciliation with his brothers. More important, Judah demonstrated an integrity that his older brothers failed to match. When their aged father gathered his sons for one last blessing, it was Judah who received the blessing of the firstborn—not Reuben, Simeon, or Levi.

Judah's privileged position suggests that character matters more than birth order.

> **DID YOU KNOW?**
>
> Judah's story was not without its own embarrassment. He once slept with a prostitute who turned out to be his deceased sons' widow, Tamar. After his first two sons had died, Judah promised to give Tamar to his youngest son, Shelah. Judah, however, reneged on his promise and ended up impregnating his own daughter-in-law without even realizing who she was (see Genesis 38).

*Enoch walked with God; and he was not,
for God took him.*
GENESIS 5:24 NASB

There are some things in the Bible we will likely never fully understand until we get to eternity. The single, simple, yet puzzling statement in Genesis 5:24 regarding Enoch's experience with God is undoubtedly one of them.

ENOCH

Man Who Walked with God

What does it mean that Enoch "walked with God"? What does it mean that God "took him" away? Scholars and laypersons alike have pondered the exact meaning of these words for thousands of years, but no one knows for sure. Most believe that "walked with God" means that he lived a godly life in close communion with God. As a result, Enoch was translated straight to heaven without experiencing death (see Hebrews 11:5).

Besides genealogies, the only other places Enoch is mentioned in the Bible are Hebrews 11:5, where he is commended as a man of faith who pleased God, and Jude 1:14, where he is said to have prophesied regarding the Lord's return.

Are you interested in growing in your spiritual life? Spend time contemplating what it might have meant for Enoch to "walk with God"—and incorporate some of those traits into your own life.

RELATED INFORMATION

Beginning a few hundred years before the birth of Jesus Christ, several works were written as prophecies of Enoch. Some of these were included in certain versions of the Bible, such as the Ethiopic Bible and the Old Slavonic Bible. It is likely that one of these books, commonly called I Enoch, is the one referred to by Jude (though this does not imply that I Enoch is inspired scripture), and the books of I Peter and Revelation may draw imagery from this book as well.

Absalom and all the men of Israel said, "The advice of Hushai the Arkite is better than that of Ahithophel." For the LORD had determined to frustrate the good advice of Ahithophel in order to bring disaster on Absalom.

2 SAMUEL 17:14

Davids son Solomon once wrote, "The eyes of the LORD keep watch over knowledge, but he frustrates the words of the unfaithful" (Proverbs 22:12). Perhaps he had in mind Ahithophel, David's former counselor who betrayed him and joined in Absalom's rebellion.

Ahithophel was apparently a trusted adviser to David, and his son Eliam was even listed among David's mighty men (2 Samuel 23:34). When Absalom staged his rebellion, however, Ahithophel chose to become Absalom's adviser against David. He failed to anticipate, however, that the Lord Himself was working against him

AHITHOPHEL

Counselor to David
and Absalom

(2 Samuel 17:14), so ultimately his counsel would come to nothing.

David sent his friend Hushai to act as a mole, deceiving Absalom into thinking he was giving him good counsel but all the while leading him into error. Against the advice of Ahithophel, Hushai convinced Absalom not to pursue David's fleeing forces immediately, and Absalom's error allowed David to escape. This rejection of Ahithophel's counsel was too great a shame for Ahithophel to bear, and he committed suicide.

SPIRITUAL INSIGHT

Ahithophel's life demonstrates that no one, no matter how learned or experienced, is wise enough to overcome the will of the Lord. It is all too easy to become puffed up with our own knowledge (1 Corinthians 8:1) and to begin to rely on ourselves to make good decisions, rather than relying on God and seeking His will.

*And Ahab the son of Omri did evil in the sight of the LORD,
more than all who were before him.*

1 KINGS 16:30 ESV

As Ahab's life shows, God's favor often has little to do with worldly success. By all worldly accounts, Ahab was a very successful leader. He ruled as king over Israel for twenty-two years (1 Kings 16:29), cementing his power through a shrewd political marriage to Jezebel, daughter of the king of Tyre. He was successful in several military campaigns and even persuaded the king of Judah to join him in his attempt to recover the city of Ramoth-gilead from the Arameans (1 Kings 22:3–4). Assyrian records recall how Ahab spearheaded a coalition of forces to fight against the Assyrians at Qarqar, and his own contribution of over half the chariots for the coalition demonstrates his great military strength in comparison to neighboring nations.

AHAB

King of Israel

So does Ahab's great success reveal that God was pleased with him? Not at all. The Bible makes it clear that Ahab sinned more than all the kings of Israel before him (1 Kings 16:30), and God was greatly displeased with him. Ahab's marriage to Jezebel led him and his people to worship Baal and other idols, and his reign was marked by wickedness. In the end, the Lord ordained that Ahab would be killed by an archer as Israel fought against the Arameans to recover Ramoth-gilead, and his wife Jezebel would suffer a shameful death as well (2 Kings 9:30–37).

SPIRITUAL INSIGHT

First Samuel 16:7 makes it clear that "the LORD sees not as man sees: man looks on the outward appearance, but the LORD looks on the heart" (I Samuel 16:7 ESV). It may have appeared to everyone else that Ahab was successful and enjoyed God's favor, but his heart was sold to wickedness, and God was not pleased with him. God is pleased when we humbly seek Him and turn from our wickedness, calling on Him to forgive us and change us to reflect His character (Micah 6:8; Romans 12:1).

*Saul sent men to David's house to watch it and to kill him
in the morning. But Michal, David's wife, warned him,
"If you don't run for your life tonight, tomorrow you'll be killed."*
1 SAMUEL 19:11

Michal's story reads like something from an ancient soap opera: romance, intrigue, feuding families, and a politically motivated lover's triangle.

Michal was the youngest daughter of Saul. She fell in love with David at a time her father was looking for a way to have him killed. Sensing his opportunity, Saul promised Michal to David in exchange for killing one hundred Philistines. Surely it was a suicide mission—except that David managed to kill *two* hundred Philistines. Not only had Saul's plan failed, but he was forced to watch his youngest daughter marry his enemy.

Saul schemed once more to take David's life, but Michal uncovered the plot and helped her husband escape. While David climbed out a window, Michal used a household idol to make it look like David was asleep in bed, underneath a garment (see 1 Samuel 19:11–16).

MICHAL

Wife of King David

After David when into hiding, Saul gave Michal to a man named Paltiel—a deliberate insult, perhaps designed to weaken David's claim to the throne. After Saul died, David demanded that Michal be returned to him—much to Paltiel's chagrin.

Michal, too, may have resented being treated like a pawn in other people's plans. Or perhaps she simply did not share David's devotion to God. For whatever reason, the love between them seemed to grow cold after David became king. Michal even mocked David's exuberant display as the ark of the covenant was carried to Jerusalem. The Bible notes that Michal bore no children after her falling out with David—which may have been due to divine punishment or simply an indication that she no longer received David's favor or affection.

Also the children of Makir son of Manasseh
were placed at birth on Joseph's knees.
GENESIS 50:23

In biblical times, Makir's name became synonymous with that of his father Manasseh, the ancestor of one of the twelve tribes of Israel. Makir was the grandson of Joseph, the last of the great patriarchs. As such, he was the subject of a recurring family ritual that may seem unusual to modern readers.

MAKIR

Manasseh's Son

Before he died, Jacob took Joseph's two sons, Manasseh and Ephraim, on his knees (see Genesis 48:12)—an ancient way of saying he adopted them as his own sons. It was a strange thing to do, particularly since Jacob was so close to death while their real father, Joseph, was alive and well. However, as Jacob's "sons," Manasseh and Ephraim were entitled to a share of Jacob's blessing. They would be forever counted among the forefathers of Israel's twelve tribes.

Years later, Joseph repeated the same ritual with his great-grandchildren, adopting Makir's offspring as his own, confirming to all present that Makir's descendants would play an important part in Israel's development.

Some of Makir's descendants became known as the Gileadites, part of the tribe of Manasseh. They were responsible for conquering and settling the portion of the Promised Land that bore their name, Gilead. Later, when the prophetess Deborah celebrated Manasseh's part in delivering Israel from the Canaanites, she actually used the name Makir instead of Manasseh. As a result, Makir's legacy was forever etched into Israel's story.

DID YOU KNOW?

Half of Makir's descendants settled on the east side of the Jordan River, in what is modern-day Syria.

*Moreover, Jacob deceived Laban the Aramean
by not telling him he was running away.*
GENESIS 31:20

Day
163

Laban spent the better part of twenty years trying to outwit his son-in-law Jacob—a man whose name was a Hebrew idiom for "the deceiver."

Laban had a natural talent for shrewdness. Long before Jacob was born, his grandfather Abraham sent a servant in search of a wife for Isaac. When the servant happened upon Laban's sister and presented her with fine jewelry, Laban took one look, saw his opportunity, and adopted the persona of an accommodating host. Laban helped to arrange his sister's marriage and received some "costly gifts" for doing so (Genesis 24:53).

LABAN

Jacob's Deceitful Father-in-Law

Laban's cunning reached new heights when Jacob arrived, shortly after stealing the birthright from his brother Esau. Jacob fell in love with Laban's youngest daughter, Rachel, and offered to serve Laban for seven years in exchange for Rachel's hand in marriage. On the wedding night, Laban managed to switch brides—Jacob awoke the next morning to see Jacob's oldest daughter, Leah, not Rachel, lying next to him! Laban agreed to let Jacob marry Rachel, too, but only after extracting the promise of another seven years of labor.

Ultimately, however, Laban's life is a reminder that people tend to reap what they sow. Not only did the con man get conned in the end, but Laban's daughter Rachel inherited her father's talent for deception and turned it against him.

Laban got years of cheap labor out of Jacob (and changed his wages several times, according to Jacob), but Jacob managed to enrich himself at Laban's expense.

DID YOU KNOW?

Laban was not just Jacob's father-in-law, he was also Jacob's uncle. Laban's sister Rebekah was Jacob's mother. In other words, Leah and Rachel were Jacob's cousins. Such incestuous marriages (in the modern view) were not unheard of in the ancient Near East.

Hiram king of Tyre had supplied Solomon with cedar and cypress timber and gold, as much as he desired, King Solomon gave to Hiram twenty cities in the land of Galilee.

1 KINGS 9:11 ESV

Great business executives are constantly on the lookout for win-win alliances with other key businesses, and King Hiram of Tyre was a business leader par excellence.

HIRAM

King of Tyre

Hiram was king over the tiny island fortress of Tyre in modern-day Lebanon, but it would be a mistake to think that his small city was also small in power and wealth. Under the leadership of Hiram and those who came after him, Tyre grew into a world-renowned trading empire, like an ancient version of the New York Stock Exchange. Tyre also capitalized on Lebanon's vast forests of highly prized cedar and its abundance of skilled carpenters and stonemasons.

During David's and Solomon's days, Hiram forged alliances with Israel, no doubt to ensure both peace with them and access to the key trade routes that passed through Israel's territory. Hiram supplied cedar, trimmed stones, and skilled labor for the building of the Lord's temple, and Solomon provided him with food as well as twenty cities in Galilee (1 Kings 5). Later Hiram would partner with Solomon in several trading expeditions to faraway places, bringing back gold, silver, and exotic goods (1 Kings 9:26–28; 10:22). These alliances and expeditions resulted in great wealth for both Hiram and Solomon.

DID YOU KNOW?

Tyre was originally two distinct cities, one located on the mainland and the other on a small island just off the coast. In 332 BC, however, Alexander the Great conquered the city by building a causeway from the mainland almost to the island fortress. Over time the causeway continued to silt up and permanently turned the island into a peninsula, as it is today.

But Peter declared, "Even if I have to die with you,
I will never disown you." And all the other disciples said the same.
Matthew 26:35

Day

165

P eter is one of the most passionate, impetuous, and volatile characters in the Bible. As such, he was simultaneously capable of great triumph and enormous failure. Peter's boundless enthusiasm was exceeded only by his love for his Master, Jesus.

Peter's original name was Simon. However, Jesus liked to call him Cephas, an Aramaic word meaning "rock" or "stone," which translated into Greek as "Peter." During the course of Jesus' ministry, Peter emerged as the natural leader among the disciples.

However, standing a head above the other disciples simply meant that Peter had further to fall—and he did. Immediately after his famous confession—which Jesus revealed was a result of divine enlightenment (see Matthew 16:17)—Peter proved equally adept at getting things wrong, contradicting Jesus' prediction of His own

PETER

Apostle of Jesus

death (Matthew 16:22). Later, Peter confidently swore that he would stand with Jesus to the bitter end—that he would die with Jesus, if the need arose. Not for the first time, though, Peter had misunderstood the fundamental nature of Jesus' ministry. When guards came to arrest Jesus, Peter reached for his sword and attacked the servant of the high priest. Peter believed the time had come to fight, not realizing that Jesus' mission was to lay down His life. Most famously, Peter wound up disowning his Master three times, much to his own dismay.

Despite all of this, Jesus never gave up on Peter. According to Mark's Gospel, the angel at the tomb mentioned Peter by name when he told the women to share the news of Jesus' resurrection. Also, John recorded a particularly touching post-resurrection scene in which Jesus restored Peter, entrusting to him the vital task of shepherding the early church.

DID YOU KNOW?

According to tradition, Peter was crucified for his faith. Some interpreters read Jesus' statement in John 21:18 ("When you are old you will stretch out your hands, and someone else will dress you and lead you where you do not want to go") as a prediction of his martyrdom. Legend has it that Peter requested to be crucified upside down because he did not consider himself worthy of being killed in the same manner as Jesus.

*May the Lord show mercy to the household of Onesiphorus,
because he often refreshed me and was not ashamed of my chains.*
2 TIMOTHY 1:16

Some of the last recorded words of the apostle Paul contain a greeting to the household of Onesiphorus, the faithful friend who sought him out in Rome.

Onesiphorus is mentioned only in Paul's second letter to his disciple Timothy, pastor of the church in Ephesus. It was to be Paul's final letter, written sometime around AD 66 or 67. Rome had burned in a great fire just a few years before, and its deranged emperor, Nero, blamed the Christians in order to avoid Rome's suspicious glare at himself. As a result, believers in Rome were subjected to horrific persecution. Some were torn apart by wild animals, while others were burned alive. Paul, who had appealed his case to Caesar sometime before the great fire of Rome, was now imprisoned, in all likelihood nearing the end of his life. He had never felt more isolated—the apostle confided in Timothy that "everyone in the province of Asia [present-day western Turkey] has deserted me" (2 Timothy 1:15).

ONESIPHORUS

Paul's Loyal Friend

It was no small injury. Paul had invested much of his ministry—indeed much of himself—into that part of the world. Ephesus had been his home for more than two years. He had spent more time there than in any other city to which his missionary journeys had taken him. Paul had made disciples there, lectured in the public hall, cast out demons, and cured illnesses. Yet now, all that seemed forgotten—more to the point, *he* seemed forgotten as he languished in a Roman prison.

But Onesiphorus had not forgotten Paul. He made the eight-hundred-mile journey from Ephesus to Rome and searched hard until he found the imprisoned apostle. Such a journey was not without risk; Nero's persecution of the church at Rome had yet to subside. But that would not deter Onesiphorus. He did not mind being associated with a condemned man in chains. Onesiphorus had been Paul's faithful friend in Ephesus—now he was his loyal companion in Rome. Having been comforted, Paul asked God's blessing on Onesiphorus.

SPIRITUAL INSIGHT

Onesiphorus lived up to his name, which means "bringing profit." While others sought to profit only themselves, Onesiphorus traveled far to bring profit to another.

*Josiah removed all the detestable idols from all the territory
belonging to the Israelites, and he had all who were present in Israel
serve the LORD their God. As long as he lived, they did not fail
to follow the LORD, the God of their fathers.*
2 CHRONICLES 34:33–34

Imagine if the Bible disappeared—lost to history, with no surviving copies to be found. How would you know how to relate to God? How could you tell if you were obeying His will?

That was Judah's dilemma when Josiah took the throne at the age of eight. The Book of the Law had not been seen or read for generations—perhaps not since Hezekiah, the last good king of Judah (and Josiah's great-grandfather). Since then, Judah had sunk to new lows, particularly during the reign of Manasseh, who sacrificed humans and defiled the Jewish temple—only to be humiliated when the Assyrians took him prisoner.

Josiah had reigned for eight years when he decided to turn things around and follow God. Still a teenager, he implemented top-down reforms with zeal, obliterating pagan worship sites and repairing the temple. But with no Book of the Law to guide him, how would Josiah know what else needed to be done?

JOSIAH

The Reformer King

While cleaning the temple, a priest named Hilkiah rediscovered the Book of the Law. It was brought to Josiah and read aloud—but rather than celebrate, Josiah lamented. Its words were a painful reminder of how far the Israelites had wandered from God's ways. Even worse, the prophetess Huldah announced that it was too late for Judah to escape judgment. The only consolation for Josiah was that he would not live to see its demise.

This, however, did not discourage him from pursuing reform. He ordered the Book of the Law read aloud to the people, renewed the covenant with God, and reinstated the Jewish feast. Unfortunately, Josiah's untimely death in battle meant the throne passed to his son, Jehoahaz—who lasted just three months.

SPIRITUAL INSIGHT

Josiah followed God, even though he knew his country was doomed. His legacy of faithfulness is recorded for all to read in the scriptures. Josiah's life serves as a reminder of the value of unwavering devotion to God, even when the whole world seems to be moving in the opposite direction.

For Demas, in love with this present world,
has deserted me and gone to Thessalonica.
Crescens has gone to Galatia, Titus to Dalmatia.
2 TIMOTHY 4:10 ESV

It's interesting how various people in the Bible have become forever identified by a single event in their lives. Enoch walked with God and was taken away, perhaps meaning he never died. Jabez prayed for God's blessing and deliverance from harm, and God granted his request. Judas betrayed Jesus to death with a kiss for thirty pieces of silver. Unfortunately for Demas, the echo that continues to ring from his brief mention in scripture is his desertion of Paul during his time of great need.

DEMAS

Coworker of Paul

Scripture does not include much about Demas, but we can infer some general impressions from what is included. In his letters to the Colossians and to Philemon (Colossians 4:10; Philemon 1:24), Paul mentions Demas in positive words and in very good company, along with Mark (Barnabas's relative), Luke (the doctor and Gospel writer), and Aristarchus (Paul's coworker and fellow prisoner). Paul's words give us every reason to believe that at that time Demas was his trusted, faithful coworker.

The only other mention of Demas occurs several years later as Paul, facing the possibility of martyrdom, asks Timothy and Mark to come to him. Paul notes that only Luke is with him, because two other coworkers have gone elsewhere, while Demas, out of love for this world, has deserted him. We never hear anything more of Demas—whether he ever returned to serve the Lord or whether he continued on his selfish path to his own destruction, we don't know. In any event, those final, sad words have largely defined Demas through history.

SPIRITUAL INSIGHT

Demas may indeed have returned to the Lord—or he may have continued in his sin. Either way, his life stands as an example of the constant need to guard against sin. If even faithful, trusted coworkers of Paul could eventually fall prey to selfish, sinful desires that lead them away from God, how much more can believers today?

Barak said to [Deborah], "If you go with me,
I will go; but if you don't go with me, I won't go."
JUDGES 4:8

F or better or worse, Barak was definitely not a lone ranger. When the Lord gave the prophetess Deborah a message for Barak and called him to fight the Canaanites under the command of Sisera, Barak basically said, "I'll do it if you will" (Judges 4:8). Deborah agreed to come but warned Barak that he would miss out on receiving glory for the victory.

BARAK

Judge of Israel

So Barak and Deborah called up the forces of Israel, and they gathered at Mount Tabor on the edge of the great Jezreel Valley. Sisera soon mustered his men and led them—along with his nine hundred iron chariots—to the Kishon River to the south of the mountain, ready for battle. Barak and his men rushed down the mountain, sending Sisera's men fleeing for their lives. The Israelites pursued the Canaanites until there was no one left, and even Sisera himself was killed by a woman as he hid in her tent. After the battle was over, Barak and Deborah sang a victory duet, recounting the story of the great battle.

RELATED INFORMATION

Despite Deborah's warning to Barak, he did still receive some glory for defeating the Canaanites. The prophet/judge Samuel referred to Barak as being among those whom the Lord sent to deliver the Israelites from their enemies (1 Samuel 12:11). The author of the New Testament book of Hebrews also referred to Barak as being among those who are good examples of faith (Hebrews 11:32).

*When all those who had formerly known him saw him prophesying
with the prophets, they asked each other, "What is this that has
happened to the son of Kish? Is Saul also among the prophets?"*

1 SAMUEL 10:11

Kish, whose name means "bow" or "power," was patriarch of the dynasty that could have been.

Described simply as "a man of standing" (1 Samuel 9:1), Kish apparently belonged to a well-respected family. That regard, however, came to an end with Kish's son, Saul.

KISH

Saul's Father

Saul's unlikely path to the throne began, oddly enough, when his father misplaced a pack of donkeys. Kish instructed Saul to accompany one of the family servants and scour the countryside until they recovered the animals. After three days of searching, Saul was ready to give up—convinced that Kish would start worrying about him more than the donkeys—but his servant urged him to consult a local prophet before abandoning the search altogether.

The prophet Samuel confirmed that Kish had grown worried for his son and was wondering what to do about him. Samuel had more pressing business, however. Directed by God, he anointed the son of Kish to be Israel's first king. Saul was disbelieving, so Samuel gave him numerous signs to watch for on his way home, in order to confirm that this was indeed God's plan for him. Among those signs was that Saul would encounter a procession of prophets and would join them in prophesying.

Things came to pass just as Samuel predicted—much to the bewilderment of those who knew Kish's son. Watching Saul prophesy, they responded with skepticism, asking, "What is this that has happened to the son of Kish? Is Saul also among the prophets?" It seems the people of Israel had difficulty accepting that Kish's son could be a prophet. The "man of standing" had passed his legacy to a man whose kingly career would end in disgrace.

DID YOU KNOW?

Kish belonged to the tribe of Benjamin. The Benjamites were renowned for their bravery—somewhat ironic, since Kish's son tried to hide during his own coronation.

But Abner the son of Ner, commander of Saul's army,
took Ish-bosheth the son of Saul and brought him over to Mahanaim.
2 SAMUEL 2:8 ESV

Perhaps a key word to associate with Abner, Saul's commander, would be *unpredictable.* He must have been an able warrior to some extent, for he continued to be Saul's commander throughout Saul's reign. But even his service to Saul seemed to have some shortcomings. He was unable to effectively respond to the challenge of the Philistine giant Goliath until the boy David stepped up to help (1 Samuel 17). He also failed to watch over King Saul's life during the night when David and Abishai infiltrated their camp (1 Samuel 26).

ABNER

Commander of Saul's Army

Abner was also somewhat unpredictable after King Saul died. Abner himself was the one who set up Saul's son Ish-bosheth as king (2 Samuel 2:8), but it appears he had aspirations of his own for the throne (2 Samuel 3:6). When Ish-bosheth confronted him about this, Abner responded in anger and threatened to hand the kingdom over to David. Soon after this he did just that.

In the end, Abner fell victim to something he himself did not predict: death at the hands of Joab and Abishai for killing their brother, Asahel. Joab sent messengers to bring Abner to the gates of Hebron as though they had some private matter to discuss, and the two brothers killed him there.

RELATED INFORMATION

Abner's death presented a dilemma for David, for it would have looked to many as though David himself had had him killed. To set the record straight, David had Abner buried in full honors and even wept aloud at his funeral (2 Samuel 3:28–39).

And Jeroboam appointed a feast on the fifteenth day of the eighth month like the feast that was in Judah, and he offered sacrifices on the altar. So he did in Bethel, sacrificing to the calves that he made. And he placed in Bethel the priests of the high places that he had made.

1 KINGS 12:32 ESV

Ask any student who's ever had a speech class, and you'll quickly see that no one wants to be first. Why? Because you become the benchmark, good or bad, for everyone who comes after you. Such was the fate of King Jeroboam of Israel. Unfortunately, he became known as a benchmark of wickedness.

JEROBOAM

First King of the Northern Kingdom of Israel

Jeroboam appears to have started out well enough. Recognized by Solomon as an able leader, Jeroboam was appointed to oversee all of Solomon's labor teams in Jerusalem. Things quickly got complicated, though, when a prophet stopped him and foretold that he would one day become king over the northern tribes of Israel. When Solomon got wind of the prophecy, he tried to kill Jeroboam, who fled to Egypt (1 Kings 11:26–40).

After Solomon died, Jeroboam returned to Israel and eventually did become king—and that's when things really began to go downhill. Hoping to keep his people from transferring loyalty back to the king of Judah (who controlled Jerusalem and the temple there), Jeroboam set up two golden calf idols within his own borders and declared that these were Israel's gods. He also set up his own religious festivals and built other pagan shrines (1 Kings 12).

From then on, Jeroboam became a benchmark of wickedness for all the kings of Israel that came after him. If they were evil, they were said to be acting like Jeroboam.

DID YOU KNOW?

Jeroboam's sin was so great that the prophet Ahijah prophesied that one day all his male descendants would be killed and left shamefully unburied (1 Kings 14:1–18). Ahijah's prophecy came true when a man named Baasha usurped the throne and killed all of Jeroboam's male descendants (1 Kings 15:27–30).

God also made the men of Shechem pay for all their wickedness.
The curse of Jotham son of Jerub-Baal came on them.
JUDGES 9:57

Jotham's brief appearance in the book of Judges proves that words can be more powerful than swords. In a tale that can only be described as a relentless cycle of betrayal and slaughter, Jotham played the part of an angry messenger to great effect.

JOTHAM

Gideon's Youngest Son

Jotham was the youngest son of Jerub-Baal, more commonly known as Gideon. Although he was one of the most celebrated judges in Israel's history, Gideon had a problem: His many wives had given him seventy legitimate sons, including Jotham. Gideon also had an illegitimate son named Abimelech. The term "sibling rivalry" does not begin to describe what took place after Gideon died.

Jotham alone survived the massacre that Abimelech orchestrated. Abimelech's intent was to slaughter all seventy of his half brothers in order to take up Gideon's mantle and govern uncontested. Jotham went into hiding but quickly emerged, incensed to learn that the people of Shechem, an important city in central Israel, intended to crown Abimelech as their king. Jotham climbed a mountain overlooking the coronation and delivered a brazen speech in which he compared Abimelech to a thornbush. The insult was not lost on Abimelech—thornbushes have no value and serve only to choke the life out of more useful plants.

Before he turned to run for his life, Jotham prophesied that Abimelech and the people of Shechem would be one another's downfall. Just as they had conspired to betray Jotham's brothers, soon they would turn on each other, at which point an even greater slaughter would commence. Three years later, Jotham's curse came to pass. The people rebelled against Abimelech, who responded with ruthless aggression. Abimelech met his end when a woman in a besieged tower dropped a millstone on his head—and Jotham's family was vindicated at last.

DID YOU KNOW?

Jotham's name means "the Lord is perfect." While his story is anything but a happy one, it serves to remind us that divine justice is indeed faultless. Even though it often seems a long time coming, God's justice does not let wickedness—like the murder of Jotham's brothers—go unpunished.

*Jehoash king of Israel captured Amaziah king of Judah,
the son of Joash, the son of Ahaziah, at Beth Shemesh.
Then Jehoash went to Jerusalem and broke down the
wall of Jerusalem from the Ephraim Gate to the Corner Gate—
a section about six hundred feet long.*

2 KINGS 14:13

J ehoash may have been battle-savvy, but that didn't make him a good guy. Despite all his military accomplishments, the Bible describes him as doing "evil in the eyes of the LORD" (2 Kings 13:11).

Jehoash was the son of Jehoahaz, who had been dominated throughout his reign by the Arameans—and who had left the army in shambles by the end of his reign (2 Kings 13:1–7). Because of God's love for His people, however, He empowered Jehoash to defeat the Arameans three times in battle and recover towns lost by his father. These victories were prophesied by Elisha, who was on his deathbed when Jehoash appealed to him for help (2 Kings 13:14–19).

JEHOASH

King of Israel

Jehoash also defeated King Amaziah of Judah at the town of Beth Shemesh and proceeded to Jerusalem to break down the wall of Jerusalem, ransack the temple and the palace, and take hostages to Samaria.

After Jehoash died, his son Jeroboam became king, and he, too, was very successful in battle (though "evil in the eyes of the LORD"), recovering much of the land that had once been ruled by King David (2 Kings 14:24, 28).

SPIRITUAL INSIGHT

It is easy to deceive ourselves into thinking that success in one area of life means that God approves of other areas of our lives. But financial success may come at the expense of the well-being of our families. And hidden bitterness toward one person is not smoothed over by being loving toward most other people. Make sure to submit every area of your life to God and seek to please Him in all things.

Day
175

When the Lord began to speak through Hosea, the Lord said to him, "Go, take to yourself an adulterous wife and children of unfaithfulness, because the land is guilty of the vilest adultery in departing from the Lord."

Hosea 1:2

I f you have ever looked through the personals section of the newspaper, it's unlikely that you found someone seeking "unfaithful female, likely to have affairs." Who would want to marry someone like that? Yet that's exactly the kind of woman God told Hosea to marry as an object lesson about Israel's unfaithfulness to God.

Hosea was a prophet to the northern kingdom of Israel, and his intimate knowledge of that land suggests he was probably from there. At some point in his life, God commanded him to marry an adulterous wife, and she bore him three children (Hosea 1). It is not known for certain whether his wife, named Gomer, was adulterous when

HOSEA

Prophet of Israel

Hosea married her or whether she only became unfaithful after their wedding. In any case, Hosea demonstrated unrelenting love for Gomer even after she left him for another lover. He went so far as to buy her back from her lover and offered her a chance to be faithful to him once again (Hosea 3:1–2).

All of Hosea's actions toward Gomer served to illustrate what God experienced with Israel, His covenant partner. Though God was faithful to Israel, the people were unfaithful to Him and chose to give themselves over to idolatry and wickedness. God sought to bring them back by sending prophets to warn them of the consequences of their sin.

RELATED INFORMATION

Hosea 11:1 says, "When Israel was a child, I loved him, and out of Egypt I called my son." There it refers to the Exodus, when Israel was led out of Egypt to follow the Lord and establish a new nation in Canaan. The Gospel of Matthew quotes this same verse to explain why Jesus' family was forced to flee to Egypt to escape Herod (Matthew 2:15).

*The king [Saul] then ordered Doeg, "You turn and strike down
the priests." So Doeg the Edomite turned and struck them down.
That day he killed eighty-five men who wore the linen ephod.*

1 SAMUEL 22:18

Loyalty is normally an admirable trait, but not if it means devotedly carrying
out the wicked orders of a man gone mad with jealousy. But such was the twisted
character of Doeg the Edomite, King Saul's head shepherd.

DOEG

Saul's Edomite Servant

Soon after David had been anointed
to be the next king and grew in popularity,
Saul grew jealous and began to threaten
David's life. David fled, stopping first at
Nob, where many of the priests and their
families lived. A priest named Ahimelech
gave David and his men some of the sacred
bread that was there, as well as the sword of
Goliath. Doeg the Edomite happened to be
there and saw David and his men.

Later, when Saul was accusing his officials of conspiring with David, Doeg
stepped forward and volunteered the information he had about David and his men
stopping at Nob. So Saul and his men went to Nob, but Ahimelech denied that
he was guilty of any wrong. When Saul ordered his men to kill all the priests, his
men refused—so Saul gave the order to Doeg, who murdered eighty-five priests
and their families (1 Samuel 21–22).

<table>
<tr><td>RELATED INFORMATION</td><td>We can only speculate why Doeg was willing to betray David and to kill eighty-five priests and their families. Perhaps he saw it as his chance to gain favor with the king and rise above his lowly role as head shepherd. It is also possible Doeg's heritage as an Edomite fostered a hatred of Israelites in general, because Saul had fought against the Edomites earlier in his reign as king of Israel (1 Samuel 14:47).</td></tr>
</table>

But Stephen, full of the Holy Spirit, looked up to heaven and saw the glory of God, and Jesus standing at the right hand of God.
ACTS 7:55

STEPHEN

First Christian Martyr

Stephen's death marked a crucial turning point for the church. Not only was it the beginning of the first great persecution of believers, but it set the stage for Saul—one of the great enemies of the church—to become one of its most important figures.

Stephen was a Hellenistic (Greek) Jew who embraced Jesus as his Messiah and quickly rose to prominence among the believers. He was renowned for his faith and became the first person outside the apostles to perform miracles in the name of Jesus. So Stephen was an obvious choice when the fledgling church needed to appoint godly individuals to oversee the care of its most vulnerable members: its widows. Unique among the seven men who were appointed, Stephen does not seem to have been confined to this task. He also ministered among the people, proclaiming Christ in public view. This, combined with his knack for debating his opponents into stunned silence, made him an easy target. Soon enough, Stephen was seized and dragged before the Sanhedrin, the Jewish ruling council.

Stephen laid the blame for Jesus' death on the Sanhedrin. At that point, they took him outside the city gates and stoned him to death. Before dying, Stephen caught a glimpse of Jesus—his advocate and his justifier—standing at God's right hand.

Stephen's martyrdom set off persecution of the church in Jerusalem—but it was precisely this persecution that scattered the disciples and helped spread the gospel throughout Judea and Samaria.

SPIRITUAL INSIGHT

With his final breath, Stephen cried out a prayer reminiscent of the words Jesus spoke from the cross: "Lord, do not hold this sin against them" (Acts 7:60). Indeed, God showed His mercy to one of the conspirators behind the murder of Stephen and the ensuing persecution of the church. Saul (later named Paul) was instrumental in both. Not even one of the greatest enemies of the church was beyond the kind of forgiveness that Stephen prayed for.

*[Rehoboam] followed the advice of the young men and said,
"My father made your yoke heavy; I will make it even heavier.
My father scourged you with whips; I will scourge you with scorpions."*

1 KINGS 12:14

Despite being the son of one of the wisest men who ever lived, Rehoboam's bluster proved greater than his competence to govern.

Rehoboam ascended to the throne immediately upon Solomon's death, but he did not have to wait long to encounter his first test. Jeroboam, who had fled to Egypt after an unsuccessful rebellion against Solomon, returned to present himself to Israel's new king. Together with the leaders from the northern part of the country, Jeroboam made just one request in return for their loyalty to Rehoboam: They asked him to lighten the oppressive load that had been placed upon them by Solomon.

REHOBOAM

Last King of a United Israel

In order to consolidate power and make Israel a regional power, Solomon had levied burdensome taxes—he had even used forced labor to build God's temple. The people had had enough and were hoping for a more benevolent ruler in Rehoboam.

How wrong they were.

Instead of listening to seasoned advisers from Solomon's court, Rehoboam turned to his friends, who seemed to think the best way for Rehoboam to assert his authority was to be even more brutish and cruel than his father. So instead of granting the people's request, Rehoboam promised the opposite.

All but the tribe of Judah abandoned Rehoboam and rallied around Jeroboam. While one of God's prophets managed to dissuade Rehoboam from all-out civil war with the northern tribes, there was conflict between the two kingdoms for the rest of Rehoboam's days.

During his seventeen-year reign, Rehoboam lost territory, wealth, and respect. Worst of all, he set a new low in terms of idolatry—a disheartening standard that would become the benchmark against which Judah's future kings were measured. In addition to erecting pagan places of worship, Rehoboam allowed religious prostitution and actively engaged in the pagan practices of the surrounding nations. Solomon's failure was made complete in his disaster of a son.

DID YOU KNOW? Rehoboam's ironic name borders on the comical. In Hebrew, it means "enlarger of the people." Sadly, Rehoboam did the opposite, reducing David and Solomon's kingdom to a fraction of its former glory.

Now Absalom had set Amasa over the army instead of Joab.
Amasa was the son of a man named Ithra the Ishmaelite,
who had married Abigal the daughter of Nahash,
sister of Zeruiah, Joab's mother.
2 SAMUEL 17:25 ESV

Perhaps Amasa's primary role in scripture is simply that he was an upright, capable warrior who fell prey to the jealous schemes of another. We first read of this nephew of David when Absalom chose him to replace another nephew (Joab) as head of Israel's army during Absalom's rebellion against his father. Yet while Amasa's loyalty to Absalom might have seemed a black mark against his character, David clearly considered Amasa worthy enough to continue in his leadership role when David returned to power.

AMASA

One of David's Mighty Men

Soon after this, another rebellion broke out in the north under the leadership of a man named Sheba—and David dispatched two other nephews, Abishai and Joab, to lead his men into battle against him. Amasa met up with them a bit later, and Joab, apparently out of jealousy, drew him close as though he were going to kiss him—but killed him instead. Then he and Abishai continued on to put down the rebellion. Later David would instruct his son Solomon to pay back Joab for his wicked slaying of Amasa and another commander (1 Kings 2:5).

SPIRITUAL INSIGHT

It's tempting to ask why God would allow a great man like Amasa to fall prey to the wickedness of someone like Joab. Ultimately we are never told why, but we can take heart in Jesus' words in the New Testament: "Do not be afraid of those who kill the body but cannot kill the soul. . . . Are not two sparrows sold for a penny? Yet not one of them will fall to the ground apart from the will of your Father. . . . So don't be afraid; you are worth more than many sparrows" (Matthew 10:28–31).

*"Micah of Moresheth prophesied in the days of Hezekiah. . . .
Did Hezekiah king of Judah or anyone else in Judah put
him to death? Did not Hezekiah fear the LORD and seek his favor?
And did not the LORD relent. . .?"*

JEREMIAH 26:18–19

Micah's listeners may have dismissed him as an outsider—a country simpleton. He was not from Jerusalem, after all—he lived in the rural foothills of southern Judah. Yet that did not stop Micah from delivering a forceful message aimed directly at the rampant corruption of Judah's elite.

MICAH

Old Testament Prophet

His prophecy was relatively straightforward. According to Micah, it was not hard to figure out why God was angry with Judah. Her wealthy landowners had committed fraud and outright theft, taking people's farms and homes, depriving them of their livelihood and inheritance (Micah 2:1–2). The authorities were systematically subverting justice and oppressing the poor (Micah 3:1–9). Judah's merchants were cheating people with dishonest scales (Micah 6:11). Even the religious leaders did not escape God's wrath, according to Micah—they had turned the sacred ministry of teaching into a commercial venture, demanding a price for their services (Micah 3:11).

Micah—whose prophecy is often compared to that of his contemporary Isaiah—was forceful and impassioned. His writing bore the marks of a divine lawsuit: God was, in effect, taking His people to court over their abuses and injustices (see Micah 6:1–2). Micah predicted that both Israel and Judah would reap calamity for their sins. Samaria would fall first, but soon disaster would reach "even to the gate of Jerusalem" (Micah 1:12).

SPIRITUAL INSIGHT

For all of Micah's doom and gloom, he also promised hope—a time of restoration when God's people would return to Him and pursue peace instead of violence (see Micah 4–5). In fact, each of Micah's three oracles of judgment was followed by a promise of restoration.

Arriving at Jerusalem with a very great caravan—
with camels carrying spices, large quantities of gold,
and precious stones—she came to Solomon
and talked with him about all that she had on her mind.
1 KINGS 10:2

According to the writer of 1 Kings, the queen of Sheba visited Solomon in order to test him. The queen's test may well have demanded the best of not only Solomon's wisdom but his diplomatic and political skills as well.

The Bible does not reveal origins or the identity of the queen of Sheba. According to one tradition, she came from Ethiopia. (Ancient Ethiopian lore claimed that Solomon and the queen had a son who grew up to become the African nation's first king.) However, archaeological findings indicate that the Arabian Peninsula is a more likely option. It is also a location that fits well with the biblical narrative.

The ancient peoples of Arabia had accumulated great wealth by importing goods from Asia and Africa and exporting them to their neighbors in the Middle East. Their trade consisted mainly of expensive spices, gold, and precious stones—in other words, the very items the queen presented to Solomon.

QUEEN OF SHEBA

Solomon's Royal Visitor

Under Solomon, Israel had become a regional power—his kingdom controlled some of the key trade routes that Sheba depended on for its prosperity. In all likelihood, this is what the queen of Sheba "had on her mind" when she tested Solomon's wisdom. Between Solomon's impressive showing—his skills at discernment and negotiation were legendary (see 1 Kings 3:16–28)—and the overwhelming display of his wealth, the queen was awestruck. She honored Israel's king with high praise and a lavish gift of gold, about four-and-a-half tons' worth. Solomon reciprocated by giving the queen "all she desired" (1 Kings 10:13). The queen of Sheba returned to Arabia, her diplomatic mission a success.

SPIRITUAL INSIGHT

Jesus taught that the queen of Sheba (to whom he referred as the "Queen of the South" in Matthew 12:42 and Luke 11:31) was more righteous than the religious leaders who opposed Him. When they skeptically demanded proof of His authority, Jesus responded that the queen herself would judge people like them. After all, at least she—though she was a foreigner—had been willing to listen to Solomon's wisdom. Jesus' words are a reminder that religious piety has no value unless it is accompanied by a humble, teachable heart.

Now the young man Samuel was ministering to the Lord under Eli. And the word of the Lord was rare in those days; there was no frequent vision.

1 Samuel 3:1 esv

It's a classic model: An enthusiastic visionary founds an organization and steers it to excellence, but over time the organization is drained dry as less dedicated leadership allows things to grow more and more lax. That must have been the general tenor of things by the time Eli's priestly ministry in Shiloh was winding down.

Eli himself is not necessarily spoken of in scripture as corrupt or sinful, but it

Eli

Priest of Israel

appears that he had let his own sons, who also served as priests, become very corrupt and abusive of their office (1 Samuel 2:10–18). Because of this, Eli's family was cursed by God—and this may be the reason that few people received special messages or visions from the Lord (1 Samuel 2:27–36).

In the meantime, God was raising up Samuel to replace Eli's sons as priests and leaders of the people. Samuel had been brought to Shiloh as a young boy and left in the care of Eli (1 Samuel 2–3). The final blow to Eli's family came when the Israelites were fighting against the Philistines. Both of Eli's sons were killed as they carried the ark of the covenant into battle, and even Eli himself fell over backward and broke his neck when he heard the news that the ark had been captured (1 Samuel 4).

SPIRITUAL INSIGHT

It is very shortsighted to think that all we need to concern ourselves with is our own spiritual walk. But this attitude leaves the spiritual lives of those who come after us in jeopardy. What are we doing to promote faithfulness to God in the lives of our children and others entrusted to our care?

Jesus straightened up and asked her, "Woman, where are they?
Has no one condemned you?"
"No one, sir," she said.
"Then neither do I condemn you,"
Jesus declared. "Go now and leave your life of sin."
JOHN 8:10–11

W hen the Jewish religious leaders dragged the adulterous woman before Jesus, He did not question her guilt. However, the entire situation reeked of injustice— which Jesus masterfully exposed in His response.

The adulterous woman provided the bait in the Pharisees' trap. Aside from this, nothing is known about her—or how the religious leaders managed to catch her "in the act" of committing adultery. They pretended to be concerned with fidelity to the Law of Moses, yet nothing could have been further from the truth. Otherwise, they would have apprehended the guilty man as well, since the Law held *both* parties accountable in cases of adultery (see Leviticus 20:10).

THE WOMAN CAUGHT IN ADULTERY

Unnamed Woman
Spared by Jesus

The religious leaders intended to use the woman's plight in order to trap Jesus in a no-win situation. If He disagreed with the suggestion that she be stoned, He would be accused of going against the Torah—the very Law He had come to "fulfill" (see Matthew 5:17). But if Jesus agreed with their sentence, He would be challenging the power of Rome, which had the exclusive authority to mete out capital punishment.

Perhaps the woman held her breath as Jesus invited the religious leaders to stone her—provided they were without sin themselves, that is. According to Jesus, only a righteous judge would do—and the only truly righteous judge in their midst (the Lord Himself) chose not to throw any stones. Instead, having silenced His opponents, Jesus sent the woman on her way, with the loving admonition to leave behind the destructive life that had gotten her into this mess in the first place.

DID YOU KNOW?

The earliest manuscripts of John do not contain this story of the woman caught in adultery. As further evidence that it was not original to John's Gospel, some experts note that the first verse (John 7:53) does not fit the preceding context. However, the story is consistent with the overall life and teachings of Jesus, leading a number of scholars to conclude that it is nonetheless authentic— just misplaced somehow. (There's even one family of manuscripts that puts the story at the end of Luke 21.)

*Julius, in kindness to Paul, allowed him to go to
his friends so they might provide for his needs.*
ACTS 27:3

To many ancient readers, Julius would have seemed like a contradiction—a kindhearted Roman centurion, though he is certainly not the only one to be found in the New Testament.

A member of the Imperial or Augustan Regiment, Julius would have had approximately one hundred men under his command. The few glimpses we get of Julius reveal an authoritative yet compassionate leader.

JULIUS

Paul's Escort to Rome

Julius was responsible for ensuring that Paul, on his way to testify before Caesar, arrived safely in Rome. It was no small task. More than one person wanted Paul dead, and even the weather seemed determined to make their journey as arduous as possible.

Along the way, Julius allowed Paul to disembark in Sidon (north of Judea on the Mediterranean coast) to visit friends—a gesture significant enough to merit inclusion in Acts 27. However, when Paul warned of a dangerous journey ahead, Julius ignored him, preferring to take his advice from the ship's pilot and owner instead.

Paul was proved right when a storm threatened to tear the ship apart. He told Julius that anyone who tried to escape would perish. This time Julius listened, ordering his men to cut the ropes that held the lifeboat. The fact that his soldiers would obey what must have sounded like a suicidal command indicates the kind of authority Julius held.

Later, when the ship ran aground, Julius's authority and compassion united in his most important decision of the journey. His men wanted to kill the prisoners to keep them from escaping the shipwreck, but Julius intervened to save Paul's life. If he had not done so, Paul never would have gotten his opportunity to preach the gospel in the very heart of the Roman Empire.

SPIRITUAL INSIGHT

Julius's refusal to kill his prisoners demanded a great deal of trust in Paul's integrity. The penalty for losing a prisoner was death (see Acts 16:27). Paul was the kind of person who could be counted on to remain true to his word, even if the price was his own freedom.

So he married Gomer daughter of Diblaim,
and she conceived and bore him a son.
HOSEA 1:3

Day

185

Gomer is one of those people we would rather not acknowledge that we know. Perhaps that's because she reminds us of ourselves in ways that we wish she didn't.

GOMER

Unfaithful Wife of the Prophet Hosea

Gomer was the wife of the prophet Hosea, whom the Lord commanded to marry an "adulterous wife" (Hosea 1:2). It is not clear whether she was unfaithful when Hosea married her or only became unfaithful after the wedding. Whatever the case, Gomer sadly demonstrated that Hosea chose correctly when he married her, for though she bore Hosea three children, she eventually left him for another lover. Later Hosea found her again and even bought her back so that she could be faithful to him once again (Hosea 3).

In all this, Gomer was a living allegory of the unfaithfulness of God's people. Israel had been chosen by God to be a covenant partner with Him, but they had been unfaithful to Him by worshipping other gods and embracing wickedness. The Lord desired for them to come back to Him, but they often refused.

SPIRITUAL INSIGHT

In what ways have you been like Gomer? How have you strayed from your commitment to be faithful to God and His covenant with you? Is He calling you to return to Him and be faithful to Him once again? Don't run from the joys that God offers His people as His bride—His faithful, covenant people.

*In his days, Nebuchadnezzar king of Babylon came up,
and Jehoiakim became his servant three years.
Then he turned and rebelled against him.*

2 KINGS 24:1 ESV

Jehoiakim's reign marked the beginning of the end for the kingdom of Judah. Jehoiakim was originally named Eliakim by his father, Josiah, but Pharaoh Neco of Egypt changed his name after he took his brother King Jehoahaz captive to Egypt and installed Jehoiakim as the new king. Jehoiakim was required to pay Pharaoh Neco a large sum of money, so he imposed a real estate tax to raise the money. The Bible characterizes Jehoiakim's reign as evil (2 Kings 23:34–36).

JEHOIAKIM

King of Judah

Later the Babylonians gained control over Judah, and at first Jehoiakim chose to make Judah a vassal, or dependent state, of Babylon, rather than risk challenging their rule. Three years later, however, Jehoiakim rebelled, and King Nebuchadnezzar exiled him and many other leaders to Babylon (2 Chronicles 36:6). Nebuchadnezzar then installed Jehoiakim's son as king, later deposing and exiling him, too, and installing Jehoiakim's brother as king. After that, the Babylonians broke down the walls of Jerusalem, and the temple itself was destroyed, bringing the kingdom of Judah to an end. For many years to come, the country would simply be a province of foreign powers.

RELATED INFORMATION

Daniel, Shadrach, Meshach, and Abednego were among those who were exiled to Babylon along with Jehoiakim (Daniel I). Though this exile was devastating to Judah as a country, and no doubt traumatic for those who were exiled, it appears that a few Judeans such as Daniel and his friends gained positions of leadership within the Babylonian government. Daniel's leadership even continued under the Persians, who conquered the Babylonians (Daniel 6:28).

*They chose Stephen, a man full of faith and of the Holy Spirit;
also Philip, Procorus, Nicanor, Timon, Parmenas,
and Nicolas from Antioch, a convert to Judaism.*
ACTS 6:5

N icolas has the distinction of being the first Gentile Christian named in the New Testament. He also helped the church overcome one of its first practical hurdles.

At a time when the church was comprised almost entirely of Jewish believers, its growing numbers brought increasing tension between two particular groups: the Hellenistic Jews and the Hebraic Jews. Hellenistic Jews were those who were influenced by Greek thought and language—they had been born far from Jerusalem in most cases. Hebraic Jews maintained close ties to the Promised Land, its language, and its culture.

Within the church at Jerusalem, the Hellenistic Jews began to feel slighted, complaining that their widows were being excluded from the church's regular food distributions. The apostles, already stretched to capacity with their teaching responsibilities, appointed seven men (Nicolas being one of them) to make

NICOLAS

Deacon of the
Early Church

sure all of the church's widows were cared for. Judging by their Greek names, all seven men were of a Hellenistic background. Such a selection surely would have won the trust of Hellenistic Jews within the church.

Even more significant, Nicolas was a God-fearer—a Gentile convert to Judaism. His presence in the church and his appointment to such an important role was a clear signal that the gospel could not be constrained by nationality or ethnicity. Nicolas was an early reminder of the great commission and Jesus' insistence that His good news is for "all nations" (see Matthew 28:19). Later, Nicolas's hometown of Antioch would become the front line in the effort to spread the gospel among the Gentiles.

DID YOU KNOW? According to one tradition, Nicolas was responsible for starting the heretical group known as the Nicolaitans, who sought a "happy medium" between Christian faith and pagan practice in order to avoid being ostracized for their commitment to Christ (see Revelation 2:6, 15). However, there is no historical evidence to link the two.

When Pilate saw that he was getting nowhere, but that instead an uproar was starting, he took water and washed his hands in front of the crowd. "I am innocent of this man's blood," he said.

MATTHEW 27:24

Pontius Pilate represented everything the Jewish leaders hated about Rome—its dominance, its oppression, and its idolatry. Yet when it came to the conspiracy to kill Jesus, the religious leaders were powerless to do anything without Pilate.

Ancient historians did not judge Pilate kindly. They saw an arrogant man who despised those he governed. Josephus noted that Pilate once tried to set up the Roman standards in the holy city of Jerusalem. Such graven images of the emperor—who claimed to be a god—were bad enough, but to have them so near the temple was an unbearable insult.

PONTIUS PILATE

Procurator of Judea

Later Pilate plundered the temple coffers to finance an aqueduct—once again infuriating the Jews. This time he had soldiers disguise themselves and mingle among the protesters gathered in Jerusalem, killing many. (Some believe this is the event Jesus mentioned in Luke 13:1–2.)

During the trial and execution of Jesus, Pilate demonstrated his disdain for the Jewish leaders—at one point deliberately provoking them by crucifying Jesus under a sign that read, THE KING OF THE JEWS. While the Roman procurator seemed in no hurry to condemn Jesus to death, his reluctance probably had less to do with any prevailing sense of justice (such a concept seemed utterly foreign to Pilate) and more to do with his desire for damage control. Pilate's subjects had already complained once to Rome about his oppressive rule. He didn't need another mark on his record, particularly at such a volatile time like the Jewish Passover festival.

Ultimately, Pilate's brutality proved his undoing when he was dismissed from office for slaughtering a number of Samaritans at Mount Gerizim around AD 37.

SPIRITUAL INSIGHT

When Pilate asked Jesus if He was a king, Jesus famously responded, "My kingdom is not of this world" (John 18:36). Jesus did not deny Pilate's authority—instead, He masterfully subverted it, refusing to play by Pilate's rules. Pilate only knew how to command by the sword. In contrast, Jesus declared that His true followers, whose allegiance belonged to a higher authority, would not fight as Rome fought.

At his gate was laid a beggar named Lazarus, covered with sores and longing to eat what fell from the rich man's table.
LUKE 16:20–21

Day
189

Lazarus has the distinction of being the only person to be named in any of Jesus' parables. Most likely a fictional character invented to illustrate a point, Lazarus nonetheless represents the plight of many.

The parable of the rich man and Lazarus is a story of contrasts. In the first scene, the rich man puts on a very public display of opulence. Lazarus, whom the rich man ignores, lies just beyond the gate—close enough to salivate over the excess from the rich man's table. Jesus raises the odds against Lazarus by adding that he is covered in sores—making him ritually unclean in the eyes of the religious establishment (see Leviticus 13).

LAZARUS THE BEGGAR

Ate Leftovers from the Rich Man's Table

When both men die in the following scene, however, Lazarus ends up in paradise while the rich man is subjected to torment. Once again, a barrier separates them—although this time it is a "great chasm" (Luke 16:26). In pleading with Abraham, the rich man lets slip that he knows Lazarus's name (Luke 16:24, 27)—making his prior apathy toward the poor beggar even more appalling. Abraham rebuffs each of the rich man's protests, noting that since he did not see fit to reverse Lazarus's fortunes in life, God has seen fit to reverse both men's fortunes in the afterlife.

Lazarus does not speak once during the entire episode. His name—a shortened form of Eleazar, which is Hebrew for "God has helped"—is a fitting choice for this parable. Jesus used Lazarus's story to teach the importance of caring for the poor and providing justice—and as a reminder that any injustices left unsettled in this life will be settled by God in the next.

There [in Corinth] he [Paul] met a Jew named Aquila,
a native of Pontus, who had recently come from Italy with
his wife Priscilla, because Claudius had ordered all the Jews
to leave Rome. Paul went to see them, and because he was a
tentmaker as they were, he stayed and worked with them.
ACTS 18:2–3

Aquila and his wife Priscilla were truly coworkers of Paul in the fullest sense of the word. Paul refers to them as his "fellow workers" in Romans 16:3, meaning they shared in his work of spreading the gospel among the Gentiles. Yet they were even his coworkers in the secular sense of being fellow tentmakers (Acts 18:3).

AQUILA

Coworker of Paul

Aquila was originally from Pontus, a region on the southeast coast of the Black Sea, but at some point he and his wife moved to Rome. Eventually they had to leave Rome, too, because they were Jews, and the emperor expelled all Jews from Rome. That is how they came to be in Corinth when Paul arrived there after delivering his speech to the Areopagus in Athens.

Paul no doubt taught Aquila and his wife the gospel well while they were with him at Corinth, and then they accompanied him to Ephesus (Acts 18:18–19). Paul left them there while he himself went on to Jerusalem and then back to his home church of Antioch. In the meantime, Aquila and Priscilla demonstrated their true understanding of the gospel by helping Apollos, a very skilled, learned Bible teacher in his own right, come to know the gospel more adequately (Acts 18:26).

At some point, the couple must have traveled back to Rome for a time, because Paul greeted them in his letter to the Romans (Romans 16:3). Then they must have returned to Ephesus, because Paul greeted them again in a letter to Timothy, whom Paul had sent to Ephesus (2 Timothy 4:19).

DID YOU KNOW?

Corinth and Ephesus were among the busiest, wealthiest cities of the Roman Empire. It is possible that Aquila and Priscilla chose to live and work in these cities because they could find abundant demand for their tent-making skills.

And all the leaders of Shechem came together,
and all Beth-millo, and they went and made Abimelech king,
by the oak of the pillar at Shechem.
JUDGES 9:6 ESV

W hen the temptation to rule over others gets hold of someone, there is no end to what that person will do to attain power. In the time of Israel's judges, a man named Abimelech even murdered his seventy brothers to become the leader of the people.

ABIMELECH

Gideon's Son and Leader of Israel

Abimelech was born to Gideon, the great leader who saved Israel from the Midianites—so one would think that Abimelech would also be a great leader. But from the start it was clear that Abimelech craved power and privilege more than leadership. After Gideon's death, his seventy sons were regarded as the leaders of Israel. But Abimelech wanted the role of leader all to himself, and he convinced the people of his hometown of Shechem to help him. They gave him money, and he hired a band of reckless men who went with him to Gideon's hometown of Ophrah to murder Abimelech's brothers—all except one.

The youngest, Jotham, escaped and stirred up discontent in Shechem against Abimelech, but Abimelech put down the rebellion and ruthlessly punished the people of Shechem. When he went to Thebez to put down more rebellion there, the people fled into a tower, and he was killed by a woman who threw down a millstone on his head after he came too close to the tower wall. The Bible points out that Abimelech's death was just punishment for murdering his seventy brothers (Judges 9:56).

RELATED INFORMATION

The story of Abimelech's death at the hands of a woman must have come to be quoted proverbially in Israel as a warning against getting too close to the wall of a besieged city, because when Joab sent a messenger to inform David about Uriah's death in battle, he anticipated that David would reference Abimelech's death and criticize Joab for letting Uriah get too close (2 Samuel 11:18–21).

And the LORD said to [Moses], "What Zelophehad's daughters
are saying is right. You must certainly give them property as
an inheritance among their father's relatives and turn their father's
inheritance over to them."

NUMBERS 27:6–7

Zelophehad's daughters pioneered significant changes in the rights of Hebrew women. Traditionally, Hebrew culture directed the property of a family to be passed along only through male heirs. Women, on the other hand, generally remained in the protection of their own families or married into the protection of another. Nestled in the pages of Numbers, however, lies the anecdote of Zelophehad's daughters. The story reveals God's concern for women and a noteworthy change in how women were treated as heirs.

DAUGHTERS OF ZELOPHEHAD

Pioneers in Women's Rights

Zelophehad was a Hebrew who lived during the time of the exodus from Egypt. While wandering with the people in the wilderness, God blessed him with daughters but no sons before he died (Numbers 27:1–11). As the people approached the Promised Land, Moses and Eleazar began plans to parcel out land assignments to the men of each Hebrew family. Since Zelophehad's family did not have a male heir, his allotment was likely to be lost—until the daughters boldly approached Moses and asked him to consider their case. They said, "Why should the name of our father be taken away from his clan because he had no son? Give to us a possession among our father's brothers" (Numbers 27:4 NRSV).

While Moses undoubtedly had many concerns related to leading millions of people, he took time to bring the women's request to God—who responded favorably to their appeal. This gift of land became legal precedent and indicated the inherent value in women as well as men in the kingdom of God.

Then they said, "Let's call the girl and ask her about it."
So they called Rebekah and asked her, "Will you go with this man?"
"I will go," she said.
Genesis 24:57–58

Day
193

P regnancy is not an easy experience—but Rebekah's was so unpleasant that she inquired of the Lord to find out why she was suffering so badly. More amazingly, the Lord answered.

After twenty years of marriage, Rebekah was finally pregnant. It had taken an answer to prayer in order for her and her husband, Isaac, to conceive. The two loved each other—the story of how they came to be married reads like an ancient romance novel. However, without a child, they would be subject to public shame. More important, God's covenant with Rebekah's father-in-law was in jeopardy. How would Abraham become the father of many nations if Isaac and Rebekah could not provide even one offspring?

When Rebekah did become pregnant, however, it was not with just one son but with two. The babies wrestled with one another in the womb, apparently causing Rebekah great discomfort. When she sought an explanation from God, she was told that the sons she bore would give rise to two separate nations. But harmonious coexistence was not

REBEKAH

Isaac's Wife

what the future held for Rebekah's sons. Puzzlingly, God informed Rebekah that the younger would triumph over the older—precisely the opposite of how it was supposed to be in the ancient Near East.

Things happened exactly as God told Rebekah they would. Of course, Rebekah played a helping hand, favoring her younger son, Jacob, over Esau. Rebekah helped Jacob trick his father into giving him the blessing that was rightfully Esau's. She wanted the best for her younger son, but the best came at a price—estrangement between Jacob and Esau. After Jacob fled on his mother's advice, it is very likely that he never saw Rebekah alive again.

SPIRITUAL INSIGHT

Rebekah stood in a long line of deceivers. Out of a desire for self-preservation, her father-in-law, Abraham, had tried to convince others that his wife, Sarah, was really just his sister—not once but twice. Rebekah's brother Laban later tricked Jacob into marrying Leah first instead of Rachel. Rebekah prompted Jacob to deceive her own husband. Unfortunately, sinful tendencies have a way of repeating themselves in successive generations. Jacob, for example, came to be regarded as one of the most famous deceivers in the Bible.

When Jesus saw Nathanael [Bartholomew] approaching,
he said of him, "Here is a true Israelite,
in whom there is nothing false."

JOHN 1:47

Cynicism and doubt are popular shields people use to fend off the gospel, but often underneath, these people are ripe to become the most faithful of believers. Bartholomew (apparently the same person as Nathanael) seems to have been just such a person.

BARTHOLOMEW

Disciple of Jesus

Only a handful of information is recorded about Bartholomew in scripture, but the little that is there probably tells a lot. As Jesus was beginning to call His disciples to follow Him, Philip came to Bartholomew and told him that he had found the Messiah, Jesus of Nazareth. Bartholomew, who himself came from a small village only eight miles from Nazareth, cynically responded, "Nazareth! Can anything good come from there?" (John 1:46).

But when Jesus saw Bartholomew coming, He immediately declared, "Here is a true Israelite, in whom there is nothing false." Why would Jesus say that? Didn't Bartholomew just demonstrate his lack of faith? But Jesus knew better. When Bartholomew asked Jesus how He knew him, Jesus told him that He could see Bartholomew even before Philip called him. Immediately Bartholomew responded in faith, declaring, "You are the Son of God; you are the King of Israel" (John 1:49). Jesus praised Bartholomew's faith over such a small miracle and assured him that he would see even greater things than that. Bartholomew did indeed see greater things than that. He became one of Jesus' disciples and witnessed His ascension to heaven (Acts 1:9–13).

For Herod himself had given orders to have John arrested,
and he had him bound and put in prison. He did this because
of Herodias, his brother Philip's wife, whom he had married.
MARK 6:17

Nothing stings quite like the truth. Perhaps that's why Herodias hated John the Baptist so much.

At the age of twenty-three, Herodias divorced her husband, Philip, who was also her uncle, and married Antipas, another uncle. Both men were sons of Herod the Great, the king who ruled over Judea and Galilee when Jesus was born. John the Baptist openly condemned Antipas for his marriage to Herodias, which caused Herodias to nurse a deep hatred of John (Mark 6:17–20). She wanted to have John killed, but Antipas regarded John as a holy man and feared what would happen if he killed him.

But Herodias's hatred was unrelenting, and eventually she found a way to have John killed. Herod held a banquet for his birthday, and Herodias's daughter danced for his guests. Herod was so pleased that he offered her anything she wished for, up to half his kingdom. Herodias told her to ask for the head of John the Baptist on a platter, and she did.

HERODIAS

Wife of Herod Antipas

Herod Antipas was very distressed at her request, but he did not want to go back on his offer in front of his guests, so he carried out her evil wishes immediately.

RELATED INFORMATION

A few years after Jesus' death, Herodias's brother Agrippa was made king over certain parts of Palestine, and she grew jealous. She urged Antipas to sail for Rome and ask Emperor Caligula for the title of king. Agrippa, however, sent letters denouncing Antipas for various misdeeds, and the emperor exiled him to the area now known as France. Herodias chose to accompany him, and she likely died there.

"This is [the Merarites'] duty as they perform service at the Tent of Meeting: to carry the frames of the tabernacle, its crossbars, posts and bases, as well as the posts of the surrounding courtyard with their bases, tent pegs, ropes. . .and everything related to their use."

NUMBERS 4:31–32

Merari was patriarch of one of three main branches of Levites, Israel's priestly tribe. As the youngest son of Levi, Merari accompanied his father and his grandfather Jacob when the latter took his family to Egypt. There Merari and his relatives were reunited with Jacob's son Joseph. More important, the family was spared from the famine that had brought the entire region to its knees.

Nothing else is known about Merari, aside from the fact that he made the journey from Canaan to Egypt. His descendants, however, played a vital role during Israel's forty years of wandering in the wilderness on their way back to the Promised Land.

MERARI

Third Son of Levi

The sons of Merari were given responsibility for much of the tabernacle's structure. Also known as the Tent of Meeting, the tabernacle had to be large enough to accommodate the Levites' priestly duties, yet portable enough to suit the Israelites' nomadic lifestyle.

Among the pieces that the Merarites looked after were forty-eight wooden frames (each of them fifteen feet long), fifteen crossbars, and ninety-six silver bases for the frames. It was the Merarites' job to keep these pieces in good condition and ensure their safe transit from place to place. In Moses' day, more than three thousand of Merari's descendants actively participated in caring for God's tabernacle.

Centuries later, when a permanent meeting place had been established in Jerusalem, King David appointed some of Merari's descendants to be professional singers, employed to make music in praise of God. The Merarites were singled out for honorable service yet again when two other kings, Hezekiah and later his great-grandson Josiah, ordered the temple to be purified of pagan instruments.

DID YOU KNOW?

In Hebrew, Merari's name means "bitter." Ruth's mother-in-law, Naomi, chose a form of this name for herself when she returned to her hometown of Bethlehem after a famine decimated her family (see Ruth 1:20).

But after Uzziah became powerful, his pride led to his downfall. He was unfaithful to the LORD his God, and entered the temple of the LORD to burn incense on the altar of incense.
2 CHRONICLES 26:16

U zziah (known in 2 Kings as Azariah) was very nearly one of the great kings of Judah. Unfortunately, his pride and reckless ambition got in his way.

Uzziah's father, Amaziah, had died at the hands of his own people in the twenty-ninth year of his reign. But unlike Israel, where new (and often short-lived) dynasties routinely replaced one another, Judah had been promised an unbroken chain of kingly succession. So Amaziah's death did not bring the end of his dynasty. Instead, Uzziah—who had probably reigned as coregent for several years—was crowned king of Judah.

Uzziah got off to a good—albeit not great—start. He received a largely favorable assessment from the writers of both 2 Kings and 2 Chronicles, even though he failed to remove the "high places" where people offered their own sacrifices. On the military front, Uzziah was an unqualified success—

UZZIAH

King of Judah

perhaps the greatest warrior-king since David. With God's help, he subdued two of Judah's longstanding enemies, the Philistines and the Ammonites. He even extended Judah's territory, regaining access to the Red Sea via the Gulf of Aqaba. His country secure, Uzziah set about strengthening Jerusalem's defenses.

Unfortunately, Uzziah—who had once taken counsel from a godly teacher named Zechariah—let his success go to his head. He became proud and sought to inject his influence into the priestly arena. Uzziah paid dearly for his overreaching. God struck Uzziah with leprosy, a humiliating disease that rendered him ceremonially unclean—unable to fulfill his kingly duties or to set foot in the temple ever again.

SPIRITUAL INSIGHT

The English historian Lord Acton famously said, "Power tends to corrupt, and absolute power corrupts absolutely." Therein lay Uzziah's downfall—and perhaps the reason that God had separated the duties of priest and king in the first place. The Bible reveals that human beings cannot be trusted with too much power over others. As the writer of 2 Chronicles reminded his readers, Uzziah was a success "until he became powerful" and forgot the Lord (2 Chronicles 26:15).

*"No razor may be used on his head, because the boy
is to be a Nazirite, set apart to God from birth,
and he will begin the deliverance of Israel
from the hands of the Philistines."*

JUDGES 13:5

People have married for a host of unusual reasons, but Samson is perhaps one of the few in history to have wedded for the express purpose of picking a fight with the bride's extended family.

Samson was born to Manoah and his wife—a righteous couple who had been barren for years. God revealed that just as Samson's birth was special, so, too, was his life to be special. He was to be set apart, bound by a lifelong Nazirite vow. In the Bible, people were set apart not just for the sake of being different—such honor always had a specific purpose. Samson's purpose was to begin the rebellion against Israel's most notorious oppressors, the Philistines.

SAMSON

Judge and Strongman of Israel

As required by the rules governing Nazirite vows, Samson was expected to abstain from three things: alcohol, contact with anything unclean (such as dead bodies), and haircuts.

Before he died, Samson probably violated all three requirements. He behaved as if he were above any rule or responsibility. Even his choice of a wife was baffling to his God-fearing parents, for Samson had demanded to be united to a Philistine woman. This, however, turned out to be one of God's strategic masterstrokes—the writer of 1 Samuel revealed that God used this marriage as an opportunity for Samson to confront the Philistines.

Samson did just that. After Samson decimated their crops, the Philistines murdered Samson's wife and father-in-law. Samson retaliated by going on a violent rampage, nearly bringing the Philistines and their Israelite subjects to full-scale war. In the end, another woman named Delilah proved to be Samson's undoing, and Samson's greatest achievement—the destruction of the temple to Dagon and the slaughter of everyone in it—brought about his own death, too.

Even though the book of Judges portrayed his life as something of a profitable disaster, Samson still managed to earn a mention—albeit a passing one—in the "faith hall of fame" found in the book of Hebrews. Samson's life is an object lesson of both the high cost of sin and God's ability to bring victory from even our greatest failures.

Eli's sons were wicked men;
they had no regard for the LORD.
1 SAMUEL 2:12

Day
199

P hinehas made a mockery of the priesthood. In the end, though, he paid dearly for his sin.

Phinehas was the younger son of Eli, a priest in the sanctuary at Shiloh before the temple was built in Jerusalem. While Eli was a reasonably honorable man—albeit an overindulgent father—the text had no kind words for his sons, Hophni and Phinehas. The two served alongside their father, but according to scripture, they were "wicked men"—literally, "sons of worthlessness" (1 Samuel 2:12).

PHINEHAS

Son of Eli

Phinehas's utter disregard for God was demonstrated by his abuse of the fellowship offering. The law made provision for a sacrifice to celebrate the peace between God and His people—this was the fellowship offering. It was unique in that all parties involved received a portion of the sacrifice. The first and best portion (including the fat and internal organs) belonged to God, while the priest and those making the sacrifice shared the remaining meat. According to tradition, the priest would plunge an instrument into the meat while it cooked. Whatever came out—however large or small—was his portion.

But Phinehas demanded his portion first, before the meat had been cooked. In doing so, he cheated both God (by claiming the best part for himself) and the person offering the sacrifice (presumably by taking more than his rightful share). Worse, if anyone challenged Phinehas's behavior, he was threatened with violence.

As if this weren't bad enough, Phinehas and his brother engaged in sexual immorality with women who served near the sanctuary entrance. It came as little surprise when God struck down Phinehas and his brother as they carried the ark of the covenant into battle against the Philistines.

SPIRITUAL INSIGHT

Eli and the rest of Israel paid dearly for Phinehas's sin. Stunned by the news of his son's death, Eli fell backward and died. Phinehas's widow named their son Ichabod, meaning "the glory has departed from Israel," accurately capturing the despair her people felt over the loss of the ark in battle. Often the consequences of our sin reach far beyond our own lives.

The next day Agrippa and Bernice came with great pomp and entered the audience room with the high ranking officers and the leading men of the city. At the command of Festus, Paul was brought in.

ACTS 25:23

Like Herod Agrippa II, people can shield themselves with all kinds of things—power, prestige, wealth, learning—but in the end, we are all stripped bare by the gospel and must ultimately answer the question, "Do we believe in Jesus?"

Agrippa II was the son of Agrippa I, the ruler over all the land of Israel. Several years after Agrippa I's death, Agrippa II was made ruler over the northern part of Israel.

HEROD AGRIPPA II

Tetrarch of Judea
and Great-Grandson
of Herod the Great

After Paul's third missionary journey, he was arrested in Jerusalem and sent to a prison in Caesarea after some Jewish leaders incited a riot against him (Acts 21–23). While he was there, the Roman governor asked Agrippa to listen to Paul's case and help him decide what to do with Paul.

Agrippa and his sister Bernice arrived "with great pomp," including an entourage of high-ranking officers and leaders of the city. Paul, however, saw right through Agrippa's grand display and spoke very directly to him about Jesus. He even asked Agrippa if he believed the prophets, at which point Agrippa tried to dodge the question by asking if Paul believed he could persuade him to become a Christian in such a short time. Paul unswervingly answered that he wished that everyone in the room would become Christians, like him (Acts 25–26).

Apparently this was too much heat for Agrippa, and he and Bernice left the room, affirming Paul's innocence. The Bible never speaks about Agrippa again, so we don't know if he ever reflected on Paul's words or not.

But one of the sons of Ahimelech the son of Ahitub,
named Abiathar, escaped and fled after David.
1 SAMUEL 22:20 ESV

The story of Abiathar underscores that life is a marathon, not a sprint—and a lifetime of good can be ruined by failing to finish strong.

Abiathar was one of the few priests who escaped the terrible slaughter at Nob by Saul and Doeg the Edomite. Abiathar fled to David, who himself was fleeing from Saul (1 Samuel 22:20). From then on it seems that Abiathar served as David's personal priest and spiritual consultant (1 Samuel 23:6, 9; 30:7–8). When Absalom rebelled against David, Abiathar was one of the priests who attempted to bring the ark of the covenant with David, but David sent them back to Jerusalem. While he remained there, he helped pass important information to David to help regain his power (2 Samuel 15).

Abiathar's story turns south, however, when we come to the end of David's life, because he chose to support Adonijah rather than Solomon, whom David had selected to be the next king (1 Kings 1). After Solomon solidified his grip on the throne, he removed Abiathar as priest and banished him to his home in Anathoth, a

ABIATHAR

A Priest during
David's Reign

suburb of Jerusalem (1 Kings 2:26–27). Abiathar's removal from the priesthood fulfilled a longstanding prophecy about his great-great-grandfather Eli, who had failed to restrain the wickedness of his two sons (1 Samuel 3:11–14; 14:3; 22:20).

SPIRITUAL INSIGHT

Abiathar appears to have done a great deal of good during his lifetime, but his bad choices at the end of his career left an indelible stain on his record of service. Abiathar's story demonstrates the need for God's people to guard against complacency. We never reach a stage in life where we can just "coast" in our spiritual life, or we will be sure to stumble, just like Abiathar. Make sure to finish strong!

"And as for Ishmael, I have heard you: I will surely bless him; I will make him fruitful and will greatly increase his numbers. He will be the father of twelve rulers, and I will make him into a great nation."

GENESIS 17:20

When we are seeking the will of God but run into a roadblock, we may start to ask, *Have I made a wrong turn? Will I miss out on God's good plan for me? Has God changed His mind? Should I come up with a plan B?* These questions were no doubt on Abraham's mind, too, as he contemplated God's plans for him and for his son, Ishmael.

ISHMAEL

Son of Abraham

God had promised to bless Abraham and make his descendants into a great nation, a chosen people of God (Genesis 12:1–3; 15:1–6). But Sarah, Abraham's wife, was about seventy-six years old and had not yet borne any children. So, in keeping with ancient Near Eastern customs, Sarah offered her handmaid, Hagar, to bear a child for Abraham—and Ishmael was born. Based on Abraham's limited knowledge at that point, he had no reason to think that Ishmael was not the fulfillment of God's promises. But later God made it clear that it would be through Sarah herself that God's chosen people would come (Genesis 17).

So what about Ishmael? Did he have any significance in his own right? Or would he simply be cast aside by God as a leftover plan B?

Not at all. Though he was not to be the ancestor of God's chosen people, Ishmael was in fact part of God's plan as well. He would become the father of another great nation (Genesis 17:20), traditionally believed to be the Arab peoples.

SPIRITUAL INSIGHT

The will of God for our future can be a difficult thing to discern clearly, and we may even find that what we thought was God's will was not. As we continue to seek His will, however, we can rest assured that God is always working, and what may seem like "wrong" turns are in fact part of God's good plan as well (Romans 8:28).

Lot's daughters did not have an easy life by any account. Raised in the city of Sodom, they were exposed, no doubt, to immorality of every kind. And when an angry mob arrived on Lot's doorstep, they found themselves to be pawns in a dangerous confrontation—their own father offering them up, like a sacrifice, so the men of the town could do whatever they wanted with them.

As they fled Sodom the next day, their mother looked back and was killed—turned into a pillar of salt, according to the writer of Genesis. Soon they were reduced to living in a cave with their ruined father. In these desperate circumstances, Lot's daughters did the unthinkable. Being in a patriarchal culture

LOT'S DAUGHTERS

Ancestors of Moab and Ammon

where women counted on husbands and sons for fulfillment and protection, Lot's daughters felt dangerously vulnerable. They stood no chance of finding partners while living in a cave. So they decided to remedy the situation by getting their father drunk and sleeping with him.

One after the other, Lot's daughters carried out their plan—and both became pregnant. Ironically, Lot's daughters owed their very survival to Abraham, who pleaded with God to spare Sodom. Yet the sons they bore by their father gave rise to the Moabites and the Ammonites—two nations that caused great trouble for the descendants of Abraham.

DID YOU KNOW?

Lot initially asked the angels to let him flee to a town called Zoar, where he thought he and his wife and daughters would be safe. However, the reason Lot and his daughters ended up living in a cave was because Lot was "afraid to stay in Zoar" (Genesis 19:30). No reason is given for Lot's fear, but apparently his judgment in choosing Zoar was as flawed as his decision to move to Sodom—to say nothing of his daughters' faulty discernment while living in the cave.

About midnight Paul and Silas were praying and singing
hymns to God, and the other prisoners were listening to them.
Suddenly there was such a violent earthquake that the
foundations of the prison were shaken.

ACTS 16:25–26

Silas was a gifted leader and a fearless adventurer. In addition, he may have aided in the composition of at least one New Testament book.

As a leader in the Jerusalem church, Silas was among those chosen to deliver the congregation's letter to Gentile believers in Antioch, Syria, and Cilicia. Silas lent credibility to the expedition, which also included Paul, Barnabas, and Judas Barsabbas. Silas, however, was far more than a letter carrier—in Antioch, he further encouraged the believers by prophesying to them. The content of Silas's teaching is not revealed in the book of Acts, but the result was that all the Gentile Christians were greatly encouraged.

SILAS

Leader of the Early Church

Later, when Paul and Barnabas parted ways over their disagreement concerning Mark (see Acts 15:36–41), Paul invited Silas to accompany him to Syria and Cilicia. Their plans changed abruptly, however, when Paul received a vision of a man begging them to come to Macedonia. With that, the pair introduced the gospel to present-day Greece. They were even imprisoned during their stay in Philippi. After a massive earthquake, however, their jailer (who was amazed to discover that Silas and Paul had not seized their opportunity to flee) converted to Christianity and invited them to his house. After that, the two were released.

Silas made an ideal traveling companion for Paul. Both were Roman citizens (see Acts 16:37), a fact that proved useful for getting out of difficult situations like the one at Philippi. Silas may have also had a way with words. Both letters to the church at Thessalonica were said to be from "Paul, Silas, and Timothy" (see 1 Thessalonians 1:1; 2 Thessalonians 1:1). Years later, the apostle Peter credited Silas with helping him write his first letter (see 1 Peter 5:12). Although he did not play a leading role himself, Silas proved a vital partner to two of the early church's greatest apostles.

DID YOU KNOW?

In three New Testament books (2 Corinthians, 1 Thessalonians, and 1 Peter) Silas is referred to as "Silvanus." Apparently "Silas" was a contraction of his full name.

But when Sanballat the Horonite and Tobiah the Ammonite servant and Geshem the Arab heard of it, they jeered at us and despised us and said, "What is this thing that you are doing? Are you rebelling against the king?"
NEHEMIAH 2:19 ESV

Geshem was afraid. Under the Persian Empire he was appointed leader of a minor Arabian people group near Judea, and it seems that he was determined to hold on to his power by making certain that no one else around him grew too strong.

But then came Nehemiah, a Jew who had served in the Persian royal court and who was now planning to rebuild the walls of Jerusalem, Judea's capital city. What would this mean for Geshem and his small nation? Would Geshem's power be overshadowed or even brought to an end by the Judeans? Something had to be done.

So Geshem, together with leaders from other surrounding nations, began to ridicule Nehemiah and his plans, even accusing him of conspiring to rebel against the Persian Empire (Nehemiah 2). But Nehemiah was not distracted from his goal, and the walls were soon completed. All that was left was to put the gates in place. Now what was Geshem going to do?

GESHEM

Arabian Leader Who Opposed Nehemiah

So Geshem and the other leaders hatched a more sinister plot: lure Nehemiah to a place outside his jurisdiction and do him harm—perhaps even kill him! They sent him several messages inviting him to meet on the plain of Ono to the northwest of Judea, but Nehemiah wisely declined. They accused him again of plotting to rebel against the Persians, but Nehemiah continued to trust in the Lord, and finally the project was completed (Nehemiah 6).

The Bible does not record anything further about Geshem, so we never learn whether his fears of losing his power were ever realized.

DID YOU KNOW?

The Persian Empire continued to rule over Judea and northern Arabia for another hundred years. Their rule came to an end around 333 BC when Alexander the Great swiftly took over the Persian Empire in about twelve years.

Then Rezin king of Aram and Pekah son of Remaliah king of Israel marched up to fight against Jerusalem and besieged Ahaz, but they could not overpower him.

2 KINGS 16:5

Solomon wisely wrote, "If a man digs a pit, he will fall into it; if a man rolls a stone, it will roll back on him" (Proverbs 26:27). This could not have been truer of King Rezin of Aram.

REZIN

King of Aram

Rezin ruled over Aram, a nation to the northeast of Israel and Judah that occasionally fought with them over territory. It seems that Rezin was trying to form an alliance of nations to resist the advance of the growing Assyrian Empire, but when King Ahaz of Judah refused to join, Rezin teamed up with King Pekah of Israel, and perhaps even with the Edomites and the Philistines, to attack Judah (2 Kings 16; 2 Chronicles 28:16–19).

In an act of desperation, Ahaz turned to Assyria to help him. He made Judah a subservient kingdom to Assyria and paid the king of Assyria a large amount of silver and gold to attack Rezin and Pekah. The plan worked. The Assyrians annexed the territory of Aram and much of Israel, and they killed Rezin. Unfortunately, this also appears to have whetted the Assyrians' appetite for the region, because they later returned and attacked Judah as well.

RELATED INFORMATION

Isaiah prophesied about Rezin's downfall to Assyria in Isaiah 7–9. He called Rezin and Pekah "two smoldering stubs of firewood" (Isaiah 7:4) and assured Ahaz that they would not succeed. Sadly, Ahaz did not trust the Lord and took matters into his own hands to gain the help of Assyria.

And there came out from the camp of the Philistines a champion named Goliath of Gath, whose height was six cubits and a span.
1 SAMUEL 17:4 ESV

Day
207

It's often who you know that makes all the difference. From business to politics to box seats at sold-out sporting events, making a simple connection to an important name is sometimes all you need to go from zero to a dream come true. But the key, of course, is *who*—whose name are you able to drop?

GOLIATH

Philistine Warrior
Killed by David

Goliath, a giant from the Philistine city of Gath, mistakenly assumed that the only names he needed were those of his people and his pagan gods (1 Samuel 17:8, 43). When the Philistines were preparing for battle against the Israelites, Goliath presented himself as the Philistines' champion and challenged the Israelites to send their own champion to fight him in order to determine which group would be victorious. He identified himself as a Philistine, and he wrongly assumed that all the Israelite warriors were merely servants of Saul (1 Samuel 17:8). But the shepherd boy David knew better. He came to Goliath in the name of the Lord, and this name would make all the difference (1 Samuel 17:43–47).

The Lord gave David victory over Goliath and the other Israelites victory over the Philistine army, and Goliath's name—and the name of his gods—would forever be associated with defeat.

SPIRITUAL INSIGHT	God has promised that those who hope in Him will not be disappointed (Isaiah 49:23), for His name is above every name, and He is the only One with the power to rescue all who call on Him (Acts 4:12). Have you called on this name for your salvation?

Day
208

*So the LORD's anger burned against Israel, and for a long time
he kept them under the power of Hazael king of Aram.*

2 KINGS 13:3

When evil people begin to oppress God's people, it's tempting to think, *Where is God? Doesn't He see what's going on? Why doesn't He do something?* But as the story of Hazael demonstrates, God is never shocked or taken by surprise by anyone— and even wicked people can only do what God has already determined that they may do.

HAZAEL

King of Aram

Though it might be hard to understand why, God had handpicked Hazael from the very beginning to be king of Aram (1 Kings 19:15), even though He already knew that Hazael would inflict terrible suffering on His people. Hazael was one of Ben-Hadad's officials and had been sent to inquire of Elisha whether the king would recover from an illness. Elisha informed Hazael that he would become king and would do terrible things to the people of Israel. Soon after Hazael returned to the king with Elisha's message, Hazael suffocated his master and took over the kingship (2 Kings 8:7–15), periodically oppressing Israel for the next forty-five years.

Hazael eventually captured all of Israel's territory east of the Jordan River (2 Kings 10:32–33), and even Judah's capital city of Jerusalem would have been attacked by Hazael had he not been paid a large sum to withdraw (2 King 12:17–18).

How could all of this happen? The Bible makes it clear: God Himself allowed Hazael to do this in order to discipline His people for their sins (2 Kings 10:32; 13:1–3). Even in the midst of this punishment, however, God was in control, ensuring that the actions did not exceed what God had decided should happen (2 Kings 13:4–5, 23).

RELATED INFORMATION

Soon after Hazael died, the people of Israel were able to recover much of the territory they had lost to Aram (2 Kings 13:24–25).

*"But charge Joshua, and encourage and strengthen him,
for he shall go over at the head of this people,
and he shall put them in possession of the land that you shall see."*
DEUTERONOMY 3:28 ESV

Moses led the people to the doorstep of the Promised Land, but Joshua helped the people walk through the door to conquer and settle the land. Though born a slave in Egypt, Joshua became Moses' primary aid and assistant (Exodus 24:13). During four decades at Moses' side, Joshua served in a variety of ways: He explored the Promised Land as one of the original twelve spies—along with Caleb, giving the only favorable report. He led the people into their first successful military battles (Exodus 17). And he joined Moses on the mountain of God (Exodus 24:13). After Moses' death and the completion of a forty-year apprenticeship, Joshua became the leader of the Hebrew people (Joshua 1–4).

Joshua assumed command during a time of military conquest. Having commissioned Moses to lead the people out of Egypt, God gave Joshua the job of leading them into Canaan. Under Joshua's leadership the people conquered Jericho, Ai, and the other people of the land

JOSHUA

Hebrew Military Leader

(Joshua 12). After the dust of battle settled, Joshua divided and assigned the land as instructed by Moses (Joshua 13–19).

Even though Joshua's legacy primarily revolves around his military exploits, each of his conquests is marked by his faith in God. Urging the people to remember the teachings of Moses, Joshua constantly reminded them of God's presence and plan. He entered into battle with a dependence on God's strength. He lived out the exhortation he received at the beginning of his days in leadership: "Have I not commanded you? Be strong and courageous. Do not be frightened, and do not be dismayed, for the Lord your God is with you wherever you go" (Joshua 1:9 ESV).

DID YOU KNOW? The name *Jesus* is derived from *Joshua*. Just as Joshua brought God's people into a physical Promised Land, so Jesus brings God's people into a spiritual Promised Land. Read more on this comparison and theme in Hebrews 4.

So the land had peace for forty years,
until Othniel son of Kenaz died.
JUDGES 3:11

As the first listed among a series of judges, Othniel's story established a pattern that would be repeated often in Israel's history.

Othniel had already proven his valor during the conquest of the Promised Land. He led the successful assault on Kiriath Sepher (in what became the territory of Judah) in order to win a girl's hand in marriage. (One detail that modern readers may find disturbing is that the girl in question was, in fact, his cousin.)

OTHNIEL

Judge of Israel

However, Israel failed to complete its conquest of the Promised Land. As a result, the pagan practices of the land's original inhabitants continued unabated. Soon the Israelites were copying their neighbors, forsaking God in order to worship Baal, the supreme Canaanite god, and Asherah, the Canaanite mother goddess, instead. As punishment, God sent raiders from Aram Naharaim (northern Mesopotamia, located in present-day Iraq) to oppress the Israelites. The punishment lasted eight years, until the Israelites remembered the real God and cried out for deliverance. In response, God raised up Othniel—one of the heroes of Canaan's conquest—to do the job.

As judge of Israel, Othniel fulfilled two functions: He served as a military commander in times of conflict and as political leader in times of peace. Othniel performed both tasks admirably. Without going into detail, the Bible simply says that Othniel overpowered the oppressors from Aram Naharaim (Judges 3:10). After that, the Israelites enjoyed a period of peace and prosperity that lasted until Othniel's death forty years later.

However, the writer did not leave Othniel's story before revealing the secret to his success as both ruler and warrior: Othniel had been filled with the "Spirit of the LORD" (Judges 3:10), empowered by God for the task at hand.

DID YOU KNOW? Othniel had heroism in his blood. His uncle was Caleb, one of only two spies (the other being Joshua) who had encouraged the Israelites to enter the Promised Land as God had commanded.

When Lamech had lived 182 years, he had a son.
He named him Noah and said, "He will comfort us in
the labor and painful toil of our hands
caused by the ground the LORD has cursed."
GENESIS 5:28–29

Among those listed in the genealogy of Seth, Adam and Eve's third son, only one is quoted directly: Lamech (see Genesis 5).

Lamech was the son of Methuselah, a man famous for little more than being the answer to a trivia question: Who was the oldest person who ever lived? Lamech, though, lived at a crucial juncture in early human history—just before God destroyed the world in a cataclysmic flood.

LAMECH

Noah's Father

Lamech's brief quote reveals an acute awareness of how much things had deteriorated since his ancestors Adam and Eve fell from grace and were expelled from the garden. God's promise of "painful toil" (Genesis 3:17; 5:29) had come true. The ground was cursed, and Lamech was looking for a reason to believe things might change for the better.

He placed that hope in his son Noah, whom he said "will comfort us." Lamech's words proved true, though perhaps not in the way he anticipated. A few years after Lamech died, God appeared to Noah and commanded him to start building an ark to preserve his family and a sampling of the animals during the judgment that was coming. It may seem like a strange way to bring comfort, but Noah also found himself on the receiving end of humanity's first covenant with God.

Perhaps more significantly, the Gospel writer Luke counted both Noah and his father, Lamech, among the ancestors of hope personified, Jesus Christ.

But when he drew back his hand, his brother came out,
and [the midwife] said, "So this is how you have broken out!"
And he was named Perez.
GENESIS 38:29

Perez was the underdog (in more ways than one) who rose to prominence among the descendants of Jacob.

To begin with, Perez was the child of a union that should never have been. His mother was Tamar, who had been married to Judah's oldest son, Er. But Er had died, so Judah ordered his younger son to father a child with Tamar so she would have a son who would be reckoned as Er's heir. Onan refused and was struck dead by the Lord.

PEREZ

King of Persia

Initially, Judah had promised his third son to Tamar but later changed his mind, afraid that his youngest son would die, too. Having no other way to ensure the survival of her family line, Tamar disguised herself as a prostitute and convinced Judah to sleep with her. The plan succeeded—Tamar conceived a child, and Judah, who initially planned to have her burned to death, was shamed into silence when he realized the prostitute was his own daughter-in-law. Tamar and her unborn child had overcome the odds and triumphed.

Months later, as Tamar prepared to give birth, it became evident she was carrying not one but two children. According to the writer of Genesis, one of the children's arms appeared, and the midwife tied a cord around it to indicate that he was the firstborn—the rightful recipient of the chief blessing. To the midwife's surprise, however, that child withdrew his arm and the second child emerged, claiming the title of firstborn. This child was named Perez. His story, though brief, echoes a recurring theme in Genesis: the weaker triumphing over the stronger and the second-born triumphing over the firstborn (or in this case, the one who was initially thought to be the firstborn). Perez overcame the odds in order to be regarded as Tamar's firstborn son.

DID YOU KNOW?

Judah's other three sons faded into obscurity (Er and Onan being dead and Shelah disappearing from the story line after Genesis 38), but Perez rose to prominence among the family line of Judah. He became the ancestor of Boaz, David, and ultimately Jesus.

David said to Abigail, "Praise be to the LORD, the God of Israel,
who has sent you today to meet me. May you be blessed
for your good judgment and for keeping me from bloodshed this day
and from avenging myself with my own hands."
1 SAMUEL 25:32–33

Everyone has needed an Abigail at some point in life—someone who, through discretion and grace, has kept us from doing something we would really regret.

Abigail was the wife of a wealthy herder named Nabal, whose name means "fool." While David was on the run from Saul, he spent some time in the area near Nabal's flocks and kept them safe from potential thieves. When the time came for Nabal's sheep to be sheared, David sent his men to receive some payment for their services, but Nabal rebuffed them and sent them away empty-handed. When David heard about this, he was furious and gathered his men to go kill every one of Nabal's men.

ABIGAIL

Nabal's Widow and David's Wife

But Abigail, whom the Bible describes as discerning and beautiful, intercepted David before he reached Nabal's men, offered him some food, and persuaded him to turn back from repaying Nabal for his affront.

David immediately recognized the wisdom in Abigail's words, turned back from his vengeance, and praised God for using Abigail to save him from doing something he would have regretted (1 Samuel 25).

When Abigail informed her husband of all that transpired between her and David, Nabal's "heart failed him and he became like a stone" (1 Samuel 25:37). Ten days later Nabal died, and David took Abigail as his wife.

RELATED INFORMATION

David once had to rescue Abigail and one of his other wives from the Amalekites, who had raided his town of Ziklag and carried off many people (1 Samuel 30).

And Jesus said to him, "What do you want me to do for you?"
And the blind man said to him, "Rabbi, let me recover my sight."
And Jesus said to him, "Go your way; your faith has made you well."
And immediately he recovered his sight and followed him on the way.

MARK 10:51–52 ESV

We don't often see miracles happening at the corner coffee shop or outside our local courthouse building. But the crowds pressing through the city gates of Jericho certainly witnessed one as Jesus passed through their city one day long ago (Mark 10:46).

By the dusty roadside near the Jericho gate sat Bartimaeus, a blind man, begging from the ground among the jostling crowd. Suddenly, he heard a large crowd moving by and learned that Jesus of Nazareth was among them. Jesus! No more begging, he began shouting, "Jesus, Son of David, have mercy on me!" (Mark 10:47). The people around him reprimanded him for his noise, but he only shouted all the louder for the merciful Son of David.

BARTIMAEUS

Blind Beggar
Who Saw Jesus

Jesus must have heard his cry, for He stopped and told the crowd to call Bartimaeus to Him. Quickly, casting aside his cloak, Bartimaeus went to meet Jesus and told Him simply, "Rabbi, I want to see." Jesus replied, "Go, your faith has healed you," and a healed, seeing Bartimaeus followed Him away from Jericho.

SPIRITUAL INSIGHT

Bartimaeus fervently called to Jesus because he recognized who Jesus was: the merciful Son of David. He was excited to be in the presence of the One who mercifully healed and worked in even the most seemingly impossible situations. Heal a blind person? Make him see? Bartimaeus had little doubt. He knew Jesus could heal him. What is our heart's attitude when we approach our Savior during difficult or traumatic times in life? Do we doubt His care, mercy, and ability to work for our good, or do we have the confidence of Bartimaeus when we call out, "Jesus, Son of David, have mercy on me"?

*Then the king placed Daniel in a high position and lavished
many gifts on him. He made him ruler over the entire
province of Babylon and placed him in charge of all its wise men.*
DANIEL 2:48

O f all the people mentioned in scripture, few are spoken of as highly as Daniel. Daniel probably came from the nobility of Judah, and he was a very young man when he was taken into exile in Babylon. Despite his traumatic beginnings, however, Daniel prospered—both as an official in the Babylonian royal court and as a follower of God.

Daniel first served in the court of Nebuchadnezzar along with his friends Hananiah (Shadrach), Mishael (Meshach), and Azariah (Abednego), and quickly distinguished himself by his great learning and understanding. Later Daniel interpreted various dreams for Nebuchadnezzar and was rewarded with promotions and wealth. Daniel also interpreted a divine message given to Nebuchadnezzar's son Belshazzar.

DANIEL

Jewish Prophet and
Royal Official of Babylon

Daniel continued his distinguished government service even after the kingdom changed hands to the Persians. Yet his devotion to God remained unshaken, as demonstrated by the fact that it was his regular times of prayer that were used by his enemies to trap him. With God's help, Daniel survived the ordeal unscathed and continued to prosper.

Daniel was also a prophet who received several visions from God, mostly about the future rise and fall of various world powers.

RELATED INFORMATION

Daniel's fame as a righteous and wise person must have been widely known even in his own day, because the prophet Ezekiel, who also lived in Babylon during the exile, spoke of Daniel's righteousness and wisdom three times in his book (Ezekiel 14:14, 20; 28:3).

*Judah recognized them and said, "She is more righteous than I,
since I wouldn't give her to my son Shelah."
And he did not sleep with her again.*

GENESIS 38:26

As a two-time widow with no other real prospects, Tamar was in a no-win situation.

Tamar was the first wife of Er, Judah's oldest son. Judah had arranged the marriage himself—unfortunately, Er was guilty of some unspecified sin and died before producing an heir. As was the custom of the day, Judah then gave Onan, his second son, to Tamar. But history repeated itself. Onan died, too, leaving Tamar still without a son. Women who had no sons or husbands were vulnerable indeed. Judah had promised his third son to Tamar—just as soon as he was old enough to marry—but the years began to pass, and it became clear that Judah had no intention of keeping his word.

TAMAR

Judah's Daughter-in-Law

One day, after getting word that Judah was out and about, Tamar covered her face with a veil and situated herself on the road, waiting for Judah to pass. Pretending to be a prostitute, she solicited her own father-in-law, who just recently finished mourning his deceased wife. Not having anything with which to pay a prostitute, Judah gave Tamar his seal—sometimes attached to a cord and worn like a necklace—and staff as a pledge of good faith.

Three months later, when Tamar was no longer able to hide her pregnancy, Judah ordered her burned alive for her adultery. This was Tamar's no-win situation: As long as she was pledged to Judah's third son, she could not enter into another man's protection, but Judah had not kept his word and had failed to provide the protection Tamar needed. Judah had been a poor father-in-law, a fact that dawned on him when Tamar produced his seal and staff, saving her own life and the lives of her twin sons. Judah was shamed into acknowledging that Tamar was more righteous than he had been.

SPIRITUAL INSIGHT

While not condoning Tamar and Judah's sexual immorality in any way, the writer of Genesis seemed far more troubled about Judah's failure to meet his obligations to his family. Judah's story is an example of what can happen when God's people forget that the second greatest command in the whole Bible is to "love your neighbor as yourself" (see Matthew 22:37–39).

The oracle that Habakkuk the prophet received.
How long, O LORD, must I call for help, but you do not listen?
Or cry out to you, "Violence!" but you do not save?
HABAKKUK 1:1–2

Day
217

With all the injustice and evil going on seemingly unchecked around us, many of us think to ourselves, *God, don't You see what's going on? Why don't You do something?* Most of us, though, are too afraid to actually speak these thoughts to God. But not Habakkuk. He boldly brought these questions to God, and God answered, though not necessarily as Habakkuk was expecting.

HABAKKUK

Prophet of Judah

We know almost nothing about Habakkuk except that, based on his prophecy, he must have lived just before the Babylonians attacked Judah and sent the people into exile. But what we do know is that he was very troubled by the wickedness going on around him, and it made him wonder whether God really cared and why He did not seem to be doing anything about it.

God answered Habakkuk's questions by assuring him that He was already raising up the Babylonians to punish the wickedness going on around him in Judah. The problem was that the Babylonians seemed even more evil than the people of Judah, according to Habakkuk—so he brought this concern to God, too.

God answered Habakkuk's second question by assuring him that one day He would punish those who have oppressed others. Habakkuk responded with a song of praise for God's mercy and salvation.

SPIRITUAL INSIGHT

When we experience pain and suffering, we may wonder why God doesn't seem to be doing anything to help us. Like Habakkuk, we should bring those questions directly to God and trust Him to answer. Otherwise we will likely breed resentment and more doubt. God does care for His people (Matthew 6:25–34, 10:29–31), and we can trust that He is always working for our good (Romans 8:28–29).

Moreover, David fought Hadadezer son of Rehob, king of Zobah,
when he went to restore his control along the Euphrates River.

2 Samuel 8:3

No amount of military might in the world is enough to stop God's people when the Lord has determined that they will be victorious. This was a lesson that was surely learned by King Hadadezer of Zobah.

HADADEZER

King of Zobah and Enemy of David

When the kingdom of Israel was firmly in David's control, he began to branch out beyond his borders and defeat enemy nations, including the Philistines and the Moabites. It seems that the Ammonites became nervous at David's victories and hired troops from the neighboring Aramean nations to fight him. King Hadadezer of Zobah, a kingdom to the north of Israel, must have been among them. When David defeated them, Hadadezer regrouped and called upon even more troops from his vassals (subservient kingdoms) in the far north, but David defeated them as well. This caused Hadadezer's vassals to abandon their loyalty to him, and he was forced to march his troops to their lands to reestablish control over them. In the meantime, David invaded Zobah itself and captured Hadadezer's kingdom (2 Samuel 10). David took a large quantity of bronze from some of Hadadezer's towns, and Solomon used this to create some of the bronze articles for the temple (1 Chronicles 18:8).

RELATED INFORMATION

David's victory over Hadadezer must have been very impressive, because the king of Hamath, just north of Hadadezer's territory, sent his son to congratulate David on his victory, and he gave him gifts of silver, gold, and bronze (2 Samuel 8:9–10). The king of Hamath had also been at war with Hadadezer.

[Jonah] prayed to the LORD, "O LORD,
is this not what I said when I was still at home?
That is why I was so quick to flee to Tarshish.
I knew that you are a gracious and compassionate God,
slow to anger and abounding in love,
a God who relents from sending calamity."
JONAH 4:2

From movies to books to workplace spats, it seems that revenge is in and mercy is out. That was true for Jonah as well. Jonah was a prophet from Israel who was called by God to preach to the people of Nineveh—the capital city of the mighty Assyrian Empire. This great empire was threatening to swallow up tiny Israel and everyone in it, and Jonah was not pleased about his new assignment.

JONAH

Reluctant Prophet to People of Nineveh

So instead of heading for Nineveh, Jonah hopped on a slow boat to Tarshish—which was located in the opposite direction. But God cared too much about both Jonah and the people of Nineveh to let him go without a fight. So the Lord sent a storm that led the other sailors to throw Jonah overboard—then He sent a fish to snatch Jonah from a watery grave. In God's grace, Jonah was given a second chance to go to Nineveh to call the people to repent—and this time Jonah took it.

For most people, that's where the story stops, but that's really only half the story. The people of Nineveh did repent, and God, in keeping with His character, relented from carrying out the destruction He had threatened for the city. Good news, right? Not for Jonah. He was actually *angry* at God for being compassionate and sparing the city!

SPIRITUAL INSIGHT

How do you respond when you are threatened or even hurt by others? Do you seek revenge? Do you pray for God to do nasty things to your enemies? Jesus calls us to pray for our enemies (Matthew 5:43–47). Since we have been spared eternal punishment for our sins (Romans 6:23), how can we wish anything else for others?

*Then the king commanded, and Daniel was brought
and cast into the den of lions. The king declared to Daniel,
"May your God, whom you serve continually, deliver you!"*

DANIEL 6:16 ESV

Though he was the most powerful man on earth during his lifetime, even King Darius of Persia was forced to recognize that ultimately only God is sovereign over all things, and we are all dependent upon Him.

The Persian Empire around the time of Darius was the greatest power the world had ever known, and Darius was the undisputed king. Yet this mighty king seemed rather gullible when it came to the crafty schemes of a few jealous officials. They were jealous of the prestige and power of Daniel, one of the Jewish nobles who had been exiled to Babylon many years earlier, because he had been promoted to second-in-command of the Persian Empire. Daniel's only "flaw" seemed to be his unwavering devotion to God, to whom he prayed three times a day. So the officials smooth-talked Darius into passing a law requiring everyone to pray only to the king for one month. Daniel, of course, continued to pray to God and was promptly arrested.

DARIUS

King of Persia

When Darius realized that Daniel would be thrown to the lions for his crime, he became distraught, because even he could not revoke anything he had signed into law. So all that was left to do was to pray that God Himself would deliver Daniel.

God did indeed deliver Daniel, and Darius rejoiced and made a new law that everyone should fear the God of Daniel.

RELATED INFORMATION

The Bible mentions a couple of different people named Darius, and both of them are described as ruling over the Persian Empire (Ezra 4:24; Nehemiah 12:22; Daniel 6; Haggai 1:1; Zechariah 1:1). All the references to Darius outside of the book of Daniel probably refer to Darius the Great, who ruled Persia from 522–486 BC. In the book of Daniel, Darius may be another name for Cyrus the Great, who ruled Persia from 559–529 BC.

But Zadok the priest, Benaiah son of Jehoiada, Nathan the prophet,
Shimei and Rei and David's special guard did not join Adonijah.
1 KINGS 1:8

Zadok, a direct descendant of Aaron, was one of David's most loyal allies, even in his darkest moments.

Aside from a passing reference in the context of David's consolidation of power (see 2 Samuel 8), Zadok first appeared in the story after David was unseated in a coup led by his own son Absalom. Zadok decided to accompany the king as he fled Jerusalem. More important, Zadok and his fellow priests meant to take the ark of the covenant with them—a powerful sign that in their estimation, David was still the rightful king and the recipient of God's blessing.

ZADOK

Priest during David's Time

David wisely counseled Zadok to turn back. He knew from previous history that the ark was no magic token—but most of all, it was meant to stay in God's chosen city, among God's chosen people. Zadok obediently returned to Jerusalem, where he paved the way for David's triumphant return following Absalom's death.

Before David died, Zadok had one more opportunity to demonstrate his loyalty to Israel's greatest king. David's intent was for Solomon to succeed him as king. However, when Adonijah moved to preemptively install himself as David's successor, a number of David's advisers—including the priest Abiathar—rallied to him. Zadok, however, stood by the dying king's wishes. Together with the prophet Nathan, Zadok had the honor of anointing Israel's next rightful king, Solomon. Zadok ended up replacing Abiathar as well.

DID YOU KNOW?

Zadok's descendants served in the temple until the destruction of Jerusalem in 586 BC. According to the prophet Ezekiel, they alone were worthy to enter God's sanctuary, because they alone had remained pure while the rest of the Israelites strayed from God (see Ezekiel 44:15–16).

When the LORD saw that Leah was not loved,
he opened her womb, but Rachel was barren.

GENESIS 29:31

It is generally not a good sign when a person's name means either "weary" or perhaps "wild cow." More than once, Leah found herself a pawn in someone else's scheme, unloved and unwanted. But God made her a pillar of His chosen people, the Hebrews.

Leah's misfortune began when her father, Laban, used her to trick Jacob. Jacob had grown smitten with Laban's younger and more beautiful daughter, Rachel, and agreed to work seven years in order to marry her. On the wedding night, Laban switched brides without Jacob realizing it until the following morning. When Jacob saw Leah—whom the Jewish historian Josephus described as "devoid of beauty"—he was furious. For the rest of his life, Jacob never loved Leah the way he loved Rachel.

LEAH

Jacob's First Wife

In response, God blessed Leah, enabling her to bear six sons and a daughter while her sister, Rachel, remained almost completely barren. Fertility was seen as a sign of divine favor in the ancient world.

Still, Jacob remained indifferent toward Leah. Initially convinced that the birth of her sons would win Jacob's affection, Leah came to terms with her situation by the time Judah was born. She contented herself with being the recipient of God's favor instead.

Years later, as Jacob prepared to meet his estranged brother, Esau, Leah received another reminder of her status. Fearful that Esau would attack, Jacob arranged his family in reverse order of importance—sending the servants and their children first, Leah and her children second, and Rachel and her son, Joseph, last. Leah was at least more valuable to Jacob than his servants, but she was still clearly the second favorite.

God's favor, however, secured an important place for Leah in Israel's history. One of her sons, Levi, became the ancestor of the Jewish priesthood, while another, Judah, was the father of Israel's lone dynasty.

DID YOU KNOW? Leah's name, along with Rachel's, was invoked in a blessing at the marriage of Ruth and Boaz—the great-grandparents of King David. The elders of Bethlehem prayed that God would make Ruth "like Rachel and Leah, who together built up the house of Israel" (Ruth 4:11).

Then Jesus answered, "Woman, you have great faith!
Your request is granted."
And her daughter was healed from that very hour.
MATTHEW 15:28

The story of the encounter between Jesus and the unnamed Syrophoenician woman has puzzled many readers. Why did Jesus appear eager to brush off the woman at first? Why did He seem to think her ethnicity was a valid reason to refuse her request—especially since it concerned the well-being of her little girl? Most of all, why did Jesus change His mind? Had He been mistaken and, realizing the error of His thinking, decided to grant the woman's request after all? Or was it all a setup designed to test the woman's persistence?

THE SYROPHOENICIAN WOMAN

Mother of a Demon-Possessed Daughter

It is unlikely, to say the least, that Jesus viewed the Syrophoenician woman disdainfully on account of her ethnicity. After all, Jesus had nearly gotten Himself killed at the synagogue in His hometown for reminding His fellow Jews of a time when God sent the prophets not to His chosen people but to people like Naaman the Syrian (see Luke 4:24–27). At the end of His earthly ministry, Jesus commissioned His disciples to take the gospel to "all nations" (see Matthew 28:19).

Scholars note that Jesus' explanation—"It is not right to take the children's bread and toss it to their dogs" (Matthew 15:26)—was not a rejection of this woman and her fellow Gentiles but a statement about the focus of Jesus' immediate ministry. He had been sent to His fellow Jews—and while this did not preclude Him from ministering among the Gentiles, His immediate focus remained on His own people.

Some suggest that Jesus may have used His exchange with the Syrophoenician woman as a test of her faith—or perhaps as a teachable moment with His disciples. Matthew noted that it was the disciples who had pressed Jesus to send the woman away. In the end, the woman triumphed—her faith and persistence mattered more than her ethnicity. Impressed by her tenacity, Jesus healed the woman's demon-possessed daughter.

SPIRITUAL INSIGHT

The Syrophoenician woman's response to Jesus' initial rebuff demonstrated not only her persistence but her quick thinking, too. Playing off Jesus' own metaphor of children and their dogs (the Greek word most likely refers to a puppy taken as a pet), the woman responded that she would accept whatever Jesus had to offer. Such unconditional acceptance was what won Jesus' admiration and respect.

*"How can a man be born when he is old?" Nicodemus asked.
"Surely he cannot enter a second time into
his mother's womb to be born!"*

JOHN 3:4

Nicodemus's faith did not appear in a moment of sudden illumination. Rather, it seems to have emerged gradually.

The Bible captures just three episodes from Nicodemus's life—all of them recorded in the book of John. In the first scene, Nicodemus sought an audience with Jesus, hoping to hear more from the popular rabbi. The nighttime setting has led many to conclude that Nicodemus feared the consequences of being seen publicly with the controversial Jesus. In His encounter with Nicodemus, Jesus told the inquisitive Pharisee that no one could experience God's kingdom without being reborn. Nicodemus, unable to distinguish between "earthly things" and "heavenly things" (see John 3:12), received a mild rebuke, accompanied by further explanation. It was to Nicodemus that Jesus revealed that faith in God's Son leads to eternal life.

NICODEMUS

Religious Leader
Taught by Jesus

John does not indicate whether Nicodemus walked away from the conversation having put his faith in Jesus, but the other two episodes featuring the religious leader are revealing. As the conspiracy against Jesus developed, some of the religious leaders rebuked the temple guards for not arresting Jesus when they had the chance. In response, the guards came to Jesus' defense, to which the Pharisees retorted that since no religious leader had put his faith in Jesus, neither should the guards. Apparently contradicting this claim, Nicodemus spoke up, challenging his colleagues for condemning Jesus without a hearing.

Once more, however, Nicodemus disappeared from the scene as quickly as he had appeared. He did not reemerge until the death of Jesus, when he, along with Joseph of Arimathea, took Jesus' body from the cross and buried it in an unused tomb—one final tribute to the Messiah who had once shared with him the secret of eternal life.

The phrase Jesus used to describe spiritual rebirth to Nicodemus can be translated "born again" or "born from above" (see John 3:3, 7). Either way, it describes a phenomenon that human beings are incapable of bringing about by their own will—we are wholly dependent on the grace of God.

From there Abraham journeyed toward the territory of the Negeb
and lived between Kadesh and Shur; and he sojourned in Gerar.
And Abraham said of Sarah his wife, "She is my sister."
And Abimelech king of Gerar sent and took Sarah.
GENESIS 20:1–2 ESV

Day
225

W e aren't doing people any favors when we bow to fear and withhold the truth from them. In fact, we may be putting them in harm's way. Just ask Abimelech.

Abimelech was the king of Gerar in southern Canaan during the time Abraham lived there. When Abraham moved into the area, he knew that someone might take an interest in his wife, Sarah—and he feared that he might be killed so that she could be taken. So Abraham told a half-truth (or rather, a partial lie) that Sarah was his sister. But he hid the fact that she was also his wife, and he told Sarah to tell people that he was her brother. So Abimelech took her with the intent to make her his wife.

ABIMELECH

King of Gerar

But before Abimelech even touched her, the Lord warned him that Sarah was already married and that he must return her to Abraham—or die. So Abimelech sent Sarah back to Abraham right away and paid him a large sum to account for any guilt he had incurred by his actions. He also invited Abraham to live anywhere in his land.

SPIRITUAL INSIGHT

Abraham lied about Sarah because he thought the people of Gerar did not fear God. Yet Abraham's dishonesty and fear revealed his own lack of fear of God and his selfish concern for his own well-being. If Abraham had trusted God to watch over him and was truthful from the beginning, he would not have unnecessarily endangered Abimelech's life and well-being.

"You should not look down on your brother in the day of his misfortune, nor rejoice over the people of Judah in the day of their destruction."

OBADIAH 1:12

Obadiah's tiny prophecy (his is the shortest book in the Bible) takes just moments to read. But for the nation of Edom—to whom it was directed—his words had a reverberating impact.

Aside from the meaning of his name, "servant of the Lord," nothing is known about Obadiah—neither his family, nor his home, nor his background is revealed in scripture. Obadiah's prophecy concerned the Edomites, longtime enemies of Israel. Centuries earlier, the Edomites had denied the Hebrews passage on their way to the Promised Land. King David eventually subjugated Edom, but the latter managed to wrest itself free from Jewish control.

OBADIAH

Prophet against Edom

The tension between Israel and Edom can be traced all the way back to their ancestors, Jacob and Esau. The two brothers were estranged when Jacob stole Esau's birthright. The Bible later reveals that God had chosen Jacob over Esau as heir to the Abrahamic covenant.

At the time of Obadiah's writing, Israel's and Edom's fortunes had been reversed. The people of Judah faced destruction, while the Edomites looked on and celebrated Judah's misfortune. Scholars have long debated whether Obadiah wrote about Jerusalem's destruction in 586 BC or some prior calamity—though the description in Obadiah 1:10–12 seems to indicate the former.

In any case, Obadiah admonished these distant cousins of the Israelites not to gloat over Judah's hardships, warning that the same fate awaited Edom. Obadiah envisioned a brighter future for the exiles of Israel, while Edom would be erased from history.

SPIRITUAL INSIGHT

The last words of Obadiah introduce what is perhaps the book's most important lesson: "The kingdom will be the LORD's," the prophet declared (Obadiah 1:21). At the end of all things, it is God—and no human power—that rules over the nations and the territories they possess.

Philip found Nathanael and told him, "We have found the one
Moses wrote about in the Law, and about whom the
prophets also wrote—Jesus of Nazareth, the son of Joseph."
JOHN 1:45

P hilip's first act as a disciple of Jesus was to recruit yet another disciple. But the few other glimpses of Philip in the New Testament suggest a man who was not quite sure of himself.

John shared four episodes involving Philip and Jesus. In the first one, Jesus issued the call to Philip to become His disciple. As Andrew had done with Peter, Philip's first impulse was to share the invitation with another—in this case, Nathanael from Cana. At first, Nathanael was skeptical, but Philip persisted; he didn't argue with Nathanael but simply told him to come and see for himself. Apparently Philip's faith in Jesus was strong enough to convince him that one encounter would forever change Nathanael's opinion of the Nazarene.

The other three episodes suggest a certain lack of confidence on Philip's part. When Jesus wanted to feed the crowd that had gathered on the shores of Galilee, He asked Philip where they could find bread— perhaps because Philip was from nearby Bethsaida and knew the area well. Philip,

PHILIP

Disciple of Jesus

however, was stumped by what he believed was the greater problem: Even if there were a place to buy enough bread, there was no way Jesus could afford the massive sum of money that would be required. Seeing only the problem, Philip missed the obvious answer to Jesus' question it was staring him in the face.

Later John noted that some Greeks approached Philip, seeking an audience with Jesus. For some reason, Philip did not take the matter directly to the Master, but went instead to Andrew, who then informed Jesus of the situation.

In one final scene shortly before Jesus' death, Philip found his courage and addressed the Master, asking Him to show them the Father—not realizing that, as Jesus would tell him, "Anyone who has seen [Jesus] has seen the Father" (John 14:9).

SPIRITUAL INSIGHT

Despite what was perhaps a quiet performance in the Gospels, Philip's faithfulness to Christ is confirmed by his presence among the disciples after Jesus' ascension to heaven. He was there when the disciples faced their first major decision: how to replace Judas Iscariot (see Acts 1:13).

*So the LORD stirred up the spirit of Zerubbabel son of Shealtiel,
governor of Judah, and the spirit of Joshua [Jeshua] son of
Jehozadak, the high priest, and the spirit of the whole remnant of
the people. They came and began to work on the house
of the LORD Almighty, their God.*

HAGGAI 1:14

When hard times come, a person can choose to wallow or to work. Jeshua definitely chose to work.

It's not that Jeshua (sometimes called Joshua) did not have plenty of reason to wallow in his troubles. He lived during the time when all the leaders of Judah and their families had been exiled to Babylon. The exile had stripped them of virtually everything they had before—property, prestige, power—and now they had recently returned to their devastated land. Surely it would have been enough to make anyone feel completely hopeless at the future that lay ahead.

JESHUA

High Priest

But Jeshua, who was the high priest, and Zerubbabel, the governor of Judah, chose instead to work. As soon as they returned to Judah, they set up the altar so that the daily sacrifices prescribed in the Law of Moses could be resumed. Immediately after this, they got to work rebuilding the temple and completed the foundation (Ezra 3–4). After a long delay in the project due to opposition from hostile neighbors, the prophets Haggai and Zechariah stirred up Jeshua and Zerubbabel to finish the temple, and the work was finally completed (Ezra 5–6).

SPIRITUAL INSIGHT

Despite all the loss they had already experienced and the hardships that lay ahead, Jeshua and Zerubbabel chose to take up God's call to rebuild the altar and the temple and bring glory to Him. We all face hard times—and we have the opportunity to make the same choice in life. In God's power, choose not to wallow but to work to bring glory to God in the midst of difficulty.

And there was a man in Maon whose business was in Carmel. The man was very rich; he had three thousand sheep and a thousand goats. He was shearing his sheep in Carmel.

1 Samuel 25:2 ESV

Some people just seem to be begging for harm to come to them—the guy who flies down the highway at ninety miles per hour, the kids who play outside during a thunderstorm, the woman who shoplifts a few things here and there. Nabal, whose name appropriately means "fool," would have found good company with these people.

Nabal was a wealthy landowner who lived in Carmel, about fifteen miles west of En-gedi on the Dead Sea, the area where David and his men were hiding from Saul. David's men had been careful not to harass Nabal's servants as they looked after his huge flocks of sheep and goats, and David's men even provided protection for Nabal's flocks against bandits in the area (1 Samuel 25:15–16). So when the time came for Nabal to shear his sheep and reap the profits, David sent his men to ask for a gratuity. Nabal, true to his name, refused—and it was only the shrewd intervention of his wife that kept David from completely wiping out Nabal and his men. In the end, Nabal was struck dead by the Lord (1 Samuel 25:37–38), and David married his widow.

NABAL

Wealthy Fool Who Rebuffed David

Everyone must submit himself to the governing authorities,
for there is no authority except that which God has established.

ROMANS 13:1

Nero is not mentioned by name in the New Testament, but his impact on the fledgling church was so notorious that some early Christians came to regard him as the Antichrist.

Nero came to power in AD 54, aided by his scheming mother, Agrippina, who had charmed her way into the affections of Claudius, the previous emperor. Nero's mother very likely instigated Claudius's assassination by poisoning—and Nero seems to have inherited his mother's homicidal tendencies, arranging her own demise a few years later.

Nero was regarded as a megalomaniac. Much to the consternation of Rome's staid nobility, Nero loved to compose his own songs and perform them publicly. Desperate for adulation, Nero made an extended visit to Greece, where his flamboyant performances were more enthusiastically received. Just prior to his suicide, Nero is said to have lamented that the world was about to lose a great artist.

NERO

Deranged Roman Emperor

As emperor, Nero proved a menace to the church. When large sections of Rome burned to the ground in AD 64, Nero blamed the fire on the local Christian sect. According to the historian Tacitus, a contemporary of Nero, Rome's displaced population suspected its own emperor of arson. As an unpopular minority falsely accused of everything from orgies to cannibalism, Christians proved an easy scapegoat. On Nero's orders, a number of believers were brutally executed. Some were covered in animal skins and torn apart by dogs, others were crucified, still others were lit as human torches.

This was the emperor to whom Paul appealed his case just a few years before the great fire (see Acts 25). As a Roman citizen, Paul had the right to personally defend himself before Caesar. While Paul's exact fate remains a matter of speculation, one early tradition held that Paul was beheaded on Nero's orders, shortly before the emperor's own downfall.

SPIRITUAL INSIGHT

Paul's teaching concerning the "governing authorities" (see Romans 13:1) is especially poignant when one considers just who the "governing authority" was at the time: Nero. Christians, Paul taught, are to be good citizens regardless of who sits on the throne.

*But Saul had given his daughter Michal, David's wife,
to Paltiel son of Laish, who was from Gallim.*
1 SAMUEL 25:44

W ith the death of Saul, Paltiel's fortunes changed dramatically. One moment, he was husband to the king's daughter, perhaps destined for a place in the royal court himself. The next moment, he was alone—having lost the bride who was not rightfully his in the first place.

Paltiel belonged to the tribe of Benjamin, the same tribe as Saul, Israel's first king. Saul had promised his daughter Michal to David in return for killing one hundred Philistines—and bringing back some rather unpleasant proof of his achievement. Saul thought he was sending David on a suicide mission; but much to Saul's astonishment, David succeeded—killing twice the required number of Philistines. Saul kept his promise, allowing David to wed Michal who was, conveniently enough, in love with David.

However, Saul continued his efforts to kill David, believing him a threat to the throne. At one point, Michal had to conspire against her own father in order to save David's life. Realizing he was no longer safe in Saul's presence, David fled, leaving Michal behind.

PALTIEL

Michal's Temporary Husband

In David's absence, Saul took it upon himself to annul David's marriage, disowning him, and giving Michal to Paltiel instead. Perhaps Saul considered Paltiel a safer choice of a son-in-law. Since he belonged to the same tribe as Saul, Paltiel was more likely to remain loyal to the king. The great irony is that Saul delivered this insult in between two encounters with David where the latter spared the king's life.

Eventually, Saul died in battle with the Philistines, and David prepared to take the throne that was his by divine appointment. When Abner, Saul's military commander, defected to David's side, the soon-to-be king made one demand: David wanted his wife back. Michal was escorted from Paltiel's house to David's, Paltiel following behind in a rather pathetic display until Abner ordered him to turn back.

DID YOU KNOW?

Michal was taken from Paltiel and returned to David on orders from Ish-bosheth, the son of Saul who attempted to sit on his father's throne until he was murdered. Perhaps sensing the weakness of his own position—or perhaps hoping in vain to appease his rival to the throne—Ish-bosheth complied with David's demand.

And all the king's servants who were at the king's gate bowed
down and paid homage to Haman, for the king had so commanded
concerning him. But Mordecai did not bow down or pay homage.
ESTHER 3:2 ESV

From lying about our accomplishments to driving ourselves into debt to "keep up with the Joneses," there is no limit to what pride can make people do. Given enough opportunity, pride could probably even lead us to do something even as sinister as what Haman did.

HAMAN

Enemy of the Jews
during Esther's Time

Haman was a high government official in the mighty Persian Empire. The Persians ruled over virtually all the known world at the time, including the land of Israel—and there were many Jews living in Susa, the capital of the empire. Haman had recently been bestowed with high honor within the government, and his heart was completely puffed up with pride. Everyone was required to bow in his presence.

When a Jew named Mordecai refused to bow down, Haman became furious and made plans to exterminate *all* the Jews in the empire. Unbeknownst to Haman, however, the new queen, Esther, was a Jew—and she was related to Mordecai. When Mordecai and Esther learned of Haman's evil plot, the queen hatched a plot herself to inform the king. At a grand banquet hosted by the queen, she revealed Haman's wicked plan to exterminate her people. In the end the Jews were saved, and Haman and his sons were killed instead.

SPIRITUAL INSIGHT

It may be tempting to think that we are above something so wicked as Haman's plot, but we are all susceptible to sin—any sin—and given the right circumstances we can be led to do things we never imagined we were capable of. What sins are lurking in your heart? Do you secretly harbor prideful thoughts? Sinful desires? Hateful grudges? Expose them in prayer before God and repent of them before your sins expose you and lead you to certain destruction.

*[David] said to Nathan the prophet, "Here I am,
living in a palace of cedar, while the ark of God remains in a tent."*
2 SAMUEL 7:2

Nathan was to David what Samuel was to Saul: a constant prophetic reminder that Israel's king was answerable to God. The only difference was that David actually listened to Nathan.

Nathan was present in three episodes of David's story. While his recorded appearances were few and far between, they suggested a closeness that existed between David and his trusted prophet. On the first occasion, David confided in Nathan his desire to build a permanent house for God to replace the portable tabernacle that had been used since the Israelites left Egypt. Nathan delivered God's answer—a refusal mixed with profound blessing. While God would not allow David to build Him a temple (that responsibility fell to his successor, Solomon), He promised to bless David with rest from his enemies and an everlasting dynasty (see 2 Samuel 7:1–17).

Sometime later, Nathan brought God's word to David once again—though under very different circumstances. David had seduced Bathsheba and arranged her husband's murder so he could take her as his own wife. Such behavior by the monarch would have been tolerated in almost any other kingdom—but not in Israel. Nathan confronted David, using the first parable recorded in the Bible to compare David to a rich man who stole a poor man's only lamb. David acknowledged his sin, but the damage was done. Nathan foretold that David and Bathsheba's first son would die—and that David and his heirs would forever be plagued by violence (see 2 Samuel 12).

NATHAN

Prophet to King David

In the final episode involving Nathan, the aging prophet worked to install one of David and Bathsheba's surviving sons, Solomon, on Israel's throne. God's favor had been with Solomon from birth (see 2 Samuel 12:24–25), so when another of David's sons conspired to take the throne, Nathan acted quickly—demonstrating shrewd political skills to match his prophetic wisdom. Together with Bathsheba, he convinced the dying King David to name Solomon heir to the throne.

SPIRITUAL INSIGHT	Nathan's story proves that even prophets get it wrong sometimes—namely, when they don't wait for God's direction. After David shared his desire to build God's temple, Nathan approved the idea without hesitation. However, when God spoke to Nathan, revealing a different plan, the prophet returned to his king—this time with the correct advice.

Then [the Israelites] turned and went up along the
road toward Bashan, and Og king of Bashan and his
whole army marched out to meet them in battle at Edrei.

NUMBERS 21:33

It's been said that the bigger they are, the harder they fall. Og certainly proved this cliché true.

Og controlled sixty cities—each of them boasting high walls and other defenses—in the territory of Bashan, which abutted the northeast corner of the Promised Land. As one of the obstacles the Israelites had to overcome before entering Canaan, Og's kingdom represented an imposing barrier to their inheritance of the land—and not just because of Bashan's well-fortified cities.

OG

Amorite King

In his farewell speech to the Israelites, Moses remembered Og as the last of the Rephaites, an ancient race first mentioned in Genesis 14 when Abraham had to rescue his nephew Lot. The Rephaites were considered giants—as tall as the Anakites, according to Moses. (Years earlier, when Moses had commissioned several spies to report on the Promised Land, they had quailed at the site of Anakites dwelling there.) As if to bring the point home, Moses reminded his audience of the size of Og's legendary iron bed: nine cubits—that is, thirteen feet long.

Og would have made a fierce enemy for Israel, except for one thing: God had promised to deliver him into Moses' hands—and not just Og, but his entire army and all sixty fortified cities. When Og and his army marched out to confront the Israelites—who had once lost their courage at the mere thought of combating giants—the battle was swift and decisive. The book of Numbers simply says, "So they struck him down, together with his sons and his whole army, leaving them no survivors" (Numbers 21:35). Og's defeat helped clear the Israelites' way into the Promised Land.

Then the king commanded Ebed-Melech the Cushite,
"Take thirty men from here with you and lift Jeremiah
the prophet out of the cistern before he dies."
JEREMIAH 38:10

T he Bible never says if Jesus was talking about a real person when He told the story of the Good Samaritan, but if He was, He certainly would have found a good model in Ebed-Melech—right down to the fact that Ebed-Melech wasn't even an Israelite.

The Bible says that Ebed-Melech was a "Cushite," meaning that he was from Cush, a land south of Egypt. Ebed-Melech was almost certainly black-skinned and would have been immediately recognizable as a Cushite. He was one of King Zedekiah's officials, so he lived during the time just before the Babylonians invaded Judah and destroyed Jerusalem and the temple.

EBED-MELECH

Judean Official
Who Helped Jeremiah

When Jeremiah warned the people that Jerusalem would soon be captured by the Babylonians, several royal officials arrested him and received permission from Zedekiah to lower him into an empty cistern. When Ebed-Melech saw him, however, he was afraid that Jeremiah would starve to death—so he received permission from Zedekiah to pull Jeremiah out of the cistern, even taking care to cover the ropes with rags to keep them from hurting Jeremiah (Jeremiah 38).

Because Ebed-Melech trusted in the Lord and saved Jeremiah, the Lord promised to save Ebed-Melech's life when Jerusalem fell to the Babylonians.

RELATED INFORMATION

Although the kingdom of Cush had several hostile encounters with Judah, there is a particularly hopeful promise about them in Psalm 87:4: "I will record Rahab and Babylon among those who acknowledge me—Philistia too, and Tyre, along with Cush—and will say, 'This one was born in Zion.'"

Day 236

This is what happened during the time of Xerxes, the Xerxes who ruled over 127 provinces stretching from India to Cush.

ESTHER 1:1

D o you ever feel as if you are completely at the mercy of godless leaders? God's people in the days of King Xerxes must have felt the same. But, as the book of Esther shows, God's plans are never frustrated by sinful people—and He can even use those same people to accomplish His will.

Clearly Xerxes was a sinful unbeliever, and he ruled over the greatest empire of his day. Over a century earlier, the lands of Israel and Judah had been conquered and Jews were scattered throughout the Near East, ruled by Xerxes. Neither Xerxes nor most of his officials worshipped God, and a plot had even been hatched to exterminate all the Jews. Where was God? What was to become of His people?

XERXES

King of Persia

Not to fear. God was still God, and Xerxes could do only what God allowed. The story of Esther describes how God orchestrated events so that Esther gained favor in Xerxes's eyes as one of his wives—and she was able to reveal the evil plot to him. In the end, God's people were saved, and Xerxes himself ordered the execution of those who had arranged for the Jews' destruction (Esther 9:14). Xerxes even promoted Esther's relative to the second highest position in the empire!

DID YOU KNOW? Xerxes is usually identified by scholars as King Xerxes I of Persia. This is the same Xerxes whose mighty army was delayed for three days at Thermopylae by three hundred Spartan warriors and whose fleet was destroyed by other Greek city-states at Salamis.

"[The LORD] has given both him and Oholiab son of Ahisamach, of the tribe of Dan, the ability to teach others. He has filled them with skill to do all kinds of work as craftsmen, designers, embroiderers in blue, purple and scarlet yarn and fine linen."
EXODUS 35:34–35

Being renowned for one's skill in embroidery may seem like a strange way to be remembered in the Bible. Yet this was Oholiab's legacy, a fleeting yet powerful reminder that the Creator—the grand designer of the universe—values artistry and beauty.

Oholiab is mentioned just three times in the book of Exodus—each time in connection with the tabernacle that was to be built so Israel could worship God in the wilderness. Oholiab was made assistant to Bezalel, who was in charge of making artistic designs for God's tabernacle using gold, silver, bronze, stone, and wood. Both men were handpicked by God—the raw talent they possessed was said to be divinely inspired.

Oholiab was identified as a "craftsman and designer, and an embroiderer" (Exodus 38:23). His media were fine linen and brightly colored, expensive yarn. Elsewhere, the text noted that Oholiab and Bezalel were blessed with the talent for sharing their knowledge with others, too (Exodus 35:34). Rather than keeping his skills to himself, Oholiab apprenticed other craftsmen so they could join him and Bezalel in creating a beautiful space for worship.

OHOLIAB

Tabernacle Craftsman

In a story where the most popular figures are mighty deliverers like Moses or valiant warriors like Joshua, Oholiab stands out as another kind of hero—one who understands that the God who invented beauty in the first place values artistry and excellence in humanity's worship of Him. Oholiab gave the very best of his artistic abilities to create an aesthetically pleasing space that would inspire the hearts of his fellow Israelites to exalt their Lord and Master.

DID YOU KNOW?

Oholiab belonged to the tribe of Dan, an otherwise obscure clan in Israel's story. Dan was so marginal, in fact, that it did not appear at all in the list of tribes in Revelation 7. Oholiab, however, stood out as a shining example of brilliance.

*Araunah said to David, "Take it! Let my lord the king do whatever
pleases him. Look, I will give the oxen for the burnt offerings,
the threshing sledges for the wood, and the wheat for the
grain offering. I will give all this."*

1 CHRONICLES 21:23

The events that led to the sale of Araunah's threshing floor to King David
were strange indeed—almost as unexpected as what God had in store next for
Araunah's tract of land.

Araunah (some translations use the name Ornan in 1 Chronicles) was a Jebusite, one of the early inhabitants of Jerusalem before David took the city and
made it his capital. Araunah owned a threshing floor on top of Mount Moriah.
A threshing floor was simply a flat piece of compacted earth or stone where grain
was separated from the inedible chaff that surrounds each kernel. Threshing was
an essential step before the wheat harvest could be made into flour. Such floors
were often located atop hills or high plains, where the winds could blow away the
chaff, leaving behind the heavier kernels of grain.

ARAUNAH

Sold a Threshing
Floor to David

David purchased Araunah's threshing
floor after a devastating plague killed about
seventy thousand Israelites. The plague
was God's punishment for David's census,
which had been conducted to determine
how many fighting men he had at his
disposal. A census was not wrong in itself—
after all, God Himself had ordered the
census recorded in the book of Numbers.
But David's census seemed to be more about his own pride and self-assuredness
than anything else. Toward the end of the plague, David came face-to-face with
the angel of the Lord as he stood at Araunah's threshing floor. David begged for
mercy, saying that he alone deserved the punishment—and the Lord relented. A
prophet named Gad then instructed David to build an altar on the site. Araunah
was happy to give David the land, along with the oxen, wood, and grain needed
for the offerings. David, however, rebuffed Araunah's generosity and insisted on
paying the full price, not wanting to offer sacrifices that cost him nothing.

Some years later, David's successor, Solomon, built the temple on the site of
the old threshing floor.

Araunah's former threshing floor was actually the perfect site for
God's temple. Being situated on top of a hill gave the temple visual
and strategic prominence amid the Jerusalem landscape. Perhaps
more significantly, threshing was a symbol of the Lord's generous
provision. Every time God's people worshipped in His temple, they
would be reminded that it was He who sustained them.

For Ezra had devoted himself to the study and observance of the Law of the LORD, and to teaching its decrees and laws in Israel.
EZRA 7:10

Ezra was a man with a very clear sense of purpose for his life: He had devoted himself to the study and observance of God's laws and to teaching them to God's people.

Ezra was both a priest and a scribe. As a priest, he was trained in the rituals and laws regarding atonement for sin and coming before God on behalf of the people. As a scribe, Ezra's chief goal was to preserve and pass on the scriptures and explain them to others. Ezra led a group of about five thousand Jewish exiles from Babylon to Judea around 459 BC, about seventy years after the first waves of exiles were allowed to return. The dangerous journey took about four months.

EZRA

Priest and Scribe
after the Exile

After Ezra arrived in Judea, he immediately began addressing wrongs that were being done in the land, and he led the people in repentance and recommitment to follow God's laws (Ezra 9–10). Soon after the walls of Jerusalem were rebuilt, Ezra read the law from morning until midday, and this sparked a new fervor among the people to follow God's laws (Nehemiah 8).

Jewish tradition also holds that Ezra founded the Great Assembly, which was the forerunner of the Sanhedrin, the council of Jewish leaders.

DID YOU KNOW? The book of Ezra, which may have been written by Ezra himself, is one of two books in the Bible that has significant portions of it written in Aramaic, a sister language to Hebrew. The other is the book of Daniel, which was also written around the time of the exile. Aramaic was the language of the Babylonian Empire.

I [Paul] appeal to you [Philemon] for my son Onesimus, who became my son while I was in chains. Formerly he was useless to you, but now he has become useful both to you and to me.

PHILEMON 1:10-11

As songwriter Bob Dylan put it, "You're gonna have to serve somebody." If Onesimus had lived in our day, he couldn't have agreed more.

ONESIMUS

A Runaway Slave Who Gained a New Master

Onesimus, a slave of a Colossian believer named Philemon, had run away from his master and somehow ended up meeting Paul. In an amazing display of the power of the gospel to change lives, Onesimus apparently became a believer and agreed to return to Philemon to face whatever consequences awaited him. At the same time, Paul sent a letter (now known as the New Testament book of Philemon) with him telling Philemon of how useful Onesimus, whose name means "useful," had become to him. In the letter, Paul urged Philemon to welcome Onesimus back as a brother rather than a slave. Paul even asked Philemon to charge to him any debt incurred by Onesimus, although Paul was quick to point out that Philemon owed his very self to Paul—most likely meaning that Paul had led Philemon to Christ.

And just in case Philemon needed some extra encouragement, Paul asked him to prepare a guest room in case he happened to stop as he passed through Colosse! Surely the thought of physically looking Paul in the eye was all the motivation he needed to do the right thing.

SPIRITUAL INSIGHT

The question remains: Who are you going to serve? If you had asked Onesimus before he became a believer, he may have bitterly answered, "Philemon," or perhaps after he fled, "No one but myself." But in the end, we all serve somebody else—either the Lord or the devil. After Onesimus became a believer, he went back to Philemon perhaps expecting to return to a life of servitude, but really he was serving the Lord. Who are you going to serve?

*"Now I will hand all your countries over to my
servant Nebuchadnezzar king of Babylon;
I will make even the wild animals subject to him."*
JEREMIAH 27:6

No pagan ruler played a more prominent role in the biblical drama than King Nebuchadnezzar of Babylon. Nebuchadnezzar's exploits are well documented in both scripture and extrabiblical sources.

After a successful career commanding the Babylonian army, Nebuchadnezzar inherited his father's throne near the end of the seventh century BC. He reigned more than four decades.

Among his many conquests, Nebuchadnezzar made numerous incursions into Jewish territory. Initially, Nebuchadnezzar allowed Judah's kings to remain on the throne, so long as they kept up their tribute payments. The first of these kings, Jehoiakim, rebelled, switching loyalties from Babylon to Egypt. In retaliation, Nebuchadnezzar removed Jehoiakim from the throne and plundered the temple. Jehoiakim's successors, Jehoiachin and Zedekiah, fared no better. Finally, in 586 BC, Nebuchadnezzar razed Jerusalem, destroyed the

NEBUCHADNEZZAR

King of Babylon

temple, and carried the surviving inhabitants into exile. The kingdom of Judah was defeated.

For all his pomp and power, though, Nebuchadnezzar was nothing more than God's instrument. The prophet Jeremiah revealed that it was God who gave Judah into Nebuchadnezzar's hands (see Jeremiah 21:7). God was responsible for his victories over Tyre and Egypt (see Ezekiel 29:17–20).

Once, in response to Daniel's successful interpretation of a dream, the Babylonian king had acknowledged the supremacy of Israel's God (see Daniel 2:46–47). Soon, however, Nebuchadnezzar forgot and attributed his successes to his own "mighty power" (Daniel 4:30). In response, God afflicted Nebuchadnezzar with temporary insanity—as He had promised earlier. Once his sanity was restored, Nebuchadnezzar acknowledged the supremacy of the Lord once more. "His dominion," Nebuchadnezzar declared, "is an eternal dominion" (Daniel 4:34).

DID YOU KNOW?

Nebuchadnezzar is a rare, pagan contributor to the Bible. The fourth chapter of Daniel is attributed to the Babylonian ruler. Nebuchadnezzar's adulation of the one true God seems to have represented something less than true conversion, as he alluded to Marduk (also known as Bel, for whom Daniel was renamed Belteshazzar) as "my god" (see Daniel 4:8).

But a Pharisee in the council named Gamaliel, a teacher of the law held in honor by all the people, stood up and gave orders to put the men outside for a little while.

Acts 5:34 esv

Gamaliel is a great example of the immense impact that a teacher—even an unbeliever—can have on the world. Gamaliel does not appear to have been a Christian, but through his student Saul/Paul he may well have had the greatest positive influence on Christianity of any unbeliever in history.

The Bible first mentions Gamaliel in connection with Peter and the other apostles, who were arrested for preaching in the name of Jesus Christ. Gamaliel, a respected teacher of Jewish law, persuaded the Sanhedrin to release the apostles and leave them alone—because if they were not from God, their cause would die out, just as many others had. But if they were from God, the Jewish leaders would be fighting against God Himself (Acts 5).

GAMALIEL

Jewish Rabbi and Paul's Mentor

The only other time the Bible mentions Gamaliel is in a speech made by the apostle Paul. When Paul arrived in Jerusalem at the end of his third missionary journey, many Jews accused him of various offenses. Paul began his defense by recounting that he was educated by Gamaliel and was thoroughly trained in the law. He zealously persecuted Christians, but later the Lord appeared to him, and he became a Christian himself. Paul's thorough training in the law under Gamaliel's teaching eventually helped Paul to see how the law points to Jesus Christ, who fulfilled the law for us. Paul's ministry has helped to spread the good news of Jesus Christ throughout the world.

DID YOU KNOW?

Gamaliel was the grandson of Hillel, a famous teacher of religious law. Among other things, Hillel, who lived shortly before the time of Jesus, became well-known for stating a saying very similar to the Golden Rule (Matthew 7:12): "What is hateful to you, do not do to your fellow: this is the whole Law; the rest is the explanation; go and learn."

Abraham agreed to Ephron's terms and weighed out for him the price he had named in the hearing of the Hittites: four hundred shekels of silver, according to the weight current among the merchants.
GENESIS 23:16

Day
243

W hile Ephron's story in scripture may not provide much in the way of spiritual lessons, his interactions with Abraham nevertheless offer an interesting window into typical business transactions in the ancient Near East. Ephron and Abraham conducted their business in keeping with what any honorable man would have done in that day.

When Abraham's wife Sarah died, Abraham was living among the Hittites near the town of Hebron, almost twenty miles southwest of Jerusalem. As an alien, Abraham did not own a proper place to bury Sarah according to the customs of that time, so he needed to buy some land for that purpose.

EPHRON

Hittite Who Sold Abraham a Burial Cave

Abraham and the Hittites wound their way through the delicate steps of business protocol, including the overture of giving the property to Abraham outright and his refusal to accept such a gift. In the end, they arrived at the sum of four hundred shekels of silver—likely the price that each expected from the beginning (Genesis 23).

Ephron's cave would serve as the permanent burial place for Abraham's family, including Abraham and Sarah, Isaac and Rebekah, and Jacob and Leah (Genesis 49:29–31).

RELATED INFORMATION

Abraham and Ephron conducted their business at the city gate, which functioned much like a local courthouse does today. There business deals were recorded and ratified, and judgments were often rendered. Other examples of similar activity taking place at the city gates include Boaz's purchase of Ruth's property (Ruth 4) and Absalom's scheming appeals to those who came with grievances (2 Samuel 15).

And he said to him, "Please, Lord, how can I save Israel? Behold, my clan is the weakest in Manasseh, and I am the least in my father's house." And the LORD said to him, "But I will be with you, and you shall strike the Midianites as one man."

JUDGES 6:15–16 ESV

In a world weaned on the idea that success comes to those who believe in themselves, Gideon is a welcome misfit. Believing in himself—or even in the power of God for that matter—seemed virtually foreign to Gideon before God used him to do great things.

GIDEON

Judge of Israel

During a time when the Midianites were oppressing God's people, the Lord appeared to Gideon and told him to rescue His people—but Gideon responded pessimistically with, "How can I save Israel? Behold, my clan is the weakest in Manasseh, and I am the least in my father's house" (Judges 6:15 ESV). When the Lord told him to tear down his father's pagan altar, Gideon did so—but at night out of fear of his family and the townspeople. As Gideon prepared to fight the Midianites, he asked God two different times to send a sign to confirm that this was His will (Judges 6:34–40).

Even with Gideon's rather meek display of faith, however, God used him to rout the Midianites. And apparently in the process, God wanted to teach Gideon a lesson in faith—because He whittled Gideon's army down from thirty-two thousand to three hundred before the battle took place. In the end, Israel was rescued from the Midianites, and Gideon became a judge over the people for the rest of his life.

SPIRITUAL INSIGHT

Gideon is living proof that it is not the greatness of our faith that makes the difference but the greatness of the One in whom we have faith. Likewise, Jesus once said, "If you have faith as small as a mustard seed, you can say to this mountain, 'Move from here to there' and it will move. Nothing will be impossible for you" (Matthew 17:20). Take courage in the great God in whom we believe.

When the priest Pashhur son of Immer, the chief officer
in the temple of the LORD, heard Jeremiah prophesying these things,
he had Jeremiah the prophet beaten and put in the stocks.
JEREMIAH 20:1–2

Day
245

Pashhur appears only briefly in the Bible, but he played the antagonist in a bitter conflict with one of Israel's most polarizing prophets.

In the years leading up to Judah's exile, the priesthood had been compromised, becoming little more than a crutch to prop up a corrupt, wayward nation. God's blessing came to be taken for granted—as long as the temple stood and priests offered the designated sacrifices, what real harm could come to God's chosen nation?

Because the people forgot that God's blessing depended on their faithfulness, the stage was set for the confrontation between prophet and priest. Jeremiah (himself a member of the priestly class) railed against Judah's unfaithfulness. None—not even his fellow priests like Pashhur—was safe from the prophet's divinely inspired rage.

PASHHUR

Priest during
Jeremiah's Time

But Jeremiah did not just preach condemnation of sin—he foretold the demise of the entire nation, too. His words were regarded as unpatriotic, even treasonous. Jeremiah's prophecies threatened to send the entire nation into a panic (see Jeremiah 26:8–9). Because of this, Pashhur used his influence as the second highest-ranking priest in the temple to intimidate Jeremiah into silence. He ordered the prophet beaten and put in restraints for a day.

Apparently, Jeremiah failed to get the message. Pashhur, however, wound up with a new identity. After being released, Jeremiah declared that from now on, God's name for Pashhur was Magor-Missabib—Hebrew for "terror on every side." Not for the last time, Jeremiah predicted the downfall of his own country at the hands of Babylon.

SPIRITUAL INSIGHT

The incident involving Jeremiah and Pashhur contains a sobering lesson. Sometimes being faithful to God means we must do the unpopular, refusing to tow the party line or say what others want to hear. Jeremiah chose the path of unpopularity at great personal cost. Pashhur, on the other hand, chose not to listen and paid dearly for his error.

Then Absalom sent secret messengers throughout the tribes of Israel to say, "As soon as you hear the sound of the trumpets, then say, 'Absalom is king in Hebron.'"

2 SAMUEL 15:10

Absalom is described in the Bible as very handsome, with no blemish in his appearance (2 Samuel 14:25)—but his heart appears to have been stained with treachery.

ABSALOM

Son of David

Absalom was David's third son, born to the daughter of the king of Geshur, located on the northeast border of Israel. Absalom first revealed his treacherous heart when his full sister Tamar was taken advantage of by Absalom's half brother Amnon, David's oldest son by another wife (2 Samuel 13). Absalom bided his time for two years without saying a word to Amnon, all the while, though, plotting his revenge. Absalom arranged for his men to kill Amnon during a sheep-shearing celebration—then he fled to his mother's home in Geshur.

Later Absalom was allowed to return to Jerusalem, and he and David were reconciled. Even then, however, Absalom was plotting more treachery—this time against his own father.

For four years, Absalom worked to gain favor with many people in Israel—then he staged an outright rebellion in Hebron, about twenty miles south of Jerusalem. David had to flee to Mahanaim on the other side of the Jordan River and even fought against Absalom's men. Eventually Absalom was killed, and the rebellion came to an end.

RELATED INFORMATION

Absalom may have staged his rebellion in Hebron because this was the town of his birth (2 Samuel 3:2–3). There were probably already people there who knew Absalom and would have been sympathetic to his desire to become king.

Ahaziah was twenty-two years old when he became king,
and he reigned in Jerusalem one year. His mother's name
was Athaliah, a granddaughter of Omri king of Israel.
2 KINGS 8:26

As every parent knows, great danger lies in store for those who choose to walk in the company of the wicked (Psalm 1:1, 6). In Ahaziah's case, that danger eventually turned into awful reality.

AHAZIAH

King of Judah

To be fair, the deck seemed to be stacked against Ahaziah from the beginning, because he was born to Athaliah, who appears to have been the daughter of wicked King Ahab of Israel (2 Kings 8:26). By arranging for his daughter to marry King Jehoram of Judah, Ahab sealed a political alliance that gave him the upper hand between the two powers. As a result, the next few kings of Judah, including Jehoram's son Ahaziah, were forced to team up with the kings of Israel on various ventures.

As Ahaziah was visiting a wounded King Joram of Israel during one of those ventures (a battle at Ramoth-gilead), Jehu, an official in the army of Israel, killed both kings and then killed forty-two of Ahaziah's relatives who were coming to visit Joram (2 Kings 9–10). Ahaziah's reign was brought to an abrupt end after one year.

RELATED INFORMATION

Unfortunately, tragedy continued to plague Ahaziah's family even after Ahaziah died. Soon after his death, his power-hungry mother, Athaliah, tried to kill off the entire royal family, and she ruled Judah for six years. Only one of Ahaziah's sons, Joash, survived—thanks to the quick thinking of Ahaziah's sister Jehosheba. Eventually Ahaziah's son was crowned king, and Ahaziah's tragedies ceased (2 Kings 11).

Day

248

At Caesarea there was a man named Cornelius, a centurion
of what was known as the Italian Cohort, a devout man
who feared God with all his household, gave alms generously
to the people, and prayed continually to God.

ACTS 10:1–2 ESV

Cornelius has the distinction of being the first fully Gentile Christian recorded in scripture. Before Cornelius's conversion, Jews and even Samaritans (half-Jews who worshipped the Lord somewhat differently) had become Christians—but the Bible does not record that any Gentiles had become Christians yet, due in part to the fact that Peter and the other apostles did not even realize they could. But with Cornelius's conversion, all that would change forever.

CORNELIUS

God-Fearing Roman Centurion

Cornelius was a centurion—a Roman military officer—which would have normally put him at odds with Jews and perhaps many early Christians as well. But Cornelius had already demonstrated that God was at work in his life, because "he gave generously to those in need and prayed to God regularly" (Acts 10:2). One day God spoke to Cornelius and told him to send for the apostle Peter in another town about thirty miles away. Meanwhile, God was working in Peter's heart as well, showing him by a vision that all people—Gentiles as well as Jews—can find forgiveness of sins in Jesus Christ.

When Cornelius's men arrived at Peter's house, Peter went with them and shared the gospel with Cornelius's household. The Holy Spirit came upon the new believers, confirming that this was indeed a work of God.

RELATED INFORMATION

Though the Old Testament places a great deal of emphasis on the Jews as the chosen people of God (Genesis 12:1–3), there are still some passages that could have made it clear to Peter that God desires for Gentiles to follow Him as well. Jonah is corrected by God for his lack of concern for the wicked people of Nineveh even when they repented (Jonah 4). Psalm 87 also celebrates that various foreign peoples will be counted among those who know the Lord and registered as residents of Jerusalem.

*"All of them are hot as an oven; they devour their rulers.
All their kings fall, and none of them calls on me."*
HOSEA 7:7

Day
249

Pekahiah did not sit long on the throne of Israel. Reigning just two years, he bears the distinction of being the seventh Israelite monarch to be assassinated.

Pekahiah's father, Menahem, had come to power through treacherous means. Menahem appears to have died a peaceful death—a rare achievement during this period in Israel's history—and was succeeded by his son.

The author of 2 Kings had little to say about Pekahiah, and none of it was good. Like every one of his predecessors, Pekahiah persisted in the sins of the northern kingdom's first ruler, Jeroboam. Aside from this, not one accomplishment—good or bad— was recorded. The writer simply notes that Pekah, one of Pekahiah's chief officers, conspired to assassinate the king. Aided by fifty Gileadites, Pekah stormed the royal compound in Samaria, killing Pekahiah and two others.

PEKAHIAH

King of Israel

Scholars speculate that the assassination was motivated by a disagreement over Israel's diplomatic policy toward Assyria, the chief power and primary threat to the region. Presumably, Pekahiah had continued his father's policy of appeasement, preferring to bribe Assyria into keeping its distance rather than having to meet its army on the battlefield. Pekah, however, wanted to take a more aggressive posture toward Assyria, preferring to confront rather than wait for an invasion that seemed all but inevitable.

Indeed, Assyrian invasion did prove inevitable—and Pekah's policies were no more effective at preventing it than Pekahiah's had been. Neither Pekahiah nor Pekah lived to see Assyria's total triumph over the northern kingdom, but Israel nevertheless continued its downward spiral during their reigns.

DID YOU KNOW?

Writing about Israel's refusal to repent, the prophet Hosea summarized the tumultuous period that included the reign of Pekahiah, noting that "all their kings fall" (Hosea 7:7). Hosea's description was bleak yet accurate: Four of Israel's kings were murdered in a span of just two decades.

*"What are you, O mighty mountain? Before Zerubbabel
you will become level ground. Then he will bring out the
capstone to shouts of 'God bless it! God bless it!'"*

ZECHARIAH 4:7

The man whose name may mean "seed of Babylon" was anything but that. Zerubbabel came from Israelite stock—indeed, he was of royal blood.

Together with a high priest named Joshua, Zerubbabel led a group of Jewish exiles returning from Babylon to their homeland. It must have been a bittersweet journey for Zerubbabel. Despite the honor of leading his people toward home— he was the last known member of the royal family to be entrusted with any kind of political authority—the painful fact remained: Zerubbabel and the nation he represented were not in control of their own destiny.

ZERUBBABEL

Led a Group of Returning Exiles

Even though Zerubbabel could not restore Judah's sovereignty, he was determined to restore its relationship with God. Once settled in Jerusalem, he and Joshua the priest set about building a new altar. The people were understandably afraid— the last temple complex had been razed as a sign of Israel's subjugation to Babylon. Would the Persian authorities that now controlled the region see the rebuilding of their religious headquarters as an act of sedition? True, King Cyrus had personally approved the rebuilding project, but kings were known to change their minds—and perhaps worse, what if a new and less agreeable king came to the throne?

Zerubbabel persevered, bravely rebuffing a disingenuous offer of help from Israel's enemies. When that failed, his enemies lobbied Cyrus's successors, who forced a ten-year hiatus on building. However, with the encouragement of prophets like Haggai and Zechariah—and eventually the blessing of Persia's King Darius— Zerubbabel and the people got back to work. The temple they built would not be as grand as the one that preceded it, but Zerubbabel completed his task, faithfully leading the people to restore the house of worship.

SPIRITUAL INSIGHT

Zerubbabel received personal encouragement from God through the prophet Zechariah. "Not by might nor by power" would Zerubbabel fulfill his mission, according to God, "but by my Spirit" (Zechariah 4:6).

*So Zimri destroyed the whole family of Baasha,
in accordance with the word of the LORD spoken
against Baasha through the prophet Jehu.*
1 KINGS 16:12

Zimri had the unenviable distinction of being the shortest-reigning monarch in Jewish history—from either the northern or southern kingdoms.

Ironically, Zimri also managed to serve as an instrument in bringing God's judgment on his predecessors—not that he was conscious of his divinely ordained role. Zimri was neither the first nor the last ungodly ruler that the Lord used to achieve His sovereign purposes.

In Zimri's case, that purpose was to bring the dynasty of Baasha to its knees. Baasha had ruled the northern kingdom of Israel for twenty-four miserable years. He was so evil that God anointed the prophet Jehu to announce his family's doom. Baasha seems to have died peacefully, but the same cannot be said for his son Elah. Two years into his reign, Zimri assassinated Elah while the latter was drunk.

ZIMRI

King of Israel

However, Zimri did not stop there. Once he had installed himself on Israel's throne, Zimri waged a campaign of annihilation against Baasha's family. None—not even Baasha's own friends—survived. According to the writer of 1 Kings, Zimri's actions were divine punishment for Baasha's wickedness. Unfortunately, Zimri was no improvement on Baasha and Elah, so God orchestrated his downfall as well.

Zimri had managed to exterminate Baasha's family, but he had not rid the nation of all of Baasha's supporters. One of those supporters was the military commander Omri, whose troops proclaimed him king instead. With that, Omri stormed the palace. Zimri, knowing he was defeated, committed suicide—just seven days into his reign.

DID YOU KNOW?

Shortly before her death, Jezebel, the widow of Ahab, tried to turn Zimri's name into an insult. When Jehu came for her, she called down from a window, "Have you come in peace, Zimri, you murderer of your master?" (2 Kings 9:31). She was referring to Zimri's extermination of his predecessor's household.

After him, Ibzan of Bethlehem led Israel. He had thirty sons and thirty daughters. He gave his daughters away in marriage to those outside his clan, and for his sons he brought in thirty young women as wives from outside his clan.

JUDGES 12:8–9

Whatever the reason for his actions, Ibzan must have been a man of firm convictions. Ibzan was a judge of Israel for seven years after Jephthah of Gilead. Ibzan was from Bethlehem, but the Bible doesn't make it clear whether this was the same Bethlehem where David was born or another Bethlehem in the far north of Israel. In any case, Ibzan had thirty sons and thirty daughters, which suggests he was very wealthy and was a man of great influence.

IBZAN

Judge of Israel

The only other significant information we know about Ibzan is that he purposely arranged for each of his children to marry someone from "outside"—giving his daughters away to men from "outside," and bringing in women from "outside" to marry his sons (Judges 12:8–10). The Bible doesn't say specifically what "outside the clan" means, but it is likely that this meant someone who was still within their tribe. It is unlikely that he would have arranged for his children to marry non-Israelites.

By marrying his sons and daughters to people outside his clan, Ibzan may have been broadening his sphere of influence within his tribe, thereby elevating his status and perhaps even leading to his installment as a judge over Israel.

RELATED INFORMATION

Jewish tradition associates Ibzan with Boaz of Bethlehem (in Judah), who married Ruth and bore a son who became the grandfather of King David.

Some women were watching from a distance. Among them were Mary Magdalene, Mary the mother of James the younger and of Joses, and Salome. In Galilee these women had followed [Jesus] and cared for his needs.
MARK 15:40–41

When asked to think about Jesus' initial followers, the twelve disciples usually come to mind first. However, Mary the mother of James and Joseph (or Joses) is proof that Jesus' followers included a larger and more diverse group than just the Twelve.

Mary's background is the stuff of speculation. She may be one of the women that Luke mentioned early in his Gospel—women who had been miraculously healed by Jesus (see Luke 8:1–3). Luke noted that these women supported Jesus "out of their own means," a point that matches Mark's description of Mary (see Mark 15:40–41).

Mary was probably a woman of wealth, perhaps belonging to an aristocratic family. As such, she supported Jesus' ministry from behind the scenes, making sure His needs were always met. But Mary did not just support Jesus from a distance—she followed Him wherever He went, her

MARY

Witness to the Resurrection

presence as a woman no doubt raising some eyebrows in a patriarchal culture. Even as Jesus hung on the cross, Mary was there, watching her Master suffer.

Following Jesus' death, it was two women named Mary—Mary Magdalene and Mary the mother of James and Joseph—who went to His tomb to anoint the body. They ventured into the open, surely risking arrest and persecution, while the twelve disciples stayed behind. Because of their courage, they became the very first witnesses to the resurrection of Jesus Christ: The two Marys were greeted by an angel and then by Jesus Himself. Stunned, they ran to tell the disciples the unbelievably good news.

SPIRITUAL INSIGHT

While men dominated Mary's world, the Gospel writers made special note of the women included in Jesus' ministry, even though doing so might have jeopardized their message. The testimony of women was not considered reliable, as evidenced by the disciples' own reaction when the Marys arrived with news of the resurrection (see Luke 24:11). On the other hand, no one deliberately fabricating an event in the first-century world would have relied on a woman's testimony, making Mary's part in the story one of many convincing reasons to believe in the resurrection.

*I have been reminded of your sincere faith, which first lived in
your grandmother Lois and in your mother Eunice and,
I am persuaded, now lives in you also.*

2 TIMOTHY 1:5

Lois is the first of three generations of unlikely believers. Paul paid tribute to her and (presumably) her daughter Eunice in a letter to his young protégé Timothy.

LOIS

Timothy's Grandmother

Paul first arrived in Lystra, Lois's hometown, during his first missionary journey. While there, Paul healed a man who was unable to walk from birth, only to be mistaken as the incarnation of the Greek god Hermes. Subsequently, Paul was stoned by an angry mob and left for dead. Apparently the visit wasn't a total disaster, though. By the time he returned on his second missionary journey, Paul found at least three believers: Timothy, his mother, Eunice, and his grandmother Lois.

Little is known about Lois, the family matriarch. Her daughter Eunice had married a Greek, which may have generated social friction between the family and the rest of the Jewish community in Lystra. (Mixed marriages with pagans were roundly criticized in the Old Testament. Ezra, for example, was "appalled" at word that some of the returning exiles had taken Gentile spouses—see Ezra 9:4.)

In any case, Lois's grandson Timothy was a paradox—steeped in the Old Testament from a young age, no doubt thanks to Lois and Eunice, yet never circumcised, perhaps due to the influence of his Greek father. In the end, it was Lois's influence that prevailed, leaving a lasting mark on Timothy. Paul, impressed by Timothy's devotion to Christ, became his mentor and eventually made him pastor of the church at Ephesus.

SPIRITUAL INSIGHT	Lois serves as a reminder that it is not necessary to play a leading role in order to have a lasting impact. Mentioned by name just once in the Bible, Lois was nevertheless vital in shaping the character and convictions of one of the early church's most influential young pastors. Those who serve God behind the scenes play no less an important role than those who serve for all to see.

Day
255

*Amos answered Amaziah, "I was neither a prophet nor a
prophet's son, but I was a shepherd, and I also took care of
sycamore-fig trees. But the LORD took me from tending
the flock and said to me, 'Go, prophesy to my people Israel.'"*
AMOS 7:14–15

Acommon accusation in the world of American politics is that someone is a
"Washington insider," meaning he (or she) is so well connected in the affairs of
the federal government that he's not in touch or concerned with the affairs of the
common voter. Instead, he is mostly concerned with using his position to benefit
himself.

There were many such "Samaria insiders"
among the prophets of Amos's day, but
Amos was clearly not one of them. As Amos
himself said, he was neither a professional
prophet nor the son of a professional prophet,
but rather, a simple shepherd and farmer of
sycamore-fig trees (Amos 7:14–15). His
chief qualification for prophesying to the
kingdom of Israel was simply the Lord's calling on his life.

AMOS

Shepherd and Prophet
of Israel

To be fair, though, Amos should not be caricatured as an uneducated country
bumpkin who had a few spiritual jabs to give Israel. Instead, his prophecies reflect
a deep understanding of God Himself and the world in which he lived. His
prophecies must have emanated from a heart and mind that had been engaged in
these two expansive thoughts throughout his simple life.

Amos's prophecies warned Israel of the coming of the great "Day of the Lord"
that would bring judgment against the injustices of both the Israelites and their
neighbors.

SPIRITUAL INSIGHT

Amos's special calling by God and his refusal to become absorbed
into the self-serving world of the professional prophets challenge
believers today to make sure they are continually being "salt and
light" to the world (Matthew 5:13) and not simply becoming
an indistinguishable part of it. At the same time, Amos's deep
understanding of God and the world around him despite his simple
vocation calls us to strive for the same, whatever our calling in life.

Two sons were born to Eber: One was named Peleg,
because in his time the earth was divided.
GENESIS 10:25

Peleg is one of just two characters mentioned in the genealogy of Genesis 9–10 to be described in any detail. (The other is Nimrod.) Peleg's claim to fame was that the earth was divided during his lifetime.

Many have puzzled over the significance of this phrase. Some have suggested it refers to a massive shift of the earth's tectonic plates, resulting in the position of the continents as they are today. More likely, however, the answer lies in the very next chapter.

Genesis 11 tells the story of the tower of Babel. The people of the earth, sharing a common tongue, decided to build a city that featured an impressive tower. The very words they spoke betrayed their arrogance. Observing the scene, God concluded that if human beings united in their prideful pursuits, their sin would reach unthinkable levels. So God scattered the people, causing them to speak different languages and forcing them to spread far and wide.

PELEG

Descendant of Noah

Whether Peleg was present at the tower of Babel, somehow involved in its construction, is not known. He simply seems to be a reference point that the writer of Genesis used to anchor the story of Babel that follows the genealogy recorded in chapters 9–10.

DID YOU KNOW?

Peleg is mentioned in Luke's genealogy of Jesus. As one of the Messiah's earliest ancestors, he provided an important link from Adam to Jesus—that is, from the first Adam to the second Adam (see Luke 3:35).

Ahaz sent messengers to say to Tiglath-Pileser king of Assyria, "I am your servant and vassal. Come up and save me out of the hand of the king of Aram and of the king of Israel, who are attacking me."
2 KINGS 16:7

It's never a good idea to get yourself out of a jam by making a deal with the devil. Just ask King Ahaz of Judah.

To make matters worse, it was Ahaz who had gotten himself into the jam. Soon after he became king of Judah, he threw himself headlong into idolatry. He practiced it, and he even promoted and supported it throughout his kingdom (2 Chronicles 28:1–4).

AHAZ

King of Judah

Because of Ahaz's idolatry, the Lord allowed Israel and Aram to attack Judah and inflict terrible losses on His people. Perhaps in a moment of desperation, Ahaz called upon the king of Assyria to help. For years the Assyrians had been slowly engulfing all the nations of the Near East into their vast empire, and Ahaz decided to make Judah a subservient kingdom to Assyria if they would attack Aram and Israel and get them off his back. He also sent the Assyrians all the silver and gold from the temple and the royal palace (2 Kings 16).

Ahaz's plan worked in the short run, but he traded Judah's independence for it instead of depending on the Lord, and his interactions with the Assyrians led to even more idolatry. He even replaced the temple altar with a new one patterned after a pagan altar from Damascus (2 Kings 16; 2 Chronicles 28:24–25).

DID YOU KNOW?

Ahaz was the king to whom Isaiah made his famous prophecy regarding the coming of Immanuel ("God with us"). The prophecy was given to reassure Ahaz that he need not fear the threats of Israel and Aram, but Ahaz refused to trust in the Lord (Isaiah 7–9). As a result, the nation became subject to Assyria.

So the word of the LORD spoken to Jehu was fulfilled:
"Your descendants will sit on the throne
of Israel to the fourth generation."
2 KINGS 15:12

Zechariah's reign marked the beginning of the end for the northern kingdom of Israel—the final, tumultuous thirty years before the Assyrian Empire finally sacked Samaria. He was the exclamation point on the last period of relative calm ever seen in the northern kingdom.

ZECHARIAH

King of Israel

Before Zechariah, Israel's monarchy had enjoyed four peaceful successions. Zechariah inherited the throne from his father, Jeroboam II, who inherited it from Zechariah's grandfather, Jehoash, who inherited it from Zechariah's great-grandfather, Jehoahaz, who inherited the throne from Zechariah's great-great-grandfather, Joash.

After Zechariah, only one of Israel's remaining kings successfully transferred power to his son. Only one died under peaceful conditions. Four, including Zechariah, were assassinated by their successors. One was carried off into exile in 722 BC, when the Assyrians descended on the land as instruments of God's judgment.

The four kings that preceded Zechariah averaged over thirty years apiece on the throne. His father, Jeroboam II, reigned for more than four decades. Together, Zechariah and the kings who followed him averaged less than seven years each. Zechariah himself only managed six months on the throne—a rather embarrassing performance, compared to the standard set by the rest of his family.

Like his royal predecessors, Zechariah did evil in God's sight—he perpetuated the sins of his fathers, worshipping false gods. By this time, though, God had had enough. The endgame had begun. Zechariah was assassinated in front of his own people. Instead of his son, Zechariah's assassin, Shallum, succeeded him as king.

SPIRITUAL INSIGHT

If Zechariah had paid more attention to God, perhaps the end would not have come as much of a shock. Years before, God had promised Zechariah's great-great-grandfather Joash that his dynasty would last four generations—God's reward to Joash (the closest thing Israel ever had to a good king) for purging the northern kingdom of Ahab's family and their idolatry. With the ascent of Zechariah, God's promise had been fulfilled—and with his death, the monarchy descended into chaos.

*When the angels had left them and gone into heaven,
the shepherds said to one another, "Let's go to Bethlehem
and see this thing that has happened, which the Lord
has told us about."*
LUKE 2:15

If a child was born into a royal family today, there would be no end to the list of dignitaries who would be expected to visit the family and congratulate them. But when Jesus, the King of kings was born, the only people who even received an announcement were some lowly shepherds who might be compared to field hands today.

THE SHEPHERDS OF THE CHRISTMAS STORY

Shepherds Who Came to See Jesus after His Birth

Because of the nature of their work, shepherds were often seen as dirty, low-class, uncivilized people in Bible times. Their full-time job, night and day, was to look after their flocks of sheep or goats, leading them to pasture and water and away from danger. At times they even acted as the doorway to their sheep pens by sleeping across the opening. Kings were often regarded as shepherds over their people, but a king's life actually had little in common with the rustic, austere life of those who looked after flocks of animals.

But it was to such people—and only to such people—that the angels announced Jesus' birth. The angels appeared to them and told them where they could find the child—and the shepherds responded in faith and went. After they visited Jesus and His family, the shepherds returned to their fields, praising God for all that they had seen and telling everyone they met about it, too (Luke 2).

SPIRITUAL INSIGHT

Thankfully, God's measure of human worth has little in common with our measure. We tend to value appearance, prestige, wealth, or power, but God does not seem to be swayed by any of these things. God regarded the presence of some lowly shepherds as fitting honor for the birth of His only Son, the King of kings.

*Joseph named his firstborn Manasseh and said,
"It is because God has made me forget all my
trouble and all my father's household."*

GENESIS 41:51

Joseph thought the sons born to him in Egypt would help him forget the family that had betrayed him into slavery. He was wrong.

Manasseh was the firstborn son of Joseph and his Egyptian wife. By this time, Joseph had experienced a series of ups and downs in Egypt. He had enjoyed success as manager of Potiphar's household—only to be thrown in jail, falsely accused of trying to seduce Potiphar's wife. After languishing in prison for at least two years, Joseph appeared before the pharaoh to interpret his dreams. Joseph accurately predicted seven years of abundance followed by seven years of famine—and rose to prominence, becoming second only to Pharaoh himself. It was during the seven years of abundance that Joseph took a wife and started a family. The hope that his new family would replace the one he'd lost years before was reflected in the meaning of Manasseh's name: "making to forget."

MANASSEH

Son of Joseph

Joseph, however, would not be allowed to forget his family for long—and this forever changed the course of Manasseh's legacy. Some time after being reunited with his brothers and his aging father, Jacob, Joseph presented his two sons to receive the family blessing. Jacob, now going by the name Israel, took Manasseh and Ephraim on his lap and announced that they would be counted among his own sons. This act secured Manasseh's place alongside Judah, Levi, Benjamin, and the others as a forefather of one of Israel's twelve tribes.

Manasseh's descendants came to be renowned for their valor. They were among the first to capture territory in the Promised Land, and commanders from the tribe of Manasseh once aided the prophetess Deborah in driving out the Midianites.

SPIRITUAL INSIGHT

The story of Manasseh's birth includes one rather curious detail: His mother, Asenath, was the daughter of Potiphera (no known relation to Potiphar). Potiphera was a priest at On, a city devoted to the worship of the Egyptian sun god, Ra. The Bible does not say whether Asenath embraced the monotheism of Joseph's family. In any case, Joseph's choice of a spouse was a brush with idolatry—something that would plague Manasseh and his descendants for centuries to come.

Saul then said to his attendants, "Find me a woman
who is a medium, so I may go and inquire of her."
"There is one in Endor," they said.
1 SAMUEL 28:7

It wasn't as if Saul didn't know better.

The Law of Moses couldn't have been clearer on the matter of divination: Don't do it. Three times the book of Leviticus warned against acting as a medium or spiritist—or seeking the counsel of one (see Leviticus 19:31; 20:6, 27). And in case that had not been clear enough, Moses repeated the admonition in his farewell speech to the Israelites (see Deuteronomy 18:9–13). Saul had even taken it upon himself to expunge the mediums and spiritists from Israel—one of the few good things he had done as king.

WITCH OF ENDOR

Necromancer Visited by Saul

One, however, survived the purge: the unnamed witch at Endor. More precisely, she was a medium or necromancer—one who consulted the spirits of the dead. Saul went to her out of sheer desperation. God had long since given up talking to the king who would not listen, and Saul needed to know what to do about the Philistine army camped nearby. In one last pathetic scene before his death in battle, Saul asked the necromancer to conjure the spirit of Samuel using her ritual pit that was dug into the earth and supposedly connected to the underworld.

The game was up as soon as Saul mentioned the name Samuel. She understood immediately—face-to-face with the man who had driven her kind from the land, she cried out in terror. With reassurances from Saul, she proceeded to conjure Samuel's spirit. Saul, however, got more than he bargained for. Scholars debate the significance of what took place in 1 Samuel 28, but the writer seemed to accept that the figure who appeared was the deceased prophet. Samuel's words were not encouraging: He revealed that God was about to take the kingdom from Saul's hands and that by the following day Saul and his sons would be every bit as dead as Samuel was. Saul's fate was sealed.

SPIRITUAL INSIGHT

Some may question why God would allow Samuel (or some manifestation of him) to appear by means of a practice that was expressly forbidden. While the practice of divination is in no way encouraged in 1 Samuel 28—in fact, the story seems to highlight Saul's humiliation in sinking to such measures—it does affirm God's supreme power over all things seen and unseen. God's sovereignty extends even to the spirit world.

*"Therefore, say to the Israelites: 'I am the LORD,
and I will bring you out from under the yoke of the Egyptians.
I will free you from being slaves to them, and I will redeem you
with an outstretched arm and with mighty acts of judgment.'"*

EXODUS 6:6

P erhaps the most significant connection that Israelites have with the Egyptians
is their deliverance *from* them. This became a defining event in the identity of
Israel, characterizing God's relationship with His people.

The Egyptians lived along the Nile River to the southwest of Israel. They
formed one of the oldest and most powerful kingdoms in the ancient world. The
land around them was desert, but the Nile River swelled its banks each spring and
enabled crops to grow.

Israel's early contact with Egypt came through Jacob, whose family eventually

EGYPTIANS

Neighbors of Israel

settled in Egypt after Joseph rose to a high
position there (Genesis 35–49). Later, however,
the Egyptians began to oppress the Israelites,
and the Lord rescued them by ten miraculous
plagues (Exodus 1–15). This deliverance was
recounted for generations as the event that
established the Lord as the God of Israel
and formed the basis for Israel's obedience to
God's commandments (Exodus 20:2; 2 Kings
17:35–39).

Israel had little significant contact with the Egyptians for many years after this,
until the Babylonians were rising to power around 609 BC. Then the Egyptians
asserted their control over Israel, but the Babylonians gained the upper hand and
took over Israel (2 Kings 23–24).

After the time of Alexander the Great, Egypt was ruled by the descendants of
one of Alexander's generals, and Israel came under their rule as well. Later Egypt
came under the rule of the Roman Empire.

*"Now you [Solomon] yourself know what Joab son of Zeruiah
did to me [David]—what he did to the two commanders of
Israel's armies, Abner son of Ner and Amasa son of Jether.
He killed them, shedding their blood in peacetime as if in battle,
and with that blood stained the belt around his waist and the sandals on his feet."*
1 KINGS 2:5

Day
263

J esus warned His followers that "all those who take up the sword shall perish by
the sword"(Matthew 26:52 NASB). If there He was thinking of anyone in particular
from the Old Testament, it very well could have been Joab. Joab's life was stained
with blood from beginning to gory end.

As commander of David's army, Joab
demonstrated great military prowess, defeating an Ammonite coalition in two separate
encounters and even giving David the glory
of capturing the enemy capital. At the same
time, however, Joab committed several acts
that seem to demonstrate a much darker
side of his character. He personally avenged

JOAB

Commander of
David's Army

the death of his brother by stabbing Abner, a rival commander, to death (2 Samuel
3:26), and he used a similar tactic to assassinate another rival commander named
Amasa (2 Samuel 20:9–10). He also stabbed David's son Absalom, despite David's
direct orders for leniency toward Absalom (2 Samuel 18). Absalom had rebelled
against David and was fighting a battle against him at that time.

Joab also went along with David's scheme to have the warrior Uriah placed in
a military situation that would almost surely result in Uriah's death (2 Samuel 11).
Finally, Joab was instrumental in staging Adonijah's unsuccessful attempt to secure
the throne of his father, David. In the end, Joab himself met a bloody death as
Solomon carried out his father's deathbed requests. David gave Solomon what seems
like an Israelite version of a "hit list," and Joab was first on the list (2 Kings 2).

DID YOU KNOW?

Joab and his brothers Abishai and Asahel were David's nephews
by his sister Zeruiah (1 Chronicles 2:13–17). David's commander,
Amasa, was also a nephew of David by his other sister, Abigail.

*In one day Pekah son of Remaliah killed a hundred and
twenty thousand soldiers in Judah—because Judah
had forsaken the LORD, the God of their fathers.*

2 CHRONICLES 28:6

Pekah ascended to Israel's throne with great ambition to neutralize the Assyrian threat to his country. He was so disastrously unsuccessful that by the time his reign ended just five years later, Israel had ceded two-thirds of its territory.

Being from the northern kingdom, it hardly bears mentioning that Pekah was a failure in God's eyes—not one king of Israel managed to remain true to the Lord. Pekah had come to power by treacherous means. When he was a royal official serving in the government of his predecessor, Pekah assassinated the king and seized the throne for himself.

Once in power, Pekah concocted a plan to push back the ever-growing Assyrian threat. Unfortunately, time was not on Israel's side—Pekah consolidated his power less than twenty years before the nation collapsed under the weight of invasion. However, Pekah was convinced that by allying himself with other regional powers, together they could defeat the Assyrians. Pekah appears to have tried in vain to coerce Judah to join the alliance, but king Ahaz of Judah resisted, probably acting on instructions from the prophet Isaiah.

PEKAH

King of Israel

In retaliation, Pekah marched against Jerusalem. While unsuccessful at toppling Ahaz, Pekah's army managed to slaughter 120,000 soldiers of Judah. Some time later, the king of Assyria marched on Israel, invading from the north. The nation was overrun—Gilead and Galilee fell, and thousands were deported. Having lost two-thirds of their territory, many in Israel must have grumbled against Pekah. One man, Hoshea, took matters into his own hands and killed the Israelite king. In an ironic twist, Pekah's short reign ended with similar bloodshed that marked its beginning.

DID YOU KNOW?

Pekah's aggression against Judah provided the original context for one of the most famous prophecies in the Bible. Isaiah, having assured the king of Judah that Pekah's invasion would ultimately fail, encouraged Ahaz to ask God for a sign. When Ahaz refused, God gave him one anyway: "The virgin will be with child and will give birth to a son, and will call him Immanuel" (Isaiah 7:14). Centuries later, Matthew applied this prophecy to the miraculous virgin birth of Jesus (see Matthew 1:22–23).

Their teaching will spread like gangrene.
Among them are Hymenaeus and Philetus,
who have wandered away from the truth.
They say that the resurrection has already taken place,
and they destroy the faith of some.
2 TIMOTHY 2:17–18

D oes theology really matter? Doesn't it actually divide the church, rather than unite it and build it up? This common criticism toward doctrine, or official beliefs and teachings of the church, may sound appealing at first—but a careful look at a man named Hymenaeus should help us see that theology is indeed important and even critical to a healthy church.

What the Bible tells us about Hymenaeus is not good. Apparently he and two other men named Alexander and Philetus were stirring up the church in Ephesus with their teaching about the resurrection. It seems that Hymenaeus was teaching that the resurrection—the day when all the dead are raised to life and eternal judgment—had already taken place. It is not certain whether

HYMENAEUS

Early Christian Who
Spread False Teaching

this means that he was saying that the day had come and gone and that they had missed the event, or that somehow the resurrection occurred as part of their acceptance of new life in Christ. In any case, it was upsetting some other believers, who were no doubt confused and concerned by all this.

So did Paul simply downplay the significance of the teaching about the resurrection? Did he say that Hymenaeus is entitled to his beliefs? No. Paul described the effect of his teaching as "gangrene" (2 Timothy 2:17). In another passage, Paul also spoke of Hymenaeus as having been "handed over to Satan to be taught not to blaspheme" (1 Timothy 1:20), which might have had to do with his teaching as well.

RELATED INFORMATION	It is not known for sure exactly what Paul meant by "handed over to Satan" when speaking of Hymenaeus's punishment. Most scholars take it to mean some form of excommunication or conditional expulsion from the church to lead him to repent of his actions.

*The sons of Japheth: Gomer, Magog, Madai, Javan,
Tubal, Meshech and Tiras. The sons of Gomer:
Ashkenaz, Riphath and Togarmah.*

GENESIS 10:2–3

The Bible doesn't say much about Gomer, son of Japheth, as a person—but history has learned many things about his descendants, who appear to have been the ancient Cimmerians.

The Cimmerians originally lived north or west of the Black Sea, but at some point early in written history they were expelled by the Scythians and migrated down into present-day Turkey and parts of Iran. Skilled at horsemanship, they helped the Assyrians conquer the kingdom of Ararat and harassed the kings of Lydia and their capital at Sardis in western Turkey—even killing King Gyges himself.

Soon after this, the Cimmerians ceased to be a recognizable force in world history. But some of Gomer's descendants formed recognizable subgroups of their own: Ashkenaz's descendants probably became the Germanic, Scandinavian, and Slavic peoples; Riphath's descendants probably became the Paphlagonians in northern Turkey; and Togarmah's descendants probably became the Armenians and/or Phrygians. The ancient Thracians may have also descended from the Cimmerians.

GOMER

Son of Japheth

Homer wrote about a people group called the Cimmerians who lived at the edge of the world in a land of fog and darkness, but it's uncertain whether he was referring to the same people.

The book of Ezekiel mentions the people of Gomer along with the people of "Beth Togarmah from the far north" (Ezekiel 38:6), giving support to the connection between Gomer and the Cimmerians.

RELATED INFORMATION

Ashkenazi Jews are descended from Jewish communities in western Germany. The name came about because medieval Jews considered Germans to be descended from Ashkenaz.

I have thought it necessary to send to you Epaphroditus
my brother and fellow worker and fellow soldier,
and your messenger and minister to my need.
PHILIPPIANS 2:25 ESV

Afriend in need is a friend indeed." This is certainly true regarding Epaphroditus's faithful service to Paul. While Paul was in prison for preaching the gospel, the church in Philippi sent Epaphroditus to him with a gift to help provide for his needs. Epaphroditus faithfully delivered the gift to Paul, but he also became very ill—perhaps from the long journey—and almost died. Epaphroditus recovered, however, and Paul planned to send him back to the Philippians so that they no longer needed to be concerned for Epaphroditus's health.

EPAPHRODITUS

Coworker of Paul

Paul commended Epaphroditus to them as a "brother, fellow worker and fellow soldier" who "almost died for the work of Christ, risking his life to make up for the help you could not give me" (Philippians 2:25, 30). He even encouraged the Philippians to "honor men like him" (Philippians 2:29).

Philippi was the first city in Europe where Paul planted a church. On the Sabbath, he went to a nearby river to find a place of prayer, and he began to share the gospel with some women who had gathered there. One of the women who responded in faith was Lydia from the city of Thyatira in Asia Minor (Acts 16:12–14). Given his warm words in his letter to the Philippians, Paul must have always had very favorable regard for the church in Philippi, and their gift to him while he was in prison reflects that the feeling must have been mutual.

So both of Lot's daughters became pregnant by their father.
The older daughter had a son, and she named him Moab;
he is the father of the Moabites of today.
GENESIS 19:36–37

The tension between Abraham and his nephew Lot foreshadowed the tension that would exist between their descendants—the children of Israel and the children of Moab.

After Abraham and Lot parted ways, resolving their disputes by putting some distance between them, Lot settled in Sodom, the city that God destroyed for its infamous wickedness. God spared Lot and his daughters—largely out of kindness to Abraham—and they fled to the mountains. There, alone and seemingly with no other prospects for marriage, Lot's daughters decided to take matters into their own hands. Determined that their family line would endure, they each slept with their father after getting him drunk. As a result, Lot's oldest daughter gave birth to a boy named Moab, who became the ancestor of one of Israel's enemies.

MOAB

Son of Lot

By the time Israel's wandering in the wilderness was drawing to a close, Moab had grown into a nation of its own. Lying just to the east of Canaan, the land of Moab was overrun by Israelites as they prepared to enter the Promised Land. Determined to stop his new neighbors from moving in, the king of Moab summoned Balaam to put a curse on the Israelites. When that failed, Moab pursued another strategy: inviting Israelite men to its pagan festivities and seducing them with Moabite women. Ultimately, that tactic failed as well. In the time of the judges, Moab tried yet a third way of dealing with Israel: invasion. Eglon, king of Moab, joined with Israel's other enemies and attacked, putting Israel under his control for nearly two decades. Tension continued between Israel and Moab, but ultimately, Israel triumphed and at times even subjected Moab to its control.

DID YOU KNOW?

According to the book of Numbers, Hebrew poets derisively referred to the Moabites as the "people of Chemosh" (Numbers 21:29). Chemosh was the chief god of Moab. The worship of Chemosh was particularly detestable, as it sometimes involved child sacrifice. Sadly, this did not stop one of Israel's most famous kings, Solomon, from building a high place for Chemosh near Jerusalem (see 1 Kings 11:7).

Epaphras, who is one of you and a servant of Christ Jesus,
sends greetings. He is always wrestling in prayer for you,
that you may stand firm in all the will of God,
mature and fully assured.
Colossians 4:12

From restaurants to hardware stores to construction companies, customers know that two simple words often make all the difference: "family owned." An organization that is managed by the same people who have invested their heart and life savings in it will be distinctly different from one that is driven by the profit margins of a faceless corporation. The same was undoubtedly true for the way that Epaphras looked after the needs of the Colossian church.

What the Bible says about Epaphras speaks a lot for his devotion to Christ and to the Colossian church. He apparently came from Colosse (Colossians 4:12) and was a coworker with Paul while he was in prison. Paul even refers to him as a "fellow prisoner" in his letter to Philemon

Epaphras

Coworker of Paul

(Philemon 1: 23), although it is not clear if Paul meant this literally or not. In his letter to the Colossians, Paul refers to Epaphras as a "dear fellow servant" and "a faithful minister of Christ on our behalf" (Colossians 1:7). It seems that Epaphras first brought the gospel to his fellow Colossians, perhaps by Paul's directive, and he reported to Paul of the Colossians' love in the Spirit (Colossians 1:8).

Epaphras's great care for the Colossians is evident in the way that he was always "wrestling in prayer for [them], that [they] may stand firm in all the will of God, mature and fully assured" (Colossians 4:12). Paul vouched for him that he was working hard for them and for the churches in their neighboring cities of Laodicea and Hierapolis.

SPIRITUAL INSIGHT

How invested are you in your care for those around you? Do you "wrestle in prayer" for them that they may grow in spiritual maturity? Do you work hard to help them grow? Be a faithful minister to the people God brings into your life.

*There was also a prophetess, Anna. . . . She was very old;
she had lived with her husband seven years after her marriage,
and then was a widow until she was eighty-four.
She never left the temple but worshiped night
and day, fasting and praying.*

LUKE 2:36–37

It's almost too hard to imagine what that moment must have been like for Anna. For probably sixty years she had been a widow living at the temple, worshipping night and day, fasting and praying, even communicating prophecies to people. No doubt many of her thoughts and prayers focused on the coming Messiah and the redemption of Jerusalem.

Then all of a sudden, there He was—the Messiah—right in front of her. She heard what godly Simeon had said about Him, about how this baby was the Lord's salvation and a light to the Gentiles. Could it really be true?

ANNA

Prophetess and Widow Who Lived in the Temple

Anna came up to Mary and Joseph, thanking God for them and for their little baby, Jesus, the Savior of the world. What else could she say to them except thanks to God? Anna had plenty to say later, though—to everyone she met who was looking forward to the redemption of Jerusalem. She told them all about the baby she had seen in the temple and the hope that He was bringing to the entire world. Anna had seen the Messiah.

Most scholars place Jesus' birth at about 5 BC, which means that Anna would have been about twenty-six years old (and perhaps recently widowed) when the independent kingdom of Israel under the Hasmoneans was overtaken by the vast Roman Empire. Perhaps this is what led her to commit herself to fasting and praying day and night in the temple for the rest of her life.

By faith Noah, when warned about things not yet seen,
in holy fear built an ark to save his family.
HEBREWS 11:7

Day
271

The unknown writer of Hebrews described Noah as a precursor of the kind of faith it would take to follow Christ. Noah's story was also a foreshadowing of the kind of redemption that God would provide for His people.

Noah lived during a time of rapidly escalating depravity. During this time, according to the author of Genesis, "every inclination" of the human heart had turned evil—much to God's anguish (see Genesis 6:5–6). As a "righteous man," Noah stood in marked contrast from the rest of civilization. Noah's righteousness was not superficial, yet it consisted of just one thing: Noah "walked with God" (see Genesis 6:9) while the rest of humanity walked in the other direction.

In Genesis, two descriptions of humanity's wickedness bookend the account of Noah's righteousness, evoking the impression that God's lone worshipper was in danger of drowning amid a sea of wickedness. God, however, had other plans—intending to drown humanity's wickedness in a sea of judgment, sparing only Noah and his family.

The details concerning Noah, the ark he built, and the flood that ensued are well-known. Acting on nothing but faith, Noah built the ark to God's exact specifications. Twice the writer noted that Noah did "all" or "everything" just as God commanded (see Genesis 6:22; 7:5).

NOAH

Builder of the Ark

As for the ark that Noah built, the Hebrew word is unique, used in Noah's story and in just one other place: the tale of the baby Moses being placed in a basket so he could escape Pharaoh's infanticide (see Exodus 2:3). Noah and his ark—and the deliverance it represented for those who follow God—anticipated the story of Moses and Israel's miraculous deliverance from the Egyptians. Also, according to the author of Hebrews, Noah's faith provided a model that all believers should follow in their devotion to Christ.

DID YOU KNOW? There are other accounts of a catastrophic flood—complete with a Noah-like hero—besides the one found in the Bible. Other examples can be found in ancient Sumerian and Akkadian literature. In the Sumerian story, the hero is named Ziusuddu or Ziusudra. In the famous *Epic of Gilgamesh,* the flood hero is named Utanapishtim.

Nebuzaradan commander of the imperial guard, an official of the
king of Babylon, came to Jerusalem. He set fire to the temple of
the LORD, *the royal palace and all the houses of Jerusalem.*
Every important building he burned down.

2 KINGS 25:8–9

Nebuchadnezzar may have been the one who conquered Jerusalem, but it was Nebuzaradan who actually set fire to the city. Nebuzaradan and his men were the hands and feet that wrought Nebuchadnezzar's destruction. He was also responsible for rescuing the prophet Jeremiah from captivity and exile.

NEBUZARADAN

Captain of Nebuchadnezzar's Army

Nebuzaradan was commander of the Babylonian military. He led the final assault on Jerusalem in 586 BC, destroying the palace, razing the temple, and burning every important building to the ground. Once the city was pounded into submission, Nebuzaradan left none but the poorest of the poor, who stayed behind to tend Jerusalem's vineyards. The rest of the survivors were carried off into exile.

On Nebuchadnezzar's orders, Nebuzaradan singled out the two leading priests—as well as Judah's military commanders and royal advisers—and had them executed. On this ignoble note, the text concludes, "Judah went into captivity, away from her land" (2 Kings 25:21).

But Nebuzaradan was also responsible for sparing the life of one of Judah's greatest prophets, Jeremiah. Chained up with the rest of the prisoners from Jerusalem, Jeremiah seemed destined for exile and perhaps death—until Nebuzaradan found him. Apparently aware of Jeremiah's prophecies concerning Jerusalem's destruction and Nebuchadnezzar's triumph, Nebuzaradan ordered Jeremiah to be set free. He even gave Jeremiah the choice between coming to Babylon where he could live under Nebuzaradan's protection or returning to his decimated homeland. Jeremiah chose the latter and remained with the poorest of the poor who were left behind among the charred remnants of Jerusalem.

DID YOU KNOW?

Both Nebuchadnezzar and Nebuzaradan's names are allusions to the Babylonian god of wisdom, Nebo. Nebuzaradan's name meant "Nebo has given seed."

The LORD had said to Abram [Abraham], "Leave your country,
your people and your father's household and go to the land I
will show you. I will make you into a great nation and
I will bless you; I will make your name great, and you will be a blessing."
GENESIS 12:1–2

Abraham is a paragon of faith. He lived in a world that regarded family and tribe as security, but the Lord called him to leave his family, people, and country and travel to a different land—and Abraham did so without question! The land that the Lord was going to give Abraham's descendants was already well settled, so how could he "inherit" this land? Finally, his wife was in her sixties—well past childbearing years—so how could he ever expect to have any descendants at all (Genesis 12)?

But Abraham trusted God and His promises, and his faith was rewarded. Abraham and Sarah eventually bore Isaac, who fathered Jacob, who fathered the leaders of the twelve tribes of Israel. Many years later, the Israelites conquered the Promised Land of Canaan and occupied it as their inheritance. God was indeed faithful.

ABRAHAM

Patriarch of Israel

Abraham was not without his times of doubt. For instance, on two separate occasions he lied about his wife in order to protect his life (Genesis 12, 20). Abraham also expressed doubt that he would bear a son to carry on his name and estate (Genesis 15:1–3). Nevertheless, when the Lord made promises to Abraham, he "believed the LORD, and he credited it to him as righteousness" (Genesis 15:6).

SPIRITUAL INSIGHT

While Abraham is certainly a great example of faith for Christians today, that is not all he is to us. We are also his very children, the descendants whom God had promised to give him and to bless. Paul makes this clear in his letter to the Galatians: "Understand, then, that those who believe are children of Abraham" (Galatians 3:7). Thank God that all His faithful promises are made available even to us who believe Him today.

*Now Mesha king of Moab raised sheep, and he had to
supply the king of Israel with a hundred thousand
lambs and with the wool of a hundred thousand rams.*

2 Kings 3:4

There was no love lost between Mesha, king of Moab, and Joram, ruler of the northern kingdom of Israel. For centuries, Israel had experienced an uneasy relationship with the Moabites, who were descendants of Lot's oldest daughter. The Moabites tried to curse the Israelites on their way to the Promised Land. During the time of the judges, one of the Moabite kings, Eglon, invaded Israelite territory. Now the tables were turned—Moab was subject to the northern kingdom—and Mesha was determined to do something about it.

During the reign of the infamous King Ahab (Joram's father), Mesha had been forced to send a massive annual tribute of one hundred thousand lambs, along with the wool of one hundred thousand rams. Such an arrangement indicated Israel's status as an important regional power at the time. With the ascent of Joram, however, Mesha sensed a power vacuum and seized his opportunity to revolt.

MESHA

King of Moab

The king of Israel, joined by the kings of Judah and Edom, decided to retaliate by invading Moab and putting Mesha in his place. What followed was an unusual story filled with strange twists of fortune. First, the invading armies nearly died of thirst in the desert. Desperate, they appealed to the prophet Elisha, who announced the miraculous provision of water, though not before taunting Joram. Next, Mesha decided he would attack first. Sensing an opportunity, he sent his forces into Israel's camp—only to be overrun.

During the rout, Mesha and seven hundred soldiers fled to a fortified city. In one last unexpected twist, Mesha sacrificed his own son to Chemosh, the god of Moab—in full view of his enemies. At this point, the chronicler wrote, "The fury against Israel was great; they withdrew and returned to their own land" (2 Kings 3:27). This cryptic statement may mean that Israel panicked, fearing the power of Chemosh and not fully trusting the Lord to deliver the promised victory. In any case, Mesha lived to fight another day.

DID YOU KNOW?

Mesha told the story from his perspective on an ancient artifact called the Moabite Stone. The stone corroborates the biblical claim that Moab was subject to Israel at the time.

The LORD within her is righteous; he does no wrong.
Morning by morning he dispenses his justice,
and every new day he does not fail,
yet the unrighteous know no shame.

ZEPHANIAH 3:5

The prophet Zephaniah was not afraid to speak truth to those in power, which is especially remarkable, considering his royal pedigree.

Other prophets had introduced themselves by identifying their fathers and perhaps even their grandfathers (see, for example, Zechariah 1:1). Zephaniah, however, felt the need to trace four generations of ancestors in his introduction—and for good reason, too. Zephaniah's great-great-grandfather was Hezekiah, one of Judah's most celebrated kings. Hezekiah was judged to be uniquely devoted to God. According to the writer of 2 Kings, "There was no one like him among all the kings of Judah, either before him or after him" (2 Kings 18:5). It is no wonder that Zephaniah identified himself with Hezekiah—it was a powerful means of establishing his credibility.

It also connected him very closely to his audience. Zephaniah prophesied during the reign of Josiah, great-grandson of Hezekiah and the last good king of Judah. In other words, Zephaniah and Josiah were relatives. This fact made Zephaniah's prophecy against Judah and "the king's sons" in particular even more daring (see Zephaniah 1:4–8).

ZEPHANIAH

Prophet of Noble Heritage

Zephaniah described an imminent judgment, which he called the "day of the LORD" (see, for example, Zephaniah 1:14). It was to be a day on which nothing could save the people of Judah—or "all who live in the earth," for that matter (see Zephaniah 1:18).

But Zephaniah also spoke of hope—of a day when the people's lips would be purified and they would once again call on God (see Zephaniah 3:9). By this time, Jerusalem's fate had been sealed, but perhaps Zephaniah took heart at Josiah's reforms and was able to foresee a day when God would once again take "great delight" in His people (Zephaniah 3:17).

DID YOU KNOW?

Zephaniah's name means either "the LORD has treasured" or "the LORD has hidden," leading some scholars to suggest that Zephaniah may have been born during the reign of Hezekiah's son Manasseh. Manasseh was said to have shed an unthinkable amount of innocent blood (see 2 Kings 21:16).

*Then after three years, I [Paul] went up to Jerusalem to get
acquainted with Peter and stayed with him fifteen days.
I saw none of the other apostles—only James, the Lord's brother.*

GALATIANS 1:18–19

J ames, often called James the Just, seems to be an enigma in virtually every way. He is at the center of several controversies surrounding the history of the early church.

What is generally agreed upon about James is that he was the leader of the Jerusalem church, and he was in contact with such leaders as Peter, John, Barnabas, and Paul. At the first church council in Jerusalem, James was instrumental in forging the church's position regarding Gentiles and the Law of Moses (Acts 15).

Beyond this, it seems like everything else is in dispute.

JAMES

Brother of Jesus and Leader
of Jerusalem Church

Regarding his relationship to Jesus, there is debate whether he was Jesus' half brother, Jesus' stepbrother, Jesus' cousin, or something else.

Regarding his theology, James's emphasis on works rather than faith alone has led some to argue that he stands in opposition to Paul's emphasis on salvation by grace through faith—but others argue that the two positions complement and balance each other.

Regarding archaeological evidence of his existence, a controversy erupted in 2002 when a tomb purported to be his was made public, but later it was deemed to be a fake by the Israeli Antiquities Authority.

Despite all these controversies, however, James's letter to the scattered believers has always been a favorite due to its very practical wisdom and instruction. It is often referred to as the Proverbs of the New Testament.

RELATED
INFORMATION

According to the Jewish historian Josephus, the Sanhedrin charged James with breaking the law and stoned him to death around AD 62.

Jotham grew powerful because he walked
steadfastly before the LORD his God.
2 CHRONICLES 27:6

Sometimes the mark of a great leader is the ability to learn from a predecessor's mistakes. This, perhaps, is the most important lesson of Jotham's relatively brief tenure as a king of Judah.

Jotham's father, Azariah—also known as Uzziah—was generally regarded as a good king, except for two fatal flaws. First, he did not tear down the high places, pagan altars scattered throughout the land. Second, in his arrogance, Azariah blurred the carefully maintained distinction between king and priest when he attempted to burn incense in the temple. As punishment, God struck Azariah with leprosy. Burdened with such an affliction, not only was Azariah unable to set foot in the temple ever again, he was forced to give up his day-to-day responsibilities as king. Jotham was installed as regent, a position he filled until Azariah's death.

Jotham officially became king at the age of twenty-five. His reign was considered a success, marked by conquest and reconstruction. He subdued the Ammonites, Judah's enemies to the east, and he rebuilt part of the temple. Jotham invested heavily in Judah's infrastructure, establishing several new towns, towers, and other fortifications.

JOTHAM

King of Judah

Still, Jotham's greatest achievement was not something he did, it was what he chose *not* to do. He wisely avoided his father's presumption and left the management of the temple to its rightful trustees, the priests. Because of Jotham's humility and faithfulness to God, he reigned powerfully for sixteen years.

SPIRITUAL INSIGHT

Despite avoiding the worst mistakes of his predecessors, Jotham failed to make a lasting contribution to his people's spiritual well-being. True, Jotham accumulated military victories and completed ambitious building projects, but he did not manage to turn the hearts of the people—let alone his own son—back to God. Which would have made for a more lasting legacy, buildings or hearts?

*Then Herod, when he saw that he had been tricked by the wise men,
became furious, and he sent and killed all the male children in
Bethlehem and in all that region who were two years old or under,
according to the time that he had ascertained from the wise men.*

MATTHEW 2:16 ESV

Herod the Great was a man of many contradictions. He was king of Judea, yet he himself was an Idumean (that is, an Edomite). He gained favor with the Jewish leaders by completely renovating the temple of the Lord and making it rival any pagan temple of its day, yet he also built many pagan gymnasiums and other Hellenistic buildings throughout Judea and Samaria. He was often particular to maintain at least the appearance of conformity to Jewish customs, yet he freely broke the sixth commandment by mercilessly killing any who threatened his rule—including his own wife and sons. This contradiction led one ancient writer to comment that he would rather be Herod's *hus* ("pig," considered unfit to eat for Jews) than his *huios* ("son").

Herod's actions regarding Jesus' birth, then, should come as no surprise to us.

HEROD THE GREAT

King of Judea

When wise men came from the East seeking to worship the newborn King Jesus, they first asked Herod where the child was. Herod led them to believe that he wanted to worship the child, too, all the while planning to kill Him. When the wise men left without telling Herod exactly where the baby was, he became furious and ordered all the baby boys two years and younger to be killed. Jesus' family escaped to Egypt until Herod had died, then returned to Nazareth, where His parents had lived before He was born.

RELATED INFORMATION

Several people were named Herod in the Bible. Herod the Great had several sons, including Antipas (who ruled over Galilee and Perea), Archelaus (who ruled over Judea and Samaria), and Philip (who ruled over the northeast corner of Palestine). Much later, Herod's grandson Agrippa ruled over much of Judea and Samaria, and still later Agrippa II ruled over portions of Palestine and Lebanon.

As [Joseph] looked about and saw his brother Benjamin,
his own mother's son, he asked, "Is this your youngest brother,
the one you told me about?"
And he said, "God be gracious to you, my son."
GENESIS 43:29

Some things never change. Brothers can fight among themselves like cats and dogs, but in the end, few other relationships are marked by greater loyalty and love than a brother for a brother. The relationship between Benjamin and Joseph may have been no different.

Benjamin was the younger brother of Joseph and the son of Rachel, the beloved wife of Jacob. Benjamin had eleven brothers in all, but only Joseph was his full brother. All the others were born to different mothers. Rachel died giving birth to Benjamin, and she wanted to name him Ben-Oni ("son of my sorrow"), but Jacob named him

BENJAMIN

Brother of Joseph

Benjamin ("son of my right hand/strength") instead (Genesis 35:18).

After Joseph had been sold into slavery by his brothers and had risen to a very high position within the Egyptian government, Joseph's brothers came to Egypt looking for food. They did not recognize Joseph when they saw him, but he recognized them. Joseph tested his brothers' hearts to see how they would respond, in the process blessing Benjamin much more than his brothers and showing his special love for the youngest. Eventually Joseph revealed his identity to the brothers and convinced them to move to Egypt with him. He continued to richly bless Benjamin with money and clothes (Genesis 45:22).

RELATED INFORMATION

Benjamin eventually became the father of a tribe of Israel by the same name, and these people were known as able warriors, many of whom were left-handed and able to sling a stone with great accuracy (Judges 20:15–16).

*But a prophet of the L<small>ORD</small> named Oded was there,
and he went out to meet the army when it returned to Samaria.*
2 C<small>HRONICLES</small> 28:9

In one of the most tragic scenes in the Bible—scarcely a decade before the northern kingdom fell—Israel and Judah went to war with each other. The battle itself was bad enough: According to the chronicler, 120,000 sons of Judah died in God's punishment for Judah's unfaithfulness. But the northern kingdom intended to pile insult on top of injury, enslaving a staggering 200,000 survivors from Judah. One prophet, however, stood in the way.

ODED

Prophet of Samaria

Oded was a prophet of Samaria, which was another name for the northern kingdom. He watched in horror as his countrymen returned from battle, having brutalized their relatives to the south. Horror turned to fury as he confronted the triumphant army on its way home. To Oded's way of thinking, divine punishment was one thing—but Israel had gone well beyond that, turning an already ugly battle into outright slaughter. Even worse, they planned to humiliate the surviving men, women, and children by making them slaves. Oded would not have it. He knew the Law of Moses: An Israelite was not to enslave another Israelite (see Leviticus 25:39–43). Politics may have separated the northern and southern kingdoms; but in Oded's eyes, they were all still fellow Israelites.

Remarkably, Oded's words had their intended effect, humbling an entire army into obedience. It helped that some of Israel's own military leaders joined Oded in condemning the army's behavior. So the prisoners were fed and clothed, their wounds were treated, and they were taken back to Judah. The incident was a reminder that no political divide could erase the Israelites' kinship with one another.

SPIRITUAL INSIGHT

Some scholars believe that Oded's story provided the inspiration for Jesus' parable of the Good Samaritan (see Luke 10:25–37). There are a number of parallels. In both stories, the victims' wounds were anointed with oil. The man in Jesus' story was placed on a donkey after his ordeal. In Oded's story, those too weak to walk back to Judah were provided with donkeys to ride. Last, the hero in each story came from Samaria. Both stories reminded their readers that no barrier—ethnic, social, religious, or political—trumps the biblical command to "love your neighbor as yourself."

There [Paul] met a Jew named Aquila, a native of Pontus,
who had recently come from Italy with his wife Priscilla,
because Claudius had ordered all the Jews to leave Rome.
ACTS 18:2

Day
281

The Roman emperor Claudius was almost certainly a complete pagan, with no care whatsoever about the God of the Bible—yet God still used him to set in motion great things for Christ's kingdom.

Claudius was emperor of Rome from AD 41 to 54. He was closely connected with Herod Agrippa I, king over most of Palestine, and Herod even appears to have been involved in Claudius's appointment as emperor.

Though it has not been confirmed by other literature, the Bible states that at some point before Paul completed his second missionary journey, Claudius expelled all the Jews from Rome. Among those Jews expelled was a Christian couple named Aquila and Priscilla. They traveled to Corinth, where they met Paul and became his coworkers in the gospel as well as in tentmaking (Acts 18).

Later Aquila and Priscilla traveled with Paul to Ephesus, where they met another Jew named Apollos. With Aquila and Priscilla's help, Apollos became a great teacher in the church there.

CLAUDIUS

Emperor of Rome

Had it not been for Claudius's edict, Aquila and Priscilla may never have met Paul, nor would they have met Apollos. God is so powerful He can use anyone to carry out His will—no matter who they are or whether they willingly follow Him.

RELATED INFORMATION

Historians often note that Claudius was an unlikely candidate for emperor, yet he eventually proved to be an able one in many ways. Apparently he suffered from some physical ailment that may have been a form of cerebral palsy.

And Gaal the son of Ebed said, "Who is Abimelech,
and who are we of Shechem, that we should serve him?
Is he not the son of Jerubbaal, and is not Zebul his officer?
Serve the men of Hamor the father of Shechem;
but why should we serve him?"

JUDGES 9:28 ESV

Many foolish ideas have been conceived in a bout of drinking and revelry, and the result is usually the same: disaster. Such was the case with a man named Gaal in the time of Israel's judges.

All we know about Gaal is that he was the son of a man named Ebed and that he and his brothers moved into the area of Shechem sometime around the time that Abimelech had become the leader of the region. Gaal must have been a man of some influence as well, because he was able to stir up the leaders of Shechem against Abimelech during a harvest festival when they were eating and drinking in the temple of their god.

GAAL

Enemy of Gideon's Son Abimelech

While Gaal was busy boasting of what he would do to Abimelech, however, the governor of the city informed Abimelech of Gaal's ambitions. Abimelech then advanced on the city in the morning, drew out Gaal and his men, and killed them in battle. The next day he ruthlessly attacked the people of Shechem for supporting Gaal, and the very short story of Gaal and his ill-conceived idea came to an end.

The ancient city of Shechem played an important role throughout the history of Israel. It was at Shechem that the Lord revealed to Abraham that he would receive Canaan as his inheritance (Genesis 12). Later Jacob bought a plot of ground there, and Joseph's bones would eventually be laid to rest there (Genesis 33:18–19; Joshua 24:32). At Shechem the people established a covenant with the Lord during the time of Joshua (Joshua 24). It was also at Shechem that the kingdom of Israel split into two kingdoms (1 Kings 12). And at a place near Shechem, Jesus spoke to a Samaritan woman at Jacob's well (John 4).

But when [Joseph] heard that Archelaus was reigning
in Judea in place of his father Herod, he was afraid to go there.
Having been warned in a dream,
he withdrew to the district of Galilee.
MATTHEW 2:22

It's interesting to reflect now and then on how certain things have influenced history and how everything might be different if something were changed.

Take, for example, a seemingly minor figure in the Bible like Herod Archelaus. He is mentioned in only one verse of scripture, and even then it is only a passing reference to him (Matthew 2:22). Yet if we think about what influence his existence has had in history, we get a tiny glimpse into just how amazing God's sovereignty is to bring everything together as it needed to happen.

Archelaus was a son of Herod the Great and was granted rule over Judea, Samaria, and Idumea by Herod's will. During this time, Jesus' family was returning from Egypt to resettle in Israel, and their decision to relocate to Nazareth, in Herod Antipas's territory, may have been due in part to the realization that Archelaus was distinguishing himself as a cruel ruler like his father. By relocating to Nazareth because of Archelaus, Jesus' family was fulfilling a prophecy (Matthew 2:23).

HEROD ARCHELAUS

Son of Herod the Great
and Ruler of Judea

By AD 6, tensions had reached a boiling point regarding Archelaus's cruel practices, and the Romans deposed him and brought his territory under direct Roman rule. This is why Jesus ultimately stood trial before the Roman governor Pontius Pilate, who condemned Him to death on a cross.

SPIRITUAL INSIGHT

The fact that God is able to bring together a whole host of seemingly insignificant things to accomplish His will should lead us to humility and worship. Praise God that He is truly sovereign and that He is able to work out His will in each of our lives as well.

Shallum son of Jabesh conspired against Zechariah.
He attacked him in front of the people,
assassinated him and succeeded him as king.
2 KINGS 15:10

When Jesus rebuked Peter, telling him that "all who draw the sword will die by the sword" (Matthew 26:52), He may have thought of men like Shallum, the fifteenth king of Israel.

Shallum's account in 2 Kings was about as brief as his time on the throne—he reigned over the northern kingdom for just one fleeting month. With the aid of unidentified conspirators, Shallum moved against the previous king, Zechariah, whose tenure was hardly more impressive than Shallum's. Zechariah lasted just six months as Israel's king.

The fact that Shallum assassinated Zechariah was not particularly surprising. Zechariah was, after all, one of four Israelite kings to be murdered in a twenty-year period. What was particularly brazen about Zechariah's assassination was the setting. According to the writer of 2 Kings, Shallum killed him "in front of the people." Shallum did not seize his moment behind closed doors or in a darkened room—he chose to carry out his treachery in full view of the Israelites. Perhaps he thought that such a bold display of violence would cow them into submission—that having seen what Shallum did to Zechariah, no one would dare interfere with Israel's new king.

SHALLUM

King of Israel

Unfortunately, the public assassination seems to have had the opposite effect, creating a large target on Shallum's back. Only weeks into his reign, Shallum himself was betrayed. Menahem, a military commander loyal to Zechariah, exacted his revenge, killing Shallum in Samaria.

DID YOU KNOW?

Shallum was a relatively common name in ancient Israel. The Old Testament includes around fifteen men who carried this name.

Mary Magdalene went to the disciples with the news:
"I have seen the Lord!"
JOHN 20:18

Mary Magdalene was one of Jesus' most devoted followers. She was among the last to leave His side after the crucifixion and the first to witness His resurrection.

It's no wonder Mary was so devoted—Luke reports that Jesus delivered her from seven demons (Luke 8:2). In the ancient Jewish world, the number seven represented completion or totality. Mary's bondage was all-encompassing—then again, so was the healing that Jesus provided. From that day on, Mary Magdalene joined several other women who followed Jesus and supported His ministry financially.

MARY MAGDALENE

Follower of Jesus

The remaining biblical references to Mary Magdalene are all connected to the death and resurrection of Jesus. Long after many of Jesus' disciples had scattered, Mary and the other women lingered at the foot of the cross (see Matthew 27:56). As Jesus' body was laid in a borrowed tomb, Mary was there, watching the somber, lonely procession (see Matthew 27:61). And it was Mary Magdalene and "the other Mary" who ventured out from safety to anoint Jesus' broken body only to find that the tomb was empty (see Matthew 28:1).

Mary had the honor of being the first person to bear witness to the resurrection. John provides an extended glimpse into Mary's encounter with the risen Christ. Her initial impression—that Jesus was the gardener—was not altogether mistaken. Jesus was, after all, the second Adam (see Romans 5:17), and the first Adam was originally a gardener. When Mary fully realized whom she was talking to, she was overcome with emotion. Jesus, however, encouraged her not to cling to Him—time was short and He had important work for her to do. Jesus entrusted Mary with the responsibility and privilege of being the first to spread the word that the Messiah had conquered death.

DID YOU KNOW?

Some of the church fathers believed that the sinful woman who anointed Jesus in Luke 7 and Mary Magdalene (introduced in Luke 8) were the same person—which gave rise to the popular myth that Mary was a prostitute. There is, however, nothing in scripture to support this. If Luke had wanted his readers to connect the woman in chapter 7 with Mary Magdalene (one of three women mentioned in Luke 8), he almost certainly would have mentioned her by name in the story of the sinful woman.

*After six days Jesus took Peter, James and John with him
and led them up a high mountain, where they were all alone.
There he was transfigured before them.*

MARK 9:2

What would it have been like to be one of Jesus' closest companions? To be able to ask Him a question anytime? To see how He handled everyday things like traveling from place to place or dealing with the weather? This was the great privilege of James the son of Zebedee.

James and his brother John were among the first disciples of Jesus (Mark 1:19–20). He and John must have been a rowdy bunch, because Jesus nicknamed them the "Sons of Thunder" (Mark 3:17). Even so, James must have held a special place in Jesus' heart, because he, along with Peter and John, were sometimes called apart separately from the other disciples to be with Jesus. As a part of this inner circle of followers, James was privy to the raising of Jairus's daughter (Mark 5:35–43), the transfiguration of Jesus (Mark 9:1–9), and Jesus' agony in the Garden of Gethsemane (Mark 14:32–42).

JAMES

Apostle and Son of Zebedee

At the same time, James still exhibited faults just like anyone else. He and John displayed what seems like selfishness by asking Jesus if they could serve as the two highest officials in His kingdom (Mark 10:35–41). They also portrayed a vengeful spirit when they asked Jesus if they should call down fire upon a Samaritan village that refused to welcome Jesus (Luke 9:52–56).

DID YOU KNOW?

James was the first apostle to suffer martyrdom. (Stephen was the first Christian martyr, but he was a deacon). James was put to death by Herod Agrippa I (Acts 12:1–2), a grandson of Herod the Great.

*So Pilate, wishing to satisfy the crowd, released for them Barabbas,
and having scourged Jesus, he delivered him to be crucified.*
MARK 15:15 ESV

Day
287

To hear it makes our blood boil: A guilty man goes free, and an innocent man is condemned instead. For most of us, this will be the only association we ever have with the name Barabbas.

All we know about Barabbas himself is that he was a notorious prisoner who had been imprisoned for insurrection and murder some time before Jesus' arrest (Matthew 27:16; Mark 15:7; Luke 23:19; John 18:40). We don't know anything about the insurrection, nor do we know what happened to Barabbas after his release.

The only other thing we know about Barabbas is that this guilty man, for no reason other than the will of God carried out by Pontius Pilate, was released and set free, and Jesus, an innocent man, was condemned and executed instead. It all happened as part of Pilate's usual custom of releasing a prisoner chosen by the crowd

BARABBAS

Prisoner with Jesus

during Passover (Matthew 27:15; Mark 15:6; John 18:39), and this time the religious leaders succeeded in stirring up the crowd to choose Barabbas instead of Jesus.

SPIRITUAL INSIGHT

It is completely right to be angry when we hear of such injustice being committed against Jesus, an innocent man. Yet if we reflect on our own salvation, every believer has stood precisely in Barabbas's place. We, being undeniably guilty in our sins, have been released from our death sentence for no reason of our own—it is simply by the gracious will of God—and Jesus has been condemned and executed in our place. From now on, when you hear the name Barabbas, praise God for the immeasurable grace He has shown every believer, and thank Him that you—though underserving—have been set free to serve Him.

*"So give your servant a discerning heart to govern your
people and to distinguish between right and wrong.
For who is able to govern this great people of yours?"*

1 KINGS 3:9

Solomon had everything going for him: wisdom, wealth, and power. Unfortunately, he had many vices as well: greed, lust, and idolatry. These combined to bring about the undoing of Israel in more ways than one.

Solomon was not the obvious choice for the throne. Nevertheless, David handpicked Solomon as his successor. While Solomon eventually took his place as one of the few truly great kings of Israel, he was very different from his father. David was a warrior, accustomed to dealing with conflict (or at least the threat of conflict) for most of his rule. By contrast, Solomon presided over the most enduring peace in Israel's history.

SOLOMON

King of Israel

Without pressures from beyond his kingdom, Solomon devoted himself to other pursuits—namely, cultivating wisdom (which he famously displayed to the amazement of his subjects and foreign dignitaries alike), forging diplomatic alliances with regional powers like Egypt, and building the temple in Jerusalem.

Solomon, however, was not without his blind spots. His wisdom (a gift from God, according to the writer of 1 Kings) did not prevent him from plunging headlong into the dangerous pursuit of wealth. He accumulated chariots and horses in violation of God's command (see Deuteronomy 17:16). He used forced labor to build the temple and taxed the people heavily in order to finance his luxurious lifestyle (see 1 Kings 5:13; 12:4). Solomon's best-known weakness, however, was his taste for women—and lots of them. Solomon famously had seven hundred wives—many of them no doubt marriages arranged for diplomatic reasons—and another three hundred concubines. Like the practice of accumulating wealth, the king's taking of many wives was expressly forbidden by the Law (see Deuteronomy 17:17), and for good reason. Over time, Solomon's pagan wives lured him away from the one true God. And as the story ends, the once wise king descends into folly.

*After the LORD had said these things to Job, he said to Eliphaz
the Temanite, "I am angry with you and your two friends,
because you have not spoken of me what is right,
as my servant Job has."*
JOB 42:7

In times of sorrow, have you ever looked to someone for understanding but found little comfort because he or she simply could not see beyond his or her own experiences and view of things? This must have been the experience of Job with Eliphaz.

When a righteous man named Job was undergoing terrible suffering for reasons that were not clear to him, three of his friends came to mourn and talk with him. Eliphaz was among those friends. He was from Teman, a city likely located in Edom, a country to the southeast of Israel.

ELIPHAZ

One of Job's Friends

Eliphaz made three different speeches to Job. In the first, he cast Job's suffering as simply another example of the suffering that all people experience as a result of sinfulness (Job 4–5). He gently encouraged Job to repent and experience God's restoration. Eliphaz's second speech came after Job defended himself against his friends' accusations, and Eliphaz became a little harsher in his rebuke (Job 15). By the time he spoke to Job a third time, he directly challenged Job as one of the wicked—but he also described the mercy that God shows to those who repent (Job 22).

In the end, God rebuked Eliphaz, not Job. The Lord even instructed Eliphaz to ask Job to pray for him, showing that Job was in the right and Eliphaz was in the wrong (Job 42:7–9).

SPIRITUAL INSIGHT

When someone comes to us for understanding during a time of trouble, one of the best things we can do is to be aware that we do *not* understand—that is, that our experiences and our way of seeing things may not exactly match up with the other person's experiences. It is often better simply to listen, reflect, and love the other person rather than to try to sort everything out for him or her.

Day
290

*[Hezekiah] held fast to the LORD and did not cease to
follow him; he kept the commands the LORD had given Moses.
And the LORD was with him; he was successful
in whatever he undertook.*

2 KINGS 18:6–7

J ust as the darkest backdrops make diamonds sparkle the brightest, the dark days surrounding Hezekiah's reign made his godly life all the more brilliant.

Hezekiah's own father had promoted idolatry throughout Judah and had made Judah a subservient kingdom to the wicked Assyrian Empire (1 Kings 16). When Hezekiah assumed the throne of Judah at the age of twenty-five, the northern kingdom of Israel was only a few years away from being sent into exile for their wickedness (2 Kings 18:9–10). These were dark days indeed.

HEZEKIAH

King of Judah

But Hezekiah determined to follow the Lord with all his heart, and the Lord empowered him to do great things for His people even in the midst of the evil forces that were still at work. Hezekiah removed idolatry from the land, including all the pagan items from the temple (2 Kings 18). He restored proper worship at the temple and sent invitations to everyone throughout the land—even people living in the northern kingdom of Israel—to come to Jerusalem to celebrate the Passover once again (2 Chronicles 29–30).

Not long after the northern kingdom of Israel fell to the Assyrians, the Assyrians attacked Jerusalem as well, but the Lord struck down 185,000 of their soldiers in a single night, and Jerusalem was spared (2 Kings 19:35–36).

RELATED INFORMATION

As part of his preparations for the Assyrian attack on Jerusalem, Hezekiah constructed a water tunnel to carry water from the Gihon Spring to the pool at the lower end of the city (2 Kings 20:20). The tunnel still exists today, and in 1838 an ancient inscription was found in it that commemorated its construction.

Cush was the father of Nimrod, who grew to
be a mighty warrior on the earth.
He was a mighty hunter before the LORD.
GENESIS 10:8–9

T oday, calling someone a "Nimrod" is an insult on par with "idiot" or "buffoon." But the original Bible character who bore that name was anything but that. He was known as a mighty warrior, perhaps even a king of old.

NIMROD

Son of Cush

Nimrod appears in the list of Noah's descendants, recorded in Genesis 9–10. While most of the names in this genealogy are given without elaboration, the writer paused at Nimrod's name to attach a brief biography. Such unique treatment in the genealogy may suggest that Nimrod was well known to the earliest readers of Genesis. Perhaps he was the subject of some other ancient piece of literature with which the ancients were familiar.

Nimrod was renowned as a "warrior" and a "mighty hunter." The second description generally referred to a hunger for animals, though on rare occasions it referred metaphorically to hunting for people (see, for example, Jeremiah 16:16). In the ancient Near Eastern culture, such a description could have royal connotations, as the roles of warrior and king often overlapped. Plus Nimrod was described as a great civilization builder, responsible for establishing a kingdom that included Babylon, Erech, Akkad, and Calneh. The writer of Genesis also credited him with building several cities, including the infamous Nineveh.

For years, scholars have attempted to correlate the biblical Nimrod to some literary or historical figure from the ancient world. Possible candidates have included Gilgamesh and Sargon, one of the earliest Akkadian kings. However, precise identification of Nimrod remains elusive.

DID YOU KNOW?

The Tower of Babel, described in Genesis 11, was built on a plain in Shinar, part of ancient Mesopotamia. Such a location places it squarely in Nimrod's territory, giving rise to the tradition (uncorroborated by the Bible) that Nimrod himself supervised construction of the notorious tower.

"For if you [Esther] remain silent at this time, relief and deliverance for the Jews will arise from another place, but you and your father's family will perish. And who knows but that you have come to royal position for such a time as this?"

ESTHER 4:14

Whether it's a fan catching a home run baseball in the World Series or a parent catching her child as she falls off a swing set, so much of life is about being at the right place at the right time. Queen Esther seemed to be at the right place and the right time to save her people, the Jews. Would she risk her life to try?

ESTHER

Queen of Persia

Esther was a Jew living in the mighty Persian Empire, which stretched from the borders of India to the borders of Europe. Many years earlier, Jews had been exiled from their homeland of Israel and scattered throughout places that would eventually be engulfed by the Persian Empire. Esther had been chosen by the king of Persia as his new queen, but she was still only allowed to come into his presence if it pleased him to do so.

When wicked Haman, a high official in the Persian Empire, devised a plan to eradicate all Jews, Esther's relative urged her to take advantage of her privileged position in the empire to save her people. At the risk of her life, she approached the king and invited him to a banquet, where she revealed Haman's plot. The king executed Haman and saved the Jews by allowing them to defend themselves against those who tried to carry out Haman's plan.

SPIRITUAL INSIGHT

We'll probably never be faced with saving God's people from total eradication—but we all encounter situations where we are placed in the right place at the right time to do something for God. Whether it is giving part of a bonus to missions or spending a free evening helping out with a church youth group event, look for opportunities to make a lasting impact on God's kingdom with the resources you have been given.

*While they were eating together there, Ishmael son of Nethaniah
and the ten men who were with him got up and struck down
Gedaliah son of Ahikam, the son of Shaphan, with the sword,
killing the one whom the king of Babylon
had appointed as governor over the land.*

JEREMIAH 41:1–2

Can there be anything more treacherous than sharing a meal with someone even as you prepare to destroy him? Such was the character of Ishmael, who fiendishly assassinated Gedaliah, the governor of Judah.

After the Babylonians conquered Judah and exiled most of the nobility to Babylon, they appointed a Judean named Gedaliah to govern the people that remained. Gedaliah appealed to the Jewish officials who remained to live at peace with the Babylonians. Ishmael, who was of royal blood (Jeremiah 41:1), was among those who came to him—but it appears that his intentions were not at all honorable, for at some point he was hired by the king of nearby Ammon to assassinate Gedaliah.

ISHMAEL

Judean Official Who Assassinated Gedaliah

Word got out about Ishmael's plans, and an official named Johanan offered to assassinate Ishmael, but Gedaliah refused to believe the rumors. Later, when Gedaliah was eating with Ishmael and his men, they rose up and killed him along with all the other Jewish and Babylonian officials who were there.

The next day some Jewish pilgrims were passing through the area on their way to Jerusalem, and Ishmael acted as though he were mourning to convince them to stop and visit. When they did, Ishmael killed most of them, except for ten of them who offered to show Ishmael where they had stored some food. Johanan pursued Ishmael and his men, but they escaped to Ammon (Jeremiah 40–41).

RELATED INFORMATION

Ishmael's treachery resembles that of Judas, who also betrayed his Lord during a meal. During the Passover with Jesus, Judas rose up and went out into the night to meet with the soldiers who would arrest Jesus and lead Him to His crucifixion (John 13).

*At this they wept again. Then Orpah kissed
her mother-in-law good-by, but Ruth clung to her.*

RUTH 1:14

Orpah did not live during a happy time in Israel's history. But Israel's troubles were not her problem—after all, Orpah was a Moabite.

Orpah was daughter-in-law to Naomi, whose family migrated from Bethlehem to Moab during a time of famine in Israel. Naomi's story, told in the first chapter of Ruth, reads like a Shakespearean tragedy. First, her husband died—tragic in any context, but potentially disastrous for a woman living in the patriarchal culture of the ancient Near East. Having a husband meant having protection—no husband meant vulnerability and perhaps abject poverty. But all was not lost, since Naomi had two sons. While living abroad, they had married Moabite women: Orpah and Ruth. However, soon Naomi's sons had died, too. Now three women were left vulnerable and destitute.

Hearing that the famine had abated in Israel, Naomi decided to return home, but she urged Orpah and Ruth to return to their families. Naomi might find

ORPAH

Ruth's Sister-in-Law

sustenance back in Bethlehem, but she could not guarantee the same for two foreigners. At first, both daughters-in-law protested, voicing their intent to stay with Naomi. However, this could easily have been a mere polite gesture, so Naomi persisted, telling Orpah and Ruth that they had no future with her.

Orpah was convinced. She kissed her mother-in-law and returned to her home—back to her own family and, presumably, to her own gods. Ruth, however, had decided that Naomi was her family now; and Naomi's God was her God.

The contrasting results of their decisions were striking. Orpah disappeared from the story, destined to become nothing more than a minor character in the biblical narrative, while Ruth rose to prominence—and ultimately became an ancestor of King David, as well as Jesus the Messiah.

DID YOU KNOW? Even though Orpah turned back, Naomi did not begrudge her. In fact, Orpah left with Naomi's blessing—a prayer that God would show kindness to her and provide another husband for her.

[Nebuchadnezzar] made Mattaniah, Jehoiachin's uncle,
king in his place and changed his name to Zedekiah.
2 KINGS 24:17

A word of advice: If you are the king of a small nation and you were put on the throne by the king of a much bigger, more powerful nation, rebellion is generally not a wise option. Unfortunately for all of Judah, Zedekiah did not heed such advice.

Zedekiah was the last king of Judah. His nephew Jehoiachin had preceded him on the throne, having the misfortune to rise to power just as King Nebuchadnezzar of Babylon decided to lay siege to the city of Jerusalem. The year was 597 BC. Time was running out for the kingdom of Judah.

Jehoiachin was forced into a humiliating surrender, after which Nebuchadnezzar looted the temple and displaced all but the poorest residents from Jerusalem. Jehoiachin was carried to Babylon, while his uncle, Zedekiah, was made king in his place.

ZEDEKIAH

King of Judah

Zedekiah, however, had little real power. He did not even have control over his own name. That had once been Mattaniah, but Nebuchadnezzar changed it when he put him on the throne. It was a simple yet profound way of reminding Zedekiah who was in charge.

Zedekiah ruled for just over a decade, and then he made the biggest mistake of his life: He rebelled against the king of Babylon. It seems that Zedekiah did not bother to seek God's direction until well after he had committed to revolt. Only when Nebuchadnezzar was beating down Jerusalem's door did the king of Judah seek advice from the prophet Jeremiah (see Jeremiah 21). Unfortunately, Jeremiah had no words of encouragement for Zedekiah. Time was up. Zedekiah and his people had nothing to look forward to but "plague, sword and famine"—and finally, total defeat at the hands of the Babylonian army.

As a final insult, Zedekiah was forced to watch as his sons were killed. Then his eyes were gouged out, and he was led to Babylon.

DID YOU KNOW?

Like Jeremiah, the prophet Ezekiel had anything but kind words for Zedekiah (see Ezekiel 17:14–16). Ezekiel seemed to marvel at Zedekiah's stupidity, noting with astonishment that it was after Nebuchadnezzar had rendered Judah "unable to rise again" that Zedekiah chose to rebel. "Will he succeed?" Ezekiel asked, his words no doubt dripping with sarcasm. "Will he break the treaty and yet escape?" The answer was a resounding no.

*Jabez cried out to the God of Israel, "Oh, that you would
bless me and enlarge my territory! Let your hand be with me,
and keep me from harm so that I will be free from pain."
And God granted his request.*

1 CHRONICLES 4:10

Imagine having a name like Pain or Trouble, a permanent reminder of the sorrow that you brought your mother at birth. Wouldn't it make you want to redeem yourself somehow in the eyes of your parents and others? This reality may be part of the background in Jabez's story.

The Bible says that Jabez was a descendant of Judah and that he was more honorable than his brothers. It doesn't even say why he was more honorable, but we can probably assume that it is because of the noble prayer he offered to God.

JABEZ

Man Who Asked
for God's Blessing

Jabez's name sounds like the Hebrew word for *pain*, which explains why his mother gave him that name when she bore him in pain. The social stigma that Jabez endured because of his name's associations must have been great, because he prayed that God would do various things that would redeem his name. He prayed that God would bless him and enlarge his territory, meaning that God would grant him even more land than that which had been granted to his family as part of their original inheritance in the Promised Land. He also asked that God's hand, presumably of blessing and protection, would be with him and that He would keep him from harm. In this way he would be free from pain.

SPIRITUAL INSIGHT

You may not have an actual name like Pain or Trouble, but perhaps your name—that is, your reputation—has become permanently associated with some other negative characteristic, and you desire to redeem your reputation. Ask God to bless you and help you to overcome whatever negative traits have been associated with your name.

*"In the days of Shamgar son of Anath, in the days of Jael,
the roads were abandoned; travelers took to winding paths."*
JUDGES 5:6

Day
297

Shamgar is perhaps the most unusual deliverer—and his account the shortest—featured in the book of Judges.

According to the author, Shamgar followed Ehud, who sneaked a sword into the palace of Eglon, king of Moab, and killed him. Following the assassination of Moab's king, Ehud led the Israelites in battle, where they killed around ten thousand Moabite soldiers. And though the Moabite threat was neutralized, the writer introduced a new danger: the Philistines who lived along the coast. They would prove to be one of Israel's most persistent and dangerous enemies. To deal with them, God raised up a man named Shamgar.

SHAMGAR

Judge of Israel

What makes Shamgar so unusual is his name—it is not a Hebrew name. Nor was his hometown, Beth Anath, a Hebrew town. Located in the territory of Naphtali, Beth Anath was a Canaanite town that was subjugated but not destroyed by the Israelites. The residents of Beth Anath had been allowed to live as forced laborers. While the text yields no further clues about Shamgar's identity, the strong implication is that he was foreign—in all likelihood a Canaanite.

The text does not bother to clarify whether Shamgar acted specifically in Israel's defense or simply out of a mutual hatred for the Philistines. In any case, Shamgar used an oxgoad—a wooden device with a sharp metal tip—to great effect, slaying six hundred Philistines. Almost as if anticipating Hebrew skepticism at the thought of a Canaanite deliverer, the writer simply states, "He too saved Israel" (Judges 3:31).

SPIRITUAL INSIGHT

Shamgar is yet another reminder of God's prerogative to use anyone—even the unlikeliest of people—to achieve His sovereign plan. God's purposes have always transcended nationality and ethnicity (see Genesis 12:3).

Once again the Israelites did evil in the eyes of the LORD,
and because they did this evil the LORD gave
Eglon king of Moab power over Israel.

JUDGES 3:12

King Eglon of Moab seems to have been a victim of his own success. His coalition of Moabites, Ammonites, and Amalekites had defeated Israel during the time of the judges and had captured the city of palms, probably referring to Jericho.

But the Lord raised up a left-handed man named Ehud to deliver His people.

EGLON

King of Moab Killed
by Ehud

Ehud carried the tribute money to Eglon at Jericho, but he took along a little something extra: a double-edged sword strapped to his right thigh under his clothes. Most people are right-handed, so Eglon's guards probably did not expect to find a weapon on Ehud's right side—since a right-handed person would draw the weapon across their body from their left side. Their failure to find Ehud's weapon may also indicate an overconfidence in their own strength, a misguided notion that no one would dare assault their king.

But Ehud dared, and he managed to slip his weapon past the guards and into the very presence of Eglon. Ehud indicated that he had a secret message for Eglon, who foolishly allowed Ehud to approach him. Ehud drew his sword and plunged it into Eglon's massive stomach. Ehud escaped to the hills of Ephraim and called out the forces of Israel to attack the Moabites. Israel was delivered from the Moabites that day (Judges 3).

RELATED INFORMATION

The Moabites, Ammonites, and Amalekites were all involved in repeated conflicts with Israel. Later King David largely annihilated the Amalekites (1 Samuel 30), but the Moabites and Ammonites remained a thorn in the Israelites' side for the remainder of their history.

But Elymas the magician (for that is the meaning of his name) opposed them, seeking to turn the proconsul away from the faith.
ACTS 13:8 ESV

Day
299

The short story of Elymas (also called Bar-Jesus), which takes up a mere seven verses of scripture (Acts 13:6–12), is filled with contrasts from start to finish.

Paul and Barnabas encountered Elymas at Paphos after traveling through the island of Cyprus. Elymas, a Jewish sorcerer and false prophet, was an attendant of the Roman proconsul in Paphos. As Paul and Barnabas tried to share the truth of the gospel with the proconsul, Elymas tried to turn him from the faith. So Paul rebuked Elymas and told him that the Lord was going to blind him for a time, which is exactly what happened. After that, the proconsul was amazed and believed in the Lord.

ELYMAS

Jewish Sorcerer Blinded by Paul

Three stark contrasts stand out in the story: First, as a Jew, Elymas was supposed to worship the Lord and refrain from practicing divination and sorcery (Leviticus 19:26; Deuteronomy 18:10–13; Ezekiel 13:9, 20; Micah 3:6–7), yet he was doing these very things in the service of the Roman proconsul. Second, Elymas was characterized by deceit and trickery (Acts 18:10), yet he wanted to turn the proconsul from the truth of the gospel. And third, Elymas was no doubt employed by the proconsul, because he offered special knowledge and power through sorcery—yet in the end Elymas himself was blinded and needed to be led by the hand.

RELATED INFORMATION

Elymas is described in the Bible as a "sorcerer," which is actually the Greek word *magos*. This is the same word (plural, *magi*) used for the "wise men" who came from the East, probably Persia or Babylonia, to worship the young Jesus (Matthew 2:1–2). By Roman times, magi had become associated with magic and divination, and many of them had flocked to the Roman Empire to profit from their practices.

"Test me in this," says the LORD *Almighty, "and see if I will not throw open the floodgates of heaven and pour out so much blessing that you will not have room enough for it."*

MALACHI 3:10

Malachi's unusual book begins with reassurance of God's love for His people—and ends with the threat of a curse.

There is no mention of the last Old Testament prophet outside the book that bears his name. The fact that the word *Malachi* means "my messenger" in Hebrew has led some scholars to suggest it was not the prophet's real name, just a title. However, since the other prophetic books of the Old Testament use the writer's personal name, there seems to be no reason to believe that Malachi's book would do any differently.

Malachi lived during the restoration—the period following Israel's return from exile. His reference to animal sacrifices (Malachi 1:6–14) indicates that the second temple was up and running by the time he wrote his prophecy. However, things were not as they should have been. Everywhere Malachi turned, he saw nothing but corruption and apathy. Priests sacrificed less-than-perfect animals, reserving the best for themselves. Israelite men married pagan women, much to the consternation of Malachi's contemporaries, Ezra and Nehemiah. The rich deprived their employees of a fair wage. Widows, orphans, and foreigners were oppressed and discriminated against. God Himself was robbed, as people simply stopped tithing. In short, Israel was living as if God didn't exist anymore.

MALACHI

Last Prophet of the Old Testament

Malachi paints a picture of people who felt slighted by God, only to reveal that they were the ones doing the slighting. Forsaking the lyrical poetry of other prophets, Malachi wrote in blunt narrative, outlining God's grievances, one by one, and mercilessly dismantling any defense the people might have raised. While Malachi ended with the threat of a curse if the people refused to change, he also wrote of a "sun of righteousness" that would "rise with healing in its wings" (Malachi 4:2). Four centuries later, Luke captured the words of an old man echoing Malachi as he anticipated the impending birth of Jesus, whom he identified as the "rising sun" that would come from heaven (Luke 1:78).

Despite the overarching theme of judgment, a vein of hope runs through Malachi. In the midst of presenting his grievances to the people, God also makes this promise: "Return to me, and I will return to you" (Malachi 3:7).

Altogether, Methuselah lived 969 years, and then he died.
GENESIS 5:27

Day
301

T here is no biblical reference to Methuselah outside of three genealogical records. Yet he is well-known as the world's longest living person, having survived, according to the Bible, for nearly a millennium.

The writer of Genesis recorded two family lines that descended from Adam and Eve. One was the family of Cain, the world's first murderer. The other was the family of Seth, to which Methuselah belonged. The two groups could not have been more different. Cain's family was industrious—playing musical instruments and working with metal—but it was also violent. Lamech, one of Cain's descendants, openly bragged about slaying two young men.

METHUSELAH

World's Longest Living Person

After chronicling Cain's descendants, the writer of Genesis notes that "at that time men began to call on the name of the LORD" (Genesis 4:26). With that, he launched into the account of the other family line—that of Seth. The most obvious characteristic of Seth's descendants was their propensity for long life spans. Five individuals mentioned, including Methuselah, exceeded nine hundred years. More important, however, this was the family that called upon God. Methuselah's father, Enoch, was the first man said to have "walked with God" (see Genesis 5:24). Methuselah's son, Lamech (no connection to the descendant of Cain), recognized God's role in their lives. And Methuselah's grandson, Noah, was found to be "blameless among the people of his time" (Genesis 6:9).

Perhaps even more remarkable than his age was the family to which Methuselah belonged—and their willingness to "call on the name of the LORD."

DID YOU KNOW?

Though Methuselah was history's longest living person, the Bible records that he died the same year as the great flood of Noah's day. The Bible doesn't record if God graciously allowed him to die before the flood or if he was one of the wicked people who perished in the flood. No matter the final outcome of his life, Luke 3 records that Methuselah was one of the ancestors of Jesus Christ.

Zechariah asked the angel, "How can I be sure of this?
I am an old man and my wife is well along in years."
LUKE 1:18

Though he may have had a rather common name (there are no less than twelve Zechariahs mentioned in the Bible), this particular Zechariah stood out as father to the forerunner of the Messiah.

Zechariah and his wife, Elizabeth, echoed a recurring theme from the Jewish story: barrenness and the accompanying sense of emptiness. In their world, bearing children meant the all-important survival of the family line. Being unable to conceive was taken as the absence of God's blessing.

However, Zechariah had been blessed in other ways, and there was no question of his integrity. A member of the Levite priestly class, he belonged to one of twenty-four divisions (his was the division of Abijah) that took turns serving in the temple at Jerusalem. According to the Gospel writer Luke, both he and his wife were blameless in God's sight. Luke wanted to make sure his readers understood that their barren situation was in no way the result of some undisclosed sin.

ZECHARIAH

Father of John the Baptist

One day during his service, Zechariah was chosen to burn incense before the Most Holy Place inside the temple. Given the number of priests available for service, it was not an honor that one received very often. For Zechariah, an already unforgettable experience was made even more unusual by the appearance of an angel who announced the impossible: Zechariah and Elizabeth would bear a son. Their son would be subject to a lifetime Nazirite vow, much like Samson, and he would be counted as the greatest of the old prophets (see Matthew 11:7–13).

Zechariah seemed to believe it was too good to be true, despite knowing the stories of Sarah, Rebekah, Rachel, and Hannah. In response to his demand for a sign, the angel gave him one: He would be mute until the child was born. Having gotten the message but being unable to share it with others (see Luke 1:22), Zechariah returned home. Everything happened just as the angel said it would.

DID YOU KNOW?

Zechariah appeared once more in the story, overruling the custom of naming the firstborn after the father in order to obey the angel's instructions. The story reveals that the naming of the child, which took place at his circumcision on the eighth day, was apparently a community affair.

*While Gallio was proconsul of Achaia, the Jews made a
united attack on Paul and brought him into court.
"This man," they charged, "is persuading the people
to worship God in ways contrary to the law."*
ACTS 18:12–13

I didn't want to get involved." It's become the all-too-common excuse for people who simply don't want to trouble themselves to help someone who is truly in need. And it seems to have been Gallio's mentality during Paul's second missionary journey.

Gallio was the Roman proconsul (or governor) of Achaia, the area of southern Greece. He was the supreme authority over the region and could impose the law as well as pass judgment on it.

While Paul was teaching in the city of Corinth, some of the Jews banded together and brought Paul before Gallio's court. They accused him of teaching people to worship God in ways that were contrary to the law. This really was a legitimate charge under Roman law, but it seems that Gallio didn't want to have to deal with it. He refused to hear the case, saying that it was merely a minor issue of varying interpretations of Jewish law.

GALLIO

Proconsul of Achaia

After Gallio drove the people from court, the mob turned on Sosthenes, the ruler of the synagogue, and beat him in front of the court. The Bible does not make it clear why the mob attacked Sosthenes, but it may have been that he, too, had become a Christian, just as Crispus (another ruler of the synagogue) had. In any case, the attack on Sosthenes even more clearly revealed Gallio's strong desire to keep from getting involved—because he showed no concern whatsoever (Acts 18).

RELATED INFORMATION

Archaeologists have excavated the judgment seat that Gallio would likely have used when the Jews brought Paul before him. It was located in the marketplace.

*But one of them, Caiaphas, who was high priest that year,
said to them, "You know nothing at all. Nor do you understand
that it is better for you that one man should die for the people,
not that the whole nation should perish."*

JOHN 11:49–50 ESV

Few things turn people's stomachs more than the abuse of power by religious leaders. Such people ought to be examples of godly, servant leadership—so when we see them clutching power and using it to serve themselves, we naturally feel angry and disgusted. Caiaphas certainly turned more than a few stomachs in his day, because it seems he was willing to do anything to retain his power.

CAIAPHAS

High Priest

Caiaphas was high priest and a member of the Jewish ruling council called the Sanhedrin. As Jesus grew in popularity and His miracles became well known, the religious leaders began to fear that the Romans would become involved. Caiaphas offered a simple solution: Kill Jesus so the rest of the nation—and no doubt his own power over it—wasn't destroyed. Caiaphas's solution eventually culminated in the crucifixion of Jesus (Matthew 26:3–4, 57; John 11:47–53).

Later, when Peter and John healed a crippled man at the temple, the religious leaders, including Caiaphas, became involved again. Peter boldly told the leaders that he and John had performed the miracle by the authority of Jesus Christ, whom the leaders had put to death. Even though the leaders recognized that their miracle was impossible to deny, they threatened Peter and John to keep them from talking about Jesus (Acts 3–4)!

DID YOU KNOW?

In 1990 twelve ossuaries—bone boxes—of the family tomb of a "Caiaphas" were discovered two miles south of Jerusalem. It is possible that this was the same Caiaphas as the one who plotted Jesus' death.

In the ninth year of Hoshea, the king of Assyria captured Samaria
and deported the Israelites to Assyria. He settled them in Halah,
in Gozan on the Habor River and in the towns of the Medes.
2 KINGS 17:6

At their height of power, the Assyrians' military might was matched only by their cruelty and ruthlessness with their defeated foes.

The Assyrians lived in the northern part of what is known today as Iraq. They were the first nation to rule over the entire Fertile Crescent, stretching from the head of the Persian Gulf up to southeast Turkey and down into Palestine. For over three hundred years they pieced together their empire (911–612 BC), and at their height made major raids into Egypt.

As far as the people of Israel were concerned, the most significant event associated with the Assyrians was their attack at Samaria and the annexation of the northern kingdom of Israel in 722 BC.

The Assyrians exiled many Israelites to faraway places and resettled other foreign peoples in Israel. As these foreign peoples intermarried with Israelites and combined their religious practices with the religion of Israel, they formed a group of people known as Samaritans. These people are spoken about later in several places in the New Testament (Matthew 10:5; Luke 17:16; John 4; Acts 8).

ASSYRIANS

Nation That Exiled
the People of Israel

The Assyrian Empire was eventually overtaken by the Babylonians around 612 BC and later by the Persians.

RELATED INFORMATION

The Bible records another important event that occurred between the Assyrians and King Hezekiah of Judah: At one point, Hezekiah refused to pay the tribute that was expected of them by the Assyrians, so the Assyrians besieged Jerusalem. One night after Hezekiah prayed to the Lord, an angel went throughout the camp and killed 185,000 Assyrians. The king of Assyria withdrew to his own country, and Jerusalem was spared destruction (2 Kings 18–19).

*Ahaz sent messengers to say to Tiglath-Pileser king of Assyria,
"I am your servant and vassal. Come up and save me out of the hand
of the king of Aram and of the king of Israel, who are attacking me."*

2 KINGS 16:7

Never make a deal with the devil. Inevitably the price you pay is far greater than any benefit you receive, just as it was for King Ahaz of Judah when he appealed to King Tiglath-Pileser of Assyria for help against his enemy.

The mighty Assyrian Empire was on the rise during the reign of Tiglath-Pileser, but up to the time of Ahaz, they had not made any real forays into Israel. That all changed once Tiglath-Pileser got a taste of what lay in store in the area—thanks to Ahaz.

At some point in Ahaz's reign, the kings of Aram and Israel teamed up to attack Judah, and Ahaz—in a moment of desperation—appealed to Tiglath-Pileser for help. Ahaz voluntarily made Judah a subservient kingdom to Assyria and paid Tiglath-Pileser a large amount of silver and gold to attack Aram and Israel. Tiglath-Pileser agreed and attacked both Aram and Israel, as Ahaz had requested (2 Kings 16:1–9).

TIGLATH-PILESER

King of Assyria

Unfortunately, however, Ahaz's actions piqued Assyria's interest in the region. Assyria would later capture all of Israel and attack Judah, as well.

RELATED INFORMATION

Isaiah prophesied about Tiglath-Pileser's attack on Aram and Israel in Isaiah 7–9. He assured Ahaz that a child would be born, and "before the boy knows enough to reject the wrong and choose the right, the land of the two kings you dread will be laid waste" (Isaiah 7:16).

So when the time came for Merab, Saul's daughter,
to be given to David, she was given in marriage
to Adriel of Meholah.
1 SAMUEL 18:19

According to the Bible, Merab served as little more than a pawn in the plans of others. First, she was offered as a reward for valor, then as bait in Saul's trap. Finally, her five sons were sacrificed to the Gibeonites to compensate for Saul's atrocities.

Merab first appeared—though she was not mentioned by name—during the confrontation between David and Goliath. Saul had promised his daughter's hand in marriage, along with riches and a lifetime tax exemption, to whoever managed to kill the Philistine giant. David, having been sent on an errand to his older brothers on

MERAB

Daughter of King Saul

the front lines, volunteered for the job, even as battle-hardened soldiers cowered. Despite killing Goliath, however, Saul did not immediately reward David as promised. Instead, while Israel celebrated its young new hero, Saul grew jealous and paranoid. Twice he tried unsuccessfully to run David through with a spear.

When that failed, Saul began sending David on dangerous military missions, promising the very reward that David had already earned: Merab's hand in marriage. "Only serve me bravely and fight the battles of the LORD," Saul insisted (1 Samuel 18:17). His real plan was to expose David to the Philistines and let them do his dirty work.

Saul's plan backfired. Not only did David refuse the invitation to wed Merab, but he continued to succeed against the Philistines, gaining more popularity with each victory. Merab was given to Adriel of Meholah instead.

Merab then went unmentioned for many years, until David was seated on Israel's throne. David had summoned the Gibeonites to find out how he could make restitution for Saul's attempt to annihilate them. (Israel had sworn an oath to spare the Gibeonites years earlier, but in an incident not recorded in scripture, Saul had attacked them.) The Gibeonites asked for seven male descendants of Saul, and David obliged, handing over five of Merab's sons, along with two other members of Saul's household. The seven men were executed and their bodies put on display as a reminder of Saul's misdeeds.

DID YOU KNOW?

Merab was the older of two daughters of Saul. The youngest daughter, Michal, fell in love with David and eventually became his wife.

In those days Caesar Augustus issued a decree
that a census should be taken of the entire Roman world.
LUKE 2:1

It is almost certain that Caesar Augustus never heard of Jesus of Nazareth during his entire life. Yet the ripple effect of Augustus's actions would affect Jesus, who would forever change the world—including the Roman Empire over which Augustus once ruled.

Augustus was the distant nephew and adopted son of Julius Caesar, the first emperor of Rome. After Julius Caesar was assassinated in 44 BC, Augustus defeated his rivals in a series of battles to secure his own rule as emperor. Augustus's reach as emperor extended all the way from Spain to the distant little territory of Palestine, the land of Israel.

CAESAR AUGUSTUS

Emperor of Rome

During his reign as emperor (27 BC to AD 14), Augustus unquestionably achieved many great things and changed the world by his accomplishments, yet it was something so simple as a census that forever linked him with the very birth of the Messiah, Jesus of Nazareth. Around 5 BC a census ordered by Augustus led Joseph and his wife, Mary, to return to Bethlehem, his ancestral home (Luke 2:1–7). While they were there, Jesus was born, which fulfilled an Old Testament prophecy about the Messiah's birthplace (Micah 5:2).

SPIRITUAL INSIGHT

Augustus never had any idea what effect his census would have on the future of the world, but that just further demonstrates how amazing our God is—that He can orchestrate such complex and minute details as the ordering of a census at just the right time to fulfill His perfect will for His people.

It was Mary Magdalene, Joanna, Mary the mother of James,
and the others with them who told this to the apostles.
But they did not believe the women, because their words
seemed to them like nonsense.
LUKE 24:10–11

There are people in the Bible who are marked by some very intriguing contrasts. Take Joanna, for example. She was the wife of Chuza, Herod's household manager—which means that she must have been very wealthy and powerful compared to most other women in first-century Palestine. This also means that her husband was directly connected to the very man who put John the Baptist to death and who played a role in Jesus' death. Yet she was also among those who followed Jesus faithfully and financially provided for Him and His disciples. Her husband must have known and likely supported her association

JOANNA

Woman Who Supported Jesus' Ministry

with Jesus. Perhaps this is one of the ways that Herod had become acquainted with Jesus' activities (Luke 23:8).

Because of her close relationship to Jesus and to the other women who followed Him, Joanna was among those who witnessed Jesus' crucifixion and were first told by angels of Jesus' resurrection. Yet her high societal status and her financial support of Jesus and His disciples did not stop the disciples from dismissing her report about the resurrection as nonsense. They insisted on going to the tomb themselves to see what was going on (Luke 24:10–11).

RELATED INFORMATION

It seems that Jesus must have cured Joanna of an evil spirit or a disease (Luke 8:2), which may be why she became such a devoted supporter of Jesus' ministry.

*Crispus, the synagogue ruler, and his entire household
believed in the Lord; and many of the Corinthians
who heard him believed and were baptized.*

ACTS 18:8

At first glance, we may think that only Gentiles responded to Paul's preaching on his missionary journeys, but the Bible makes it clear that many Jews became believers as well. Crispus is a prime example.

Crispus was the ruler of the synagogue in Corinth, meaning he was the leading elder over the synagogue. After Paul preached the gospel at Athens, he traveled to Corinth, a very wealthy port city in southern Greece. Following his normal custom,

CRISPUS

Synagogue Ruler in Corinth

Paul spent several weeks preaching in the synagogue, showing Jews that Jesus was the Messiah. Eventually, however, some of the Jews became angry and abusive toward Paul, leading him to direct his primary efforts toward the Gentiles. Despite the resistance of these Jews, however, Crispus and his entire household believed in Jesus and were baptized—and so did many other Corinthians, presumably including Jews from the synagogue (Acts 18:1–8).

Crispus and his household must have continued on in the faith, because Paul later made reference to him in 1 Corinthians (1 Corinthians 1:14).

RELATED INFORMATION

The city of Corinth had a long and distinguished history, and it was strategically located near the isthmus that connected southern Greece to the mainland. Every two years the Isthmian Games, similar to the Olympics, were held just outside the city. Partially due to the fact that it was a port city, Corinth had become renowned for its immorality, a problem that is reflected in the issues that Paul had to address later in the church.

Day
311

Josiah's servants brought his body in a chariot from Megiddo to Jerusalem and buried him in his own tomb. And the people of the land took Jehoahaz son of Josiah and anointed him and made him king in place of his father.
2 KINGS 23:30

It's difficult to find any other word than tragic to describe the life of King Jehoahaz of Judah. The only bright spot in his life seems to be that he was born to Josiah, the great king of Judah who brought religious reform to Judah during the dark days immediately before the Babylonian exile. But even his father's connection was still marked by sorrow, for it was Josiah's tragic death in battle that led to Jehoahaz's ascension to the throne.

JEHOAHAZ

King of Judah

After Josiah died trying to stop Pharaoh Neco of Egypt from advancing to help the Assyrians, the people of the land—probably meaning the clan leaders—took Jehoahaz and made him king. Jehoahaz only reigned for three months, though, because Pharaoh Neco dethroned the new king and took him away to Egypt, where he eventually died. Then the Egyptians installed one of Jehoahaz's brothers as king instead and imposed a heavy tax on the people (2 Kings 23).

RELATED INFORMATION

Jehoahaz was one of the last of the descendants of David to rule over Judah. Only three other kings ruled after him, and after that the Babylonians invaded the land, exiling most of the nobles to Babylon (2 Kings 23–24).

Then Mary took about a pint of pure nard, an expensive perfume;
she poured it on Jesus' feet and wiped his feet with her hair.
And the house was filled with the fragrance of the perfume.

JOHN 12:3

Mary was definitely a woman whose heart was given to Jesus. She seemed completely consumed by Jesus' presence when He visited her house, and her loving act of anointing His feet revealed just how deeply she was devoted to Him.

Mary was the sister of Martha and Lazarus, and they lived together in the village of Bethany just outside of Jerusalem. Jesus apparently stayed with them from time to time when He was visiting Jerusalem.

Once when Jesus was visiting, Martha was busy attending to all the preparations—and she became frustrated that Mary was choosing instead to sit at Jesus' feet and listen to Him. She asked Jesus to tell Mary to help her, but instead Jesus affirmed Mary's choice to spend time in His presence.

MARY

Sister of Martha and Lazarus

Another time, not long after Jesus raised Mary's brother, Lazarus, from the dead, Mary's deep love for Jesus was made even more public when she took a pint of expensive perfume, poured it on Jesus' feet, and wiped His feet with her hair. When Judas rebuked her for this seemingly wasteful act, Jesus instead praised her for preparing Him for burial and showing her great value of the short time that He would be with them.

SPIRITUAL INSIGHT

When is the last time you have *lavished* love on Jesus, doing something that "fills the air" of those around you with a sense of your deep care for Him? Are you making the most of your time with Him? Or do you continually choose the daily things of life over Him?

Then the people of the land killed all who had plotted against King Amon, and they made Josiah his son king in his place.
2 KINGS 21:24

Day
313

Read enough novels or watch enough movies and you will quickly see that most people—including Christians—long for a world where people get what they deserve in the end. But is this *really* a good thing? It certainly wouldn't have been the best thing for the people of Judah during the reign of Amon.

Amon was the son of Manasseh, a notoriously wicked king who promoted idolatry throughout Judah. It comes as no surprise, then, that Amon, too, was a wicked king and worshipped idols just as his father had. He forsook the Lord and did not obey Him.

So when we read that Amon's own officials conspired against him and assassinated him in his own palace, it seems like fitting, poetic justice. In fact, doesn't Amon's wickedness call for his descendants to be barred from ruling over Judah as well?

AMON

King of Judah

After all, like father like son, right? But instead, the people of Judah rounded up all of Amon's conspirators, executing them and installing Amon's son Josiah in his place. Why would God allow the dynasty of such a wicked person to continue?

The answer is simple: God is faithful to His promises. He had promised that David's descendants would always rule over His people (2 Samuel 7), and Amon was one of David's descendants. Removing Amon's descendants from the throne essentially meant nullifying God's promise to David. The people of Judah must have recognized that God's desires supersede our hunger to give people what we think they deserve.

RELATED INFORMATION

As it turns out, Amon's son Josiah was one of the godliest kings in the history of Judah (2 Kings 21–23). He fought idolatry and wickedness throughout the land and refurbished the temple. He even expanded Judah's borders to include much of the land of Israel that had been lost to Assyria.

*But Ruth replied [to Naomi], "Don't urge me to leave you
or to turn back from you. Where you go I will go, and where you
stay I will stay. Your people will be my people and your God
my God. Where you die I will die, and there I will be buried."*

RUTH 1:16–17

Going the extra mile for someone can be difficult, even when life is going well. But when there is adversity and personal turmoil, making an extra effort to help someone else can seem impossible. In the character of Ruth, however, we see a shining example of someone doing the impossible.

During the time of the judges in Israel, the family of Elimelech and Naomi moved to Moab to escape a famine in Judah. While they were there, one of their sons married a Moabite woman named Ruth. After ten years of marriage and the earlier death of her father-in-law, Ruth's husband also died.

RUTH

Moabite Daughter-in-Law of Naomi

Naomi, also widowed, decided to return to Judah with her husbandless daughters-in-law. On the way, Naomi told them both to return to their mothers' homes, while she continued on alone to Judah. One daughter-in-law agreed, but Ruth adamantly refused to leave Naomi. She stayed with her and helped to provide food for herself and Naomi in Judah by gleaning in nearby fields—where she eventually met and married Boaz, the landowner, a relative of Elimelech. Boaz and Ruth later had a son, Obed, who became the grandfather of King David.

SPIRITUAL INSIGHT

Even though Ruth may have been suffering tremendous grief over the death of her husband, she didn't return home to the possible comfort of her own family and people. She went with Naomi to a strange land with strange customs, providing comfort and help to her mother-in-law. In our own times of personal distress, would we show others this same selfless kindness? We can rely on God to provide for all our emotional and physical needs—so that we can then demonstrate His love and care to others.

Barak came by in pursuit of Sisera, and Jael went out to meet him.
"Come," she said, "I will show you the man you're looking for."
So he went in with her, and there lay Sisera
with the tent peg through his temple—dead.
JUDGES 4:22

The story may be gruesome, but Jael is a hero nonetheless. She single-handedly slew the commander of the Canaanite forces who were battling God's people.

During the days of Deborah, a judge of Israel, a Canaanite king named Jabin was oppressing God's people, and the commander of his powerful army was named Sisera. Through Deborah, the Lord raised up a man named Barak to fight against Sisera, and the Israelites were victorious. Sisera, however, fled from the battle on foot. He stopped to rest and hide in the tent of a woman named Jael, because he was on friendly terms with her husband's family. Sweet Jael kindly poured him some milk and tucked him into bed like a tired child after a hard day—and then crept up to him while he slept and drove a tent peg through his temple! When Barak came by in pursuit of Sisera, Jael simply flagged him down to show him what she had done.

JAEL

Woman Who Killed a Canaanite Commander

As jarring as it is to read her story, Jael is a woman to be celebrated and praised as a deliverer of God's people just as we praise young David for killing mighty Goliath. For the sake of God's people, she mustered up her courage and did the unthinkable—bringing an end to twenty years of their oppression.

RELATED INFORMATION

Jael's husband is described as a Kenite, a group of people apparently the same as the Midianites (see Numbers 10:29 and Judges 1:16). This group, whose name means "smiths," were not related to the Israelites—but they lived in peace among them at the southern edge of the Promised Land.

Then Bildad the Shuhite replied: "How long will you say such things? Your words are a blustering wind."

JOB 8:1–2

Bildad thought he had it all figured out—about God, about Job, about life—but in the end God showed that he was wrong on all three counts.

Though Bildad knew Job to be successful in all things, he watched as Job became the victim of unbearable suffering. Together with two mutual friends—Eliphaz and Zophar—Bildad arrived at Job's home to mourn with him and speak with him.

Job's friends started out right by simply sitting silently with Job in his pain for seven days. After that, however, everything went downhill. Eliphaz spoke first, gently suggesting that Job must have sinned to bring about his suffering. After Job replied to him, Bildad spoke. Bildad was even more direct than Eliphaz in accusing Job and his family of wrongdoing. His second and third speeches reiterated this assertion, which basically assumes that all suffering is a direct result of a person's sin—so Job must have been hiding some unconfessed failure. Even Bildad's recognition that God will restore the repentant is barely noticeable (Job 8:20–22).

BILDAD

One of Job's Friends

After everyone, including the Lord, had finished speaking, God rebuked the three friends for what they said about Job. He instructed them to offer a sacrifice and ask Job to pray for them so they wouldn't be punished for their foolish words about him. The three friends did so, and the Lord was merciful to them.

SPIRITUAL INSIGHT

When we see someone suffering, our primary concern should be to love and help that person—rather than simply judge him according to the way we think things must work with God. That's not to say that someone's sin or faulty understanding of God should never be addressed. But, unlike Bildad, we should always keep love for others as our guiding principle.

*And Jephthah made a vow to the LORD: "If you give the
Ammonites into my hands, whatever comes out of the
door of my house to meet me when I return in triumph
from the Ammonites will be the LORD's, and I will
sacrifice it as a burnt offering."*
JUDGES 11:30–31

I n the book of Ecclesiastes, the teacher wisely instructed his listeners, "Do not be
quick with your mouth, do not be hasty in your heart to utter anything before God.
God is in heaven and you are on earth, so let your words be few" (Ecclesiastes 5:2).
Unfortunately for Jephthah and his daughter,
the teacher didn't write those words until
long after this story in Judges.

JEPHTHAH

Judge of Israel Who
Made a Foolish Vow

Jephthah lived during the time of Israel's
judges, an outcast among his own family because he was the son of a prostitute. Still,
he had the opportunity to make a name for
himself when the leaders of Israel needed
help fighting the Ammonites, who were op-
pressing them. Jephthah agreed, but with the condition that he rule the people if
he was victorious over the Ammonites. As he was preparing to battle the enemy—
no doubt calculating the high stakes of the outcome—Jephthah made a rash vow
to the Lord: He promised to sacrifice the first thing that came out of his house to
greet him if he won.

Jephthah was indeed victorious over the Ammonites, but when he returned
home, he was shocked to find his daughter, rather than some chicken or goat,
running out to greet him first. So Jephthah offered his daughter as a sacrifice
(Judges 11).

RELATED INFORMATION

In another battle against some of his fellow Israelites, Jephthah
and his men capitalized on a pronunciation difference between the
Ephraimites and the Gileadites. Whenever a person wanted to cross
one of Jephthah's checkpoints, he would have to pronounce the
word "Shibboleth." An Ephraimite could be detected immediately,
because he would be unable to pronounce the *sh* sound and would
pronounce the word as "Sibboleth."

Moses built an altar and called it The Lord is my Banner.
He said, "For hands were lifted up to the throne of the Lord.
The Lord will be at war against the Amalekites from
generation to generation."
Exodus 17:15–16

The Lord will be at war with you forever." Could there be any greater curse placed on a people? This was the curse God gave to Moses about the Amalekites.

The Amalekites were an ancient nomadic people who generally lived at the southern border of Judah and in the northern Sinai region (Genesis 14:7; Numbers 13:29; 1 Samuel 15:7; 27:8). Israel's first contact with them came while the Israelites were traveling from Egypt to Mount Sinai to receive the commandments of the Lord. The Amalekites attacked them at a place called Rephidim, but the Israelites defeated them. Because of the Amalekites' aggression against Israel, the Lord declared to Moses that He would blot out their name and be at war with them forever (Exodus 17:8–16).

AMALEKITES

Desert Enemies of Israel

After Saul became king, Samuel instructed him to carry out the Lord's curse on the Amalekites and devote the entire nation to destruction. Saul attacked them, but he did not carry out God's commands completely, allowing the king of Amalek and the livestock to live (1 Samuel 15).

Later David attacked the Amalekites again after they raided his town of Ziklag and carried away some people as captives (1 Samuel 30).

It seems that a remnant of Amalekites remained even as late as Hezekiah's time, but essentially they ceased to exist as a significant population (1 Chronicles 4:41–43).

RELATED INFORMATION	It is somewhat ironic that Saul, who failed to destroy all the Amalekites, called for an Amalekite to kill him and put him out of his misery (2 Samuel 1:8).

And the hand of the Israelites grew stronger and stronger
against Jabin, the Canaanite king, until they destroyed him.
JUDGES 4:24

D avid once sang, "Some trust in chariots and some in horses, but we trust in the name of the LORD our God" (Psalm 20:7). David's timeless words would have been just as fitting for Jabin—two hundred years earlier—as they were for himself.

King Jabin of Hazor had plenty of horses and chariots—nine hundred to be exact (Judges 4:3)—but they were not enough to stop God's hand leading His people to victory against him. When Jabin began to oppress God's people, the Lord instructed his prophet Deborah to call for a man named Barak to lead God's people

JABIN

Canaanite King Who Oppressed God's People

into battle. Barak led his men to Mount Tabor, while Jabin's commander, Sisera, led his forces toward him in the valley of Jezreel along the Kishon River. Barak's men rushed down the mountain and routed Sisera's forces, chasing them all the way back to their homes. Even Sisera had to flee on foot and was eventually killed by a woman as he slept (Judges 4–5).

That battle appears to have marked the beginning of the end for Jabin's rule over the Israelites (Judges 4:24).

RELATED INFORMATION

Mount Tabor and the valley of Jezreel were the site of another important battle during the time of the judges. Gideon and his small army of three hundred men were victorious in a battle against the vast Midianite army in this area (Judges 8:18). Hundreds of years later, Alexander the Great captured a fortress called Itabyrium located on the top of Mount Tabor.

"For even the Son of Man did not come to be served, but to serve, and to give his life as a ransom for many."

MARK 10:45

The list of paradoxes about Jesus seems endless—born to die, fully God and fully man, served others though He was King of kings, betrayed to death by a kiss—but perhaps the greatest paradox is also the most wonderful for us: He died so that we might receive life.

Even Jesus' beginnings are difficult to describe, because as the third person of the Trinity, He has always existed (see John 1:1–3; 8:58). In terms of His earthly life, however, Jesus was born to Mary and Joseph, who descended from King David himself (Matthew 1–2; Luke 2–3). Jesus grew up in the town of Nazareth and became a carpenter, like Joseph (Matthew 13:55; Mark 6:3).

JESUS

Son of God

Jesus began His public ministry of teaching and healing around age thirty (Luke 3:23), and His ministry lasted about three years. At the end of His ministry, some jealous Jewish leaders, looking for a way to get rid of Him, accused Him of treason before the Roman governor for His claim to be the Messiah, the King of the Jews. The Romans crucified Jesus along with two bandits, and He was buried in a borrowed rock tomb (Matthew 26–27).

Three days later, God raised Jesus to life again, just as He had promised. Later Jesus ascended to heaven until the time comes for Him to return to take His followers with Him to heaven (Matthew 28; Luke 24:50–53).

SPIRITUAL INSIGHT

To read the bare facts about Jesus' life and death can mislead us into seeing Him as another tragic victim of an evil world—but the truth is that the world was merely carrying out the plan of God for the salvation of His people (Acts 2). Through Jesus' death, the price for sin was paid, and we can be made right with God (Romans 5). Praise God for sending Jesus to bring us eternal life in Him!

Keep yourselves in God's love as you wait for the mercy
of our Lord Jesus Christ to bring you to eternal life.
JUDE 1:21

Jude is a relatively obscure figure in the New Testament—which is quite remarkable, given his family connection to the Messiah.

In all likelihood, Jude was the half brother of Jesus, yet he made no effort to peddle his relationship in order to gain attention or influence. In his letter to fellow believers, Jude introduced himself, not as the brother of Jesus, but as the "brother of James," another of Jesus' half brothers. Jude did not even claim the privileged title of "apostle," instead referring to himself as a mere "servant of Jesus Christ" (Jude 1:1).

Jude's humility and lack of ambition can be seen in his purpose for writing the New Testament letter that bears his name. Jude set aside his own agenda—that is, his desire to write about "the salvation we share" (Jude 1:3)—in order to address more pressing matters that were affecting his audience.

JUDE

Half Brother of Jesus

Apparently, false teachers were infiltrating the church, telling all who would listen that once saved by God, they could live however they wanted—because they were already covered by grace. Jude responded with a brief history lesson, reminding believers that even though God once saved the Hebrews from slavery in Egypt, He still punished those who rebelled against Him in the wilderness—those who, according to Jude, "did not believe" (Jude 1:5).

Jude regarded these false teachers as a threat to the very gospel his half brother had come to proclaim. He described them as "blemishes at your love feasts," "clouds without rain," and "twice dead" (Jude 1:12–13). Yet, despite the urgency of his message, Jude did not resort to using his connection to Jesus as a club with which to beat his audience into submission. Instead, he relied entirely on the truth and power of what he called the "most holy faith" (Jude 1:20).

DID YOU KNOW? Jude can be found in the Gospels—but you have to look closely. In Mark 6:3, people respond to Jesus' teaching in His hometown, Nazareth, by asking, "Isn't this Mary's son and the brother of James, Joseph, Judas and Simon?" Judas is a variant of the name Jude—and most likely a reference to the New Testament author.

*Nevertheless, for David's sake the L*ORD *his God gave
him a lamp in Jerusalem by raising up a son to succeed
him and by making Jerusalem strong.*

1 KINGS 15:4

It would be interesting to know how often we are delivered from painful consequences for the sake of someone else. How often has God honored the prayers of our parents to watch over us even while we were acting foolishly or even sinfully? How often has God stopped us from speaking wrongly toward our kids because He was sparing them from the hurt that our words would cause? Abijah was spared the worst of consequences for his sins—removal from the throne—because God chose to honor the covenant He made with David many years before.

ABIJAH

King of Judah

Abijah was the son of Rehoboam, who was the son of Solomon. The Bible makes it clear that Abijah "committed all the sins his father had done before him; his heart was not fully devoted to the LORD his God" (1 Kings 15:3). These sins included the idolatry that caused the Lord to drive out the pagan nations from Canaan centuries earlier (1 Kings 14:23–24).

Despite Abijah's wickedness, however, the Lord remained faithful to His covenant with David to build up a lasting dynasty. Because of this, Abijah was allowed to continue to reign as king—and his son was allowed to carry on the Davidic dynasty after him.

RELATED INFORMATION

The Bible records a battle between Abijah and Jeroboam to determine the boundary line between their two nations. Abijah captured three towns, pushing the boundary line deep into the former territory of the northern kingdom (2 Chronicles 13:3–20). Eventually the boundary line would move farther south again and be firmly settled during the reign of Abijah's son Asa (1 Kings 15:9–22).

And at that time, when Jeroboam went out of Jerusalem, the prophet Ahijah the Shilonite found him on the road. Now Ahijah had dressed himself in a new garment, and the two of them were alone in the open country.

1 KINGS 11:29 ESV

Like all true prophets of the Lord, Ahijah told it like it was—good news or bad. We first hear about Ahijah when he prophesied to Jeroboam the good news that he would one day become king over the northern tribes of Israel. He even told Jeroboam that the Lord would establish a lasting dynasty for him if he obeyed the Lord (1 Kings 11:29–39). Eventually Jeroboam did become king, but he failed to obey the Lord and even promoted idolatry throughout Israel (1 Kings 12:28–33).

Then came the bad news. When Jeroboam's son Abijah fell sick, Jeroboam sent his wife to ask Ahijah what would happen to the child. Jeroboam must have already known that his wicked behavior would not have put him in Ahijah's good graces— and he apparently thought the way to a prophet's heart was through his stomach, because he told his wife to disguise herself and bring some sweets for Ahijah. The ruse

AHIJAH

Prophet of Israel

failed, however, because Ahijah's spiritual sight was far greater than his physical blindness. He immediately knew the woman was Jeroboam's wife, and didn't mince words about their impending fate: Their son would die, and eventually all their male descendants would be killed and left shamefully unburied (1 Kings 14:1–18). Ahijah's prophecy came true when a man named Baasha usurped the throne and killed all of Jeroboam's male descendants (1 Kings 15:27–30).

RELATED INFORMATION

Ahijah was from Shiloh, a town where the tabernacle was located until the Philistines captured the ark of the covenant in battle and apparently overran the town (1 Samuel 4).

But Lot's wife looked back,
and she became a pillar of salt.
GENESIS 19:26

Lot's wife garners only a single verse in all of scripture, but her actions and punishment raise some very significant questions. Did she look back longingly for what she was leaving? Or did she look back to see the punishment that was befalling those who did not escape Sodom?

Lot was the nephew of the patriarch Abraham, who accompanied him to Canaan. At some point in their time in Canaan, the two men decided to separate to avoid conflicts over land for their vast herds. Lot chose the lush valley of the Jordan River and Dead Sea, so he moved to Sodom, which was likely located along the eastern coast of the Dead Sea (Genesis 13).

LOT'S WIFE

Wife of Abraham's Nephew Lot

Sodom was a wicked city, and eventually the Lord destroyed it by raining burning sulfur down on it. Before He did, however, He sent two angels to lead Lot's family to safety away from the city. While they were leaving the city, Lot's wife disobeyed the warning of the angels and looked back—and she was turned into a pillar of salt (Genesis 19:17, 26).

The Bible does not make it clear *why* she looked back, so we are left wondering exactly why she was punished. One thing is clear, though: When the Lord leads us away from sin and its consequences, there is nothing to be gained by looking back.

RELATED INFORMATION

In the New Testament, Jesus tells His listeners to "remember Lot's wife" on the day when the Lord comes for His people (Luke 17:32). In that context, He seems to suggest that Lot's wife was looking back in longing for what she was leaving behind.

And there was war in heaven. Michael and his angels fought
against the dragon, and the dragon and his angels fought back.
REVELATION 12:7

Day
325

Michael is one of the most mysterious figures in the Bible. One of just two angels mentioned by name (the other being Gabriel), Michael is the only one specifically identified as an archangel.

Michael plays a variety of roles in the Bible—from Israel's protector (Daniel 10, 12) to heavenly warrior (Revelation 12:7) to the herald of Christ's return (assuming that 1 Thessalonians 4:16 is a reference to Michael). In every case, Michael is at the center of a conflict raging in an unseen realm.

MICHAEL

Archangel

Perhaps the most cryptic reference to Michael is found in the book of Jude. Writing to the early church, Jude quoted an apocryphal story in which Michael and the devil fought over the body of Moses. The original significance remains a mystery, but Jude used the story to make a point about respect for angelic beings. Apparently some false believers had rejected all forms of authority and had even begun to "slander celestial beings" (Jude 1:8). In response, Jude noted that the archangel Michael refused to accuse the devil, a fallen angel, but instead left the rebuking to God.

In the Old Testament, Daniel described an encounter with a mysterious being who was detained by an evil spirit while on his way to visit the aging prophet. It was only when Michael came to the being's aid that he was able to complete his journey (Daniel 10:12–14). Later, the mysterious being described Michael as "the great prince" who protected Israel in the midst of its distress (Daniel 12:1).

When it comes to understanding Michael, the unknown almost certainly outweighs that which can be known. However, one thing is certain: The world we see and touch is not all there is. Michael's story reminds us that angelic conflict continues unseen.

SPIRITUAL INSIGHT

While Michael engages in real conflict with demonic forces, the final outcome of the battle between good and evil is certain. Revelation predicts Michael's victory over "the dragon and his angels," driving them out of heaven (Revelation 12:7). In the end, success depends not on Michael, but on the all-powerful God. As John writes, "They overcame [the accuser] by the blood of the Lamb" (Revelation 12:11).

Day
326

*Then Jesus replied, "Have I not chosen you, the Twelve?
Yet one of you is a devil!" (He meant Judas, the son of Simon
Iscariot, who, though one of the Twelve, was later to betray him.)*
JOHN 6:70–71

Scholars have long debated the real reason for Judas's betrayal of Jesus—suggesting as possible motives everything from greed to disillusionment.

Some believe Judas did it for the money. The blood payment, thirty pieces of silver, equaled four months' salary. According to John's Gospel, Judas was a thief who liked to "help himself" to money set aside to support Jesus' ministry (John 12:6).

Another theory notes that Judas was one of the only non-Galilean disciples. His surname, Iscariot, likely indicates his birthplace—Kerioth, a town in southern Judah. As an outsider, Judas may have felt alienated from the group.

JUDAS ISCARIOT

King of Persia

Others insist that Judas was a Zealot, part of a Jewish guerilla movement bent on driving out the Romans by any means necessary. As it became clear that Jesus had no intention of waging a war, Judas grew disillusioned or fearful (or both) and began looking for a way out.

A variant on this theory suggests that Judas didn't mean to betray Jesus at all—that Judas was merely trying to force His hand, convinced Jesus would give the call to arms once He was confronted in the garden of Gethsemane.

Still others chalk it up to demonic possession, noting—as Luke does—that "Satan entered Judas" shortly before the betrayal (Luke 22:3) and leaving it at that.

Whatever the real reason (or reasons), it is clear that Judas did not see the world as Jesus did. In one of the only stories to mention Judas outside of his betrayal, he scoffed at the so-called waste of expensive perfume by the woman from Bethany (see John 12:1–11). Jesus saw the woman's gift as an act of devotion, preparing Him for His impending death and burial. Judas only saw money being poured down the drain—money he wanted for himself. Judas demonstrated greed, hypocrisy, and an unwillingness to associate himself with Jesus' death—values that have no place in God's kingdom.

DID YOU KNOW?

The disciples' first order of business after Jesus' ascension was replacing Judas. In the book of Acts, Luke chose not to spare his readers the grisly details of Judas's suicide, noting that the betrayer's "body burst open and all his intestines spilled out" (Acts 1:18).

*Then Jesus told him, "Because you have seen me, you have believed;
blessed are those who have not seen and yet have believed."*
JOHN 20:29

Thomas is best known for his doubting tendencies, but the disciple of Jesus also known as Didymus was capable of demonstrating courage and resolve, too.

When his friend Lazarus died, Jesus set out for Bethany, near Jerusalem—not to pay His last respects, but to raise Lazarus from the dead. However, doing so meant walking straight into His enemies' lair. The disciples were aware of the dangers. Jesus had already alluded to His death (see John 10:15), and of course they were not blind to opposition of the religious leaders. They knew going to Bethany was risky. Yet Thomas alone spoke in favor of Jesus' plan, saying that if their Master was going to die, the rest of them may as well die with Him.

THOMAS

Doubting Apostle

This episode of courage is overshadowed by Thomas's infamous display of doubt following the resurrection of Jesus. Thomas had been away when Jesus first appeared to the disciples. Upon hearing the news, he refused to believe it—until Jesus appeared yet again, astonishing the skeptical disciple.

It is easy to judge Thomas harshly. However, to do so is to forget that bodily resurrections were not exactly an everyday occurrence in the first century. Even the fact that Thomas had seen his Master raise others from the dead could have been forgotten easily in the grief and confusion that followed Jesus' crucifixion.

Thomas was not condemned by Jesus, nor was his belief rejected. Nevertheless, the risen Lord used the occasion to bless those who would believe in Him even without seeing.

DID YOU KNOW?

There are competing accounts of Thomas's life following the resurrection of Jesus. According to one tradition, he ventured as far as India. However, the early church theologian Origen wrote that Thomas brought the gospel to Parthia, which included parts of present-day Turkey, Iraq, and Iran. He is said to have died in Edessa, present-day Turkey. Whatever his contribution to the spread of Christianity may have been, Thomas was almost certainly a part of it. After all, he was present with the other disciples after Jesus ascended to heaven (see Acts 1:13).

*Meanwhile, the officials of the king of Aram [Ben-Hadad]
advised him, "Their gods are gods of the hills. That is why they
were too strong for us. But if we fight them on the plains,
surely we will be stronger than they."*

1 KINGS 20:23

Theology matters. From Bible professors to the person sitting next to you on the bus, we all think certain things about God, and this will affect how we live and act. Unfortunately for King Ben-Hadad of Aram, he got his theology very wrong—and it led to a stunning defeat of his army.

There were several kings of Aram named Ben-Hadad, and all of them fought with Israel at one time or another. The one who fought against King Ahab of Israel was Ben-Hadad II, likely the son of Ben-Hadad I.

BEN-HADAD

King of Aram

Ben-Hadad mustered a vast coalition of forces and besieged Samaria, the capital city of Israel. He called for Ahab to surrender, but Ahab refused. Instead, he launched a preemptive attack that caught the drunken Arameans by surprise, and Ahab won a great victory.

Ben-Hadad's officers must have been looking for some excuse as to why they were unable to defeat Ahab's forces, so they offered a bit of bad theology to Ben-Hadad: The God of Israel is a god of the hills. Attack them on the plains, and you will win. They couldn't have been more wrong. When the Arameans attacked Israel again the next year, Ahab's forces defeated them again, killing one hundred thousand of them in a single day!

SPIRITUAL INSIGHT

The world is fond of portraying theology as a bunch of ivory-towered musings of the socially irrelevant elite. But in the end, how we think about God affects everything we do. Our beliefs about God will either lead us to our salvation or our demise. Don't be like Ben-Hadad—know the God of Israel and live.

These were the Levites who were counted by their clans: through Gershon, the Gershonite clan; through Kohath, the Kohathite clan; through Merari, the Merarite clan.
NUMBERS 26:57

When we think of a noble calling, it is unlikely that we think of jobs such as janitors, maintenance workers, and security guards. But in Bible times, these were the very jobs that were specifically set aside for the descendants of Gershon, who helped to maintain the tabernacle and temple and assist the priests with their duties.

The tabernacle, and later the temple, was the place where God's presence was most visibly represented among His people, Israel. There the people would bring their sacrifices and offerings, and the priests would come before God on behalf of the people. It was arguably the most holiest on earth at that time.

GERSHON

Ancestor of
Gershonite Levites

But this structure required a great deal of work to maintain, and not just anyone was allowed to do it. Only descendants of Levi were allowed to help with this—and even this large group was separated into different clans that were assigned specific tasks for the tabernacle. The Gershonites, the descendants of Levi's son Gershon, were responsible for carrying many of the items when they were being transferred, and they also guarded the entrances to the tabernacle once it was set up and functioning (Numbers 3:23–26; 4:22–28). If they didn't do their jobs properly, the tabernacle would not be set up correctly—or the whole structure might become defiled by a ceremonially unclean person entering the area.

RELATED INFORMATION

The Gershonites were under the supervision of the priests, who were also descendants of Levi, but more specifically they were descendants of Aaron, Moses' brother (Exodus 28:1).

*Abraham left everything he owned to Isaac. But while he
was still living, he gave gifts to the sons of his concubines
and sent them away from his son Isaac to the land of the east.*
GENESIS 25:5–6

Midian was the fourth son of Abraham by his second wife, Keturah. Abraham married Keturah some time after Sarah, his first wife, had died. Elsewhere, Keturah was described as "Abraham's concubine" (see 1 Chronicles 1:32).

Before Abraham died, he sent Midian and his brothers away from him. Just as he had done with Hagar and Ishmael years before, Abraham wanted to put some distance between Isaac and his half brothers. In keeping with the covenant God had made, Abraham could have but one true heir, and that was Isaac. So Abraham gave Midian and his brothers unspecified gifts and sent them to a land east of Canaan.

In that eastern land—probably Arabia—Midian's offspring grew into a nation. His descendants would have intermittent contact with the Israelites for centuries to come—sometimes for good, sometimes for evil. Moses' father in-law, Jethro, was a Midianite priest who worshipped God. Despite their estrangement from the chosen family, at least some of Midian's descendants seem to have followed in the faith of Abraham. Later, however, the Midianites played the foil to Israel's story. Together with the Moabites, they tried to curse the Israelites on their way into the Promised Land. They also invaded Israelite territory during the time of the judges. The enmity between Israel and Midian can be seen in passages like this: "Do to them as you did to Midian. . . . May they ever be ashamed and dismayed; may they perish in disgrace" (Psalm 83:9, 17).

MIDIAN

Son of Abraham and Keturah

DID YOU KNOW?

The Midianites also played a brief but important part in the story of Joseph and his brothers (see Genesis 37). The brothers sold Joseph to a caravan of Midianite merchants, who took him to Egypt, where they in turn sold Joseph as a slave.

And a woman was there who had been subject to bleeding for twelve years. She had suffered a great deal under the care of many doctors and had spent all she had, yet instead of getting better she grew worse.
MARK 5:25–26

She was out of money, still sick, and nearly out of hope—except for Jesus. The Bible tells an interesting story about a woman who seems to appear as an interruption in another story about a little girl who needed healing.

The woman had been suffering from some sort of bleeding illness for twelve years. Besides taking a terrible physical toll on her, such an illness would have rendered her ritually unclean all this time (Leviticus 15:25–28), leaving her essentially cut off from worship at the temple. She had spent all she had on doctors, but to no avail. She had only grown worse, and now it seemed she had nowhere else to turn for healing.

THE WOMAN WITH ILLNESS

Woman Healed after Twelve Years

At this same time, Jesus was on His way to heal a young girl, and crowds were following Him closely. The woman, too, heard about Jesus—and boldly approached Him from behind to touch His cloak, trusting that this would be sufficient to heal her. The Lord rewarded her faith, and she was instantly healed. When Jesus insisted on knowing who touched Him, the woman came forward and confessed. Instead of rebuking her, Jesus praised her for her faith (Mark 5:24–34).

SPIRITUAL INSIGHT

This story clearly teaches that Jesus has the power to free us from suffering if He chooses to reward our faith in Him. At the same time, we must also keep in mind that, as with Paul (2 Corinthians 12:7–9), God sometimes chooses to give us grace to endure our suffering rather than releasing us from it. If you are suffering from an illness, seek God's healing in faith—but rest assured that God will provide all that you need in Him.

*"Son of man, behold, I am about to take the delight of
your eyes away from you at a stroke; yet you shall
not mourn or weep, nor shall your tears run down."*

Ezekiel 24:16 esv

How do you speak truth to people who have no interest in hearing it? This was as much a dilemma in the time of Ezekiel as it is today. And the solution was the same then as it is today: We speak with our lives.

Ezekiel was a priest who was taken into exile in Babylon along with many other people of Judah (Ezekiel 1:3). For many years he prophesied to the people in Babylon, giving them messages of both condemnation and hope. The Lord called him to tell the people that they were in Babylon because they had sinned greatly against the Lord—and Ezekiel often used very harsh words and powerful illustrations to make the people listen. There were times, though, when it seemed the only thing people would heed was Ezekiel's very own life before them.

EZEKIEL

Prophet of Judah

Perhaps the most moving life-message that Ezekiel gave the people was a warning of the destruction that awaited Jerusalem. The Lord told Ezekiel that his wife, "the delight of [his] eyes," would soon die—and Ezekiel was not to publicly mourn her death. Instead, he would only be allowed to grieve within himself. This prophecy foretold how God was about to destroy Jerusalem, the delight of the people's eyes, and they would not be free to mourn over the city but would waste away inside, reflecting on their own sins. Only after Ezekiel and his people had been notified of the city's destruction would Ezekiel be allowed to speak.

SPIRITUAL INSIGHT

In terms of people's hearts, we live in a world that is not all that different from the world of Ezekiel's day. People's hearts have been hardened by sin, and their eyes have been blinded to the truth. The only message that many people will ever willingly accept is the testimony of our lives. What message about God is your life communicating?

The king talked with them, and he found none equal to Daniel,
Hananiah, Mishael and Azariah; so they entered the king's service.
DANIEL 1:19

When the Babylonian king scrutinized Hananiah, Mishael, and Azariah, he found them "ten times better" than all of his sorcerers and astrologers (Daniel 1:20). Their secret was simple: The king could transplant them to pagan Babylon—he could even give them pagan names— but Babylon would not remove God from their hearts.

As members of the Jewish aristocracy, these men were taken to Babylon about two decades before Jerusalem and its temple were destroyed. In Babylon, they were trained to serve the court of King Nebuchadnezzar. Their Hebrew names, which honored God, were replaced with names that honored Babylonian idols and their new king. The change was intended to remind them that they now belonged to Nebuchadnezzar, and that his goal was their assimilation—a natural reponse since the king interpreted his triumph over Jerusalem as the triumph of his gods over the Hebrew God. These friends were now expected to pay homage to the victorious idols of Babylon.

HANANIAH, MISHAEL, AND AZARIAH

Also Known as Shadrach, Meshach, and Abednego

The religious devotion of these men came under fire at least twice. The first test came when they were ordered to eat from the royal table even though Nebuchadnezzar's food and drink had been offered to idols first. Clearly, eating this food would have signified submission to the Babylonian gods. The three friends refused—and were later vindicated when their spartan diet of vegetables and water proved superior to the choicest meals from the king's table.

Later these men—along with the rest of Babylon— were ordered to bow down to a golden image erected by Nebuchadnezzar. Once more they refused to trade their God for Babylonian idols, and once more they were vindicated. After Nebuchadnezzar had the trio thrown into a fiery furnace, they emerged without so much as the smell of soot on them.

SPIRITUAL INSIGHT

Daniel 2 reveals how these three men were successful at resisting Babylon's influence. While all the king's astrologers relied on superstition and idolatry, these men relied on prayer (see Daniel 2:17–18). Rather than look to the stars to reveal truth, they looked to the One who made the stars.

So [Philip] started out, and on his way he met an Ethiopian eunuch, an important official in charge of all the treasury of Candace, queen of the Ethiopians. This man had gone to Jerusalem to worship.

ACTS 8:27

Once in a great while it happens. Someone begins asking us questions about God or the gospel, and before we know it, he or she has virtually rolled out the red carpet to be led to Christ. That's the situation with the Ethiopian eunuch whom Philip encountered on the road to Gaza.

Ethiopia was the same country that was called Cush in the Old Testament. It was located south of Egypt in Africa, hundreds of miles from Israel. During the time of the Babylonian conquest of Judah, many Jews fled to Ethiopia to escape. Their influence may have been what led to a large following of native Ethiopians to worship the God of Israel.

THE ETHIOPIAN EUNUCH

Official Met by Philip

By the time of the New Testament, Ethiopia had been ruled by several queens, all taking the title Candace—much like the title Caesar of the Roman Empire. The eunuch was an official of this kingdom, and he had just been to Jerusalem to worship there. The Lord led a Christian leader named Philip to go down to Gaza, where he met the eunuch reading the scriptures in his chariot. As they began to talk, the eunuch asked Philip to explain who was being talked about in Isaiah 53—and Philip told him that this referred to Jesus. The eunuch became a believer, and then he was baptized. Philip was then led by the Spirit to Azotus, and the eunuch went on his way rejoicing (Acts 8:26–40).

RELATED INFORMATION

Though it is only speculation, it is possible that the Ethiopian eunuch was actually looking for a passage in Isaiah 56:3–4, and he may have only unrolled the scroll as far as chapter 53 by the time Philip met him.

*When the Ammonites saw that they had become a
stench to David, Hanun and the Ammonites sent
1,000 talents of silver to hire chariots and horsemen
from Mesopotamia, from Aram-maacah, and from Zobah.*
1 CHRONICLES 19:6 ESV

W hen Hanun picked a fight with David, he definitely bit off more than he
could chew. Hanun's father, Nahash, was king of the Ammonites, and apparently
he had maintained good relations with David, who was king of Israel. When
Nahash died, his son Hanun became king, and David sent a delegation to express
sympathy for the death of Hanun's father. Hanun, however, chose to interpret
David's gesture as a spy mission—and he
essentially threw down the gauntlet by
humiliating David's men and sending them
back to him (2 Samuel 10).

HANUN

Ammonite King Who
Rebuffed David

David, of course, prepared for war. In
the meantime, Hanun made preparations of
his own by hiring mercenaries from three
other countries to the north. But David's
commander, Joab, proved too capable for
Hanun's coalition, and the Ammonites were defeated. Later the Ammonites and
their allies regrouped, mustering even more men from other lands—but David
and his men defeated them a second time. After that Hanun's allies refused to
help him.

*But God, who comforts the downcast, comforted us by the
coming of Titus, and not only by his coming but
also by the comfort you had given him.*
2 CORINTHIANS 7:6–7

On more than one occasion, Titus proved a vital partner in Paul's "ministry of reconciliation" (see 2 Corinthians 5:18).

In Paul's mind, Titus provided the answer to a burning question that motivated his letter to the Galatians: Was it necessary for Gentile converts to Christianity to be circumcised in order to be received into the body of Christ? According to Paul, Titus was living, breathing proof that the answer was no.

TITUS

Paul's Ministry Partner

Titus is not mentioned by name in the book of Acts, though some have suggested (with good reason) that Titus was at the center of the circumcision debate described in Acts 15. In any case, Paul peppered his letters with numbers of references to Titus, demonstrating how important he was to Paul in their mutual ministry.

During his first missionary journey, Paul became the first church leader to systematically reach out to Gentiles wherever he went. At the close of this expedition, he returned to Jerusalem, presumably to join the debate over the need for Gentile circumcision (compare Galatians 2:1 with Acts 15:1, though some think Paul was referring to the visit alluded to in Acts 11:30). Some in the church at Jerusalem argued that circumcision was a necessary prerequisite for salvation. Before long, the same idea was circulating among believers in Galatia. Paul reminded his readers that not only had the church leaders in Jerusalem endorsed his ministry to the Gentiles, they had declined to make Titus—a Gentile believer who accompanied Paul to Jerusalem—undergo circumcision. In Paul's mind, Titus's example settled the matter.

In the years that followed, Titus continued to be a catalyst for reconciliation. Titus was Paul's emissary to the church in Corinth during a particularly difficult time in the relationship between it and the apostle. Much to Paul's relief, Titus returned to him with a positive report of comfort, "godly sorrow," and reconciliation (see 2 Corinthians 7:5–13).

Titus continued to work alongside Paul, traveling with him to Crete, where they seem to have parted for a time. Nevertheless, Titus continued to serve God faithfully, reconciling people to Him and to each other.

DID YOU KNOW? Titus eventually wound up ministering in Dalmatia, a Roman province on the other side of the Adriatic Sea from Italy.

But the king of Assyria discovered that Hoshea was a traitor,
for he had sent envoys to So king of Egypt, and he no longer
paid tribute to the king of Assyria, as he had done year by year.
Therefore Shalmaneser seized him and put him in prison.
2 KINGS 17:4

King Shalmaneser reigned over Assyria for only five years, but in that time he changed the land and the people of Israel forever.

The northern kingdom of Israel was already a subservient kingdom to Assyria when Shalmaneser became king, but eventually Israel's leader, Hoshea, rebelled. He turned to King So of Egypt to support him and refused to pay tribute money to Assyria. As a result, Shalmaneser invaded Israel and laid siege to Samaria for three years.

SHALMANESER

King of Assyria

Eventually the city fell, and the Assyrians deported many Israelites to faraway places in the Assyrian Empire (2 Kings 17). Unlike the southern kingdom of Judah, which would experience exile later, Israel would never truly recover from its exile. Instead, foreign peoples were resettled in Israel, and the resulting mixing of the population and their religions created the Samaritan people and religion. Israel would be dominated by these people and other non-Jews for the rest of biblical history, including the time of Jesus.

RELATED INFORMATION

The Samaritans are spoken of several times in the New Testament. Jesus told a story about a Samaritan man who acted as a neighbor by helping a Jew who had been attacked by robbers (Luke 10:25–37). Jesus healed a Samaritan man of leprosy (Luke 17:11–19). Jesus also spoke with a Samaritan woman at a well near Sychar (John 4). Peter and John preached the gospel in several Samaritan towns (Acts 8:25).

One of those listening was a woman named Lydia, a dealer in purple cloth from the city of Thyatira, who was a worshiper of God. The Lord opened her heart to respond to Paul's message.
ACTS 16:14

LYDIA

First Believer from Paul's Ministry in Europe

Lydia has the great distinction of being the first person in Europe to respond to Paul's presentation of the gospel.

Paul met Lydia in the city of Philippi while he was on his second missionary journey. He had just sailed from the city of Troas in Asia Minor to the port city of Neapolis, which is near Philippi in Macedonia (northern Greece). There must not have been very many Jews in Philippi, because Paul did not go to a synagogue on the Sabbath as he usually did. Instead, he went to a nearby riverbank, where any Jews who did live there would likely have met for prayer.

There he found several women, including Lydia, a "worshiper of God," which usually meant a Gentile convert to Judaism. She was actually from the city of Thyatira in Asia Minor and was likely wealthy, since she was a dealer in purple cloth. When Paul began to speak to the women about the gospel, Lydia responded, became a believer, and was baptized. Later she invited Paul and his companions to stay with her family. Still later, after Paul and Silas were released from prison, they returned to Lydia's house, encouraged the fledgling church that was started there, and then left to travel farther throughout Macedonia.

RELATED INFORMATION

By the time of Paul, Philippi, while not large, was a significant Roman city—home to many retired Roman soldiers and granted exemption from most taxes.

So he died, according to the word of the LORD that
Elijah had spoken. Because Ahaziah had no son,
Joram succeeded him as king in the second year
of Jehoram son of Jehoshaphat king of Judah.
2 KINGS 1:17

D EAD END. That's probably the most concise way to sum up the brief reign of King Ahaziah of Israel. He was born the son of Ahab, and like his father, is described as "evil in the eyes of the LORD" because he worshipped idols. The only two events that the Bible mentions during his brief two-year reign are his failed venture with Jehoshaphat and his encounter with Elijah, who prophesied judgment on him for consulting Baal about an injury.

Many years earlier, King Solomon had launched trading ships from Ezion Geber on the Red Sea, at the extreme southern border of Israel, and they returned with gold, silver, and exotic goods from faraway lands (1 Kings 9:26–28; 10:11–12). It seems that Ahaziah and Jehoshaphat planned to

AHAZIAH

King of Israel

do the same thing from Ezion Geber, but their ships were wrecked in port before they ever set sail (1 Kings 22:48–49).

Sometime later Ahaziah fell through the lattice of his upper room in Samaria and severely injured himself. He sent messengers to consult Baal-Zebub in the Philistine city of Ekron to see if he would recover. The prophet Elijah, however, intercepted his messengers and informed them that Ahaziah would die before ever leaving his bed. Elijah's words came true, and Ahaziah died without leaving an heir—so his brother Joram was made king instead (2 Kings 1).

RELATED INFORMATION

The name Baal-Zebub probably means "Lord of the Flies" and has become associated with Satan. The English title has gained renewed fame in recent decades with the publication of William Golding's book by the same title.

Asa then took the silver and gold out of the treasuries of
the Lord's temple and of his own palace and sent it to
Ben-Hadad king of Aram, who was ruling in Damascus.
2 Chronicles 16:2

Like a lion stalking its prey until the moment is right to pounce, pride can creep up on us over time—slowly, almost imperceptibly—until suddenly we are overtaken by sin. This must have been how pride got the best of Asa.

In general, the Bible speaks very highly of King Asa of Judah. His first ten years of rule were marked by peace and by his efforts to remove idolatry from Judah. He strengthened Judah's defenses and even defeated a great army from Cush (modern Sudan) that had come up against him (2 Chronicles 14). Later a prophet named Azariah encouraged him to continue following the Lord, and Asa's efforts to remove idolatry grew. It became so evident that the Lord was with him that many people from the northern kingdom of Israel left their country to join him in Judah (2 Chronicles 15).

Asa

King of Judah

But even as Asa grew in his accomplishments, pride must have been growing in him as well. This first became evident when Asa was at war with King Baasha of Israel. Instead of relying on the Lord to help him, Asa bribed the Arameans, who bordered Israel on the northeast, to attack Israel. When the prophet Hanani rebuked Asa for this, Asa became enraged and put him in prison. He also began to brutally oppress some of the people. A few years later, Asa contracted a foot disease and refused to seek help from the Lord, relying instead only on physicians (2 Chronicles 16). The pride in Asa's heart had come to full flower.

SPIRITUAL INSIGHT

Asa allowed pride to creep up in his heart even as he was doing great things for the Lord. Perhaps it was these great deeds themselves that led Asa to become prideful. Is pride gaining a foothold in your heart? Find your security in God and not in your own accomplishments.

Day 341

Then I said to them, "You see the trouble we are in: Jerusalem lies in ruins, and its gates have been burned with fire. Come, let us rebuild the wall of Jerusalem, and we will no longer be in disgrace."
NEHEMIAH 2:17

Nehemiah had probably never set foot in his homeland when he took it upon himself to rebuild Jerusalem's wall. The city had been destroyed a century before his time.

But Nehemiah was ideally suited to the task—driven, determined, and unafraid to confront any obstacle. After all, this was a man who put his life on the line every day, serving as the Persian king's cupbearer.

NEHEMIAH

Persian Cupbearer and Jewish Reformer

As cupbearer, Nehemiah would taste the king's food and wine before giving it to him, making sure it had not been poisoned. Cupbearers enjoyed a revered status in the royal court, and Nehemiah took advantage of his close relationship with the king to make a bold request. Having been informed by his brother that Jerusalem was in a state of disrepair—despite the return of many exiles—Nehemiah requested a leave of absence to lead the rebuilding effort in his homeland. The king obliged, appointing Nehemiah as governor of Judah.

Upon his arrival in Jerusalem, Nehemiah set his sights on the city's most pressing need: a protective wall. Officials from Judah's neighboring provinces, including Sanballat, governor of Samaria, scoffed at the idea—first ridiculing Nehemiah's efforts, then plotting to undermine them by force. When these efforts failed, Sanballat accused Nehemiah of sedition. Such rivalry among Persian governors was not uncommon. In any case, Nehemiah persevered over the opposition from his enemies, completing the wall in less than two months.

SPIRITUAL INSIGHT

Nehemiah shared God's heart for the poor and His passion for justice. In order to pay the Persian king's tax, Jerusalem's poor had to borrow from the wealthy. But the wealthy smelled opportunity for enrichment and charged interest, forcing many to mortgage their own lands just to survive. In keeping with God's law (see Exodus 22:25–27), Nehemiah ended this practice, accusing the nobility of sending their own people into yet another form of exile: economic exploitation.

But [Eleazar] stood his ground and struck down the Philistines till his hand grew tired and froze to the sword. The LORD brought about a great victory that day. The troops returned to Eleazar, but only to strip the dead.

2 SAMUEL 23:10

Eleazar must have been incredibly tenacious. He wasn't going to give up ground to the enemy under any circumstance.

Eleazar is listed among David's mighty men—an elite group of valiant warriors who distinguished themselves in battle in various ways (1 Samuel 23; 1 Chronicles 11). Apparently the deed that vaulted Eleazar into this group was his unrelenting defense of a barley field during a battle with the Philistines.

ELEAZAR

One of David's Mighty Men

It is not certain exactly which battle was being fought when Eleazar stood his ground. The Bible says it occurred at Pas Dammim, which is the same location where young David defeated the Philistine giant Goliath. It is located in the valley of Elah, a shallow valley in the foothills that lie between Philistia and the hill country of Israel. Nevertheless, at some point in the battle, the Israelites withdrew from the field, but Eleazar stood his ground and struck down so many Philistines that his hand grew weary and apparently clung to the sword even after the battle was over. The Israelites defeated the Philistines in battle that day (2 Samuel 23:9–10; 1 Chronicles 11:12–14).

RELATED INFORMATION

Because the fertile valley of Elah formed a natural pathway between Philistia and Israel, both people groups vied for control over it. The Philistine city of Gath stood at the western end of the valley, while the Israelite city of Azekah stood at a key bend in the middle.

Absalom and all the men of Israel said, "The advice of
Hushai the Arkite is better than that of Ahithophel."
For the LORD had determined to frustrate the good
advice of Ahithophel in order to bring disaster on Absalom.
2 SAMUEL 17:14

D avid had some very interesting—yet loyal—friends during his reign as king of Israel. Hushai is among the more intriguing ones, largely due to the fact that he may not have even been a native Israelite.

While David was fleeing from Saul, he occasionally took refuge among non-Israelite peoples, such as the Philistines and the Moabites. During this time, he may have forged some lasting relationships, because some of the names listed among David's most loyal soldiers and friends do not appear to be Israelite (2 Samuel 23).

HUSHAI

Friend of David

Hushai is described as an Arkite, a name that is associated elsewhere with Canaanites and other non-Israelite peoples (Genesis 10:15–19; 1 Chronicles 1:13–16). Even so, Hushai demonstrated himself as a faithful friend of David during the rebellion of David's son Absalom.

As David was fleeing Jerusalem, he sent Hushai back to the city to act as a mole in the service of Absalom. When Absalom was seeking advice regarding whether he should pursue David, Hushai was able to foil the wise advice of Ahithophel and keep Absalom from overtaking David. He also sent messengers to notify David of the situation (2 Samuel 16–17). Because of Hushai's advice, David was kept safe—and eventually Absalom was killed.

RELATED INFORMATION

Other associates of David who may not have been Israelites include Igal from Zobah (a kingdom north of Israel), Zelek the Ammonite (a kingdom to the east of Israel), Uriah the Hittite (Canaanites who lived all along the eastern Mediterranean coast), and the Kerethites and Pelethites (who appear to have been associated with the Philistines along the southwest coast of Israel).

Some time later Abraham was told, "Milcah is also a mother;
she has borne sons to your brother Nahor."
GENESIS 22:20

Nahor's kinship to Abraham does not seem to have influenced his religious faith. But the lives of Nahor's descendants would become intertwined with the lives of Abraham's children and grandchildren.

Nahor was Abraham's younger brother. The writer of Genesis introduced Abraham and Nahor and their respective marriages in the same breath, but he added one crucial detail that distinguished Abraham and his wife: They were unable to conceive. Later the writer revealed that Nahor's wife and concubine had given him twelve sons. These children eventually became the patriarchs of twelve Aramean tribes.

One of Nahor's sons—and his children—played a particularly important part in the Jewish story. When Abraham wanted to find a wife for his son Isaac, he

NAHOR

Brother of Abraham

sent a servant to the family of his brother, Nahor. Rebekah, the chosen bride, was Nahor's granddaughter. Years later, when Jacob fled his brother's wrath, he took refuge with Laban, another of Nahor's grandchildren. Both of Jacob's brides, Leah and Rachel, were great-granddaughters of Nahor.

Nahor impacted Abraham's family in other ways, too. When Laban and Jacob parted ways, Laban made his oath to Jacob in the name of "the God of Abraham and the God of Nahor" (Genesis 31:53). In all likelihood, Laban was not referring to one God, but to two separate deities. Whereas Abraham had abandoned the gods of his father, Terah, to forge a new relationship with the God of the Bible, Nahor maintained his devotion to the household gods (see Joshua 24:2). Nahor's idolatry was passed down to Rachel, who stole the household gods (see Genesis 31:19) when Jacob's family fled from Laban. That connection to paganism would haunt Abraham's descendants throughout the Old Testament.

> **DID YOU KNOW?**
>
> Twelve is an important number in the Bible—particularly in the story of Abraham and Nahor. Just as Nahor was the ancestor of twelve tribes, so, too, were Abraham's son Ishmael and his grandson Jacob. The number twelve was often a symbol of God's divine purpose at work—as is the case, for example, with the twelve tribes of Israel and the twelve apostles.

It was about this time that King Herod arrested some
who belonged to the church, intending to persecute them.
He had James, the brother of John, put to death with the sword.
ACTS 12:1–2

T he old saying is often true: "The apple doesn't fall far from the tree." Or in the case of Herod Agrippa I, the apple doesn't fall far from the grand-tree, Herod the Great.

Herod the Great, who was king over the land of Israel when Jesus was born, was notorious for his ruthlessness toward those who appeared to threaten his rule. Upon his death, the Romans divided his territory among some of his sons, who also took the title "Herod." Three other sons, including one named Aristobulus, were killed as the family members fought among themselves for the crown.

HEROD AGRIPPA

King of Judea and
Grandson of Herod
the Great

After Gaius Caligula became emperor of Rome, he appointed Agrippa, the son of Aristobulus, as king over the land of Israel and eventually granted him virtually all the land that his grandfather Herod the Great had ruled.

Unfortunately Agrippa appears to have acquired his grandfather's ruthless political jealousy. As the church began to grow, Herod Agrippa must have regarded these followers of Jesus as a threat to his rule, and he began to persecute them. He even killed James, the brother of John. Once Agrippa saw that this gained him favor with the Jewish leaders, he arrested Peter, but an angel allowed Peter to escape from prison unharmed.

Herod was struck down by an angel of the Lord when he allowed people to praise him as a god (Acts 12).

RELATED INFORMATION

Gaius Caligula and Agrippa had been raised together in Rome, where they became friends. Agrippa continued to support the promotion of Gaius as emperor, which explains why Gaius granted Agrippa rule over so much land in Israel.

This is the account of Esau the father
of the Edomites in the hill country of Seir.
GENESIS 36:9

T hough the Edomites were closely related to the Israelites, it seems that when the Israelites needed their help the most, the Edomites did more harm than good.

The Edomites were the descendants of Esau, who was the son of Isaac and the twin brother of Jacob (Genesis 32:3). The Edomites settled in the mountainous region to the southeast of Israel (which was called Canaan at the time), driving out the Horites who were there (Genesis 36:9).

The shaky relationship between Israel and Edom becomes evident very early, when the Israelites were seeking permission from the Edomites to pass through their territory on their way to the Promised Land of Canaan. The Edomites denied them permission to pass through and threatened to attack the Israelites if they tried to do so (Numbers 20).

EDOMITES

Descendants of Esau
and Neighbor of Israel

Years later, Saul and David fought against the Edomites, and David eventually brought them under the rule of Israel (1 Samuel 14:47; 2 Samuel 8:11–14). After Israel split into two kingdoms, the Edomites remained under the rule of Judah for a time and even helped King Jehoshaphat of Judah fight against Moab (2 Kings 3). But later the Edomites regained their independence during the reign of King Jehoram of Judah (2 Kings 8:20–22).

When the Babylonians attacked Judah in 586 BC, the Edomites displayed disloyalty to their relatives again. Instead of helping them, it seems that they capitalized on Judah's weakened state and made raids on them as well (Obadiah 1:1–21).

By the time the Jews returned from exile in Babylon, many Edomites had moved into southern Judah, and it became known as Idumea.

RELATED INFORMATION

At the time when Jesus was born, Herod the Great was king of Judea, but he was not even fully an Israelite. He was an Idumean.

[Peter] went to the house of Mary the mother of John,
also called Mark, where many people had gathered and were praying.
ACTS 12:12

In the earliest days of Christianity, there were no church buildings. Believers met in each other's homes. And one of the first house churches recorded in the Bible gathered under the hospitality of a woman named Mary.

Mary was the mother of Mark, sometimes called John, who later became one of Paul's traveling companions and the author of the second Gospel. She was also the aunt of Barnabas, one of Paul's other ministry partners.

Evidently, Mary was a woman of some means, wealthy enough to employ a servant named Rhoda. Mary graciously opened her house to members of Jerusalem's Christian community—perhaps at great personal risk, since it was around this time that Herod Agrippa began persecuting the church in Jerusalem (see Acts 12:1). After executing James, the brother of John, Herod moved against Peter, throwing the apostle in jail with the intent of putting him on trial during Passover.

MARY

Mother of John Mark

God, however, intervened, making possible Peter's miraculous escape from prison. Mary's house was the first place Peter went—a strong indication that it was already a well established gathering place for Christians. Peter lingered only long enough to tell Mary and the other believers what had happened. Apparently not wanting to put Mary and her family in greater jeopardy, Peter then left for "another place" (Acts 12:17).

DID YOU KNOW?

Mary's house provided the backdrop for one of the truly comedic moments in the Bible. When Peter arrived at her home, he knocked on the door, only to be answered by Rhoda, Mary's servant. Rhoda was so excited at the sound of Peter's voice, she ran to tell the others who were gathered there—without bothering to let Peter in!

Now Naomi had a relative on her husband's side, from the clan of Elimelech, a man of standing, whose name was Boaz.
RUTH 2:1

It is often in the smaller, less noticeable things we do that our true character is revealed. Do we impatiently stare at the checkout clerk working the long line ahead of us? Do we decide not to help with the new church ministry because we don't like the person in charge?

Surely Boaz faced similar decisions in his everyday life, but the Bible details various ways he showed unselfishness and concern for others—even at his own expense.

The book of Ruth recounts how Boaz, a farmer in Bethlehem, was a wealthy man, yet he took time to talk to others, such as his harvesters. He also took special notice of a young woman named Ruth who was gleaning in his fields, and he learned that she was the daughter-in-law of Naomi, the widow of his deceased relative Elimelech. Boaz made sure Ruth was protected and treated honorably while she gleaned in his fields. He provided her with abundant food and water and even instructed his men to purposely leave stalks of grain for her to gather.

BOAZ

Wealthy Bethlehemite Who Married Widowed Ruth

Later Ruth appealed to Boaz that he marry her and purchase the land that had belonged to Naomi's husband so it would remain within the family. Boaz was certainly interested, but honorably and selflessly presented the offer first to a relative who was more closely related to Naomi. When the other relative declined, Boaz gladly acquired the land and Ruth as his wife.

Boaz and Ruth later had a son, Obed, who became an ancestor of David and ultimately an ancestor of Christ.

RELATED INFORMATION

By purchasing the land and marrying Ruth, Boaz acted in the Old Testament role of kinsman-redeemer. In ancient Israel, God's covenant with His people included the offer of a portion of the Promised Land as an inheritance, so it was critical that everything be done to prevent the loss of one's land. The kinsman-redeemer could help a struggling relative by purchasing his or her land to ensure that it remained with the family.

The Sadducees say that there is no resurrection, and that there are neither angels nor spirits, but the Pharisees acknowledge them all.
ACTS 23:8

The Sadducees were one of two groups—the other being the Pharisees—that famously came into conflict with Jesus. Of the two, however, Sadducees did not have as much direct contact with Jesus, perhaps because their values and ideals were even further removed from Jesus than were those of the Pharisees.

Unlike the Pharisees, who found favor with the common people of Palestine, the Sadducees were "men of the world." They moved comfortably along the halls of power, rubbing shoulders with the religious and political elite. Whereas the Pharisees stood out for their strict adherence to the Law, Sadducees had a talent for blending in—they were happy to accommodate their Roman overlords in order to maintain their own grasp on power. Many Sadducees were thought to be members of the priestly class. As a political party, the Sadducees held sway over the Sanhedrin, the Jewish ruling council.

SADDUCEES

Jewish Religious Leaders

In terms of their theology, Sadducees were, once again, men of the world. According to the New Testament, they did not believe in the immortality of the soul or the existence of angels or spirits. According to them, this life is all there is—and they sought to make the most of it.

Without doubt, the more prominence Jesus gained, the more of a threat He became to the Sadducees' comfortable arrangement with Rome.

DID YOU KNOW?

> Paul brilliantly used the polarizing subject of the resurrection to send the Sanhedrin into an uproar when he was made to appear before them. When he claimed that he was on trial because of his belief in the resurrection, he angered the Sadducees who were present, while gaining the sympathy of their rival Pharisees (see Acts 23:1–11).

"Martha, Martha," the Lord answered, "you are worried and upset about many things, but only one thing is needed. Mary has chosen what is better, and it will not be taken away from her."

LUKE 10:41–42

It seems like it's the same every holiday. We have good intentions of reflecting on the true meaning of the special day and focusing on Jesus, but inevitably we can never seem to fit this in amid all the busyness of preparing food or visiting family or buying gifts or whatever. We are too much like Martha and not enough like her sister, Mary.

Martha was the sister of Mary and Lazarus. The three of them lived near Jerusalem in a small village named Bethany. Because of their friendship with Jesus and their proximity to the holy city, Jesus seemed to regularly stay with them while he was in the area.

MARTHA

Sister of Mary and Lazarus

On one of these visits, Martha worked hard at serving Jesus and grew indignant when her sister, Mary, sat beside Jesus rather than help with the preparations. Jesus gently rebuked Martha instead, telling her that she was not choosing the most important thing: being in Jesus' presence.

Martha's busy nature can be seen again at a meal given in Jesus' honor in their home. Martha served while Lazarus reclined and ate with the other guests at the dinner. Mary later demonstrated her love for Jesus by pouring perfume on Jesus' feet and wiping His feet with her hair.

SPIRITUAL INSIGHT

Though we should be careful not to write Martha off completely as someone only consumed with daily chores and uninterested in spending time with Jesus, she does stand as a bit of a negative example to believers today. We should make sure that we are always keeping the main thing the main thing: spending time with Jesus and enjoying Him.

*But when they did not find them, they dragged Jason
and some other brothers before the city officials, shouting:
"These men who have caused trouble all over the world
have now come here, and Jason has welcomed them into his house."*
ACTS 17:6–7

Day
351

W e've all heard of those who take great risks and suffer persecution to advance the gospel and build up Christ's kingdom. Usually the people that come to mind are missionaries, jungle pilots, or smugglers of Bibles into restricted countries. But have you ever considered what danger might lie in store for. . .a host? In Paul's day, a man named Jason was dragged before the city officials by an angry mob and accused of treason—all because he simply hosted Paul in his home.

JASON

Host of Paul and Silas
in Thessalonica

During Paul's second missionary journey, Paul and Silas stayed for a few weeks in Thessalonica at the home of Jason. At the local synagogue, they were teaching that Jesus was the Messiah. Some Jews believed, but others became upset at Paul's teaching and went to Jason's house to find him. When they couldn't find him there, they dragged Jason before the officials instead and accused him of harboring those who were loyal to a king other than Caesar.

The city officials were thrown into turmoil about these accusations, but in the end they released Jason on bail to await trial later. Meanwhile Paul and Silas were whisked away to Berea, where they continued spreading the gospel.

SPIRITUAL INSIGHT

We are all called to work for God's kingdom, whatever role we perform. Our job may not seem as glamorous as, say, a foreign missionary or an evangelist, but our service to Christ is every bit as important. Even so, like Jason, we just never know what incredible things we might experience while we are helping to build God's kingdom!

What [Onan] did was wicked in the LORD's sight;
so he put him to death also.
GENESIS 38:10

Onan's story is understandably baffling to many readers today. The second son of Judah, Onan appears in a strange account, one that serves as an interlude to the tale of Joseph.

Onan's older brother, Er, had been deemed guilty of an unspecified offense—perhaps idolatry, a distinct possibility, since Onan and Er's father had married a Canaanite. In any case, Er's sin led God to strike him down, after which Judah ordered Onan to sleep with Er's widow. What seems like such an inappropriate command today was rather customary in the ancient Near East. The practice, known as levirate marriage, would later be enshrined in the Law of Moses (see Deuteronomy 25:5–6).

ONAN

Son of Judah
Struck Down by God

When a husband died leaving no heir, the dead man's brother was to take the widow as his own wife, with the aim of providing an offspring. There was just one catch: The firstborn son would be regarded as the offspring of the deceased brother, not the one who married his widow. As a result, the dead brother's name would endure, and his inheritance would pass to the child who was regarded as his own. The system was also designed to afford some protection to widows, who were quite vulnerable in the ancient Near East. With the inheritance that passed to the offspring of such marriages, widows could be provided for in the years to come.

Onan found that the prospect of a son who would not be his own was more than he could bear. So he refused to sleep with Er's widow in a way that would allow a child to be conceived—and, more important, no heir would be produced to claim Er's inheritance. God was furious with Onan and his utter disregard for justice. Like his brother before him, Onan was struck down by God.

DID YOU KNOW? Onan's name means "vigorous"—perhaps an ironic wordplay. A man whose stamina and vigor should have easily helped produce children for Er's widow had instead refused his God-given responsibility. In the end, Onan lost not only his vigor but his life, too.

This is what the LORD says: "I will return to Zion and dwell in Jerusalem. Then Jerusalem will be called the City of Truth, and the mountain of the LORD Almighty will be called the Holy Mountain."
ZECHARIAH 8:3

For ten years, Jerusalem's most important construction site fell silent as work on the second temple ground to a halt. Zechariah was one of the prophets who stepped into the silence and summoned the people back to work.

Zechariah served a dual function in Jewish society: He was both prophet and priest. The grandson of Iddo had been born in exile. As such, he had not participated in the sin that brought God's wrath and led to the destruction of Jerusalem and its most precious building, the temple. Until his return to Jerusalem sometime in the 530s BC, Zechariah had been without a homeland. Even upon his return, he was still without a place to carry out his divinely appointed profession. Zechariah was a priest without a temple.

ZECHARIAH

Prophet

Work on the new temple began almost immediately after Cyrus, king of Persia, allowed the first delegation of exiles to return home. However, some of their neighbors objected to the new temple and managed to convince the royal authorities that the Israelites had a long history of rebellion and could not be trusted. As a result, work on the temple stopped for a full decade.

That all changed, however, when Zechariah began to prophesy, encouraging the people to resume work on the temple. According to the prophet, the completion of the temple would be a confirmation of God's presence. It did not matter that the new structure would not match the glory of Solomon's temple—the "day of small things" was not to be despised (see Zechariah 4:8–10).

Having been persuaded to return to work, the people of Jerusalem completed the temple in four years. Zechariah—who, according to Ezra, was instrumental in motivating the people to carry on—was there with "the priests, the Levites and the rest of the exiles" to dedicate the new structure to the God who had brought them back from despair (see Ezra 6:13–18).

DID YOU KNOW? Zechariah was not the only person to prophesy in favor of rebuilding the temple. Another prophet named Haggai—Zechariah's contemporary—also wrote and spoke to encourage the exiles in their most important work.

In bitterness of soul Hannah wept much and prayed to the LORD.
And she made a vow, saying, "O LORD Almighty, if you will...
not forget your servant but give her a son, then I will give
him to the LORD for all the days of his life."

1 SAMUEL 1:10–11

O ne of the most moving passages of scripture is the story of Hannah, the mother of the prophet Samuel. In the span of two simple chapters, we find such heartfelt themes as the pain and longing of childlessness, the joy of childbirth, and the surrender of a child to God's service.

When we first read about Hannah, she has been unable to bear a child and is being taunted for this by her rival, Peninnah, who is the other wife of Hannah's husband. Hannah's sorrow and longing lead her to pray earnestly to God for a son, whom she promises to dedicate fully to God's service (1 Samuel 1).

HANNAH

Mother of Samuel

God answers Hannah's prayer, and she gives birth to Samuel. True to her word, Hannah brings Samuel to the tabernacle after he is weaned and gives him over to God's service there. Instead of expressing sorrow at her loss of Samuel, however, Hannah praises God for answering her prayer for a son (1 Samuel 2:1–10). Hannah eventually bears more children, and Samuel becomes a great prophet and judge over Israel.

DID YOU KNOW?

When Hannah promised to give her son over to God's service (1 Samuel 1:11), she was probably offering to make him a Nazirite for his entire life. People dedicated as Nazirites were not allowed to cut their hair or drink alcohol (Numbers 6).

Then the people of Israel were split into two factions;
half supported Tibni son of Ginath for king,
and the other half supported Omri.
1 KINGS 16:21

Tibni's struggle for the throne of the northern kingdom is barely mentioned in the Bible. In the end, he lost out to the far more powerful Omri.

Tibni's rival had already dispatched Zimri, the shortest reigning monarch in Israel's history. Zimri managed just one week on the throne before Omri avenged the murder of Zimri's predecessor. ("King of Israel" was one of the most hazardous occupations in the country at this time. It's a wonder that Tibni aspired to it in the first place!)

Nothing is known about Tibni or what he did before laying claim to the throne. However, he was considered well enough qualified that roughly half the nation supported his bid for power. It was not enough, though. The writer of 1 Kings does not bother to document one detail concerning the struggle between Tibni and Omri. It is only by the process of deduction that it can be determined that the struggle went on for roughly four years (compare 1 Kings 16:15 and 23). Even Tibni's fate remains a mystery. Whether he survived the conflict or was slain by Omri is unknown—though death in battle seems the more likely outcome. It seems the biblical writer regarded Tibni as too inconsequential to bother with him any further.

TIBNI

Challenged Omri
for Israel's Throne

DID YCU KNOW? Even if Tibni had succeeded in his quest for the throne, he probably would have wound up becoming as much of a failure as king as Omri proved to be. Not one ruler in the entire history of the northern kingdom was judged to be a good king in the eyes of God.

"Simeon and Levi are brothers—
their swords are weapons of violence. . .
Cursed be their anger, so fierce, and their fury, so cruel!"
GENESIS 49:5, 7

S imeon was the second son born to Jacob by his wife Leah. Though she was convinced that her son's birth would win Jacob's affection, in the end her son Simeon revealed a violent streak that endangered the entire family.

When his sister, Dinah, was raped by a neighboring Hivite named Shechem, Simeon was furious. Perhaps just as outrageous to him as the original offense was the fact that his father, Jacob, did nothing in response. The writer of Genesis seemed sympathetic to Simeon and his brothers' reaction, calling Shechem's crime a "disgraceful thing. . .that should not be done" (Genesis 34:7). However, Jacob's reaction was understandable, too. Yes, his daughter had been violated—but if he struck against his more powerful neighbors, he might put the whole family in jeopardy. That, however, was not enough to pacify Simeon. It is no wonder that he and Levi led their brothers in their quest for revenge. They—along with Reuben, Judah, Issachar, and Zebulun—were Dinah's full brothers. So when Shechem brazenly asked for Dinah's hand in marriage, the brothers devised a cunning scheme. They demanded Shechem and his fellow Hivites circumcise themselves. Three days later, while they were still writhing in pain, Simeon and Levi led the slaughter. Simeon's only other significant contribution to the story in Genesis was as a hostage in Egypt. When Joseph sent his brothers home to fetch Benjamin, Simeon was detained, kept back as collateral to ensure the brothers' return.

SIMEON

Son of Jacob

After that, Simeon faded into obscurity—literally. Just as his father, Jacob, predicted on his deathbed, Simeon's descendants were scattered, their allotment in the Promised Land being surrounded on all sides by Judah.

DID YOU KNOW?

The sons of Simeon had at least one fleeting moment of glory. In the waning days of the southern kingdom—during the rule of Hezekiah—the Simeonites waged assaults against a number of Israel's enemies, including the dreaded Amalekites (see 1 Chronicles 4:41–43). After the exile, however, the tribe of Simeon was never again mentioned by name (except briefly in Revelation 7:7).

Then they cast lots, and the lot fell to Matthias;
so he was added to the eleven apostles.
ACTS 1:26

Day
357

W hat if, after all the primaries and campaign speeches, the president of the United States was to be decided by a coin toss?

You might ask, *How could the most powerful person in the world be chosen by such a random process?* Yet that is similar to the process used to decide who would fill one of the most important offices in the history of the world—the twelfth apostle of Jesus Christ.

MATTHIAS

Disciple Chosen to
Replace Judas Iscariot

While Jesus was ministering throughout Israel, He gathered many followers who had varying levels of commitment. Some belonged simply to the thousands that came and went. Others belonged to a group of seventy-two that were sent out by Jesus to minister to people (Luke 10:1, 17). Still others belonged to an inner circle of twelve who followed Jesus almost constantly and were privy to most of his teaching and deeds (Mark 3:16–19).

When Judas Iscariot, one of the Twelve, committed suicide after betraying Jesus to death, the eleven remaining disciples recognized the need to fill Judas's role as a witness to Christ. They stipulated that any candidates would need to have been with Jesus from the very beginning of His ministry.

After narrowing the candidates down to two men—Matthias and Joseph—the disciples "cast lots," meaning they used some process such as throwing dice or drawing straws, to make the final selection. In this way, they handed the final decision over to God, who oversees even things that we regard as chance. The lot fell to Matthias, and he became the twelfth apostle (Acts 1:15–26).

SPIRITUAL INSIGHT

While it is tempting to see this passage as undermining the necessity of wisdom in making decisions, it is important to recognize that the disciples did not simply put a bunch of names in a hat and pick one out. They used their own discretion to narrow the number of candidates down to two fully qualified people, and then they handed the final choice over to God.

*After this, his brother came out, with his hand grasping
Esau's heel; so he was named Jacob. Isaac was sixty
years old when Rebekah gave birth to them.*

GENESIS 25:26

It's not uncommon for parents to give their children names that express the hopes they have for them or the attributes they associate with them: Joy, Hope, Victor, Hunter, and so on. So how about the idea of *Deceiver?* That's exactly the sentiment expressed by the name Jacob.

Jacob, also called Israel, was the son of Isaac and the father of the twelve patriarchs of Israel. He and his older brother, Esau, were twins—and when they were born, Jacob was grasping the heel of Esau (Genesis 25:26), so he was given the name Jacob ("heel holder"). In ancient Israel, to "grasp the heel" meant to deceive or supplant, which was somewhat fitting for Jacob's personality throughout much of his life.

JACOB

Son of Isaac and Father
of the Israelite Tribes

Some of the ways that Jacob deceived or supplanted others include convincing Esau to trade his birthright for a bowl of stew (Genesis 25:29–34), tricking Isaac to gain the blessing he wanted to give Esau (Genesis 27) and fooling his uncle Laban to increase his flocks (Genesis 30). Later, after Jacob wrestled with a man of God at the Jabbok River, his name was appropriately changed to Israel, meaning "one who strives with God" (Genesis 32).

One of Jacob's twelve sons was Joseph, who rose to a position of second in command of Egypt, and Jacob and his family moved to Egypt to live with him there. After Jacob had grown very old, he blessed his twelve sons and died (Genesis 37–50).

RELATED INFORMATION

Once, even Jacob the Deceiver was deceived by his uncle Laban. Jacob had worked for seven years to pay the bride price for Rachel, but Laban gave Jacob Rachel's older sister, Leah, instead. Jacob had to work another seven years for Rachel (Genesis 29).

So the LORD saved Hezekiah and the people of Jerusalem from the hand of Sennacherib king of Assyria and from the hand of all others. He took care of them on every side.

2 CHRONICLES 32:22

There are wicked people in this world who wield great power, and it can seem at times as if they are on the verge of completely overwhelming God's people. But we must always remember that God is infinitely more powerful than any human being—even someone so powerful as King Sennacherib of Assyria, the greatest power the world had ever known.

Up to the reign of Sennacherib, the Assyrian Empire appeared to be unstoppable. It was gobbling up virtually the entire civilized world of the Near East, and it had annexed the northern kingdom of Israel into its territory as well. After King Hezekiah of Judah refused to submit to Assyria and pay the tribute owed, King Sennacherib came and attacked the towns of Judah. Nearly all the fortified towns of Judah had fallen to Assyria—except for the capital city of Jerusalem. The Assyrians were besieging the city, and Hezekiah and

SENNACHERIB

King of Assyria

his people were desperately crying out to the Lord to save them (2 Kings 18:13–19:34).

The Lord answered their prayers by sending an angel throughout the Assyrian camp—killing 185,000 troops in a single night! As a result, Sennacherib broke camp and returned to Nineveh, where his own sons killed him (2 Kings 19:35–37). Such is the amazing power of God.

RELATED INFORMATION

Among the ruins of Assyria's palaces in Nineveh, archaeologists have found wall reliefs depicting the siege of Lachish, one the towns of Judah captured by Sennacherib.

Paul replied, "Short time or long—I pray God that not only you but all who are listening to me today may become what I am, except for these chains." The king rose, and with him the governor and Bernice and those sitting with them.

ACTS 26:29–30

There is not enough room in the Bible to record everything about every person who encountered the gospel during Paul's ministry, but it's interesting to speculate about what some must have been thinking. For example, what was going on in the heart of Bernice when Paul was directly urging her to embrace the gospel?

Bernice was the daughter of Agrippa I, who was the grandson of Herod the Great, the king who reigned over Judea when Jesus was born. She was also the sister of Agrippa II.

Bernice had several short-lived marriages and eventually spent most of her time in the company of her brother Agrippa, which generated rumors of impropriety in their relationship. That was her situation when she encountered Paul at Caesarea.

BERNICE

Sister of King Agrippa II

Paul had been imprisoned at Caesarea because of a dispute with the Jewish leaders at Jerusalem. While he was there, Festus, the Roman governor, invited Agrippa and Bernice to hear Paul's case and help him decide what to do about Paul. Agrippa and Bernice arrived in great pomp, and Paul was allowed to speak. In the process, he boldly urged Agrippa and Bernice to become Christians! Agrippa and Bernice immediately left the room, declaring Paul to be innocent.

We hear nothing further about Bernice after this episode. Perhaps she was not moved at all by Paul's invitation. But perhaps she was. We can only hope.

RELATED INFORMATION

A few years after Paul's appeal to Agrippa and Bernice, the Jews revolted against the Romans, and the couple traveled to Jerusalem to appeal to the Romans to be merciful to the Jews. Their appeal was unsuccessful, and the Jews forced them to flee to Galilee, where they eventually gave themselves up to the Romans.

*[Menahem] did evil in the eyes of the LORD. During his
entire reign he did not turn away from the sins of
Jeroboam son of Nebat, which he had caused Israel to commit.*
2 KINGS 15:18

After a period of upheaval that saw back-to-back assassinations, Menahem restored a degree of stability to the northern kingdom of Israel—but the price was astronomical.

Only months before Menahem's rise to power, a man named Zechariah had taken the throne. His murder ended a dynasty that had lasted four kings—an impressive period of stability for such a volatile nation. Zechariah's murderer was a man named Shallum, who seized Samaria's throne for himself.

But it was not to last. Menahem—who probably commanded a military force based in nearby Tirzah—had been loyal to Zechariah. Barely one month into Shallum's reign, Menahem marched on Samaria and killed the usurper.

MENAHEM

King of Israel

It has been said that power corrupts people. Such was the case in Menahem's story. His path to the throne clear, the avenger became the usurper. Menahem placed himself in command—the fourth king to sit on Israel's throne in less than a year.

Menahem's reign was characterized by brutality and cowardice. When one of the cities of Samaria refused to acknowledge his legitimacy, Menahem not only sacked the city, but the writer of Kings reports that he "ripped open all the pregnant women" (2 Kings 15:16). Such brutality was designed to send a message to the next generation of would-be insurgents.

Eventually, however, every aggressor found himself confronted by a larger, more powerful aggressor. Menahem met his match in Tiglath-Pileser III, king of Assyria—known in the Bible as Pul. The Assyrians invaded and demanded that Menahem pay tribute, acknowledging Tiglath-Pileser as his overlord. Menahem obliged, raising the necessary funds—a breathtaking one thousand talents of silver—from Israel's wealthy class. Menahem's ability to collect such an amount suggests that the northern kingdom enjoyed great prosperity at the time.

DID YOU KNOW? Menahem, who reigned for ten years, is mentioned outside the Bible. The records of Tiglath-Pileser confirm the accuracy of the Bible's account, noting that Menahem was one of several regional rulers who paid tribute to Assyria.

*To Timothy my true son in the faith: Grace, mercy and peace
from God the Father and Christ Jesus our Lord.*

1 TIMOTHY 1:2

The uncircumcised son of a Jewish mother and a Gentile father, Timothy was the last person one would have expected Paul—a former Pharisee—to choose as his disciple.

The fact that Timothy was the product of a mixed marriage would have been enough cause for a scandal among his fellow Jews. It was probably Timothy's father who kept him from being circumcised as a baby—Gentiles in the Greco-Roman world considered it a mutilation of the male human figure, which was revered as one of the highest forms of beauty. In any case, Timothy's uncircumcised state is a strong indicator that his father was not just a Gentile, but a pagan as well.

TIMOTHY

Disciple of Paul

Without the mark of the circumcision, Timothy probably was not fully welcomed by the Jewish community in his hometown of Lystra, in present-day Turkey. He may have been labeled a *mamzer*—regarded as an illegitimate child in the eyes of his fellow Jews. Nevertheless, Timothy devoted himself to the Old Testament scriptures, aided by his devout mother and grandmother, Lois.

When Paul—who had once believed that circumcision and the law were all that mattered—arrived in Lystra, Timothy caught his attention. Hearing nothing but praise from the Christians already present there, Paul decided that Timothy should accompany him on his journey. In order not to cause unnecessary offense among the local Jews, Paul had Timothy circumcised—apparently this is the kind of thing that becoming "all things to all men" involved. Perhaps more than anything else, the fact that Timothy was willing to undergo such a painful procedure as an adult indicates the depth of his devotion to Christ and His church.

Timothy went on to become the pastor of the church at Ephesus, approximately 250–300 miles west of his hometown. The assignment brought its share of challenges, but Timothy had the writings of his mentor, Paul, to encourage him along the way.

SPIRITUAL INSIGHT

Timothy is a well-known reminder that age is not a barrier to serving God's kingdom. Paul famously encouraged Timothy, who was by this time assigned to the church at Ephesus, not to "let anyone look down" on him because of his youth. Anyone—no matter how young—can set an example for all of God's people.

Greet Priscilla and Aquila, my fellow workers in Christ Jesus.
They risked their lives for me. Not only I but all the churches
of the Gentiles are grateful to them.
ROMANS 16:3–4

P riscilla and her husband, Aquila, were refugees who had been driven out of Rome by persecution. But their upheaval opened the door to a new life and a new calling.

PRISCILLA

Prominent Woman
in the Early Church

Priscilla was a Jewish woman who lived in Rome. Whether she was native to the city is not known—her husband was originally from the distant region of Pontus, located on the southern Black Sea, in present-day Turkey. Sometime around AD 50, Emperor Claudius expelled all of Rome's Jewish residents. The reason for the order, according to the Roman historian Suetonius, was an ongoing disturbance regarding someone named Chrestus—in all likelihood a misspelled reference to Christ. Word of Jesus had spread to Rome, polarizing the Jewish community and threatening to turn the city upside down.

Whether Priscilla and her husband became Christians before or after their encounter with Paul is not known, but it is clear they grew to be two of Paul's strongest allies in his ministry. Together they journeyed across the Aegean Sea to Ephesus. While Paul continued on from there, Priscilla and Aquila stayed behind. By this time they were so deeply rooted in the Christian faith that they were able to instruct another powerful teacher named Apollos, who had also come to believe that Jesus was the Messiah.

Touched by their friendship, Paul mentioned Priscilla and Aquila in three of his letters. His greeting to them at the end of Romans suggests they were able to return to their home city at some point. However, by the time Paul wrote his second letter to Timothy—perhaps his final letter—the pair seemed to have taken up residence in Ephesus once again.

DID YOU KNOW?

Priscilla is mentioned first in five out of the Bible's seven references to the famous couple. Scholars debate the precise significance, though it is generally noted that the order of names was important. Priscilla may have had a more forceful personality, she may have been of a higher social rank than her husband, or she may have played a more prominent role in the early church.

[Reuben] was the firstborn, but when he defiled his father's marriage bed, his rights as firstborn were given to the sons of Joseph son of Israel; so he could not be listed in the genealogical record in accordance with his birthright.

1 CHRONICLES 5:1

Reuben's life was a tragic tale of honor lost and never quite regained. Reuben forfeited the double portion of the inheritance that should have been his by right as the firstborn of Jacob by his first wife, Leah. More important, Reuben was forced to relinquish his prized position as the leader among the twelve tribes of Israel.

After Rachel died while giving birth to Jacob's youngest son, Benjamin, the family moved south to Migdal Eder. There Reuben did the unthinkable: He slept with his father's concubine, Bilhah.

Bilhah had been Rachel's servant. Years earlier Rachel had offered her to Jacob to be his concubine, in the hopes that Bilhah would bear the children that Rachel was unable to conceive. By sleeping with Bilhah after Rachel's death, Reuben did more than commit an act of sexual immorality—he signaled his rejection of Jacob's authority as family patriarch. In the ancient world, one way to challenge a king's rule was to sleep with one or more of his concubines. Such an insult—usually committed by another family member—communicated one's own claim to the throne and invariably severed ties with the king. Reuben, perhaps sensing his father's weakness, overstepped his bounds as firstborn and presumed to supplant his father as head of the family.

REUBEN

Son of Jacob

The other episodes from Reuben's life reveal a more honorable character. When his brothers conspired to murder Joseph, it was Reuben who intervened, persuading them to throw Joseph in a cistern instead. Before Reuben could rescue Joseph as he had planned, his brothers sold the boy to a passing caravan of Midianite merchants.

DID YOU KNOW?

Jacob never forgot his son's betrayal. While commending him for his honor and strength, the aging patriarch told Reuben that he would no longer excel. The blessing of preeminence passed to Judah, while Joseph's sons inherited the rights of the firstborn.

David reigned in Jerusalem thirty-three years,
and these were the children born to him there:
Shammua, Shobab, Nathan and Solomon. These four
were by Bathsheba daughter of Ammiel.
1 CHRONICLES 3:4–5

According to the writer of 1 Chronicles, Nathan was one of more than nineteen sons that were born to David and his eight wives. This number did not include the unnamed offspring of David and his concubines.

Nothing is known about Nathan's life. It is possible—though entirely speculative—that he was named in honor of the prophet who served David so well throughout his reign.

What is most remarkable about Nathan is that he was one of four sons born to David and Bathsheba, the wife who never should have been his. David committed adultery with Bathsheba, after which he sent her rightful husband, Uriah, to the front lines in battle with the Ammonites. As a result, Uriah was killed as planned, clearing the way for David to make Bathsheba his own wife.

NATHAN

Son of David

David's crime, however, did not escape notice. The prophet Nathan confronted the king. David confessed, but he and Bathsheba were punished with the loss of the child that had been conceived in the adulterous affair. At this point, David might have easily scorned Bathsheba, regarding her as too painful a reminder of his indiscretion. Instead, David chose to comfort his bereaved wife, and in His mercy, God gave the couple four sons—one of whom was Nathan.

DID YOU KNOW?

The Gospel of Luke traces Jesus' genealogy through Nathan, son of David and Bathsheba (see Luke 3:31).

INDEX OF PEOPLE

Scripture Index